A History of American Higher Education

A History of American Higher Education

Second Edition

John R. Thelin

The Johns Hopkins University Press
Baltimore

© 2004, 2011 The Johns Hopkins University Press
All rights reserved. Published 2011
Printed in the United States of America on acid-free paper
9 8 7 6 5 4 3 2 1

The Johns Hopkins University Press
2715 North Charles Street
Baltimore, Maryland 21218-4363
www.press.jhu.edu

Library of Congress Cataloging-in-Publication Data
Thelin, John R., 1947–
    A history of American higher education / John R. Thelin.—2nd ed.
        p.   cm.
Includes bibliographical references and index.
    ISBN-13: 978-1-4214-0266-6 (hardcover : alk. paper)
    ISBN-10: 1-4214-0266-1 (hardcover : alk. paper)
    ISBN-13: 978-1-4214-0267-3 (pbk. : alk. paper)
    ISBN-10: 1-4214-0267-X (pbk. : alk. paper)
    1. Education, Higher—United States—History. 2. Universities and
colleges—United States—History. I. Title.
    LA226.T45 2011
    378.73—dc22   2011011298

A catalog record for this book is available from the British Library.

Special discounts are available for bulk purchases of this book. For more information, please contact Special Sales at 410-516-6936 or specialsales@press.jhu.edu.

The Johns Hopkins University Press uses environmentally friendly book materials, including recycled text paper that is composed of at least 30 percent post-consumer waste, whenever possible.

For Sharon

Contents

viii   Contents

Preface

A journalist, after completing a nationwide tour of American campuses, noted, "At every one of the fourteen universities I visited, I was met with the remark, 'You have come to us at a critical moment. This university is just now in a transition stage.'"[1] It's a statement that resonates with the uncertainties and changes that college and university presidents face in 2011. What may be surprising to contemporary readers is that the remark was made a century earlier—in 1910—by Edwin Slosson when he was finishing the field work for his classic anthology, *Great American Universities.*

Whether 1910 or 2011, an element of continuity is that our colleges and universities are constantly changing, both by accident and design. The temptation is for each generation of academic leaders to consider its own time to be *the* critical juncture. This historical myopia is especially evident to me when the crises of today are seen as surpassing those of an earlier period—especially in the recent past, such as 1981. One needs historical context to counter the egocentrism of present college and university presidents. As one who has been a faculty member and administrator at both endpoints in this thirty-year span, my best estimate is that one reason the problems of 1981 seem manageable, perhaps even quaint, in 2011 is that colleges and universities survived a severe storm of financial and political problems thanks to some remarkable displays of imaginative adjustment, academic soul searching, and sound educational thinking. How bad were the good old days? The years 1978 to 1981 were a time when the staid Carnegie Commission on Higher Education made the sobering projection that about 25 percent of American colleges and universities were soon going to cease operation. A historical message, then, is that the problems facing American higher education in 2011 are not necessarily unprecedented in their gravity. But this time around the insights and priorities that might have led academic leaders to good solutions do not seem to be surfacing as well and creatively as they did in 1981.

Troubling today is that for those who are seeking to understand and solve the problems now facing colleges and universities, there does not seem much inclination to seek genuine historical perspective about higher education as a lens. For example, in November 2010 the *Chronicle of Higher Education* and *Inside Higher Ed* reported that Yale University's School of Management was going to work with India's Institute of Management at Kozhikode to train university leaders.[2] The M.B.A. was the model for setting higher education aright. As such, there was little indication that in-depth historical analysis would have an integral part in the kinds of readings and projects associated with an M.B.A.-style curriculum. The problematic and unanswered question, then, was what role the history of higher education ought to play in the education of future academic leaders?

I resist invoking the academic adage attributed to George Santayana: "Those who cannot remember the past are condemned to repeat it." My hunch is that the real genesis of this bold claim was that a wise, pragmatic senior warned some lazy sophomores, "If you don't study for your History 101 exam, you will fail the course and will have to repeat it!" That sound advice was not quite as earthshaking as Santayana's dramatic version. My modest argument is that colleges and universities are historic institutions—and this is a characteristic that warrants careful consideration for those who live, work, and even lead there. Consider once again the insights from a century ago, as journalist Edwin Slosson (himself a chemist) observed about the material and physical environment of higher education: "But it is impossible to ignore history in dealing with the University of Pennsylvania. One cannot get away from it. All the walls are covered with it. The buildings are genealogical museums. Paintings, bas reliefs, inscriptions, windows, relics, manuscripts, and similar memorabilia catch the attention of the visitor wherever he goes."[3]

Most established American colleges and universities share this legacy of architecture and artifacts. The irony is that often the most *unhistorical* offices tend most to invoke historic motifs. Often it is the main administration building that is home for the relics and paintings—even though few presidents or board members have a deep grasp of the history of higher education. Reasonable doubt about the efficacy of history

is kindled as one walks around and through a campus and pays attention to the people and values that are honored in the memorial plaques
and naming of buildings. Sitting in the Board Room of a renovated historic administration building, the gallery of presidential portraits often
are underwhelming and uninspiring. Why this lackluster impression?
Perhaps it is because the patina of heritage wears thin and is exposed as
merely an accumulation of mediocre-quality oil paintings of old white
guys sitting in high-backed chairs, wearing academic gowns with hoods
and medallions that bring to mind lodge initiations rather than serious
ideas or excitement about education.

The good news is that in recent years a number of colleges and universities have dared to revisit their heritage with fresh, critical eyes. At
Brown University in 2003 the president appointed a broad-based committee of faculty, administrators, and undergraduate and graduate students to investigate the university's history "with regard to slavery and
the transatlantic slave trade"—an exploration that was indelibly linked
to the university's namesake Brown family. This Steering Committee on
Justice spent three years researching and discussing the "complex historical, political, legal and moral questions posed by any present-day
confrontation with past injustice." It led to the creation of a memorial
that was no less than "a living site of memory, inviting reflection and
fresh discovery without provoking paralysis or shame."[4] What was refreshing about this project was that it showed how the history of colleges and universities could be ongoing, as a source of both renewal and
rediscovery. It provided a welcome alternative to a widespread tendency
for institutional histories to avoid or deny controversial episodes—and
for present and future generations of the campus community to gain
strength and purpose from the informed research and reflection.

In a similar vein, there are promising signs that historians who are
writing institutional histories are including and addressing characteristics that may today be unflattering. A good example is James Axtell's
2006 *The Making of Princeton University*, a history that ranged from
Woodrow Wilson's presidency up to the early twenty-first century.[5]
Axtell was remarkably candid in noting that the Princeton of Wilson's
presidency was intolerant of Jews and other religious minorities, as well
as exclusive in its formal and informal restrictions facing women, African Americans, and those from modest income as students, as faculty,
and as administrators. Yet the important sequel is that over time Princeton confronted internally and externally these biases—and learned from

them, ultimately and continually changing so that Princeton enhanced both its academic stature and its appropriate commitment to equity and social justice. Brown and Princeton, then, have provided models for harnessing heritage in ways that are simultaneously thoughtful and useful for present institutional policies and practices.

Resurrecting history to face all dimensions of the institutional past will, of course, require initiative and commitment, especially from a president and other academic leaders, in conjunction with grassroots ideas and energy from students and alumni. And, although Brown and Princeton have led by example in showing how a college or university might replace superficial celebration of the past with a complex, timely presentation of institutional heritage, it will not necessarily be easy for other institutions to follow suit. This is because there are numerous problems facing even those presidents, board members, and alumni groups who wish to keep history vital in higher education. One disturbing development is logistical. Colleges and universities have been losing their institutional memory because dedicated, knowledgeable archivists often now have less and less resources, professional staff, and space for preserving the artifacts and records of campus life, especially in the realm of student culture. The justification for this shift in mission is that in an "information age" campus archives have been required to devote increasing time and resources to serve as custodians of official records and institutional files, in both electronic and paper form. Meanwhile, photographs, yearbooks, student posters and publications, sample student term papers, examinations, diaries, and memoirs from recent years have a shrinking place in the institutional memory.[6]

The bricks and mortar of colleges and universities are impressive yet inconsistent in their ability to instill respect for the past. The emphasis on building and expansion is central to American higher education. One journalist noted in 1985 that more than 75 percent of campus buildings had been constructed in the preceding twenty years, leading him to conclude that "the true campus symbol for the tumultuous decade of the 1960s wasn't a picket line; it was a construction crane."[7] This building tradition has meant that American colleges and universities are simultaneously major sources of historic preservation and major destroyers of historic buildings, as illustrated by George Washington University, which razed late eighteenth-century row houses to create space for its office-retail complex enterprise.[8]

Transformations in campus architecture are symptomatic of changes

—and problems—in American higher education. A century ago nationally famous architectural firms competed for the honor of being selected to design and build handsome campus environments. In recent decades, however, the trend has been toward what historian Gay Brechlin called the drift from "Classical Dreams to Concrete Realities."[9] By the 1950s campus construction at public universities often was determined by state agency low-bid contract guidelines. Today campus architecture is large but often neither inspired nor inspiring. The American campus has become a prisoner of its own success and growth. A century ago it was praised as a beautiful, amenable place to walk and visit; today it is more likely to be about the hardest place for a visitor to find parking—and sometimes so large that students are not able to reach one side of the campus from the other during class breaks. A football stadium and basketball arena used to be built adjacent to one another in the heart of the campus, similar to metropolitan train stations. Illustrative of the transformation of the American campus away from being an integrative, cohesive environment in the twenty-first century is that campus design is more likely to resemble the logic of airports, with athletic complexes built far away from the campus core.

The most disturbing aspect of the historical myopia of American higher education today is the belief by presidents and boards that, if only they had more money, then their institutions would be great. Equally plausible is that, with more money, the institutions would be merely larger, more complex, and less coherent. When gauged by the standard of the history of higher education from the seventeenth century to the present, the problems are more those of confused purpose than lack of resources. I gain reinforcement for this view from one of my favorite authors and books—the late Clark Kerr's *The Uses of the University*. Kerr had no fewer than five opportunities to write a new preface in which he could defend or amend the insights he made in his original work. In his final preface, published in 2001, he concluded that American higher education in the twenty-first century had become uncertain and unclear in its direction and mission.

One manifestation of this institutional malaise has been shown during the past decade in the conventional wisdom of college admissions offices, especially at academically selective institutions. Annual increases in college enrollments nationwide have been accompanied by an even greater growth in the number of applications for undergraduate admissions that colleges receive. It is indicative of what has been called "application inflation," which college presidents ascribe to the belief that "bigger numbers mean better students." As Eric Hoover has questioned, however, where are the signs that college officials have considered "When is enough enough?"[10] Evidently a number of colleges gain reflected glory in their record for denying even highly qualified applicants. It is a syndrome that is commensurate with the research arms race in pursuit of federal grants—pursuits that at some point become counterproductive and dubious in educational propriety. Illustrative of the unfortunate abuses of the syndrome is its encouragement of indulgent consumerism. High school seniors, for example, tend to be encouraged to apply to ten to twenty undergraduate programs—a behavior made increasingly easy by the availability of internet on-line common application forms. In addition to inflating and clogging the admissions and selection channels, this collective behavior most likely favors students who already have advantages in terms of college counselors and educated parents. It may help some colleges buoy their statistics and ratios in such rankings as those published by *U.S. News and World Report.* On balance, however, it does little to increase genuine access, choice, and affordability to students from underserved constituencies. It represents a peculiar, furtive behavior on the part of established colleges and universities that begs the question of significant educational issues.

How should we gauge the most significant historical changes that will have implications for the twenty-first century? I think that universities, contrary to a stereotype of being stodgy and belatedly mimicking companies and commercial organizations, have often led the way in an organizational transformation that is consequential for American life. The university model, in sum, has been increasingly attractive as a structural and legal arrangement for what once would have been categorized as commercial ventures. The truism used to be, "Why can't a college be run more like a business?" On closer inspection one finds that pragmatic entrepreneurs have discovered that the smart money opts for a business to be run more like a college—or, more specifically, like a university.[11] Often overlooked is that, in legal and technical terms, all the designation "nonprofit" means is that an organization does not offer stocks and dividends to investors. Nonprofit status is relatively silent on matters of compensation and earnings. It is relatively easy to gain status as a 501(c)3 nonprofit, tax-exempt entity. Hence, any enterprise even remotely related to educational, scientific, and service-oriented activities has a good chance to qualify as a privileged nonprofit entity. This has certainly been an attractive option for numerous enterprises associated with health care services and commercial applications of research and development. To suggest the flexibility of this legal arrangement, one might consider that even the National Collegiate Athletic Association enjoys nonprofit standing, despite its highly lucrative and commercial ventures into broadcasting and spectator sports. As a recent Stanford University study concluded, when it comes to gaining nonprofit status, the American model is that "Anything Goes!" The downside has been that universities are less distinctive and less special in how various levels of government treat them.

If the institutional conduct in inflating admissions applications were not sufficiently suspect regarding college and university priorities, events of the past decade involving endowments and investments have suggested what truly is a world turned upside down. Or, stated another way, it has been a strange world in which university values about stewardship have been inverted so as to be wrong-headed. A decade ago Yale's chief investment officer, David Swensen, wrote the influential book *Pioneering Portfolio Management*—with the interesting subtitle "An unconventional approach to institutional investment."[12] According to Andrew Delbanco's 14 May 2009 essay review in the *New York Review of Books,* Swensen's principal case to his professional academic investment managers was that he had discovered no less than the formula to assure university endowments high yields with low risks.[13] Indeed, this worked—for awhile. Perusing the annual editions of the *Chronicle of Higher Education*'s special almanac year-by-year over the past decade, one does indeed find a three- or four-year run in the middle of the decade when numerous universities reported annual enrollment growth of 10 percent, 15 percent, and even 20 percent. But look again—by 2008 and 2009 the double-digit numbers are intact, except that by these years they had turned from gains to losses. What is ironic in terms of sound academic values is that philanthropy and higher education, including the wise and sound stewardship of endowments, evidently has come to mean in the twenty-first century that it is imprudent for a university to spend 10 percent or 15 percent per year on academic improvement and enhancements to assure quality and affordability for students. Evidently, however, it is all right—or, at least, understandable and forgivable—for the same institution to lose 10 percent to 30 percent on its endowment through risky investment strategies. Are our universities off course in their gyroscope of values and priorities and goals when it is acceptable to lose a large part of the endowment due to greed and risk-taking investments but off base and spendthrift when "investing" in the present and future by spending substantially more than the customary albeit unworthy limit of 5 percent spend-down per year to solve problems and provide solutions to educational concerns? That is a dilemma of endowments and philanthropy for American higher education in the twenty-first century that calls out for historical complexity and context to shape present and future deliberations. One imperative for this brand of informed, rigorous self-scrutiny of development and endowment policies is the sobering fact, according to the *New York Times* in November 2010, that universities will be challenged to reconsider "business as usual" because donors have retrenched. One reason for this change in giving behavior is evidently due to a loss of confidence in colleges and universities, with the result that "donors, especially major donors, ask tougher questions about institutions than they did when they trusted leadership throughout society."[14]

The kinds of enterprising organizational behavior found in admissions, fund-raising, and endowments have yet another, related significant consequence for the blurring line between educational and commercial activities in American higher education. An Achilles heel in large-scale academic research is that the private or commercial sector, as represented by pharmaceutical companies, has been able to evade a great deal of expense and risk. That situation has been allowed to persist because federally sponsored research usually directed toward university-based research centers has been well funded, leaving campus-based scientists to take on the burden of expensive, time-consuming, and precarious basic research. But the indefinite, generous support of campus research has become increasingly uncertain and fragile. Over the long run this cobbled relationship of corporations and campus has become harmful or at least skewed, in that it obligates federal resources to projects that might be directed elsewhere within higher education for other goals.[15] The most troublesome consequence is that these dynamics propel universities to act increasingly as if they were commercial rather than educational institutions.

Acknowledgments

I've been fortunate to receive help from many colleagues while working on this book. Geraldine Joncich Clifford, professor emeritus at the University of California, Berkeley, has been my mentor since 1969. Frederick Rudolph, professor emeritus at Williams College, has shared materials from his own projects dealing with the history of American colleges and universities. Professor Jack Schuster, Claremont Graduate University, started talking with me about this topic when we both were graduate students at Berkeley—a conversation that has been going for three decades. Scholars who frequently gave me insights on higher education include James Axtell of the College of William and Mary; Thomas Dyer, Jr., of the University of Georgia; John T. Casteen III, of the University of Virginia; Bruce Leslie of the State University of New York, Brockport; Kathryn Spoehr of Brown University; Lawrence Wiseman of the College of William and Mary; James W. Thelin of the University of Tennessee; Peter C. Thelin of West Valley Community College; and Alan W. Blazar of the Marquandia Society for Studies in History and Literature. The late Howard Bowen of Claremont Graduate School encouraged me to write about the history of colleges and universities. Donald Warren, my trusted dean at Indiana University and fellow historian of education, has long supported my work. Edward Kifer of the University of Kentucky patiently read chapter drafts, with concern for my understanding of statistical analysis and public policy as part of the historical record.

My writing has benefited from longtime membership in two groups: the History of Education Society and the Association for the Study of Higher Education (ASHE). I owe special thanks to fellow members who have compared research notes over many years. These include Linda Eisenmann of the University of Massachusetts, Boston; Maresi Nerad of Berkeley and the University of Washington; George Keller; Katherine C.

Reynolds of the University of South Carolina; Jan Lawrence of the University of Michigan; Ann Austin of Michigan State University; Jana Nidiffer of the University of Michigan; Edward McClellan of Indiana University; and Hugh Hawkins of Amherst College.

Graduate students with whom I have worked demonstrate the adage that ultimately the teacher becomes the taught. At the College of William and Mary, Marsha Van Dyke Krotseng co-authored numerous articles with me and contributed original scholarship on governors and higher education. Barbara K. Townsend, Louise Robertson, Jane Minto Bailey, Robert Seal, Bill Wilson, Deborah DiCroce, Elizabeth Crowther, and Todd Cockrell were research assistants on various aspects of higher education's history. When I was teaching at Indiana University, David Campaigne briefed me on all aspects of academe, literally ranging from *A* to *Z* (athletics to zoology). Gerald St. Armand kept me posted on contemporary higher-education issues. Gayle Williams educated me on religion in American colleges and universities. Doctoral students at the University of Kentucky—Amy E. Wells, Eric Moyen, Robin Geiger, Chris Beckham, Dexter Alexander, Richard Trollinger, and Jason Edwards— have been research assistants and co-authors on a variety of publications. The original contributions that all these have made in their own scholarly works provide a good sign of vitality for teaching and research about higher education.

One reason I was able to complete writing this book was the generous support provided by the University of Kentucky in the 2000–2001 academic year when I was named University Research Professor. I am grateful to Professor Alan DeYoung for having nominated me for this honor, and to Vice President James Boling and Kathy Stanwix-Hays of the University of Kentucky Research Foundation, who were advocates for my book project. I owe special thanks to Vice President Wendy Baldwin and to Dean James Cibulka, Associate Dean Robert Shapiro, and to Professor Jefferey Bieber of the University of Kentucky's College of Education for providing funding for editing and indexing expenses.

I wish to thank the following individuals and institutions for their kind permission to reproduce original sources as illustrations: Martha Mitchell of Brown University's Archives and Special Collections; Craig Kridel of the University of South Carolina's Museum of Education and its Hawley Higher Education Postcard Collection; Susan Snyder of the University of California, Berkeley's Bancroft Library; Mary Cory of Illini Media Company Publications and *The Illio* yearbook of the University of Illinois; Stacy Gould, university archivist of the College of William and Mary's Department of Special Collections; Daria D'Arienzo, head of Special Collections and Archives at Amherst College; and Hilary Johnson of Time Pix and the Time and Life Picture Corporation for the covers of *Life* magazine; and MCA Home Video, Inc., for the 1932 Marx Brothers movie poster. Terry Birdwhistell and Tom Rosko of the University of Kentucky have helped me out on numerous questions about campus archives, oral histories, and special collections.

For the first edition, Sharon Thelin-Blackburn read chapter manuscripts, with particular attention to improving my transitions. Dan Vantreese, director of graphics for the College of Education at the University of Kentucky, excelled at taking care of technical arrangements for the book illustrations. Mary V. Yates skillfully copyedited the manuscript. Alexa Selph drafted the index. Jacqueline Wehmueller, executive editor at the Johns Hopkins University Press, combined expertise and support at all stages of the project.

Some authors complain that writing is difficult. Not me. Thanks to these thoughtful colleagues, I have enjoyed writing this book. I hope they enjoy reading it.

I am especially grateful to Ashleigh Elliott McKown of the Johns Hopkins University Press for her encouragement and expertise in making the second edition come to fruition so as to be a timely part of American higher education in the twenty-first century.

Introduction
Historians and Higher Education

A beleaguered public-relations officer at a White House press conference once fended off a reporter's tough question with the arch quip, "Hey, that's history!" The implication was that placing an issue in the historical domain destined it to the dreary insignificance associated with obsolescence. For politicians and journalists, it effectively closed the case. And since American higher education today is a formidable modern enterprise, academic leaders can easily overlook its past. However, my response is markedly different. For me, the discussion of timely higher-education topics starts—not stops—with history.

Colleges and universities are historical institutions. They may suffer amnesia or may have selective recall, but ultimately heritage is the life-blood of our campuses. I take my cue from a passage in a 1963 Harvard admissions brochure sent out to prospective undergraduate applicants. Its succinct insight was that "wealth, like age, does not make a university great. But it helps." That candid observation was bolstered by some thoughtful reflection. The admissions brochure elaborated: "Obviously age does not guarantee excellence. It may produce simply smug somnolence and hardened arteries. But the University has grown with the country. It has maintained over three centuries an extraordinary vitality and a tough-minded awareness of changing conditions. Its ability to survive and grow strong over these three troubled centuries and its deep roots in the American past have given it an unusual mixture of perspective, confidence, and continuity of purpose."[1]

I find this to be a healthy attitude for approaching the history of higher education. In this book I will introduce the topic by relating some stories that I hope will prompt readers to think historically about events whose outcomes were neither clear nor certain to the participants when the events were taking place. The aim is to gently upset some conventional notions about how colleges and universities have developed and behaved, especially in such volatile matters as institutional costs and effectiveness; admissions and access; and the character of the curriculum and extracurriculum. This undertaking will mean exhuming forgotten facts and overlooked data to persuade readers to suspend contemporary notions about academic prestige as well as academic problems.

History does matter. Even the basic facts—names, numbers, and dates—are subject to contemporary confusion and debate. At the inauguration of a college president, institutional representatives usually line up according to the age of their respective institutions, with seniority conferring the privilege of marching at the front of the academic procession. Seldom does anyone in Europe question the right of the delegate from the University of Bologna to lead the procession, because, after all, it was founded in the thirteenth century. Nor do many representatives from colleges in the United States have the audacity or ignorance to step in front of Harvard, with its charter of 1636. After that, however, things get a little more tense when, for example, the delegate from Hampden-Sydney cuts in line in front of Brown University's representative. How does a historian resolve the dispute as to whether both were chartered in 1764?[2]

Consider the recent dispute between two colleges as to which had the right to use a historic name. In 1996, Trenton State College announced that henceforth it would call itself the College of New Jersey. This was the original name for what is now Princeton University. Although Princeton had not used that title for over a century, it "filed trademark applications to try to retain rights to the name and strip it from Trenton State College."[3] This was no trifle, as Princeton's vice president for public affairs explained in a letter to the editor of the *Chronicle of Higher Education:*

> The only college president to sign the Declaration of Independence was John Witherspoon, from the College of New Jersey. The first meeting ever of the New Jersey State Legislature took place 220 years ago this summer on the campus of the College of New Jersey. The only U.S. Presidents educated in New Jersey, James Madison and Woodrow Wilson, were students at the College of New Jersey. The first intercollegiate football game was played between two New Jersey teams, including one wearing the orange colors of the College of New Jersey.
>
> Much important U.S., New Jersey, and collegiate history took place at the College of New Jersey. So it is not surprising that Trenton State College

wishes to wrap itself in that history by taking over a name that, for 150 years, was the name of what is now Princeton University. We are proud of our history and proud of our original name, and we will do everything we can to prevent someone else from taking it from us.

In its efforts to improve quality, we wish Trenton State every success, as we do all other colleges and universities in New Jersey. But we hope the trustees of Trenton State will proceed under a name of their own, not under ours. At a minimum, if they decide to change let them think about becoming the College *for* New Jersey, not the College *of* New Jersey, and leave our history to us.[4]

Eventually the two institutions reached an agreement to allow Trenton State to call itself the College of New Jersey. Soon thereafter, the "new" College of New Jersey asserted its heritage with a preamble that had Princeton's tone, but fleshed out with different facts: "At the College of New Jersey, you will find that traditions are important. The college's history reaches back to 1855. It was established by the state legislature as the Normal School, New Jersey's first, and the nation's ninth, teacher training school. The school flourished in the latter 1800s and the first baccalaureate program was established in 1925. This change marked the beginning of TCNJ's transition to a four-year college."[5] Each institution had a different story for the same name. Both cases demonstrated that justifiable institutional pride in the past was essential for purpose and confidence in the present.

From time to time presidents and trustees at colleges and universities face pressure from politicians to alter their institutional history because of its potential to contribute to civic or state pride. For example, in 1948 the mayor of Louisville undertook a prolonged campaign to "push to relocate the founding of the University of Louisville back to 1798" instead of its conventional date of 1837. He underwrote "energetic chronological research" in a quest for documents that would confirm his point. According to the university historians, "He kept a vertical chart listing the founding dates of the earlier universities, the U of L coming at the end. Then as his search through the documents enabled him to attain a fresh conclusion, he'd push the position of the U of L a few slots up on the chart and cry out, 'We're gaining on them.'"[6]

These examples illustrate that historical writing about higher education is constantly subject to new estimates and reconsideration. If we find serious disagreements about the names of institutions and their founding dates, then it is reasonable to expect complexity and uncertainty when we try to reconstruct and interpret the most significant issues and episodes of higher education's past. The historian of higher education, then, is both an umpire and an analyst. Given scholarly license and latitude, historical writing can enhance the significance and appeal of contemporary policy issues associated with higher education. My professional passion is to write history for nonhistorians. The logic, methods, and complexities that historians encounter in reconstructing the past of colleges and universities can inspire as well as inform higher-education leaders and decision-makers.

To suggest how fragile some of our contemporary practices and assumptions are, consider, for example, that in the 1890s Harvard used its medical school as a safe place to admit those sons of wealthy alumni who could not pass the undergraduate college admissions examination. One will not find such data in the official university catalogue of the era, for it is a "tale told out of school" by the eminent Harvard philosopher George Santayana in *The Last Puritan*, the only novel he ever wrote.[7]

If this kind of an anecdote seems to be an aberration and is insufficient to alter our familiar view of academic prestige and positions, I bring attention to an account of faculty deliberations at the University of Pennsylvania in the 1880s: the professors in the established liberal arts college rejected proposals to invite the new departments of history, government, and economics into their ranks. Hence the rejected departments sought an institutional home elsewhere—namely, in the newly founded Wharton School. Unfortunately, historical tensions and debates are often overlooked today as a generation of scholars assume that such seemingly prestigious disciplines and fields have been long established in their familiar settings—when such is not the case at all.[8]

Historians can be useful in saving contemporary decision-makers from rushing to judgment about seemingly obvious (yet incorrect) inferences from documents. For example, one comes across a *Life* magazine cover photograph featuring screaming, intense Berkeley students (figure 1). A predictable immediate impression is that of a graphic memento of student unrest, a confirmation of the stereotype of the University of California, Berkeley, as the crucible of strident undergraduate rebellion and demonstrations. This impression might be correct if the *Life* magazine were from 1968, but this is not the case. In October 1948 the editors of *Life* focused on Berkeley as the archetypal large state university, with a cover photograph of undergraduates amid a stadium crowd of seventy thousand urging their powerhouse California Golden

Figure 1. Student unrest at Berkeley? Cover of Life *magazine, 25 October 1948 (TimePix, Inc.)*

Bears football team to run up the score, on the way to a conference championship and a trip to the Rose Bowl. Later in the year those same students would cheer for their "Cal" baseball team, which won the NCAA championship by defeating a Yale squad led by first baseman George Bush. In sum, historical documents have complicated our understandings of the complex multiversity. The reader is then left with the historical puzzle of reconciling the images of Berkeley in both 1948 and 1968 as part of the autobiography of an institution.

These selected vignettes at the start of the book are intended to convey the diversity and change in American higher education by suggesting "reasonable doubt" about the permanence of many present-day policies and practices. The best way for people who analyze higher education—whether as presidents, deans, board members, professors, or concerned parents—to acquire this sense of discovery and fascination with the complexities of their institutional past is to "get dirty with data," to work with unwieldy sources and disparate materials in archives and files.

The stakes of this charge become higher when college and university presidents invoke historical cases to dramatize a contemporary problem. Presidents of state universities lament that their annual appropriations from the state legislature are now inadequate. The typical historical evidence is that state support had been 75 percent of the university's operating budget in 1910 but had fallen to about 20 percent in 2000.[9] On close inspection, the logic of this presidential argument is dubious, and sometimes disingenuous. A legitimate comparison of past and present campus budgets calls for additional work. First, a cardinal rule among statisticians is that comparing percentages over time without including the actual dollar amounts is incomplete and potentially misleading. Second, the dollars in one era must be indexed for inflation if comparisons with dollars in another era are to be meaningful. And, in the case of the state university budget's changes between 1910 and 2000, it's important to add some historical context. The contemporary president is probably hinting that the state government has become stingy. In some states that might be true. In most states, however, the actual dollar amounts appropriated for the state university have increased each year. A state university in 1910 probably received such a high percentage of state support simply because the numerous other sources of funding we rely on today were either minuscule or nonexistent. Federal research and development grants, federal student financial aid transfers, alumni fund contributions, interest from large endowments, and major private donations have all been added to the university operating budget in recent decades. Furthermore, most accounts of the financing of higher education in 1910 indicate that state university presidents considered their governors and legislators to be both frugal and unpredictable.[10] Teaching loads were relatively heavy, and few state universities provided much in the way of sophisticated laboratories, libraries, or resources for doctoral programs. The residual point is that in American higher education, nostalgia for the past needs to be tempered with some careful analyses. What started out as an "obvious" comparison of higher education's past and present

finances has turned out to be a thorny, complex issue that resists simplistic judgment.

In 1968, sociologists Christopher Jencks and David Riesman noted in
their introduction to their remarkable book, *The Academic Revolution,*
that serious writing and systematic research about higher education had
surged since about 1960. They recalled, "When we began studying higher
education more than a decade ago, the number of scholars in the field
was small enough so that we could know almost all of them personally
and keep up a correspondence with them. Today this is no longer possible. Even keeping up with published reports is a full-time occupation,
especially if one defines 'the problem' to include not only higher education, but its relationship to American society."[11] This proliferation of
scholarship about colleges and universities has continued over the past
three decades. Given this remarkable energy, one aim of my book is to
bring together the fresh research by historians who since about 1970 have
made interesting contributions to our understanding of higher education. Heretofore these works may have not always been acknowledged as
part of the broad interpretation of American higher education.

Hence the account I present relies greatly on a synthesis of articles,
books, and monographs by dozens of established historians. In particular, I owe a debt to Frederick Rudolph for his 1962 classic, *The American
College and University: A History.* My book is, in essence, an attempt to
acknowledge Rudolph's work—not in the sense of being an imitation
but rather in an effort to try my own hand and to carry out some suggestions made in the introductory essay I wrote in 1990 as part of a reissue
of his influential book.[12]

The need for a new book now is twofold. Rudolph's 1962 classic work
has some limits. First, it stops with coverage around 1960, and we now
have more than four decades of additional events and episodes that
call for incorporation into our historical analysis—not just as "current
events." The same characterization holds true for the exemplary two-
volume anthology of primary sources and documentary history that
Richard Hofstadter and Wilson Smith edited in 1961.[13] Second, and perhaps most difficult to fuse into the higher-education "memory," is that
since 1960 there has been an interesting, often underappreciated flow
of historical scholarship not just analyzing events since 1960 but rather
dealing with the entire history of higher education. These works and
their authors have not been fully acknowledged or incorporated into an
overarching synthesis. I hope this book redresses that imbalance.

Frederick Rudolph's classic work devotes most of its attention to established colleges and universities. My account extends the domain to include analysis of the historical significance of other understudied institutions, such as community colleges, women's colleges, and the historically black campuses. I also try to give some discussion to proprietary schools and freestanding professional colleges. These campuses, whether familiar or understudied, are all part of what I call "vertical history" because they are the familiar landmarks that stand upright in our institutional consciousness. I also try to expand the perspective so as to bring explicit attention to what I call "horizontal history": the founding and influence of institutions and agencies that cut horizontally across the higher-education landscape. These include private foundations, government agencies, and regional boards. The horizontal perspective is a lens that is especially crucial to understanding the interplay between organized philanthropy and higher education.[14] It also provides a good way to integrate a history of public policies with one of colleges and universities. This important addition acknowledges the role of external government programs at local, state, and federal levels that had significance for higher-education institutions.

My approach to writing a history of American higher education emphasizes the notion of the organizational *saga*—a term drawn from sociologist Burton Clark's influential analysis of distinctive colleges in the early 1970s.[15] By *saga* I mean the proposition that institutions are heirs to various historical strands. On one level, there is the "official" chronology as presented in board meetings and formal documents. At the same time, other constituencies transmit the embellished history associated with legends, lore, and heroic events. This history includes the informal yet powerful memories of students, quite apart from official documents or accounts. For example, there is no formal record to confirm that in 1819 Daniel Webster tearfully said to the Supreme Court about Dartmouth, "It is, sir, but a small college—and yet there are those who love it." Despite this lack of formal documentation, the embellished account has had an enduring, powerful impact on how Americans think about colleges as historic, special places. It is a strand of institutional memory that warrants inclusion in any substantive historical account.

Architecture is essential for capturing and conveying the historical motifs that each campus projects via its monuments and memorials. Forty years ago historian Allan Nevins described the importance of campus architecture for institutional saga: "One of the more difficult obligations of these new institutions has been the creation of an atmosphere, a tradition, a sense of the past which might play as important a part in the education of sensitive students as any other influence. This requires time, sustained attention to cultural values, and the special beauties of landscape and architecture. . . . This spiritual grace the state universities cannot acquire quickly, but they have been gaining it."[16]

Understanding the role of architecture sometimes means paying attention to buildings apart from the conspicuous great campus construction of bell towers and arches. For example, a university's historical saga often depends on certain shrines for enduring inspiration not because they are magnificent architecture but rather because they are hallowed ground of important events. So although Stanford University includes the impressive Mediterranean-revival chapel that the founders had built in honor of their son (and the institution's namesake), the complete institutional saga must also celebrate the modest rented garage near the campus where in the late 1930s two young Stanford alumni, William Hewlett and David Packard, worked out their innovations in electrical engineering that ultimately helped to spawn the computer industry of Northern California's "Silicon Valley."

My approach is to consider key historical episodes that have enduring implications for colleges and universities. Emphasis will be on the social, political, and economic factors that have shaped the structure and life of higher-education institutions. So along with acquiring background on institutional histories, the reader will gain experience in making sense out of a range of historical documents and data. The intent is not to train expert historians but rather to provide nonhistorians with at least a sampling of the problems and pleasures associated with attempts to reconcile information from the past and the present. The text will draw from secondary sources and scholarly research. It will also rely on primary materials such as institutional records, biography, fiction, memoirs, legends, lore, photographs, monuments, journalism, government reports, statistical summaries, and Hollywood movies to try to reconstruct the issues and debates that comprise higher education's interesting and significant past.[17]

My reliance on fiction and memoirs about college life coexists with an equally strong interest in the use and abuse of historical statistics about higher education. In 1984 I wrote an article on "Cliometrics" for a quantitative research journal, *Research in Higher Education*.[18] I want to revive and expand a theme I developed in that article—namely, to provide alternatives to dubious examples of historical analysis stemming from sloppy statistics. I found, for example, that most institutional annual reports on enrollments and budgets were flawed, and that such economists as Seymour Harris often took the data at face value.[19] I want to acknowledge the contributions of such works as Colin Burke's remarkable 1982 study in which his reconsideration of fundamental data on college founding dates has prompted a dramatically new view of the health of institutions in the early nineteenth century.[20] I also wish to bring a new generation of readers to consider such underappreciated works as Margery Somers Foster's 1962 economic history of Harvard College in the colonial era.[21] My hope is to encourage contemporary scholars to undertake fresh analysis of historical statistics, especially in the economics of higher education and in the enrollment and retention patterns of students at colleges and universities. To accomplish this I have presented financial data in two ways: first, in the actual dollar amounts reported in documents at the time; and second, in figures adjusted to account for inflation.[22] Even this procedure requires a caveat: making sense out of finances from a past era ultimately must be grounded in an understanding of the circumstances of economic and social customs of each historical period. A thoughtful economist who compares college tuition charges of 1800 with those of 2000 might also ask probing questions about purchasing power, forgone income, and reliance on barter and exchanges of goods and services other than currency. This is the attention to detail that makes the history of higher education simultaneously complicated and interesting.[23]

No author can succeed at narrating a wholly comprehensive chronology of American higher education in a single, concise volume. My interpretation is admittedly selective. Nor do I think trying to present all the facts and dates about colleges and universities is even a desirable goal for most readers. Instead of emphasizing mastery of information, my aim is to promote an interest in and appreciation for working with documents and secondary sources. I hope this relatively concise work about a long sweep of time will show how historical analysis of higher education may be transformed from a passive spectator sport into an active intellectual pursuit. The varieties of records about institutional heritage, including the numerous versions that are written and rewritten by new generations and multiple audiences, hold out the promise of American higher education's lively, enjoyable past.

A History
of American
Higher
Education

I   Colleges in the Colonial Era

Colleges and the Colonial Revival

The historic colleges founded in the colonial era enjoy a special place in our national memory. Our oldest corporation, for example, is Harvard College, not a commercial business. Not only are these colleges old, they also are influential and vivid in the American imagination. When President Dwight D. Eisenhower visited the Dartmouth campus in 1953 he exclaimed, "Why, this is how I always thought a college should look!"[1] Most Americans understood his response and shared his sentiment. Red brick Georgian buildings with slate roofs, white trim, and mullioned windows, clustered around a green, provided an academic archetype indelibly linked with a real and imagined colonial past.

This presence meant that the surviving colleges founded before 1781—familiar today as Harvard, William and Mary, Yale, Princeton, Columbia, Brown, Dartmouth, Rutgers, and Pennsylvania—stand out as institutions that have acquired prestige along with longevity. Their oldest buildings, including Princeton's Nassau Hall, Brown's University Hall, Harvard's Massachusetts Hall, Yale's Connecticut Hall, and the Wren Building at William and Mary, have become monuments that convey dignity and command respect. These buildings ascend to the status of national shrines because early on, their academic operations were heroically fused with the larger events of social and political history. Their space was transformed dramatically to play a central role in the American campaign for independence. Classrooms became sites of legendary patriotic oratory, and dormitories were pressed into service as hospitals and barracks for troops during the Revolutionary War. As one alumni society's bumper sticker proclaimed in 1981, they were the "Alma Mater of a nation."

I

The obvious prestige that the colonial heritage gives to these colleges today, however, has been neither inevitable nor unbroken. The historic colleges themselves had from time to time been indifferent to connections between their past and present. In other words, it has only been since around 1890 or 1900 that the colleges founded in the colonial era rediscovered and then asserted this legacy as part of their contemporary educational mission and appeal. Once again, the architectural record provides a good clue to this change. Most of their original buildings from the seventeenth and eighteenth centuries had been either torn down or destroyed by fire. Those that survived into the nineteenth century were in disrepair. Many of their original design elements became hidden over the years as college officials, for example, added a porch in the 1850s or plastered over windows in the 1870s. Photographs of the academic building at the College of William and Mary from as late as 1925 show the original college edifice, constructed in 1695, with plaster crumbling, electrical cords dangling from the ceiling, and window frames rudely covered by either brick or plywood.

The important element of the colonial success story is that between 1890 and 1960, Americans, including officials at the old colleges, rediscovered and then revitalized their colonial heritage. The momentum was provided in part by the centennial celebration of 1876, and by 1890 it had gained formal status with the creation of such organizations as the Daughters of the American Revolution.[2] In numerous cities and states along the Atlantic coast, voluntary associations formed groups dedicated to "preserving antiquities," and the old colleges benefited from this movement, which energetically combined historical preservation, ancestor worship, and patriotism. Renovating the handful of surviving seventeenth- and eighteenth-century college structures was the first step, with attention to sprucing up the neglected sites, and the preservation ethos dictated that this was to be done so as to convey some approximation of allegedly *authentic* historic forms and colors. The growing fascination with and respect for the colonial connection surfaced in other visual forms, too. When Brown University, for example, celebrated its sesquicentennial in 1914, its official poster depicted a thoughtful colonial gentleman in a tricorn hat kneeling next to a modern scholar wearing a mortarboard and academic gown (figure 2).

Resurrection of colonial motifs as part of academic strategy gained appeal elsewhere. In Williamsburg, Virginia, the college campus benefited from the colonial restoration sponsored by the Rockefeller family

Figure 2. Brown University sesquicentennial poster, 1914 (Brown University Archives and Special Collections)

starting in the late 1920s.[3] Not only was the academic building restored; there was also a commensurate restoration of ceremonies and rituals as students and administrators increasingly emphasized colonial roots in college publications and public events. Festive colonial costume balls were initiated, as well as such solemn events as "Charter Day," with readings from original college documents. Before the 1930s, catalogues, diplomas, and library stamps had shown little connection with historic names and often referred to the institution as William and Mary College. But now names and titles were codified and standardized to reflect a distinguished past. Henceforth the institution would be known as the College of William and Mary in Virginia. The official language on diplomas took the historicism an additional step: deference to the real and imagined classical curriculum of the eighteenth century meant that the twentieth-century parchment would carry the name Collegium Guillamus et Marius, even though the study of Latin had long ceased to be a requirement for the bachelor's degree.

At the College of William and Mary, revitalized historic pride also displayed itself in the name and tone of the student yearbook, *The Colonial Echo*. Editors of the 1936 edition showed their admiration for the founding fathers by using seventeenth-century typefaces and spelling in a volume "in which Ye editors attempt to intensify the reverberations of the Glorious Past of The College" (figure 3). The college president reinforced the spirit of the student project as he noted in his preface to the yearbook, "Like a great Artery throbbing and pulsing from the Heart of Life, the Aims, the Obligations, the Courage and the Will of 1693 animate the William and Mary of 1936."[4]

Indeed, 1936 was a very good year for colonial celebration. At the same time that William and Mary was echoing its seventeenth-century heritage, to the north in Massachusetts, Harvard was celebrating its three hundredth anniversary with a yearlong slate of academic ceremonies, special events, and guest speakers. At all the historic colleges, officials began to update their admissions brochures and "view books" so as to draw increasing attention to an account of founding, of struggle and perseverance, a mix of heroic events and legendary figures.

Why is it important to delineate this colonial revivalism as part of the colleges' self-characterization in the twentieth century? First, one must bear in mind that invoking an inspired colonial heritage had become potent but had not always been so. For example, in 1888, representatives of William and Mary urged Virginia's legislators to fund this historic institution that had fallen on hard times.[5] Surely the legislature would recognize its duty to help the college reclaim its original colonial commitment to the liberal education of future leaders. This historical imperative might have been self-evident to the college representatives, but they were surprised to find that their campaign held little appeal to the Virginia General Assembly. Legislators ignored the case for colonial res-

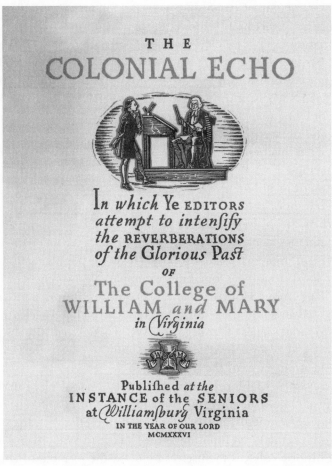

Figure 3. The Colonial Echo, *yearbook of the College of William and Mary, 1936 (The College of William and Mary Archives and Special Collections)*

urrection and instead opted to provide annual subsidies so that the historic college could tend to the immediate and modern problem of educating a cohort of white male schoolteachers to staff the state's emerging public school system. Fifty years later, though, invoking a colonial legacy would become effective in both academic fund-raising and admissions.

A second reason to consider closely the historic colleges as part of a larger movement of colonial revivalism is that the movement fostered standards of academic honor and imitation. Brown University reminded prospective students of its heritage with the following reminder in its 1956 admissions brochure: "Brown is an old institution—older, actually, than the nation itself—and it derives great strength from its rich tradition and heritage. There is a distinctive flavor about very old colleges, something that comes from vast experience, from the durability of ancient ideas and ideals, from a spirit that has persisted long before the memory of living man and even from the ivy which climbs the walls."[6] Colleges and universities of all ages and types across the United States acknowledged this heritage and often attempted to incorporate it into their own ethos.

The American public, as well as academics, has subscribed to this characterization of colonial tradition as a source of educational excellence. When the historic colleges banded together to form an "Ivy League" athletics conference in 1956, the group was nicknamed the "Ancient Eight" by sportswriters. Jumping from the popular activities of spectator sports to movies, one finds a comparable awareness of collegiate heritage among Hollywood studio executives. In 1934 a movie director insisted on sending an entire film crew to from Los Angeles to New England to shoot scenes of "college life." When asked to justify the inordinate time and expense involved, he said bluntly, "I want the richness, the fine old atmosphere of the Ivy League."[7]

A good example of this revivalism and emulation took place at Miami University of Ohio. The university's splendid Marcum Conference Center combines a twentieth-century interior and amenities with an exterior that reproduces the Wren Building of the College of William and Mary. Even the historic colleges themselves followed the formula of colonial revivalism. For example, Thomas Mott Shaw, one of the primary architects of the colonial Williamsburg town restoration, also designed new residential quadrangles at Brown University. In 1934, William and Mary replaced a nondescript field with a colonial-style "sunken garden" to complement its newly renovated Wren Building. By the time Harvard was ready to celebrate its tercentennial in 1936, it had completed an extensive neo-Georgian environment, relying on the architectural firm of Coolidge, Shepley, Bulfinch, and Abbott to create its new residential "house" system, which would accommodate over thirty-five hundred undergraduates. Here as at other historic colleges, it was not sufficient merely to renovate existing buildings. When new construction was required, even it had to look old.

Exhuming and Examining the Glorious Past

Although campus visitors and yearbook editors may have been satisfied with the atmosphere and imagery of the glorious past projected by the colonial colleges, the revivalism movement merely starts our historical inquiry. Monuments and motifs are important, but they are only one layer of historical analysis. The challenge here is to use the colonial celebration as the lens through which to look critically and closely at the substance of these institutions founded prior to the Revolutionary War.

The first research question the colonial-revival colleges raise is, What were the distinctive features and contributions of these colleges that make them central to the *American* heritage? Reconstructing the collegiate past gets increasingly complicated when this question coincides with another finding: the attraction of the early American colleges is in part due to their historic association with England. For example, a recent guide to Harvard's architecture described Holden Chapel (built in 1744) as a "Georgian Gem" that stands out as a "solitary English daisy in a field of Yankee dandelions."[8] When academic leaders at William and Mary completed their historic college building they called it the Sir Christopher Wren Building, even though there was no record that the great English architect had anything to do with its construction or that his name was ever used to describe it in the seventeenth and eighteenth centuries. So we are left with the reminder that American heritage included a formidable strand of Anglophilia. It was, after all, a colonial region that included a self-proclaimed "New England."

Anglophilia is a recurring theme in the history of American higher education. One important interpretation is that the distinction and success of the colonial colleges was associated with their having transplanted the Oxford-Cambridge ideal to America. This was the intriguing argument made by historian Frederick Rudolph in his classic account of the "collegiate way."[9] It is also a theme often presented by the colleges themselves today. In 1963, Harvard College described the legacy as follows: "Students lived together in the college building in constant contact with their teachers. They worked and played together, creating the very special kind of community which has been characteristic of the American residential college ever since. American colleges, following Harvard's early example, have adopted the Cambridge-Oxford pattern rather than that of the continental universities."[10] The late George W. Pierson, longtime historian of Yale, summed up the legacy with this account of the "college system":

> Another essential in Yale's code from the start was the collegiate ideal. That is, young men should eat, sleep, study, play, and worship together, make friends, compete against each other and learn to stand on their own two feet, in loyalty always to the larger community. As at Oxford and Cambridge, books were to be but a part of the education. Or, as Yale's younger Timothy Dwight (1886–99) would insist, the truth can be "but dimly seen by the intellect alone."
>
> Whatever the present differences of opinion on this matter, the historic fact is that from the earliest times the College had tried to keep all of its students together—and the youthful society thus formed had promptly and enthusiastically set to work to create its own system of self-improvement, a second or social curriculum.[11]

This intriguing interpretation, persistently presented by a formidable group of college historians, however, is not the whole story. In order to understand precisely what was being praised and invoked as the model for the American colonial colleges, it is useful to reconstruct the character and condition of Oxford and Cambridge in the seventeenth and eighteenth centuries.

Oxford and Cambridge in Perspective

It is true that the "collegiate system" of mixing living and learning was at the heart of the Oxford and Cambridge pedagogy, and this vision was seminal in the plan for higher education that college-founders pursued in the American colonies. Equally true, however, was that Oxford and Cambridge were distinctive in their governance and formal legal structures. This unique arrangement was that the "colleges" were privately endowed, relatively autonomous units that were linked in a federation. In short, the twelve or so residential "colleges" of eighteenth-century Oxford and Cambridge were the famous sites of student learning and living. College names, including Balliol, Trinity, Clare, Caius, Pembroke, Emanuel, Magdalene, Oriel, and Christchurch, were the primary sources of affiliation for students and faculty alike. The overarching structure— the "university"—was the degree-granting entity, defined and protected by a royal charter. At Oxford and Cambridge, students may have had their academic instruction and extracurricular activities centered in their respective "colleges," but it was the "university" that conducted examinations and awarded degrees.[12]

Why is this important? First, the American colonial colleges fused instruction with certification—a practice wholly alien to Oxford and Cambridge. Second, Oxford and Cambridge were remarkable in that within each university there was a honeycomb network of "colleges," each with its own heritage, tradition, funding, and emphases. According to Cambridge University's historical brochures, by 1596 it included sixteen endowed colleges, and "the founders of colleges were various—but all were extremely wealthy."[13] In contrast, no American institution ever went beyond providing a single "college," and founding donations were modest when measured against the standards of benefactions for England's universities. America's colleges took a long time—more than two centuries—to match the appearance of Oxford and Cambridge. Construction of the Harvard "houses" and the Yale "colleges" in the 1930s was a belated architectural fulfillment of this collegiate ideal.

Architecture also is a useful approach to reconstructing the colonial colleges because the surviving buildings graphically display both the strengths and the limits of the Oxford-Cambridge model in America. The defining form for the Oxford and Cambridge educational and "collegiate" system was the quadrangle: an enclosed, total institution with a courtyard or grassy interior. The historic colonial academic buildings, for all their grandeur, also demonstrated the limits of transplanting England's academic architecture to the New World. Each building was at the time of construction probably the largest, most expensive structure in its host colony. At the same time, neither the architecture nor the pedagogy could completely replicate the Oxford-Cambridge ideal. In most cases the colleges ran out of money before they could complete the construction of a planned quadrangle that would extend behind and around the main building to create the "total environment" for living and learning associated with the "collegiate way." King's College (now Columbia University) in New York City first used Trinity Church Schoolhouse for its instruction. There is no compelling evidence of plans for elaborate construction of quadrangles. In Philadelphia, local fund-raising was intended to pay for what was called New Building, a large preaching hall and charity school. Work on this monumental structure, hailed as the city's largest building, was suspended first for lack of money and later for hospital and military operations during the Revolutionary War.

Even from its origin it carried out the distinctive educational ideas and plans of Benjamin Franklin, who hardly sought to emulate the English residential college curricular scheme.

Reservations about the extent to which the colonial academics sought to create truly residential collegiate environments are found in Virginia. The early statutes for William and Mary explicitly stated that students who were paying their bills were *not* required to live at the college: "We leave their parents and guardians at liberty whether they shall lodge and eat within the college or elsewhere in the town, or any country village near the town. For it being our intention that the youth, with as little charge as they can, should learn the learned languages and the other liberal arts and sciences; If any have their houses so near the college, that from thence the college bells can be heard and the public hours of study be duly observed, we would not by these statutes hinder them from boarding their own children, or their friends, or from lodging them at their own houses."[14]

Adaptation to scarcity was part of the story. Running out of money was a pervasive problem, but not the only factor. Even if the New World college-founders had acquired additional resources, they would not necessarily have considered Oxford's architecture of the eighteenth century to be a very pleasing model. Accounts from England indicate a great deal of self-indulgent, ostentatious building at the universities. Magnificent stables for gentleman scholars who brought more horses than books to university was one Oxford contribution. Laboratories and provisions for scientific research were marginal at Oxford, if provided at all. Libraries were built more for the sake of monumental decor than utility. Diaries of university scholars indicate time and time again that for well over a half-century, commitment to serious scholarship had ceased to be "fashionable" among Oxford undergraduates and masters alike.[15] In conclusion, although Oxford and Cambridge influenced and inspired the college-founders in America, the British universities also provided some examples of educational practices that the colonists deliberately rejected. The colonial colleges were both more and less than "little Oxfords and Cambridges."

This general claim about the "collegiate way" must be tempered by a close look at varieties of historical evidence. First, institutional transplants seldom have been perfect, so for all the invocation of a "New England," well-intentioned college-builders fell short in their efforts to recreate Cambridge or Oxford in America. Furthermore, the various colonial colleges also embodied indigenous efforts at innovation and reform. In fact, the American colleges of the colonial era were remarkable and complex, a hybrid of legacies, transplants, deliberate plans, and unintended adaptations. As historian James Axtell has argued, the New England colonists aspired to create a "school upon the hill" as part of their social ideal of a "city upon the hill."[16] The preceding brief profile of seventeenth- and eighteenth-century Oxford and Cambridge has already hinted at some defining characteristics of the colonial colleges. It is a good preface to a detailed consideration of religion, philanthropy, governance, curriculum, and student life up to the Revolutionary War.

Governance and Structure

Understanding the philosophy and structure of the colonial colleges requires consideration of legacies beyond Oxford and Cambridge. For example, although the residential "collegiate way" appealed to the New World college-founders, they detested the sloth and autonomy of the Oxford scholars. They therefore looked to the Scottish universities' reliance on an external board—rather than faculty control—to give legal definition to the college as an incorporated institution. In matters of charters and academic codes, the medieval universities of the Continent also had an influence that has often been underappreciated by historians. And given the range of Protestant denominations accommodated within the colonies, one would do well to look at the influence of England's "dissenting academies": institutions of advanced learning founded by Methodists and other groups that were ineligible for royal charters and hence excluded the power to confer degrees.[17]

This provision for ultimate control by an external board built in a mechanism for continual accountability. Equally important was the board's vesting the office of the college president with administrative authority. This was a radical departure from academic governance at the historic British universities. In England the custom had been that the colleges were self-perpetuating associations of faculty, with perhaps some rotational authority given to a master who would be "first among equals." The English universities had no strong central administrative officer. Even to this day it remains an Oxford pastime to try to decipher what precisely, if anything, the chancellor is expected to do. The American colleges could not have been more different.

Whereas Oxford and Cambridge masters had endured and ignored kings, queens, and bishops for centuries, the colonial college faculty faced daily scrutiny by, and little indulgence from, a stern governing board and its appointed administrators. A president reported to the board of trustees or the board of visitors, not to the faculty. Reading through the early college statutes and bylaws, one finds other evidence of a systematic effort to confine faculty authority. For example, at one institution there was official provision for a "College Senate," but the bylaws defined its membership as being drawn exclusively from the board of visitors and college governors, not the faculty. Little wonder, then, that academic freedom and instructors' rights in matters of hiring and firing received minimal consideration. This element in the structure and accountability of the colleges was an innovation that had enduring consequences. One could argue that the creation and refinement of this structure—the external board combined with a strong college president—is a legacy of the colonial colleges that has defined and shaped higher education in the United States to this day.

College Finances

During an extended period in which colonies were saturated with taxes from the British crown, it seems remarkable that colonial revenues were used to support the colleges at all. Relative to other civic or public services, each college tended to be blessed with government funding. The General Court of the Massachusetts Bay Colony dedicated one-fourth of the colony's annual tax levy—about £400—to help Harvard College get started. The College of William and Mary, which enjoyed the privilege of a royal charter, was the most abundantly assisted institution, King William having provided almost £2,000 and other subsidies for founding the college in 1693. Either crown or colony provided the colleges with land. In several cases, when founders of a new college grew unhappy with its original site, they considered moving elsewhere. Such cases gave rise to battles between towns, with the host town literally fighting to keep the college in its original place. If persuasion or incentives did not work, townspeople relied on other means. Citizens of Saybrook, Connecticut, "unhitched the Oxen, [and] broke down some bridges" in an effort to block that colony's college from carting its books to New Haven.[18] Meanwhile, rival New Haven offered incentives of land and subsidies to persuade a college to relocate. In New Jersey the town of New Brunswick lost out to Princeton in the competition to be the home of the Presbyterians' College of New Jersey. This did not deter the New Brunswick contingent, which eventually persuaded the Dutch Reform church leaders to build their new Queen's College (now Rutgers) in their town.

Bridge tolls, surcharges on licenses, tobacco poundage, lottery proceeds, and gifts of land were among the varied and sundry subsidies colonial governments relied upon for collegiate funding. But if the system and intentions were strong, the actual record of regular support was erratic and (at least from the colleges' perspective) marginal if not insufficient. From the start, then, American colleges perpetually depended on tuition payments and donations as well as subsidies to operate.[19] The colleges also learned through experience the need for accountability and good record keeping, particularly as they came to acquire substantial resources. During the Revolutionary War, for example, Harvard's treasurer absconded with college funds, an action that one economic historian has described as "disturbing."[20]

Religion and the College

Religion occupied a central but confined place in the colonial colleges. Although the New World provided some opportunities for religious freedom not found in England or Europe, it does not follow that the colonies were hospitable to religious tolerance. Rhode Island was an anomaly on two counts. First, its founding by a Baptist put it outside the orbit of not only the Church of England but even the "accepted" learned Protestant denominations. Second, its allowance for religious practice by a number of groups was exceptional. This tolerance worked its way into Rhode Island's collegiate charter, with the explicit provision that "there shall never be admitted any Religious Tests but on the Contrary all members hereof shall forever enjoy full free absolute and uninterrupted Liberty of Conscience," and that "the Sectarian differences of opinions shall not make any Part of the Public and Classical Instruction."[21]

Even this accommodation had strict limits. The colonies were a Christian world, and more accurately a Protestant world. Well into the eighteenth century, few colonial governments accommodated Quakers. We find no establishment of a Roman Catholic–affiliated college in the colonies. Judaism did not enter into the discussions, even though college scholars sometimes studied Hebrew. Appointments to the governing board of the tolerant College of Rhode Island were set by statute to follow a strict formula that limited membership to Baptists, Presbyterians,

Congregationalists, and Anglicans. New Jersey—along with Rhode Island, probably the most diverse and tolerant of the colonies—was home to two colleges: the College of New Jersey, founded by and for Presbyterians, and Queen's College, tied closely to the Dutch Reform denomination. At the College of William and Mary all masters and scholars were required to take an oath of allegiance to the crown and to the Church of England. What we find, then, especially in the seventeenth and early eighteenth centuries, is a precarious balance in which each colony and its college were staked out by followers of a particular Protestant denomination.

Was this a "theocracy"? Contrary to conventional wisdom, it was not. The Massachusetts Bay Colony had restrictions on clergy and government. Harvard College's statutes for appointments to the college's board made a clear distinction between "ministers" and "magistrates." Although divines were influential and powerful figures in the life of the colonies, including the colleges, ordained clergy could not hold government office. Hence there were some structural checks and balances with respect to clerical power. This provision, however, did not prohibit one religious group from dominating institutions. The College in Connecticut, later renamed Yale, was founded by Congregationalists who had become displeased with what they thought was theological laxity of the Harvard divines. In their new venture as "wilderness prophets," they soon faced some bad news: college board members were surprised to discover that their newly selected rector and their one tutor, upon whom they had relied to uphold a strict Congregational orthodoxy, had publicly declared for Episcopacy. Anglicans were not welcome in Connecticut or at its college. Illustrating the power of the external board, both the rector and tutor were dismissed immediately, and henceforth all those who were appointed to the faculty were required to subscribe to a "confession of Congregational orthodoxy."

There was an important change in the politics of religion and colleges by the mid-eighteenth century. The aim at some of the newer colleges was to allow some diversity and balance of representation among sects in an effort to keep any single group from gaining hegemony. The original proposal for the creation of King's College in New York had called for it to be an Anglican institution, but by 1753 a group of Presbyterians, many from the nearby College of New Jersey, had effectively blocked this measure. The compromise was that the charter required the King's College president to be Anglican, but its board members were to be drawn from other Protestant denominations, and its admissions requirements showed no favoritism toward any one sect.

These episodes and resolutions indicate that within the ranks of the colonial colleges there was no love lost and little tolerance extended between competing denominations. According to historian Jurgen Herbst, the religious disputes in matters of college governance were a result of the proliferation of Protestant denominations, which led to increased diversity within the colonial population, especially in the Middle Atlantic region. Colonial governments tried to avoid social disruption by encouraging denominational tolerance, even in college admission policies. In the mid-eighteenth century, however, this practice broke down when the dominant denomination at a particular college clashed with the varied mix of Methodists, Baptists, and Quakers among students and their parents. Herbst claims that the breakdown of interdenominational tolerance in college governance laid the groundwork for the nineteenth-century trend in which each religious group would seek to found its own colleges.[22]

Philanthropy

Philanthropy was closely tied to religion — a partnership of which colleges were major beneficiaries. This partnership worked in several interlocking ways. First, devout donors in England who may not have been specifically interested in endowing a college were nevertheless intrigued by the prospects for missionary work among the American Indians. Such donors were generous in their support of programs designed to provide a Christian education to those they considered to be savages. Colonial colleges were an available, appropriate vehicle to administer such funds and to carry out these charitable programs.[23]

Resourceful college officials were adept at gaining permission to implement flexible interpretations of wills and bequests. Perhaps the best illustration of this sort of philanthropic windfall is the estate of the wealthy English chemist Sir Robert Boyle. Boyle's will designated that rents from his estate, the Brafferton, were to be used to support "pious and charitable works." The executor of the estate had license to define this directive as including scholarships for Indian students in the wilderness of America. And representatives of two colonial colleges — Harvard and the College of William and Mary — were eager to let the executor know that their colleges were available to help carry out Boyle's charitable wishes. In addition to the scholarship funds, each college also claimed a sum for operating expenses (probably a forerunner to "overhead" accounts). Later, ingenious college officials argued successfully that the scholarships could also be used to educate colonial students who aspired to become missionary teachers among the Indians.

Assessing the motives and measure of early donations is not easy. John Harvard and his fellow Cambridge University alumni, whose early gifts of books and money were crucial to the founding of the college in the Massachusetts Bay Colony, are depicted as devout and serious of purpose. The college's fund-raising prospectus indicated that good works — namely, support for a college — might help one to a place in heaven. This was not always the only incentive for generosity, as some donors sought and received their rewards immediately on earth. In London, for example, three convicted pirates agreed to give the College of William and Mary a gift worth £300, and in return they were spared the gallows.[24]

At best a college donor could simultaneously gain both perpetual fame and eternal salvation. One fascinating glimpse at the biographical profile of a philanthropist who combined the two goals comes from the epitaph that Elihu Yale wrote to describe himself before his death in 1721:

> Born in *America,*
> in *Europe* bred,
> In *Africa* Travell'd,
> and in *Asia* wed,
> Where long he liv'd,
> and thriv'd;
> at *London* dead.
> Much good, some ill, he did;
> so hope all's even,
> and that his soul,
> through mercy's gone to heaven.
> You that survive,
> and read, take care
> For this most certain exit to prepare:
> For only the actions of the just
> Smell sweet
> and blossom in the dust

Elihu Yale, described by George Pierson as a "London Yankee who had been a nabob in India," gave the financially struggling collegiate school in Connecticut a gift of "nine bales of goods" worth about £562, along with 417 books and a portrait and arms of King George I.[25] Although this donation represented only a small part of his mercantile wealth, the college trustees changed the institution's name to Yale College as a sign of both gratitude and hope for additional gifts from this new namesake patron. But much to the college officials' disappointment, Yale's will did not mention the college. Unknown to college representatives at the time, Elihu Yale had never really considered the college to be a primary interest among his numerous projects and philanthropies. Religion also probably played a role. As an Anglican he had reservations about being benefactor for a college that represented a dissenting denomination.

Donations to support faculty were rare during the colonial period, but there were some landmark episodes. At Harvard in 1721, Thomas Hollis donated money to endow a chair of divinity. This was an important, controversial area of scholarship, and the gift ushered in a classic battle between college and donor over who had the right to define the curriculum and to pick the scholar to occupy the chair. The legacy of this episode of philanthropy was charges on both sides of abuse and self-dealing.[26] The acrimony that the episode generated was fortunately dissipated when Harvard readily accepted, and adhered to the conditions of, Hollis's later gift to endow a faculty chair in the sciences and mathematics.

One can piece together from ledgers and journals the skeletons of college budgets. However, the records are incomplete and misleading.[27] First, currencies varied greatly in their worth. Silver and gold coins from England were worth more than domestic currency of comparable face value. Second, economic historians rely on rough estimates based on "comparable worth" from one era to another. This strategy runs into problems when an item that might have been essential in the eighteenth century is in little demand in the twentieth. Third, a great deal of a college's income was in the form of "country pay"—namely, gifts in kind of crops, firewood, or livestock. Before one dismisses such practices as obsolete, it is worthwhile to note that even in the twenty-first century the practice of prosperous farmers and ranchers donating livestock for university football team dining halls persists as a generous and welcome custom.

The colonial colleges were lean operations. Salaries for most instructors (called "tutors") were marginal, often less than the wages for artisans. Professorial positions were scarce. The one academic appointment that commanded good compensation was that of college president. The salary was relatively high and was often paid directly from the colonial general courts. The job's perquisites included a house and grazing rights in the college yard for one's cows.

Colleges subsisted from year to year and were dependent in part on paying students. However, according to most estimates, charges for tuition plus room and board were relatively modest, and no college could have paid all operating expenses from student fees. When Samuel Johnson wrote an advertisement for the opening of King's College in 1754, he went on eloquently about lofty aims "to teach and engage the children to know God in Jesus Christ, and to love and serve him in all sobriety, godliness, and righteousness of life." Then he closed with the less lofty but very emphatic note, "The charge of the tuition is established by the trustees to be only 25 s[hillings] for each quarter."[28] Another source of income was endowed scholarships for "poor but able youth." The colleges seem to have worked hard at keeping tuition low and to have used financial aid to recruit applicants. What is remarkable about the colonial colleges is that they managed to survive despite their lean budgets. This was due in part to their fiscal conservatism and also to the legal protections and occasional subsidies provided by governments of the era. But most of all they owed their survival to their tireless fund-raising efforts.

The Curriculum

We have few written records to help us reconstruct the colonial curriculum. Each college published admission requirements and usually spelled out the specific classical languages, ancient authors, and levels of mathematics the student was expected to have mastered. Published requirements are one matter, but strict adherence is quite another. Entrance examinations were usually administered verbally by the college president. Since there was no reliable system of primary or secondary education in place, precisely how prospective college students were to gain a preparatory education remained uncertain. Sometimes the colleges simply allowed boys to matriculate, often as young as fourteen or fifteen years old. Most of the colonial colleges both bent admissions requirements and provided preparatory and elementary instruction as a way of gaining revenues and cultivating future student cohorts.

As for pedagogy, students faced a mix of classroom recitations and oral disputations in which they were subject to immediate critical evaluation by both masters and fellow undergraduates.[29] Often the motivation for a young man to put aside games and indolence in order to study biblical texts, solve mathematical problems, or conjugate Latin verbs was to avoid the jeers that greeted poor public speaking, flawed logic, or faulty translations. The capstone event of the academic year was the series of speeches and disputations presented during commencement week. Varied accounts indicate an impressive level of intellectual discourse and critical analysis. One newspaper account of the commencement exercises at King's College in 1758 praised the presentations dealing with such topics as metaphysics. Contemporary science was given a central place, with the audience hearing a treatise on the revolution of the earth around the sun that was based on both astronomical observations and the theory of gravity. Although the college had made concessions to the vernacular by allowing disputations to be conducted in English, guardians of standards were reassured to learn that the valedictory oration was in Latin. The program ended with prayers and blessings, reconciling secular learning with Christian faith. The newspaper writer concluded that all was well with the young college and urged citizens to "promote so useful, so well regulated an institution."[30] What the newspaper account did not mention was that in addition to the academic events, commencement exercises were often an occasion for extended celebrations and drinking by both town and gown in the colonial era.

The kinds of lectures and presentations that were central to the King's College commencement ceremonies illustrated exciting international developments. At the highest levels of their scholarship and pedagogy, the colonial colleges were influenced by the academics at Edinburgh and Glasgow more than by the practices of Oxford or Cambridge.[31] Political oratory based on classical allusions and sound logic helped to develop the critical analytic skills that defined political economy as a discipline, a discipline that would be central to the college education of future statesmen in the New World.

There also was a fluidity in the collegiate environment that indicates a breadth of learning and inquiry beyond the formal course of study. Undergraduates, including a young Thomas Jefferson, noted in diaries their lessons and discussions with mentors in such fields as law or even medicine, even though such subjects were not always a central part of the official curriculum. (King's College in New York claims to have established a medical school in 1767, but this was an exceptional innovation.) The College of Rhode Island was adventurous in its relatively broad intentions for the curriculum. Its charter explicitly stated that "the

Public teaching shall in general respect the Sciences."[32] At all the colleges the young scholars who served as tutors evidently had interests and learning far beyond the requirements of their formal teaching. From time to time there is evidence that they pursued on their own studies in "natural philosophy," forerunner to our contemporary notion of the physical sciences.

One peculiar characteristic of the colonial colleges in their first decades is that there was little emphasis on completing degrees. Many students matriculated and then left college after a year or two, apparently with none of the stigma we now associate with "dropouts." College students probably constituted less than 1 percent of the population. Enrollments were modest even in terms of the eighteenth-century population. When the College of Rhode Island opened in 1765, only one student enrolled. Two years later, the total enrollment was ten. By 1707 Yale College had conferred bachelor's degrees upon a total of eighteen students. At the College of William and Mary so few undergraduates petitioned for graduation that in 1768 a new governor of Virginia, Lord Botetourt, resolved to provide both a push and a pull to the conferring of the bachelor of arts degree. His strategy was to put up substantial prize money and medallion awards for commencement week oratory contests. The governor, who surprised both himself and the colonists by his unexpected fondness for the college, insisted on the interesting requirement that only degree candidates were eligible to participate. Botetourt's plan was appealing. Several students completed degrees, and the fortunate few who won prizes left the college wiser and wealthier than their less academically ambitious fellows. Historian Phyllis Vine has argued that the ascent of commencement ceremonies as a solemn, prestigious event coincided with the increased recognition by colonial leaders that a college education signaled a young man's entry into a position of power and responsibility in adult life.[33]

Reconstructing the academic life of colonial instructors and students is surprisingly difficult because although many of the elements seem familiar, colonial practices were in fact markedly different from their modern counterparts. For example, one pervasive mode of instruction was classroom recitations. In more advanced courses, lectures on such topics as political economy found favor among both instructors and students. This was probably the clearest link to the remarkable teaching legacy of the universities of the Continent and Scotland. At the same time, the colonial colleges did draw from the pedagogy associated with

Oxford and Cambridge: reliance on tutors and tutorial sessions. Across all these instructional variations, books and paper remained dear commodities, so most work was oral. Instead of the written examinations familiar to us today, declamation and oratory dominated the educational life of the colonial colleges. Colleges took great pride in their book collections, but these collections remained small and were hardly intended to be a library in the modern sense, with volumes circulating to undergraduates.

Even the most prosperous and successful colleges — namely, Harvard, Yale, the College of New Jersey, and the College of William and Mary — remained small as to enrollments and limited as to constituency and mission. There is little evidence that any of the colonial colleges ever enrolled more than a hundred students in a single year. Many of the colleges expanded their courses of study to include a grammar school as well as the bachelor of arts course. The bachelor of arts curriculum did not include fine arts. Some of the colleges' charters and documents talk about intentions to add advanced studies in, for example, theology, but such plans seldom if ever materialized. A fictionalized example of the curricular limits of undergraduate studies may be found in Kenneth Roberts's bestselling historical novel of 1937, *Northwest Passage*. The narrator is a young man who has been expelled from Harvard and ends up serving as a cartographer with the famous Rogers Rangers in the British wars against the French and Indians. He was forced to leave Harvard for violating two college regulations: he had first ridiculed college masters and then, to compound this crime of disrespect, had drawn caricatures of the president and instructors. Neither art nor insubordination had a place in the college.

The incident, although fictional, is telling because it illustrates the extent to which colonial college life was characterized by perpetual tensions between students and faculty.[34] Despite the glorification of the "collegiate way" as a haven for youth and a harmonious arrangement for learning, it also was a recipe for conflict characterized by student riots and revolts. These outbursts frequently were triggered by what we would call "consumer complaints" about matters ranging from bad food in the dining commons to restrictions on student activities and autonomy. Presidents, assisted by tutors, were constant disciplinarians. Student offenders were subject to a range of punishments. "Rustication," for example, meant that a student literally had to "go to the country" — that is, move his person and possessions off the college property for some stated period of time. A more enduring, formal punishment was "degradation," the lowering of a student's ranking in his class. The dispensing of academic penalties in the colonial colleges appears to have lacked the humor and goodwill that often characterized student life in the medieval universities. In fourteenth-century Paris, for example, a young scholar found guilty of some offense such as speaking in the vernacular or missing vespers might be "punished" by having to provide wine for masters and fellow students alike.

Food and discipline did not exhaust the list of student complaints about college life. In addition to these perennial sources of student malaise, by the mid-eighteenth century an increasing number of intense, thoughtful students had become restless and critical of the collegiate order and curriculum. This shift was promoted in part by a change in the nature of student misconduct. Whereas in 1720, for example, college students often were boys guilty of childish mischief, by 1770 or thereabouts an older and more politically savvy generation of students were young men who challenged the principles and premises of their elders. There was a growing student interest in Republicanism and ideas outside the academic orthodoxy. Furthermore, a tendency for college officials to be loyal to the unpopular crown escalated the conflicts between students and administration.[35]

The elaborate extracurriculum of athletics teams and musical groups later associated with the "collegiate way" were not part of the colonial colleges. There was one important organized activity, however, that did flourish in the latter part of the colonial era: student debating and literary societies. The first such group, Phi Beta Kappa, was founded at William and Mary in 1776. Accounts indicate that this student society met and drafted its charter and bylaws in the Apollo Room of the Raleigh Tavern, not on the college grounds or in a college building. Its spirit of fraternity and political discussion was evident in its provision for welcoming fellow students at other colleges to join in starting their own chapters. Hence by 1781, undergraduates at Yale and then Harvard had accepted the invitation to establish their own Phi Beta Kappa chapters. In a similar spirit, undergraduates at the College of Rhode Island formed their own "Society of the Federal Adelphi" to promote literary discourse and scholarly fellowship.[36]

Whatever the boundaries of the formal academic course of study, American college students had from the start exhibited an interest in political discussion and oratory. When a college happened to be located near its colonial capital, it provided a convenient outlet for the young gentleman to observe and emulate the leading lawyers and statesmen of the day. The interest in politics and law, both within and beyond the formal course of studies, also signaled another important change in the colonies and the colleges: the gradual but persistent decline of clergy as public leaders, with a drift toward the ascendancy of the lawyer as statesman.[37]

Although the social composition of the collegiate student body was relatively homogeneous, there were clear reminders of social class. College rolls listed students not alphabetically but by family rank. And, following the Oxford tradition, academic robes identified socioeconomic position. "Commoners"—literally, those students who dined in commons—wore long robes, as distinguished from the short academic robes of "servitors," scholarship students who waited on tables. Little wonder, then, that the College of Rhode Island was considered a bit radical in 1769 when the broadside for its commencement exercises bore the headline, "Nomine alphabetice disposita sunt." Although the college had retained the curricular elitism of Latin, it had made a concession to democracy by publishing the names of its graduating students in alphabetical order. Elsewhere, Harvard and the other colleges continued to list graduates by social rank.[38]

College Students: From Christian Gentleman to Gentleman Scholar

The preceding account of the collegiate curriculum has, naturally, included some observations about student life and the composition of the student body. The characteristics of these students reveal a great deal about the purposes of the colleges, and about the reasons for colonies being established in the first place. If one looks at the colonies associated with the founding of Harvard, Yale, and Princeton, it is evident that college-building was serious business. Congregationalists and Presbyterians—what might be collectively described as Puritans—had definite ideas about collegiate education as part of a large, important social, religious, and political vision. As a group, Puritans had tended to be dissenters in matters of religion. This put them at odds with the crown and often meant that their sons were not eligible to matriculate at the royal universities. From time to time all Oxford students were required to swear an oath of allegiance to the monarchy and to the Church of England. The former was acceptable to Puritans; the latter was not.

The family background of the students at colonial Harvard, Yale, and Princeton tended to be one of mercantile wealth. Prosperous and successful, the Puritan merchants were also devout. They hardly wanted to lose their sons to the depravity of Oxford, where "Cavaliers" and "rakes" represented the worst of two worlds: indecent behavior combined with Anglican affiliation. From time to time during the lengthy wars of religion and civil wars of the Tudor and Stuart reigns in England, the Puritans might gain a foothold in the universities. As a general rule, though, the two historic universities, especially Oxford, were not hospitable to the Puritan sense of propriety, religion, or education.

The Puritans as college-founders were committed to a rigorous, demanding education of young men who would become Christian gentlemen. They were in line to inherit family commercial enterprises in shipping and selling. The tradeoff was that fathers wanted assurance that Congregationalism or Presbyterianism was integral to their sons' daily and eternal life. So the early collegians were sons of privilege who at the same time were expected to inherit grave responsibilities as leaders and men of influence in a new world where their religion was central and not subject to government or ecclesiastical constraints. Learning was serious, and there was great emphasis placed on the ability to analyze and to be articulate. The crucial ingredient, though, was that all learning ultimately was to coalesce into the values and actions of a Christian gentleman.

Who went to the colonial colleges? As the preceding profile suggests, it was a relatively privileged group of young men who were expected to be serious about their studies and their religion. In the early decades, college tuition charges were not prohibitive, and there was some scholarship money available for poor, able youth. However, in the seventeenth and early eighteenth centuries, economic conditions in the Massachusetts Bay Colony and Connecticut were austere. Few families could afford the loss of an able-bodied young man from the family farm or business.

There were significant differences among the colonies that shaped their respective colleges. South of New England and the Middle Atlantic area, patterns of settlement in Virginia and what was known as the Chesapeake were markedly different from what one would have found in

Cambridge or New Haven. By the late seventeenth century, Virginia had attracted and nurtured a conspicuous planter class—a group whose religious heritage was Anglican and whose ancestors had been large landholders in England, gentry who loved horses and hunting. Not surprisingly, these legacies shaped their notion of colony and college. Plantations and waterways, not townships and roads, defined the colonial world in Tidewater Virginia and into the coastal Carolina region.

By the mid-eighteenth century, colonial economies in all the regions, ranging from New England to Virginia, enjoyed substantial growth and prosperity. Local communities had each developed their own networks and hierarchies of regional elites and favored families. By about 1750 or so a college affiliation connoted prestige and high social status. The combination of forgone income and the cost of two or three years of college tuition and expenses made a college education unaffordable, or at least unappealing, to the vast majority of colonists. Class distinctions within the colony were sharp, and the colleges became increasingly distant from the world and experience of most American families. Clearly, a main purpose of the colleges was to identify and ratify a colonial elite. The college was a conservative institution that was essential to transmitting a relatively fixed social order.[39]

The colleges' acquisition of this enhanced role in creating a colonial elite was not altogether direct or immediate. According to Phyllis Vine, there was widespread concern among colonial leaders and elders that parents were not always providing the appropriate upbringing for boys who were likely to hold responsible positions when they became adults. One solution was to shift the socialization function away from the family to formal institutions, including grammar schools and, ultimately, the colleges. The colleges, with their concentration of strong male adults— ministers, alumni, government officials, and tutors—were charged with transforming little boys into little men.[40] The historical importance of this enhanced responsibility for the colleges is that it marked a significant transition in colonial society. In 1960, Bernard Bailyn's seminal work *Education in the Forming of American Society* prompted a generation of scholars to regard families as the primary agents to educate children both in literacy and in social values.[41] Vine does not reject that perspective, but she concludes that by the early eighteenth century the college had supplemented, and perhaps replaced, the family as the transmitter of social lessons.

Given this socializing role, one challenge in accurately analyzing the

colonial colleges is to try to look beneath the pejorative modern conno-
tations of *elitism*. In other words, the remarkable feature of the colonial
colleges was not their elite character. Rather, it was the fact that established wealthy families and frugal colonial governments and representatives of the crown put so much discretionary time and resources into
trying to impart to their privileged sons a sense of responsibility and
public service. It is true that the colonial colleges ratified and perpetuated an elite that would inherit positions of influence in communities.
One could also argue that the son of a wealthy Virginia planter or Boston
merchant was going to be wealthy and powerful whether he went to college or not. The colonial college was an insurance policy guaranteeing
that these favored young men would acquire not only literacy but also a
sense of leadership and service by about their twentieth birthday. Democracy in the modern sense of the word had little support among colonial leaders—a disparity that remains difficult for us today to accept.
The forthright statement of one Virginian sums up the worldview of the
young men who typically went to the colonial colleges: "I am an aristo-
crat. I love liberty; I hate equality."[42]

The colleges stepped in to nurture and harness this attitude. King's
College described its mission as being to provide to future colonial
leaders an education that would "enlarge the Mind, improve the Understanding, polish the whole Man, and qualify them to support the brightest Characters in all the elevated stations in life."[43] A comparable commitment and justification were conveyed by John Witherspoon in 1772
when he wrote about the founding and mission of the College of New
Jersey (later renamed Princeton) to prospective donors in the West Indies:

> The children of persons in the higher ranks of life, and especially of those
> who by their own activity and diligence, rise to opulence, have of all others
> the greatest need of an early, prudent and well-conducted education. The
> wealth to which they are born becomes often a dangerous temptation, and
> the station in which they enter upon life, requires such duties, as those of
> the finest talents can scarcely be supposed capable of, unless they have been
> improved and cultivated with the utmost care. Experience shows the use of
> a liberal Education ... to those who do not wish to live for themselves
> alone, but would apply their talents to the service of the public and the good
> of mankind.[44]

Did the colonial colleges in fact provide their communities with an
effective, responsible elite? If one looks at the disproportionate contribution of colonial college alumni to the discussions, debates, and political

activity associated with the Revolutionary War and the creation of the United States, it is not unreasonable to give the colleges high marks. College alumni certainly did not monopolize the intellectual and political leadership of the Revolution, but they were a formidable presence. Secular leadership characterized by the ability to debate in the public forum and to write effectively on matters of political philosophy and law was no small achievement.

The religious emphasis of the college-founders raises some questions about collegiate purpose. It is important to dispel the stereotype that the colonial colleges were largely concerned with the education of clergymen. The seventeenth-century document "New Englande's First Fruits," in which Harvard officials stated their "dread fear" of leaving future generations an unlettered ministry, is frequently cited as proof of Harvard's central commitment to the education of the clergy.[45] In fact, this interpretation is inaccurate because it fails to acknowledge the tone and context of the document. "First Fruits" was essentially a fundraising broadside, distributed in England as an emotional appeal to potential donors who had little if any firsthand knowledge of the New World, let alone its colleges. It emphasized the religious element because college-founders knew this commitment would be especially appealing to potential donors.

The argument that colonial colleges were devoting a substantial part of their curricula to education of the clergy runs into trouble when one considers that these colleges did not confer divinity degrees. Nor did they ordain ministers or priests. In Virginia, for example, although the royally chartered College of William and Mary was loyal to the crown and the Church of England, it would have been impossible for the college to serve as a seminary. Ordination of an Anglican priest had to be carried out by a bishop. Any aspirant would have had to sail back to England for examination and other ecclesiastical requirements. One must also consider the important distinction between collegiate plans and collegiate achievements. The charter for the College of William and Mary referred to a course of study in divinity, an advanced curriculum following the bachelor of arts degree, but there is no record that the program was ever implemented.

This debate about the relation between the colleges and the ministry was connected to issues of conservative elitism, as discussed earlier. Colonial leaders had an unabashed distrust of an unlearned clergy. Since colleges were the necessary prelude to advanced divinity study and clerical ordination, they were the thin line that protected the colonies from the excesses of populist religion. Harvard College did not ordain ministers, but about half of its graduates eventually entered the clergy. The hope among the governors of the Massachusetts Bay Colony and their counterparts in Connecticut, New Jersey, and other colonies was that college alumni who became clergy would provide an antidote to the threat of uneducated or "unlettered" revivalist preachers. The cautious, critical, scholarly clerics of Presbyterianism and Congregationalism were concerned that "enthusiasm," not reasoned belief, would come to dominate colonial religion and society. What the established clergy did not see was that by the mid-eighteenth century their influence even among the traditional college constituencies had started to erode, with power and prestige becoming increasingly concentrated among an educated secular leadership. There was, in short, a discernible separation of the state from colleges and churches by the end of the colonial era.

Religious Revivalism and the Colonial Colleges

A number of prominent historians, including George M. Marsden, have argued that the colleges and universities of today have unwisely ignored the importance of religious belief or abolished its place in the core of higher education.[46] One variation of this lament is that faculty and curricula have been allowed to stray from the original religious, and specifically Christian, values of the "founding fathers." The implication is that reform is in order—that it would be good to restore the religious spirit and emphasis of the original colleges.

What is problematic about such revivalism as a reform mandate is that its historical references and antecedents are unclear, and perhaps dubious. First, the "founding fathers" of the colleges must not be confused with the "founding fathers" of the nation. As noted earlier, by the time of the Revolutionary War the collegiate mission had already undergone a discernible shift away from religious orthodoxy toward secular learning and leadership. The leading educational thinkers of the mid-eighteenth-century colonial colleges were hardly of a single mind on the primacy of some set of religious beliefs. Benjamin Franklin and Thomas Jefferson, for example, were worlds apart from John Winthrop or Increase Mather. Above all, it is not evident that the values espoused by the Puritan college-builders were especially humane or tolerant. The college-founders were impatient with or at best indifferent to disagreements within Congregationalism and Presbyterianism, and they were down-right hostile toward Anglicanism and Roman Catholicism.

A recurring pattern in the progression of college-founding is that disputes over religious beliefs were a driving force for groups either to be expelled from an established college or to leave it because they felt that it had fallen from religious grace. Cotton Mather, dissatisfied with both the religion and the politics of Harvard College, saw the young Collegiate School in Connecticut as a welcome opportunity to restore to Congregationalism the purity that he and others felt Harvard had lost. The subsequent efforts of Connecticut's Congregationalists to purge the colony and its college of Anglican stirrings demonstrated that the fusion of religion and higher education in the eighteenth century placed more importance on orthodoxy than on interdenominational goodwill. The later founding of the College of New Jersey by New Light Presbyterians was in large measure an effort to create an institution that acknowledged some elements of the Great Awakening, as established Harvard and Yale did not. Indeed, the College of Rhode Island stands as the major exception to this relative lack of tolerance and accommodation within collegiate communities of the seventeenth and eighteenth centuries. To reiterate a point made earlier in discussing Jurgen Herbst's scholarship on college governance of the mid-eighteenth century, the concerted efforts of colonial governors to promote denominational tolerance in college admissions in the Middle Atlantic region ultimately failed.

On balance, then, the religious policy of most colonial colleges was one of favoritism toward established denominations, with a drift toward exclusion of dissenters and evangelicals. This policy would leave a legacy of conflict and fragmentation. Dissatisfaction and departure were precedents established early in the histories of these colleges. Just within the confined world of Protestantism, they were characterized by distrust, wrangling, and crystallization into warring factions. As such, they provide a dubious model for the restoration of religion to a central place on the American campus of the twenty-first century, especially in a society characterized by religious diversity.

Expansion and Experimentation: The Limits of Student Diversity

Instead of being preoccupied with conjecture about the colonial colleges as clerical seminaries, a fresh historical account ought to include attention to activities that extended the scope of the colleges. Experiments such as grammar schools and Indian schools indicate the pragmatism and creativity that the early college presidents and boards brought to the task of devising plans to increase the enrollments and resources of their institutions. Once again, philanthropy was center stage, as the education of Native Americans, including their conversion to Christianity, had great appeal to donors in England. The problem was that such experiments were usually disastrous, and most enterprising college officials who got involved in these ventures quickly looked for ways to get out.[47] Most of the Indian students who showed up at the colleges succumbed either to measles, consumption, or alcoholism. Pedagogically and philosophically, they became trapped between worlds. After a few years of high attrition among Native American students, the colleges had to construct a strategy for holding on to the missionary endowments while shifting attention away from educating heathens and back toward instilling knowledge and responsibility into young gentlemen. Tellingly, the council of Indian chiefs who had initially agreed to send their sons to the colleges felt that the colonial education had rendered their future chiefs "good for nothing." They refused the colleges' offers to renew the scholarship program and politely suggested that colonial officials might want to send young Englishmen to the tribes for a truly beneficial education in leadership.[48]

If a missionary zeal for the Christian education of Native Americans characterized the colonists and their working connections in England, there is little evidence that this commitment extended to a comparable concern for African Americans. Nothing in their attitudes or actions with respect to race relations or slaveholding sets college officials and alumni apart from other colonists. There is no record of colonial commitment to the collegiate education of black students, whether in the regular course of study or at special affiliated schools.

Women were excluded from the colleges by statute. There are occasional accounts of young women who were considered for entrance examinations — strange, because there would never have been any intention to allow the woman to matriculate, even if she had excelled in the admissions examination. For example, George W. Pierson wrote about one "Miss Lucinda Foote whose knowledge of classical authors and New Testament scripture in 1784 was declared to be worthy of admission by the Yale President. She was given a parchment to document that achievement"—and nothing else.[49] One is left, then, with several intriguing historical riddles: What was the reason for this partial acknowledgment of talent without conceding educational opportunity? What would Lucinda Foote gain or do with the consolation prize that gave testimony to her academic skill? Equally mysterious are the alternative modes of education that enabled at least a significant minority of women to acquire a high level of literacy and professional skills, no thanks to the formal schools or colleges.

The Limits of Institutional Purpose and Educational Mission

From time to time historians have uncovered fragmentary records that prompt a reinterpretation of the colleges' scope and mission. For example, is there evidence that such "applied" fields as engineering and science had a place at the college? My curiosity about this possibility was aroused when I learned that the College of William and Mary issued a surveyor's license to George Washington. Was this evidence that the eighteenth-century college had perhaps provided instruction and certification in civil engineering? In fact, the evidence did not support the hypothesis. The issuing of a surveyor's license by the college proved to have no connection with the curriculum. It was merely a convenience that benefited the college: the crown and the colonial government allowed the college both to issue the license and, more important, to keep the licensing fee as well as some percentage of the proceeds from a surveyor's land sales.

Furthermore, there is not much evidence that the colonial colleges provided advanced instruction in the learned professions. A college might have had a professor who delivered lectures on law, but the subject was combined with such topics as "police," a field that was most likely a forerunner to what is known today as political science and public administration. There were no law degrees or coherent courses of legal study. Going to college was not a prerequisite to the practice of the learned professions. Learning often took place outside the academy in various forms of apprenticeship.

In short, the established colleges were not the only places where advanced learning took place in this era. The fact that a college degree was seldom if ever a prerequisite for the practice of any learned profession, including law and medicine, underscores the limited mission and scope of the colonial colleges. The colleges did, especially in the mid- and late eighteenth century, undertake admirable ventures to assure that undergraduates studied mathematics, history, natural sciences, political economy, and moral philosophy. They were not averse to innovation, as indicated by accounts from the 1750s about disputations sometimes being held in English as well as in Latin. But advanced scientific inquiry and what we would call "research" were beyond the resources (if not the intentions) of the colleges. Probably the best opportunities for such endeavors were in private societies, museum groups, or investigations by independent naturalists and investigators. The separation of advanced professional study and certification from the American college was not inherently a problem. Why *not* have other institutions—Inns of Court, teaching hospitals, apprenticeships, or a College of Surgeons or Royal Society—handle such pursuits?

Attempts to reform and expand the academic curriculum usually met with failure. One conspicuous case was Thomas Jefferson's failure to persuade his alma mater to embrace new fields of study, let alone a comprehensive plan of educational reform. The so-called Jeffersonian Reorganization of the College of William and Mary in 1779 was an earnest attempt to transform the historic college into a "university." But here as elsewhere, conservatism among the board of visitors and the unfortunate timing of the war meant that many such innovative reforms had to be tabled or scrapped. Jefferson would have to wait several decades to put into place his plan for an "academical village."

External Relations and the Paper Chase

Constructing a clear picture of the colonial colleges can be problematic for historians in the twenty-first century because these institutions did not adhere to the categories of "public" and "private" that shape our thinking about organizational taxonomies today. Even though Harvard, Yale, Brown, and Princeton all claim to be "independent" institutions today, in the seventeenth and eighteenth centuries each was indelibly linked to its colonial government. This linkage was reflected in the original names. Princeton was the College of New Jersey, Brown was the College of Rhode Island and Providence Plantations. No Harvard commencement ceremony could begin without the procession led by the sheriff of Middlesex County, and no degree could be awarded without approval of a board whose membership by statute included the governor of Massachusetts Bay Colony. The academic procession outlined for King's College specifically mentioned the lieutenant governor's place in the marching order. The charter of the College of William and Mary explicitly recognized the crown and royal emissaries. In most colonies only a single institution received a charter, and overproliferation of new colleges was strongly resisted. Herein lie the roots of an interesting and significant cluster of government-campus relations, ranging from oversight to financial support.

The accounts of the founding and early decades of the nine colonial institutions attest that college leaders were constantly required to plunge into external politics. Many college presidents were skilled at this endeavor and seemed to relish the intrigue and negotiations with constituencies outside the college. The earlier discussion of institutional governance and philanthropy hints at a distinctively American tradition of college relations. It was in the external relations of college-founding and then college-building and political involvement that the leaders of the colonial colleges most conspicuously displayed their genius and expended their energies. On balance, the American college was an indigenous and exciting institution that historian Jurgen Herbst has perceptively called the "Provincial College."[50]

One finds in the numerous early accounts of colonial college life a stark split within the ranks of presidents. There seem to have been many who were temperamentally unsuited to the job or who misread its emphases. In this category one places the hapless presidents who were mired in the policing of student life or, to an even more depressing extreme, intent on gouging students through petty abuses such as skimping on the dining commons or levying fines. Numerous diaries and other accounts indicate that those students often literally voted with their feet and gave such presidents the boot.

In contrast, such presidents as James Manning of Rhode Island College, James Blair at William and Mary, Thomas Clap at Yale, and Eleazar Wheelock at Dartmouth understood and relished the essentially political character of the institution. They grasped the opportunities and understood the problems that accompanied this new American institutional form: its strong legal protections, the alliance of an external board with a strong administrative president. And they understood its peculiar challenge: funding was not so much meager as uncertain and subject to vacillations. This indigenous form of American leadership was personified in Benjamin Franklin, founder of the Publick Academy of Philadelphia (later known as the College of Philadelphia and later still as the University of Pennsylvania). In short, the American college president from the start had to be an entrepreneur in the broadest and best sense of the word.

The successful presidents were indefatigable. James Blair, who persuaded his board of visitors to have him named president-for-life, coexisted with colonial governors over the course of decades and usually gained an advantage for his beloved College of William and Mary. James Manning, who served as president of the College of Rhode Island from its founding in 1765 until his death twenty-six years later, established a reputation as a civic leader, as the pastor of an influential urban congregation, and, in 1786, as a member of Congress. He was an expert stonemason and scythe-wielder as well as a superb conversationalist and orator, and students held him in high esteem as an instructor. Manning cultivated the enduring financial and political support of the Brown family, Providence's leading commercial family for whom the college was eventually renamed.

Perhaps the most intriguing member of this group of lively, long-term college presidents was Eleazar Wheelock. His grasp of the political life of the colonies was matched only by his opportunism. He parlayed Moor's Indian School, chartered in Connecticut, into Dartmouth College in New Hampshire. Later, when farmers and merchants in the western part of Massachusetts expressed resentment at their exclusion from the politics and privileges of the Boston-Cambridge area, Wheelock advanced a bold proposition: he urged the dissidents to secede from Massachusetts and create a new colony. His contribution would be to bring with him the collegiate charter for Dartmouth — on the condition that he would then be installed as governor of the new colony.[51]

The paper chase and the thrill of the hunt, whether for charters, donors, or political allies, were the lifeblood of the colonial college presidents who endured and whose institutions thrived.[52] Architects are fond of debating the relation between form and function. The same concept can help us understand how and why an institutional model allegedly transplanted from Oxford and Cambridge ended up so markedly different in its dynamics. At Oxford and Cambridge, where the endowed "college" was the crucial unit, the structure was comparable to that of a lobster: a strong external shell (including a hefty endowment) that provided the sustenance and armor to allow the growth and vitality of the institution to take place inward. In contrast, the radical structural innovation of the American colonial college left it with a strong skeleton, yet its growth and activities took place externally. American college presidents, who had no counterpart at Oxford or Cambridge, did not have the luxury of retreating inward. Their charters and statutes may have protected them from their faculty and students, yet these instruments also gave them both the freedom and the obligation to tend to matters with legislatures, governors, sheriffs, bishops, merchants, and monarchs.

Timing, of course, was important in charting college presidential fortunes. By the eve of the Revolutionary War, many college presidents were in an untenable position. On the one hand, if their charters or funding were at all dependent on loyalty to the British crown, their flexibility to negotiate in provincial and local matters was obviously constrained. The advantage associated with being president of an institution called King's College or Queen's College in 1766, for example, had most likely become a local liability by 1776. Americans (including Tories) of the 1770s have been described as "vexed and troubled Englishmen"[53] — a mood that did not bode well for any of the colleges whose charters included an oath of loyalty to the crown.

Indeed, the advent of revolution and war put the colonial colleges in a paradoxical position. On the one hand, it was a heroic time for the colleges. They provided students and alumni to serve as soldiers and political leaders, as well as academic buildings to serve as barracks and hospitals. On the other hand, the War of Independence suspended academic operations and, predictably, drained off funding for the war effort. And, of course, support in the form of the royal taxes that had once come from the crown was forfeited. By the end of the war almost all the colleges either had closed down or were greatly reduced in resources and energy. Queen's College probably fared the worst of the historic colleges. A proposal to save the struggling college by merging it with the College of New Jersey was voted down in 1793. Two years later the trustees considered moving to New York, but lacking both funds and tutors, they closed the institution. The timing of the war explains in part the colleges' failure or inability to respond to the exciting ideas about curricular expansion and institutional innovation put forward by Thomas Jefferson and others who wanted to create a distinctive modern university for a new nation.

The Essence of the Colonial Colleges

On balance, then, what was distinctively "American" about the colonial colleges? Here we encounter a series of paradoxes if not contradictions. In the aggregate, the colonies and their colleges showed some religious diversity, but not necessarily religious tolerance. The colleges were concerned with educating their students for "public service," but these students were neither egalitarian nor democratic.

Oscar and Mary Handlin captured the subtleties of the collegiate role in their profile of the young John Adams:

> For young men like Adams, the value of a higher education lay not in professional training but elsewhere. It derived from the belief that a course of learning endowed those who completed it with cultural attributes that were signs of superior status. This was by no means a crude, calculating attitude, but rather one composed of multiple, scarcely conscious, sets of values. The ability to quote a Greek maxim in a legal brief was not essential but helpful. More important was the prevailing conviction that those who had sharpened their minds on the complexities of Greek thought would be better able as a result to deal with the day-to-day problems of trespass and contract. Most important was the awareness that colonial society still put a premium on and assigned practical rewards to people who could display such signs of gentlemanly rank as command of the classics.[54]

Along with refining the politically ambitious and financially privileged young men of the colonies, colonial college-building made a significant, positive contribution to the ideas and actions of the generation that shaped the American Revolution. As Gordon S. Wood has argued, impact of the colleges stands out when one contrasts the aspirations of fathers and sons in the mid-eighteenth century. Thomas Jefferson, for example, inherited from and shared with his father the benefits of life as a Virginia planter. Yet many of the founding fathers attended college and were the first in their families to do so. A college education with its emphasis on informed argumentation, classical languages, and political economy supplemented the landed gentry's ethos with a political and intellectual awareness largely absent from the previous generation. Wood elaborated:

> Both the Scottish and North American leaders felt compelled to think freshly about the meaning of being civilized, and in the process they put a heightened emphasis on learned and acquired values at the expense of the traditional values of blood and kinship. Wanting to become the kind of gentlemen that their contemporaries Jane Austen and Edmund Burke idealized, they enthusiastically adopted the new enlightened eighteenth century ideals of gentility—grace without foppishness, refinement without ostentation, virtue without affection, independence without arrogance. They struggled to internalize the new liberal man-made standards that had

come to define what it meant to be truly civilized—politeness, taste, sociability, learning, compassion, and benevolence—and what it meant to be good political leaders—virtue, disinterestedness, and an aversion to corruption and courtier-like behavior.[55]

The colonial college, then, was the right institution in place at the right time to nurture this predisposition. Its impact was neither complete nor infallible, nor even indispensable. It was, however, significant. The preamble to the charter for the College of Rhode Island and Providence Plantations (later renamed Brown University) captured the convictions of the college-builders: "Institutions for liberal Education are highly beneficial to Society, by forming the rising Generation to Virtue, Knowledge and useful literature and thus preserving in the Community a Succession of Men duly qualified for discharging the Offices of Life with usefulness and reputation."[56] There is a touching sense of high purpose in the mottoes adopted by these small, struggling institutions: "Veritas," "Lux et veritas," "In deo speramus," "Vox clamantis in deserto." These were admirable voices crying out in the New World wilderness, looking for light and truth—and not without strong Christian faith combined with secular resolve. No right-minded builder of a new, better world could disagree with the University of Pennsylvania's motto: "Leges sine moribus vanae" (Laws without morals are useless). Despite numerous obstacles and poor odds, these colleges educated several generations of bright, articulate young men, and probably did so far more effectively and efficiently than their academic counterparts in England during the same era.

Historical memory is, of course, dominated by the perspectives of those who survived and triumphed. Harvard College's founding in 1636 shines brightly today because the college endured. This contrasts to the false start or stillbirth of college-building in Virginia in 1619. The Virginia Company had endowed ten thousand acres of land and arranged with King James I to receive donations of £1,500 for founding a university and an Indian School near Henrico. However, the educational plans were abandoned after Indians massacred 347 settlers, including the deputy in charge of the college lands.[57]

It is difficult to find a wholly satisfactory explanation as to why colleges were established in some places but not in others. For all the commerce, trade, agriculture, and population that existed south of Tidewater Virginia, for example, why did wealthy planters not found a college in Savannah or Charleston for their sons? Was Maryland's strong Catholic composition a factor that prompted either an Anglican monarchy or adjacent Protestant governors to block a college there? The absence of colleges in such underserved colonies as Georgia was not due to lack of effort. Thomas G. Dyer has reconstructed the prolonged campaign by the evangelist George Whitefield from about 1755 to 1770 to have Bethesda School in Savannah enhanced in its mission so that he could petition the English crown to have it chartered as Bethesda College. For a while Whitefield's attempts to gain the college charter seemed well timed because the idea was attractive to constituencies both in England and in Georgia. Georgia's colonial government was intrigued by the prospect of having a bona fide college close to home so that the colony's future leaders would not have to head north to Princeton or King's College to be educated. According to Dyer, the crown's distrust of a college with evangelical roots was evidently the primary obstacle to the granting of a charter.[58] Even though this attempt at college-founding came to nothing, the commitment that the Bethesda College plan commanded reinforces the general observation that creating a college was an important proposition in the southern colonies as well as in the north.

Contrasts in Colonization and Colleges: New England and New Spain

Thus far our historical discussion has been limited to the British colonies. To put the experience of these colonies in perspective, it is useful to look at other parts of the North American colonial world. In 1538, almost a century before the founding of Harvard College in the Massachusetts Bay Colony, Spanish settlers in the Caribbean had established the University of Santo Domingo. As early as the mid-sixteenth century one finds that Spanish settlers had utilized the support of both the king of Spain and the pope to open universities in their colonies, including the Universidad Nacional Autonoma de Mexico and the Universidad Nacional Mayor de San Marco in Peru, both established in 1551. Some records indicate that the oldest continuously operating American university is in Mexico: the Colegio de San Nicolas Hidalgo.[59] By the early seventeenth century the Spanish had established universities in Chile, Argentina, and Bolivia.[60]

Imperial Spain probably surpassed Britain in its commitment to institution-building, educational programs, and missionary work among indigenous peoples in the New World.[61] And although the collegiate architecture of the British colonies was impressive, it paled in comparison with the network of missions—elaborate "total institutions"—that Franciscan monks from Spain established along the Pacific Coast at about the same time that the British colonists were founding colleges. The Spanish colonies had the advantage of a concentrated official policy of both crown and church to fund and supervise distinct programs and goals. But although the Spanish settlers may have built magnificent coordinated systems of churches, missions, and forts, it was as part of an imperial blueprint that was not strongly committed to bringing settlers from the Old World to establish civilian towns and to pursue agriculture and local trade. And the Spanish imperial model evidently had little if any provision for founding and nurturing universities as part of the colonial vision in the vast area of America north of Mexico.

The missions in what we know today as California warrant some comparison with the Indian Schools that were a feature of many colonies on the Atlantic coast. The California missions administered by the Franciscans were well organized and dedicated (although not always effective) in their efforts to "educate" Native Americans, in the sense of converting them to Roman Catholicism and socializing them into a work ethic tied to raising and processing local agricultural crops. In contrast, the Indian Schools at Dartmouth, Harvard, and William and Mary relied on uncertain private donations and were characterized by reluctant commitment. But when one looks beyond missionary efforts and into the realm of higher learning, the Spanish educational initiatives in California are dwarfed by those of the British colonists. The colleges stretching from the Massachusetts Bay Colony to Tidewater Virginia were distinctive in the imperial scheme. The contrast between the British and Spanish colonies in North America reinforces the point that college-building was not inevitable, and the efforts and achievements of college-founders in the British colonies gain in historical significance as exceptional endeavors.

After the Revolution: Colonies and Colleges in a World Turned Upside Down

When the British troops of Cornwallis surrendered to George Washington at Yorktown, the fifers for the defeated army were ordered to play "A World Turned Upside Down." True, the victory of the colonists over the imperial troops upset the conventional political order. Long before that, however, the colonial colleges had turned the educational world upside down. And they had taken the Oxford-Cambridge corporate structure and turned it inside out by shifting control from faculty to an external board of trustees and a president. They had founded and maintained eight colleges in a country where higher education might not necessarily have been a high priority. The most incredible finding of all is an obvious and basic one: each colony built its beloved "school upon a hill" as a *college,* without a strong, coherent base of elementary and secondary education even among its elite families, let alone its general population.

By the close of the colonial period the American colleges were characterized by two features: their charters and legally incorporated structures were strong; and their structures and protections ensured flexibility and endurance. This was fortunate because the college's future survival and health would depend on their capacity for resilience.

An interesting postscript to this discussion of the legacies of the colonial colleges is that the "colonial revival" impetus that started around 1890 ultimately proved to be limited in its ability to invigorate a university. In 1960 a Harvard faculty report on admissions suggested that college brochures and publicity items needed a change of tone. The report warned that "chilly Puritan prose" might be sending the message that Harvard was seeking only "eggheads."[62] In other words, the prestige of historic Harvard was in danger of losing its appeal to talented, lively prospective students. Evidently the report made an impact on the graphics and images projected by the historic institution. In 1970 one commentator observed the shift away from somber prose and colonial motifs: "Until very recently Harvard's official publications looked to have been designed by a Pliocene typographer whose idea of the beautiful was different from our own. Most of them still are in appearance strongly reminiscent of another epoch. Though brave new things are announced within them, they proclaim by the grayness of their pages, that the University is stoutly resisting change. But a few official publications have turned over a new leaf and put a bold face on it."[63]

So, in both 1780 and 1980, academic leaders at the historic colleges realized that reliance on heritage without attention to the changing social and political environment was a blueprint for institutional erosion. How American colleges fared under the auspices of a new nation and a new set of legal ground rules after the Revolutionary War is the next theme for consideration.

2 Creating the "American Way" in Higher Education
College-Building, 1785 to 1860

College Mottoes and American Aspirations

College mottoes of the colonial period proclaimed noble purposes. "Veritas" conveyed Harvard's quest for truth, and "Lux et veritas" (Light and truth) Yale's commitment to revelation and reason. Brown placed its hope in God with "In Deo Speramus." New institutions founded after the Revolutionary War continued this custom of high-minded purpose expressed, of course, in Latin. Thus, the University of North Carolina, chartered in 1790, adopted the motto "Lux libertas" (Light and liberty). The new South Carolina College founded in 1801 (later renamed the University of South Carolina) set a standard for long and lofty Latin with "Emollit mores nec sinit esse feros," which may be loosely translated as "Learning humanizes character and does not permit it to be cruel."

Uplifting as these individual expressions were, however, they do not completely capture the spirit of the era. For American higher education in the late eighteenth and early nineteenth centuries—a period often called the "new national period"—a more fitting motto might have been "Caveat emptor" (Let the buyer beware). It was a period of extreme innovation and consumerism, with virtually no government accountability or regulation. Yet it was not a period of chaos for higher education, because the colleges displayed a pattern of both initiation and response that was very much in tune with the nation's changing geographic, demographic, and economic character.

Higher education would become America's "cottage industry." In 1800 there were twenty-five degree-granting colleges in the United States. By 1820 the number had increased to fifty-two.[1] This was steady and substantial proliferation, but it would be dwarfed by the college-building boom of the next three decades, which by 1860 had brought the total number to 241 (a figure that does not include 40 colleges that had been founded and then ceased operation).[2] In addition to the expansion of college foundings, the period saw the creation of other diverse kinds of institutions offering formal programs: universities, academies, seminaries, scientific schools, normal schools, and institutes. Creativity in the naming of institutions was carried to an extreme in the upper Midwest, where in 1817 a new "University of Michigania" was proposed (the official designation had originally been the "Catholepistemiad"). Fortunately, for the sake of pronunciation, this name did not catch on elsewhere and eventually fell into disuse even in Michigan.

The innovations of this period included internal changes as well as new institutions. Within colleges, curricula were from time to time extended beyond the liberal arts to include medicine, law, engineering, military science, commerce, theology, and agriculture. Institutions whose purpose was to enroll previously excluded groups—women, blacks, and Roman Catholics, for example—surfaced on the higher-education landscape in the first half of the nineteenth century. Far from being moribund, higher education was a robust albeit complex activity.

A New Nation without Nationalism

One conspicuous feature of the new United States was the widespread distrust of a strong national government. That aversion was accentuated by intense regional rivalries between the North and South. The result was that most proposals for truly "national" initiatives were defused. Banking, for example, remained a state activity. Numerous visionary proposals to create a "national" university were either delayed or diluted despite the advocacy of, and even the funding sometimes provided by, such nationally respected figures as George Washington, Thomas Jefferson, James Madison, and Benjamin Rush. When James Madison was president he made specific recommendations for this proposal in his four annual messages. Its greatest prospect for success came in 1817, when a bill to create a national university was brought before Congress and even received endorsement from a congressional committee. It was, however, voted down by the House of Representatives.

An important exception to the absence of "national" institutions was the founding of two service academies: the United States Military Academy at West Point, New York, in 1802 and the United States Naval Academy at Annapolis, Maryland, in 1845. Both were created by acts of the

United States Congress. The federal government also had some presence in advanced research and scholarship, the most notable example being Congress's establishment of the Smithsonian Institution in 1846, thanks to a generous gift of $500,000 ($9.6 million in 2000 dollars) from the estate of Joseph Smithson several years earlier.[3] Otherwise, formal education programs—and especially the power to grant a charter for a college or university—almost always rested with the states, and to a lesser extent with municipalities within states.

Historians of higher education often refer to the institutions of the early and mid-nineteenth century as "antebellum colleges." But it would be more accurate to describe them as a product of the entire period, 1785 to 1860, in which the "new nation" was being navigated and negotiated. Both old and new colleges were included in these negotiations.

Charters and Changes

Many of the former colonies that became states made relatively few changes in the charters of their existing colleges. Obviously, in governance and in names, any references to monarchy were altered. In New York, for example, King's College was renamed Columbia. In 1792 the historic charter of Yale was amended to make several members of the Connecticut state government ex officio members of the Yale Corporation. This change also opened the door for Yale to receive state funds. The most obvious significant change was that the chartering of colleges and other educational and literary institutions now fell under the auspices of state governments, not a national or federal domain.

One other major policy change represented little less than a revolution in how colleges and governments interacted. Whereas in colonial America, as in England, receiving a charter had been difficult, those privileged few institutions that were granted a charter could then count on enduring, generous support. In contrast, in the new United States—especially in the South and the West—the granting of charters came to be regarded as an aspect of political patronage and the spoils system. It was an easy, inexpensive way for legislators and governors to reward supporters. An important corollary of this new approach was that the granting of a charter carried no promise, explicit or implicit, of financial support from the state government. This fact set into motion a perennial quest for funding from diverse, mixed, and often transient sources. Hence by the litmus test of two crucial variables—the difficulty of obtaining a charter, and the likelihood of a charter being accompanied by reliable government or public funding—American higher education was being shaped by a new deal.

Some statistical summaries hint at the transformation of the legal, political, and financial environment of higher education during this period. In England—a highly populated and politically powerful, established nation that was the hub of an empire—only a handful of institutions, namely Oxford, Cambridge, and the University of London, had charters and the power to grant academic degrees. Similarly, in the American colonies, chartered institutions had tended to be limited to one per colony. In contrast, by 1860 the state of Ohio alone was host to twenty-seven chartered colleges, with nineteen in Pennsylvania and fourteen in Kentucky. How to explain this growth? And how did these colleges manage to survive to carry out their work?

What one finds is an array of innovations in both the financing and the curricula of colleges and related institutions. This large umbrella of new, diverse institutions warrants emphasis because it amends the conventional interpretation. The usual approach by historians writing in the 1950s and 1960s was to focus on one type of institution—the small, underfunded church-related liberal arts college—as the prototype of the first half of the nineteenth century. A corollary to this interpretation was that such colleges allegedly were inefficient, ineffective, stubbornly conservative, and an obstacle to the creation of a "truly modern" network of "real" universities. True, the small church-related college was a crucial unit in higher education in the early to mid-nineteenth century, but it was not the whole story. Furthermore, its role may have been underappreciated by a generation of American historians writing in the decades immediately following World War II. The most important contribution of recent historical scholarship has been to reconsider the alleged fragility, rigidity, and mortality of the numerous new American colleges. A half-century ago historians concluded that the small, underfunded church-related colleges founded in the early nineteenth century faced a failure rate of about 80 percent. Over the past two decades, however, a succession of careful analyses of archival data by such historians as Colin Burke, James McLachlan, and Roger Geiger indicate that American colleges in the era 1800 to 1860 were relatively resourceful. Their hardiness is attested to by a survival rate in some cases estimated at slightly more than 80 percent.[4] This high estimate is debatable because it is based on incomplete records and a relatively small statistical sampling.[5] Nonethe-

less, it raises strong doubt about the extremely low survival rates estimated by historians of the 1950s and 1960s.

Historical Memory and Institutional Anniversaries

Given the difficulties of institutional survival in the nineteenth century,
it is no wonder that longevity has become a source of prestige in higher
education today. An interesting legacy of the "new national period" is the
question, Which institution can claim to be the first *state* university?
More than two centuries after the fact, the matter is a source of dispute
between the University of Georgia and the University of North Carolina.

In 1985 when the University of Georgia celebrated its bicentennial, it
gained renown as the "first state university in the United States." This
landmark status was publicized far and wide because university alumni
were able to purchase state license plates that carried that bicentennial
message, tastefully presented with the university's architectural motifs.
What better example could there be of a historic university using modern means to project its heritage, and in cooperation with its state government? The celebration of this heritage soon created some interstate
tension, for the University of North Carolina, founded in 1795, also
claimed the distinction of being the "oldest state university." This claim
was reinforced by the United States Postal Service, which commemo-
rated it in the form of a special issue post card. Heritage, rather than
football, became a source of intercollegiate rivalry. If the sports pages did
not pick up on this competition, such national newspapers as the *Wall
Street Journal*, the *Washington Post*, and the *Chronicle of Higher Education* did. It was undisputed that the University of Georgia had received
its formal, legal charter from the state of Georgia in 1785. The University
of North Carolina had received its charter in 1789, laid the cornerstone
for its first building in 1793, and admitted its first student in 1795. The
basis for North Carolina's claim to seniority was that Georgia did not
actually enroll a student until 1801.[6]

Whether one sides with the University of Georgia or the University of
North Carolina, the episode is important, for several reasons. It com-
memorates the start of an interesting and distinctive period of college-
building throughout the entire area that then constituted the United
States. It also reveals Americans' mixed feelings about higher education,
ranging from immense pride to indifference and even hostility. Finally,
it demonstrates the problems posed by the incompleteness of historical

statistics on American colleges and universities, whether for ascertaining founding dates or analyzing annual operating budgets and graduation rates.

More Institution-Building in the South

The University of Georgia and the University of North Carolina do not represent the entire range of developments in the South. There are also the three important institutions that Merle Borrowman examines in his 1961 study of the forerunners of the comprehensive modern university: Transylvania, South Carolina, and Nashville, all of which enjoyed initial success and then fell from favor.[7] And any survey of the impressive new institutions of the South must consider the University of Virginia. The example of these Southern universities dispels the facile observation that the early-nineteenth-century colleges tended to be pedagogically unimaginative and disconnected from the major social and political trends of the era.

Transylvania University

Located in the western region of Virginia in what was then known as Kentucky County, Transylvania University received its charter in 1780, when Thomas Jefferson was governor of the commonwealth. Twelve years later, the region would be granted statehood as Kentucky.

According to some historians' interpretation of surviving documents and records, Transylvania was not only an early college, it could claim to be the oldest state university. In any event, Transylvania was highly regarded as a pioneering institution and was sometimes called the "Tutor to the West."[8] During the period 1818 to 1826, thanks to the energy of its president, Horace Holley, Transylvania demonstrated both success in its enrollments and innovation and excellence in its curriculum. Holley, a transplanted New Englander, recruited faculty from the Northeast and also from England and the Continent. Although the original sponsors of the college had been Presbyterians, during Holley's term as president Transylvania moved toward a Unitarian orientation. Curricular innovations included the addition of the sciences, especially botany, to the course of study. In addition to a college of liberal arts, Transylvania had a flourishing law school and medical department. Henry Clay, a young attorney from Virginia, taught for several years in the law department. Indeed, Thomas Jefferson cited Transylvania's example to his own Virginia legislature as evidence that Virginia had lost many good students to this impressive institution because the commonwealth had dawdled in founding its own university.[9]

One measure of Transylvania's success was the number of early national leaders it educated: 50 United States senators, 101 members of Congress, 36 governors, and 34 ambassadors. Other prominent alumni included Jefferson Davis, president of the Confederacy; the abolitionist Cassius Clay; and Stephen Austin, governor of Texas. If the case of Transylvania illustrates the potential for energetic innovation in the early nineteenth century, it also shows the risks of a meteoric rise and the erratic nature of fortune. Its location in Lexington, known at the time as the "Athens of the West," attracted a distinguished faculty and president, and they were the toast of this prosperous town. The price Transylvania paid was that its reputation as a flourishing center of the arts and sciences, its adoption of a Unitarian character, and its location in the most affluent town in the region ultimately alienated it from the rest of the state. This alienation was reflected in the punitive measures later taken by the Kentucky legislature, which was largely dominated by rural constituencies and was also an arena for bitter denominational disputes. Unitarian Transylvania became the object of attacks by legislators representing rival religious groups, and support shifted to other Kentucky colleges. Despite its eventual institutional deterioration, Transylvania remained a significant regional and national presence for several decades.

South Carolina College

Known today as the University of South Carolina, South Carolina College was founded in 1801 and opened in 1806. There is little disagreement among historians about its potency as an institution, especially in having influenced several generations of political leaders. Whether this was a "good" influence for a college to render remains a source of debate.

At the time of the college's founding, the lowlands of South Carolina, which included the city of Charleston, were probably the most prosperous region in the United States. It was the haven of a plantation aristocracy whose fortunes had been made in rice, indigo, and shipping. Their aim was to create a college that would keep their sons at home, far from the dangerous notions circulating at a Harvard or a Yale. The municipally chartered College of Charleston was one possibility. Its promise, however, was soon surpassed by that of a new college located in Columbia, the state capital. This campus site helped accomplish two goals. First, proximity to the legislature and governor provided a superb laboratory for college students who aspired to be future state politicians. Second, Columbia was close to the lowlands, and thus geographically and psychologically distant from the different socioeconomic and religious constituency of the state's mountain region. The new college was positioned to be an exclusive, powerful crucible that would confirm the existing planter aristocracy's succession of power and its extension of an eighteenth-century political orthodoxy.

The college was off to a good start, and in 1820, under its second president, Thomas Cooper, it began a dramatic ascent as an attractive and highly political institution. Cooper, an Englishman, gravitated to the political and social elite of the city and the state. He honed and perfected a liberal arts curriculum that emphasized distinctive forms and substance. The aim of a South Carolina College education was to socialize the planter aristocracy's scions into a tradition of leadership whose skills included oratory and argument. Public speaking was the medium, and the content was the political theory of nullification and states' rights.

The educational plan worked well. South Carolina College was the alma mater of several generations of governors of Southern states—not only South Carolina but also Florida, Alabama, Georgia, and Louisiana—and its alumni were disproportionately represented in the United States Senate and House of Representatives. John C. Calhoun became the icon of the college and its political tradition and national presence. Whereas Thomas Dew, president of the College of William and Mary in Virginia, was credited with having written the intellectual defense of slavery, South Carolina College educated several generations of the South's proslavery, antifederalist advocates in Congress. Like Transylvania, South Carolina proved that the South could create its own distinctive academic institutions.

Student diaries and memoirs allow us to reconstruct not only the instruction in the classroom but also the larger sphere of student life. First, tuition charges were high, effectively restricting the college to the sons of the region's wealthy families. Second, the formal curriculum emphasized a didactic method centered on the specific philosophy of states' rights and nullification theory. Third, literary societies reinforced those lessons and became coveted affiliations inviting students and alumni to debate their views and sharpen their rhetorical skills. South Carolinians were regarded as the most loquacious orators in the nation. Fourth, in marked contrast to student life elsewhere, the code of student conduct emphasized honor—its maintenance and defense. Duels, whether fought with pistols, swords, or fists, were accepted as the normal, even obligatory way of settling disputes involving insults to personal honor. The honor code of South Carolina's collegiate life was a rehearsal for adult public life, as is evident in the infamous incident on the floor of the United States Senate in 1849 when, in the course of an intense debate over abolition and states' rights, the senator from South Carolina caned the senator from Massachusetts. Evidently the South Carolinian had learned his collegiate lessons well.

Jon Wakelyn has probed education and student life by examining the correspondence between fathers and their college sons enrolled at South Carolina and other colleges in the South. He found that fathers, of course, indulged and forgave youthful indiscretions—a "boys will be boys" response. But their letters also expressed the commitment and aspiration that "boys will be men," in the best sense of the word. The fathers, usually planters, consistently expressed concern that their sons were coming to understand the gravity of adulthood—the idea that inherited wealth and position also carried responsibilities and called for sound values.[10]

Cooper, the college's charismatic president, remains an enigmatic figure. He was a friend and colleague of Thomas Jefferson, with whom he shared a belief in deism. Some historians of higher education have hailed Cooper as a builder and an innovator who eventually ran out of good fortune or goodwill (or both). Others have paid more attention to his excesses than to his commitment to responsible innovation.[11] In any case, Cooper ultimately overplayed his hand. He insisted on making polemical speeches against the clergy—a disastrous stance in a state in which organized religious denominations were strong. His anticlericalism continued to hamper his career. After he was forced to resign his presidency at South Carolina, religious leaders in Virginia effectively blocked Jefferson's suggestion that Cooper be considered for a faculty appointment at the University of Virginia. Despite Cooper's personal descent from fame and influence at South Carolina College, the institution continued its tradition of education for political leadership in the South up to the Civil War.

The University of Nashville

Whereas South Carolina developed a "home-grown" philosophy and practice for the education of future leaders, an opposite approach was undertaken in Tennessee, under the leadership of Philip Lindsley. Lindsley was educated at Princeton and served for a time as its vice president, but he turned down presidency offers by Princeton and several other established colleges in the Middle Atlantic region. He saw himself as an educational missionary whose calling was to create a truly modern secular university in the frontier of what was then known as the South and West.

In 1824 Lindsley accepted the presidency of the University of Nashville. Central to Lindsley's vision was his belief that families in the South were making a mistake when they sent their sons to colleges in the Northeast. His major fear was that a student who went away to college would probably forfeit respect upon his return to his home state. Instead of depending on distant colleges whose political and social climate was so different from that of the Southern states, he thought the region could create a responsible local leadership by bringing to it the best teaching and curricula in the arts and sciences. However, to do so required a new university that was urban and nonsectarian.

Unlike Thomas Cooper at South Carolina College, Lindsley was neither an anticleric nor a deist. Nor was he an atheist. Indeed, he had strong ties to the Presbyterianism associated with Princeton. But his personal commitment to Christian education coexisted with a pragmatic concern about the political economy of higher education — namely, that religious sectarianism and denominationalism were impediments to creating educationally attractive, financially sound colleges. He commented forcefully in his 1829 baccalaureate address:

> A principal cause of the excessive multiplication and dwarfish dimension of Western colleges is, no doubt, the diversity of religious denominations among us. Almost every sect will have its colleges, and generally one at least in each State. Of the score of colleges in Ohio, Kentucky and Tennessee, all are sectarian except two or three; and of course few of them are what they might and should be; and the greater part of them are mere impositions on the public. Why should colleges be sectarian, any more than penitentiaries or than bank, road or canal corporations, is not very obvious. Colleges are designed for the instruction of youth in the learned languages — in polite literature — in the liberal arts and sciences — and not in the dogmatical theology of any sect or party. Why then should they be baptized with sectarian names?[12]

Lindsley was an articulate advocate. His speeches and articles received nationwide press coverage, and colleges in the North continued to try to recruit him as a president. His plans for his university in Nashville were impressive, and his commitment remained strong for several years. Unfortunately, he misread the consumerism of the region. People really did prefer the small denominational colleges. Nashville's curriculum, which included an array of professional fields as well as the arts and sciences, received commendation from college presidents across the nation, but it failed to attract a substantial number of students or donors within Tennessee and surrounding areas.

The University of Virginia

The University of Virginia, "Mister Jefferson's University," stands out as a model and marvel of planning, in both its educational mission and its architecture. Its greatness is in large measure a function of its distinctiveness. It was a counterpoint to conventional thinking and presumptions. The famous "academical village" and such well-designed buildings as the Rotunda provided the setting for an innovative curriculum that eschewed the usual nomenclature of academic classes, degrees, and course requirements. At the University of Virginia, courses of study included modern languages, science, and architecture. Faculty were hand-picked, coming from international universities as well as leading American institutions. There was no daily chapel, no links to religious denominations. Students were to be full citizens in a self-governing community. The conventional system of demerits and petty rules of discipline was supplanted by a unique student code—a code that was literally by and for students. Faculty received explicit instructions that being a professor was to be their sole and total commitment.

The vision projected by the impressive architectural and curricular plans, however, overshadowed the realities of living and learning at the new University of Virginia.[13] Even Jefferson acknowledged this fact. Some of the disappointments were prosaic, predictable, and relatively unimportant. For example, Jefferson had envisioned a combination of living and learning that would combine the study of foreign languages with immersion in the cultures of other nations, including their cuisine. This idea never really reached fruition, and cooking as well as conduct tended to remain in the realm of regional rather than cosmopolitan habits. It was acceptable to have some familiarity with the classics, modern languages, and the liberal arts, but serious scholarship or any intense commitment beyond the scope of a gentleman's life received little encouragement within the student culture.

The gap between the ideal and the reality of the new University of

Virginia was due in large measure to the conduct of its students. Like their counterparts at South Carolina College, they were overwhelmingly drawn from wealthy planter families in Virginia and other Southern states. Tuition was the highest of any university in the country, which added a financial obstacle to the strong social class tracking that was in place — a peculiar feature in light of Jefferson's professed commitment to an "aristocracy of talent."

A gravitation toward regional and provincial elitism rather than toward genuine merit and international or neoclassical norms was evident in student attitudes, values, and conduct. Virginia's students were the sons of a landed gentry, and they brought with them to Charlottesville their slaves, servants, and horses and their fondness for drinking, gambling, and guns. Faculty were essentially powerless to discourage such pastimes. Because Jefferson had allowed students such great powers of self-determination, the University of Virginia's early decades were shaped by a code of honor that had few checks or balances. It was considered appropriate for students to challenge professors, to take umbrage at alleged insults by faculty. And, most important, the student code defined academic citizenship in a peculiar, wrong-spirited way: "honor" meant never betraying a fellow student — hardly a spirit conducive to promoting the highest values of a university.

It would be fair to say that by 1860 the University of Virginia had become successful at transmitting the distinctive code and culture of the nineteenth-century Virginia gentleman to its students, and to the South's future leadership. Whether this educational success included fostering an aristocracy of talent as envisioned by Thomas Jefferson is dubious at best.

A Variety of Institutions and Innovations

The building of new colleges in the South was the most substantial evidence of higher education's growing appeal throughout the new, expanding United States. But geographical extension was only one dimension of the changes that were occurring. What follows is a gallery of the principal new types of institutions and programs of advanced instruction that characterized the diversity of American higher education, whether in the Northeast or the Southeast, in the first half of the nineteenth century.

New England's "Hilltop Colleges"

In New England one finds substantial evidence of institutional and student diversity. David Allmendinger's *Paupers and Scholars* focuses on the early decades of the "hilltop colleges" of Amherst, Williams, Bowdoin, Dartmouth, and Wesleyan to reconstruct a demographic profile of their students. Allmendinger found that many were older than the "traditional" college age of eighteen to twenty-one, and most were from modest-income families and were required to earn their way through college while preparing for careers as teachers and ministers.[14]

These findings about the students at the small New England colleges reflect an interesting connection between higher education and the regional economy and demography. Adherence to the Anglo-Saxon common law of inheritance meant that New England farm families would not subdivide agricultural land among several sons. Furthermore, agriculture in New England was often subsistence farming, in contrast to the plantations of the South. The result was that by the early nineteenth century the rural areas had a surplus of young men who, in the language of the day, "had no prospects." For these young men, college was an attractive option.

Geographically accessible and financially affordable local colleges, then, provided a safety valve to reduce pressure on land and families. It became attractive and acceptable for the second- and third-born sons of New England families to go to college, both for self-improvement and for increasing their professional options. Teaching and the ministry, for example, were fields that needed educated recruits. The "nontraditional" college students—older and poorer than the traditional college men—responded earnestly and enthusiastically to the opportunities. The strength of Congregationalism and its emphasis on a learned clergy gave the "hilltop colleges" identity and appeal, especially as an alternative to "godless" Harvard with its Unitarian character and big-city location. Under the leadership of such educators as Williams College's longtime president, Mark Hopkins, they would become nationally respected models for liberal arts colleges.

Medical Colleges and Law Schools

One estimate is that there were about 175 medical schools offering classes at one time or another during the first half of the nineteenth century. They stand as a paramount example of American society's fondness for education and simultaneous aversion to strict standards. Few of these medical schools had any substantive admission requirements. There was no notion that a prospective medical student should be required to have a high school diploma or college degree. In such urban areas as Philadelphia, New York, and Boston there appears to have been some tradition for physicians to graduate from college and then study medicine, but this sequence was neither typical nor required.

Most medical schools were freestanding—what we would call "proprietary schools." Some had a loose nominal affiliation with a liberal arts college, but there was little interaction. Instruction, curriculum, faculty, students, budget, and site were functionally separate. The course of study varied greatly from place to place, ranging from one to three years. Instruction usually included a mix of lectures on anatomy, discourses on theories of disease, and other topics left to the discretion of instructors. Apart from these rudimentary lessons, the medical curriculum had little if any connection with new scholarship in chemistry and the biological sciences.

Medical schools were usually located in cities, relying on rented buildings rather than permanent facilities. They had no laboratories, although access to a cheap, steady supply of cadavers was imperative. Dissection, usually optional and apart from lectures, was pursued by small groups of students—usually at night. Instruction was offered strictly on a pay-as-you go basis. Finances were so central to medical school faculty that students were required to purchase a nonrefundable ticket to each lecture. Another source of revenue was the exam fee, paid directly to the professor. And at some medical schools, students were required to take the final examination twice. The aim could conceivably have been to assure high quality of academic work, although the obsession with revenue is a more plausible explanation, for the student had to pay a separate fee for the second, perfunctory examination.[15]

The field of law was in some respects comparable to medicine. It was a popular profession, so much so that European visitors in 1820 commented on the pervasiveness of lawyers and law practices in the United States. Law, however, was a field that had only incidental connection with academic studies offered by colleges and universities. Most lawyers acquired their grounding in the field by serving as clerks and apprentices for a law office or judge. Provisions for state licensure and bar exams were uneven, and none required an academic degree, whether a bachelor of arts or a law degree such as the LL.D. or J.D. This is not to say that there were few lawyers who either had a college degree or had studied at a law school — rather, there simply was no requirement for such preparation or certification. One tentative estimate is that there were about thirty-six distinct law schools in operation between 1800 and 1860, most of which were opened for instruction in the latter decades of that sixty-year period.

It is difficult to chart with precision the evolution of education for the law. For example, some colleges established chairs or professorships for such fields as "police" or "jurisprudence," terms that probably designated some combination of law and what we would call "political science." The role of such innovations in the education of future lawyers was not fixed at the time, and it is even more ambiguous to historians of the twenty-first century. If college presidents and boards in the first half of the nineteenth century were indeed concerned about attracting paying students to enroll in courses of study that had appeal in American society, one wonders why law as an explicit field did not have more of a presence in the colleges.

Higher Education for Women

Enrollments of women in the "new national period" were small compared with those of men. But this disparity is less significant than the net gains that had been made in providing young women with formal opportunities for advanced study. There is no record of a woman of the colonial period having received a degree. In contrast, between 1800 and 1860 at least fourteen institutions enrolled women for advanced studies in what is thought to have been "college-level" work.[16]

Records, admittedly incomplete, indicate that the earliest women's colleges, those opened in the 1840s and 1850s, included Knox University in Illinois; Wesleyan Female Seminary in Macon, Georgia; and Masonic University in Selma, Alabama. The Midwest appears to have been the region most hospitable to women's colleges, with Michigan, Wisconsin, and Ohio having three each. Oberlin Collegiate Institute would gain fame for its double commitment to coeducation according both to gender and to race. Mount Holyoke, founded by Mary Lyon in western Massachusetts in 1837, is usually cited as the most thorough and academically advanced women's college. It was noteworthy because its pedagogy, curriculum, and living arrangements were integrated and coherent. According to Helen Lefkowitz Horowitz, one reason Mary Lyon's pioneering work at Mount Holyoke stands out is that the seminary / college had the combination of a dedicated leader and sufficient resources to create a distinctive institution. Its architecture, for example, reflected a deliberate educational philosophy. Lyon's "plain and simple" design combined features of an institutional asylum and a family home with a course of study that was both expansive and practical in an era in which opportunities for women were limited.[17]

In most cases, including that of Mount Holyoke, tracking down origins requires functional analysis of curricula and estimates about levels of scholarship, since most were not originally called "colleges" but rather went by such names as "academy," "female institute," or "seminary for women." Christie Anne Farnham's research on nineteenth-century higher education for women in the South supports this observation. Farnham found that elite families in the South invested substantially in creating institutions for their daughters that tried to provide advanced academic work while emphasizing preparation for such conventional feminine roles as household hostess, supervisor, wife, and mother.[18] This profile pieced together from numerous historians' case studies may understate women's enrollments because a substantial number of normal schools also opened during this period, to offer formal instruction and certification for teachers. Analysis of catalogues, courses of studies, and memoirs left by instructors and students indicate that the "female seminaries" were usually comparable in academic rigor to the colleges for men in the same area. Some evidence suggests that the curriculum for women usually emphasized English and modern languages over classics — not unlike the parallel offerings at men's colleges in the "bachelor of science" track.

Diploma Mills

In addition to the familiar unit of colleges, it is important to bring into the historical narrative an account of a distinctively American contribution: "diploma mills." A favorite form was the "medical college." This peculiar entity usually had no campus, no laboratories, no faculty, and no curriculum. It did have the power to confer degrees, especially to those who had made donations to particular campaigns and causes. Such examples are significant for contemporary discussions of quality and accreditation because they call into question the assumption that modern standards of academic rigor have slipped from those of an earlier era.

A case study of one such college and its main proponent in the 1830s provides insight into the general phenomenon of the opportunistic "diploma mill." John Cook Bennett, a native of Massachusetts, moved to Ohio and he received a state license to practice medicine there after claiming to have served an apprenticeship with his uncle, who was a physician. Known as an itinerant peddler, a fraud, and a forger, Bennett in 1832 took on the added role of "chancellor" of newly opened Christian College in New Albany, Indiana. Bennett helped draft the college's by-laws, which included a provision that allowed the college to confer doctorates in fifteen fields, even though no established university in the United States yet offered doctoral programs. His next contribution to academic innovation was to change the name of the institution to the University of Indiana.

Bennett's major reform to medical education was to assure that experience, not mere completion of a prescribed course of formal instruction, was the ultimate standard for assessing professional merit. He had a good point, and later generations of educators would espouse learning by objectives, credit for demonstrable life experience, and measures of achievement other than classroom endurance. In practice, though, Bennett used this change in methods of certification to his own advantage, and to the public's disadvantage. He took upon himself the task of conferring M.D.'s upon those he felt to be qualified or who had passed examinations. He then traveled through several states, conferring a range of academic degrees for fees ranging from $10 to $25 ($172 to $430 in 2000 dollars) per diploma.

After numerous complaints, Christian College severed its ties with Bennett, by now known as the "diploma peddler." It was discovered that he had not only ignored any tests of merit in conferring his degrees but had also pocketed all the fees for himself, handing over nothing to the college. He next became an agent for Willoughby University in Ohio, whose trustees asked him to start a medical college for them. But his unsavory reputation caught up with him, and he was discharged from Willoughby. He resurfaced in yet another academic position, this time as a lecturer at the Literary and Botanical Medical Society in Cincinnati. Eventually he moved to Illinois and persuaded a Mormon group to seek incorporation for a Nauvoo University, with Bennett himself, of course, as president. A year later he was expelled from the Mormon Church and returned to his native Massachusetts. According to one historical biographer, in his last great venture he shifted from medicine to agriculture. The high point of this endeavor came when he sponsored a poultry conference in Boston that attracted ten thousand visitors. This success prompted him to write a popular book on poultry that led to the national fad known as "hen fever."[19]

Bennett's schemes to use a chartered college as a base from which to sell a variety of degrees was outright fraud and represented the excessive spirit of enterprise in an era in which state regulation was marginal at best and largely unenforceable even when present. At the same time, diploma peddling raised some interesting issues pertaining to educational policy. Should a degree be based on classes attended and examinations passed at a set physical place? Or should a demonstration of proficiency and merit be the criterion? Worth noting is that in the mid-nineteenth century, academic degrees were not required for professional practice, whether in law or in medicine. Licensure was an activity of the state government, quite separate from instruction and colleges.

It is easy to dismiss Bennett's itinerant diploma peddling as an aberration. However, the case illustrates inability or disinclination of state governments to require accountability from chartered institutions. Dependence on market forces made American higher education susceptible to innovations, and even to abuses. Furthermore, although the selling of academic and professional degrees for a fee was a suspect practice, the fact that it occurred demonstrates the latitude institutions had in managing their activities and affairs. Almost all established colleges and universities did rely from time to time on a related practice: the conferring of honorary degrees. Yale University tested the boundaries of legitimacy in the late eighteenth century when it conferred upon one generous benefactor the honorary degree of M.D. This did not mean that Yale had established a medical college. Rather, the M.D. stood for "Multum donivat"—"He gave much."[20]

The "Useful Arts": Science, Engineering, the Military, and Agriculture

Although most occupations, including the professions, required little formal certification or training, one finds in the "new national period" significant signs of interest in providing options for formal training in such fields as agriculture, the military, science, and engineering. Most established colleges that had any discretionary funding and any inclination to be "current" in their offerings made some provision for the natural and physical sciences. Consider the first prospectus published by the young University of North Carolina to attract candidates for faculty appointments: "The subjects to which it is contemplated by the Board to turn the attention of the students on the first establishment are — the study of languages, particularly the English — History, ancient and modern — the Belle Lettre and Moral Philosophy — the knowledge of the mathematics and Natural Philosophy — Agriculture and Botany, with the principles of Architecture. . . . Gentlemen conversant in these branches of Science and Literature, and who can be well recommended, will receive very handsome encouragement by the Board."[21] At Harvard and some of the wealthier institutions, donors established, and the board approved, endowed chairs in the sciences and natural philosophy. If the new sciences were seen as intrusive in the bachelor of arts curriculum, a college might establish a "parallel course" leading to the bachelor of science degree. Eventually some liberal arts colleges created distinct "scientific schools," complete with their own curricula, faculty, and degrees.

In addition to expanding the curricula within liberal arts colleges, one finds evidence of commitment to creating wholly new kinds of institutions. Our earlier discussion of the federal government's limited forays into higher education mentioned the founding of the military and naval academies. Comparable institutions were founded by private donors or by state governments across the nation — for example, Norwich Academy in Vermont, the Citadel in South Carolina, and Virginia Military Institute. The military academies are important because they made another contribution that often is obscured by the formal, primary mission and name. They were significant as schools of engineering and applied science.

Cadet diaries from West Point in the 1830s predictably went on at length about discipline, demerits, barracks life, marching, and tactics. Sprinkled among the complaints about field drills are recurrent discussions of instruction in mathematics and engineering. As one cadet wrote in 1833 to his brother, "We have finished our course for this year and are now reviewing; we went as far as Spherical Projections in Descriptive Geometry, it is a study which is studied no other place but here, the object is to represent all Geometrical Problems on planes, the objects are given in space, we have to find the Projections of them on planes. I drew yesterday the intersections of two cylinders." One of his fellow cadets entered in his diary, "We shall [have] a very busy time between now and next June, it will take about a week to examine my class, next June we shall have so many subjects to be called upon, Civil engineering is the most important of them, and the one to which I shall pay the most attention. The number of Railroads constructing in all parts of our country will furnish employment for many engineers, and if I do not get stationed at West Point, I think I should try to get employed on some one of them for a while."[22]

The cadets' concerns about the uncertainties of a military career were warranted. During peacetime, most cadets who completed their course of study were unlikely to receive both a commission as a lieutenant and a post. In an era of railroad and bridge construction, civil engineering was a sensible, marketable skill. Even for those West Point graduates who received posts as commissioned officers, army assignments often included the building of forts, dams, and bridges. Formal instruction and advanced study, then, were not necessarily unrelated to "real work" in the early nineteenth century.

"That Old-Time Religion": The Denominational Colleges Reconsidered

In 1980 the Commonwealth of Kentucky erected a historical marker in downtown Lexington to commemorate the site of a sixteen-day debate held in 1831 and moderated by the famous United States senator Henry Clay. The event was exclusively devoted to the issue of denominational differences with respect to doctrines related to infant baptism and salvation. The debate drew crowds numbering in the thousands each day. Lexington was at the time considered a highly literate urban community—the "Athens of the West," home of the prestigious liberal institution Transylvania University. This was no backwater event for an illiterate population who had few options for pastimes or recreation. Its attendance figures and the press coverage devoted to it illustrate well that issues of religious doctrine were central matters to the American public in the mid-nineteenth century.

Given the historical fact of the primacy of religious denominations in public life of the "new national period," is it any wonder that churches and denominations would be integral to college curricula and any attempt to define the values and attitudes associated with the collegiate education of American youth? And since neither state nor federal governments were providing dependable, ample financial support for higher education, few entities were likely to surpass Protestant denominations as sources of college-building and college-funding. Even though historians of the mid-twentieth century may have lamented the inordinate presence of churches in nineteenth-century college activities, churches were among the few available agencies to enter into the educational arena. Indicative of their philanthropic role was the formation in 1843 of the Society for the Promotion of Collegiate and Theological Education of the West, a vehicle whereby the generosity of East Coast donors was directed to such designated colleges as Marietta in Ohio, Wabash in Indiana, and Illinois College.

One irony of historical memory is that institutions that were innovative in their own time often come to be seen as stodgy and ordinary by a later generation. Historians writing in the 1950s and 1960s often referred disparagingly to the "old-time college," by which they meant the church-related colleges founded in the nineteenth century. Ironically, those colleges, both literally and as a type, were not "old"; they were young, and at the time of their founding they were an innovation. For example, in the early nineteenth century probably the most dramatic change in higher education was the new interest that evangelical denominations showed in founding colleges to educate the sons (and later, the daughters) of their faith. Even more surprising was the decision of Methodists and Baptists to provide for the formal education of a new generation of ministers, as demonstrated by their founding and funding of their own colleges and theological seminaries. Prior to the early nineteenth century, the established college-builders had been Anglicans, Congregationalists, and Presbyterians.[23] However, by 1820 the Methodists and Baptists had become belated but enthusiastic participants as well. This development was unexpected because heretofore such denominations had been viewed as favoring an unlettered clergy. Revelation and inspiration, not formal study and degrees, had formed the Methodist and Baptist clergy of an earlier generation. In sum, the allegedly "old-time college" of this era was actually a new type.

These institutions faced a paradox of popularity. It often appeared as if enthusiasm for founding them had spread to every church in every small town. Not surprisingly, such colleges tended to be small in enrollments, lean in operations, and poor in endowments. Since their constituents were drawn from families with modest incomes, tuition and hence revenues were sparse. According to David Potts and James McLachlan, the denominational origins of these colleges did not always mean exclusion. Many became "local" colleges, serving students from a variety of Protestant denominations.[24]

Although denominational differences were sometimes glossed over in order to serve an expanded local constituency, denominational beliefs were often more important to a college's founders and factions than was mere institutional survival. The apparent fragility of young colleges was often a function of religious disputes within a campus — or rather within its host denomination or board of trustees. Although Presbyterians had been powerful in controlling Transylvania University in the late eighteenth and early nineteenth centuries, such leverage was subject to vacillations. It made sense, then, that when Unitarians — a relatively new religious group, regarded as "godless" by established denominations — gained influence at Transylvania, the Presbyterians withdrew from the established institution and moved thirty miles to Danville, Kentucky, to set up a new, purified Presbyterian institution, Centre College. Similar episodes characterized college-building and college-leaving in this era.

Colleges in the Midwestern states of Illinois, Wisconsin, and Iowa showed some important differences from the Southern colleges with respect to denominational disputes. In the Midwest, the tradition of college-building by the historic college-founding denominations — Presbyterians and Congregationalists — remained dominant. One new adaptation was that with increasing frequency, these two denominations merged forces and put aside doctrinal differences so as to cooperate in sponsoring colleges.

The Protestant denominations and their colleges typified the voluntary organizations, ever endorsing and supporting their favorite causes, that Alexis de Tocqueville described in his profile of the young United States as a "nation of joiners." The colleges were models of devoted effort. Almost every college president would leave the campus for weeks or months at a time for a "canvassing trip" to distant towns and other states as a fund-raising effort. Congregations would continuously raise monies for their affiliated college. Most college presidents were ministers. Experience in passing collection plates and persuading parishioners to tithe was apt preparation for the hardscrabble course of persistent fund-raising that a college demanded.

This invaluable contribution was not the sole legacy that the churches brought to American philanthropy and higher education. One attractive inducement for churches to support collegiate education was that it was seen as a means of recruiting and educating future clergy. This was the genesis of one important type of "horizontal" philanthropic agency: the nationwide scholarship fund. Most notable among these was the American Education Society, whose scholarship awards were distributed to needy young men enrolling at small colleges in New England and the Middle Atlantic area. Such incentive programs probably meant the difference between institutional life and death for many provincial colleges. One estimate is that at the "hilltop colleges" of Amherst or Williams College, as many as 25 – 40 percent of the students were receiving some form of missionary fund scholarship. Usually the financial aid came with conditions. For example, a student would agree to serve as a minister, missionary, or teacher in an underserved region after having graduated from college.[25]

The Established Colleges and "Campus Life"

Our discussion about this era has so far focused on the new institutions and their innovations. What, then, of the historic, established colleges during the first decades of the nineteenth century? A small number of older, wealthier institutions located in urban centers became increasingly homogeneous and socially exclusive. Ironically, they became increasingly local in character even though they enjoyed a national renown. For example, the memoir of alumnus Henry Adams and the later account by the literary historian Van Wyck Brooks pointed to the increasingly Bostonian character of Harvard College between 1830 and 1860. Adams recalled the distinctive "Harvard Stamp" from his own student days in the late 1850s: "For generation after generation, Adamses and Brookses and Boylstons and Gorhams had gone to Harvard, and although none of them, as far as known, had ever done any good there, or thought himself the better for it, custom, social ties, convenience, and above all, economy, kept each generation in the track. Any other education would have required a serious effort, but no one took Harvard College seriously. All went there because their friends went there, and the College was their ideal of social self-respect."[26]

It should be pointed out that Adams's insights were shaped by his idiosyncratic pessimism. Despite his understatement of Harvard's institutional stature and educational influence, the college was increasingly strong and increasingly envied throughout the nation. Whatever the dominant tenor of undergraduate life, Harvard was able to attract faculty with wide-ranging academic interests and perspectives. We do learn from Adams some straightforward things about Harvard in 1858: It was small, with about one hundred students per class, for a total enrollment of about four to five hundred. Its faculty enjoyed high local prestige yet were not especially well paid. The aim of a Harvard education was apparently to instill a habit of self-criticism, even self-doubt. The intent was not to impart advanced or specialized knowledge but to shape a character of balance and measure, quietly liberal and outwardly reserved.

Comparable contraction toward a local urban elitism took place at Columbia, Yale, and the University of Pennsylvania as each became its host city's "preferred college." Among the original colonial colleges of the Northeast, Yale and Princeton stand out because they were both privileged and influential. Their alumni founded an inordinate number of new colleges. Both institutions maintained a strong commitment to religion and to a conservative curriculum. Both attracted a significant number of students from outside their region. Princeton, for example, was usually considered the northernmost college to which elite families in the South would consider sending their sons. This accumulation of characteristics and tendencies meant that Princeton and Yale were watched and emulated elsewhere.

Nowhere did the influence of such established colleges as Princeton and Yale manifest itself more than in the interesting chemistry of student culture and campus life, the blend of formal and informal, curricular and extracurricular. This theme is explored at length in Frederick Rudolph's seminal interpretation.[27] The task of making formal studies appealing to youths in late adolescence was not easy. Critics of the college curriculum of that era point out that the standard pedagogy—daily recitations and a punitive system of grading—was intellectually uninspiring and had the effect of encouraging elaborate cat-and-mouse games between students and instructors. The typical curriculum was that described in the influential Yale Report of 1828: a bachelor of arts curriculum that emphasized the study of classical languages, science, and mathematics with the aim of building character and promoting distinctive habits of thought.

Educational reformers of the era were particularly alarmed by the apparent gulf between students and studies. They were concerned that the collegiate culture tended to discourage students from taking any genuine interest in the concepts they encountered in their formal studies. Many colleges did, from time to time, try to spark student interest by offering something new in the way of teaching styles or subject matter, affording at least a partial reprieve from the main diet of memorization and recitation drills. One wonders, though, whether any institutionalized form of instruction or course of study could have attracted and maintained the interest and enthusiasm of American youths between the ages of sixteen and twenty-two. What was the root of the problem? Had the expectations of American undergraduates of what a college should offer in the late eighteenth and early nineteenth centuries undergone a dramatic transformation? There were instances of student demonstrations, revolts, and acts of sabotage, rebellious incidents in which students seemed to be expressing genuine dissatisfaction with archaic administration, disrespectful faculty, and a dull course of study irrelevant to the issues they would face as adults. To undergraduates, Republicanism had growing appeal, ranging from a post–Revolutionary War interest in individual rights and self-determination to students' vicarious fascination with the ideas and social movements they associated with the French Revolution. Leon Jackson has insightfully characterized this complex mix of student motives and initiatives as the task of distinguishing the "Rights of Man" from the "Rites of Youth."[28] These incidents of rebellion were also an expression of youth's typical impatience with its elders, of the "war between the generations." Such conflicts were disruptive, but probably inevitable.

What emerges is a remarkable pattern of student life in which undergraduates—especially at the established colleges, and then to some degree at colleges elsewhere that emulated the established model—created an elaborate world of their own within and alongside the official world of the college. For many undergraduates, compliance with the formal curriculum was merely the price of admission into "college life." It was an accommodation that simultaneously enriched the content of campus life and allowed for a precarious coexistence of students with college presidents and professors. To paraphrase Frederick Rudolph, student-initiated activities had a discernible life cycle.[29] In the initial stage, an activity would surface informally and even spontaneously among undergraduates. If a particular activity enjoyed sustained popularity, it attracted scrutiny from the administration and then attempts at either official abolition or control. Such administrative efforts usually failed and the activity would resurface in the form of a renegade organization. Ultimately the administration would try to control or co-opt the activity by assimilating it into the formal structure (and covenants) of the college.

Today the conventional belief is that since colleges in the nineteenth century were relatively small, they were cohesive communities and "total institutions." In fact few colleges had the requisite resources to provide on-campus housing for all their students. A typical campus often included three or four buildings: a multipurpose "Old Main" building flanked by a residential "college" and perhaps a chapel or one other structure. Students often had to fend for themselves, finding lodging off campus in private homes or boardinghouses—a feature of campus life that thwarted the administration's ability to control student conduct. Similarly, one finds at Yale, Princeton, and other colleges a mix of arrangements for meals. Not everyone dined at commons. Students often formed "eating clubs," transient and highly pragmatic arrangements whereby a group of friends banded together to pool resources, hire a steward or cook, and rent a dining room near campus. Years later such associations might crystallize into enduring social organizations, but in the 1800s they had not yet been elevated to permanence or prestige.

This account helps explain the pattern of student life and extracurricular activities that evolved at Yale and Princeton and then diffused to other New England "hilltop" colleges such as Amherst, Bowdoin, and Williams. It also illuminates the mix of coexistence and contention in the distinctive student code of the elite Southern universities such as Virginia and South Carolina. And, shifting from institutional diffusion, it is a good lens through which to look at the proliferation of such student organizations as literary societies, debating clubs, discussion groups, Greek-letter fraternities, campus publications, athletics, libraries and reading collections, secret societies, honor groups, and even religious groups.[30] As mid-twentieth-century behavioral scientists confirmed, the potency of student groups has always been formidable.

The proliferation of student organizations also meant that if undergraduates found the formal curriculum to be stultifying, they at least had reasonable odds of finding or initiating interesting pursuits outside the classroom and the formal course of study. Taken as a whole, campus life in the first half of the nineteenth century was limited in terms of facilities and resources. The same could be said for life about anywhere in the United States at that time, but at the colleges there was at least a reasonably good prospect of experiencing some significant affiliation or compelling intellectual or social pursuit.

Most colleges were relatively small and tried to promote cohesion through membership designations of academic class: freshmen, sophomores, juniors, and seniors. In practice, though, these official designations were inadequate, and most campuses became subdivided into other important groupings, as suggested by sociologists Martin Trow and Burton Clark, who identified such student subcultures in the 1960s. Helen Horowitz has traced the evolution of the "college men"—the consummate "insiders" who dominated the prestigious groups, whether literary societies or Greek-letter fraternities.[31] Standing in sharp contrast to the "college men" and their extracurricular orbits were the "outsiders"—students who usually were from modest economic backgrounds and were not offered membership in the established enclaves. The low-income students were ridiculed as "blue skins"—pious rubes who were often suspected of currying favor with instructors and officials. At times the overt discrimination by the wealthier undergraduates prompted college board members and presidents to consider creating separate theological seminaries that would give formal recognition of and protection to low-income students.

The dichotomy of "insiders" versus "outsiders" had some interesting variations in the colleges. The "outsiders" often formed their own groups. For example, at colleges that had a mix of wealthy and impoverished students, there was a recurring organizational pattern. The scholarship students who worked part-time jobs and lacked the clothes and accessories of gentlemen were often preparing to be ministers or teachers. They were generally excluded by the elite student associations, but they created enclaves of their own: religious discussion societies. And from time to time, when religious revivalism became a general college movement, their "outside" groups might for a while achieve popularity and stature in campus life.

One theme that emerges in alumni memoirs is that for all its limitations, the early-nineteenth-century college offered variety to its constituents. Among the most grateful alumni were those scholarship students who, although they may have endured snobbery and exclusion within the campus culture, still encountered experiences, friendships, learning, and associations they would have been unlikely to find elsewhere.

Consumerism and the Colleges

Constructing a balanced, accurate view of the health of the early-nineteenth-century colleges calls for making sense out of puzzling data. For example, Colin Burke's painstaking study of college foundings and closures in the antebellum period suggests that colleges were more hardy than had been thought by historians in the 1950s.[32] Often, what appeared to be a closing was in fact a merger. Historians looking at this era must also consider the "school and society" riddle: Will a college necessarily flourish if it meets what its sponsors believe to be "societal needs"? If so, why did so many attempts to create a "useful" and "modern" curriculum meet with so little interest on the part of students or donors? And, to another extreme, perhaps we should consider the proposition that for many Americans, the demand was not for a modern university but for a denomination-based undergraduate college.

It is tempting to say in hindsight that colleges of 1820 or 1830 should have provided a modern, useful course of study. The problem is that the historical record shows that such prescriptions would not necessarily have been effective. There is an uneven pattern of modern subjects and institutional appeal. Yale, the foremost champion of ancient languages and a conservative curriculum, enjoyed prestige and popularity. It had the largest enrollment of any institution in the country. In contrast, Columbia's experiments with adding an engineering course of study had little appeal to prospective students. Meanwhile, in upstate New York, Union College combined a traditional liberal arts offering with a parallel track in the applied sciences and engineering, with great success. Although innovations in science and technical education attracted some interest among higher-education donors, the most important philanthropic trend of the era was for the manufacturing and mercantile wealth of New England to commit generous endowment gifts to liberal arts education, often with a religious emphasis. On balance, there was no guaranteed formula for a college to attract either donors or paying students.

A peculiar feature of the college-building impulse is that it took place prior to, and with more enthusiasm than, the initiative to establish primary- and secondary-school systems. The names of college towns on the frontier reflect this lofty though sometimes premature zeal: Athens in Ohio and Georgia, Oxford in Ohio and Mississippi. Civic "boosterism" for establishing a town with a college probably led to an excessive proliferation of colleges. The popularity of the "booster college" movement also meant that even an ostensibly "church-related" college founded by a particular denomination might end up serving as a local "community college" that cut across denominational lines.

How do these examples coalesce into an overall profile of American higher education between 1785 and 1860? First, there were important regional differences between New England, the Middle Atlantic region, the South, and what today we call the Midwest. The greatest growth in college-building and enrollments took place in the South and West. Contrary to our assumptions about public access and affordability, in the Southern states the state universities were exclusive and expensive. South Carolina College and the University of Virginia were foremost examples. If higher education in the early nineteenth century had any role in providing social mobility to young men from modest backgrounds, it was in the small church-related colleges of rural New England and the newly settled states of Ohio, Illinois, Pennsylvania, Tennessee, Kentucky, North Carolina, and South Carolina.

On the whole, most nineteenth-century colleges were not exclusionist or elite in matters of admission. Entrance requirements were flexible, and tuition charges were low. In fact, even if most small colleges had been able to collect total tuition charges from all their enrolled students, the resulting revenues would have been inadequate for annual operations and faculty salaries. Philanthropy, financial aid, and fund-raising were central to the educational philosophy and strategy. What these colleges did contribute to American life was a reasonably affordable entree into a new, educated elite. They helped to create an elite rather than to confirm one. The professions of the ministry, teaching, law, and engineering were their staples.

How attractive were the colleges to prospective students and their parents in the early- and mid-nineteenth-century economy? Certainly the proliferation of new colleges was one sign of appeal. However, student enrollments are usually cited as a better proxy for consumer interest. Some recent estimates suggest that college enrollments doubled between 1800 and 1860, indicating growing appeal. However, this claim warrants careful consideration. If correct, it meant that going to college attracted about 0.6 percent of American men between the ages of sixteen and twenty-five in the early 1800s, a figure that increased to about 1.75 percent over the next half-century. The records from which the statistical compilations were derived are incomplete and not completely trustworthy.[33] Even an optimistic interpretation of the data indicates that a college education remained a scarce commodity and a rare experience in the "new national period."

Given that tuition, room, and board charges at many colleges were minimal, why did more young men and women not opt to enroll? The American economy provides two very different explanations. On the one hand, many families could not afford tuition payments, however low; more important, they could not afford the forgone income or forfeited field labor of an elder child who went from farm to campus. On the other hand, in those areas where the American economy showed signs of enterprise and growth, a college degree—even if affordable and accessible—was perceived as representing lost time for making one's fortune. This perception held for such high-risk ventures as land development, mining, and business. It also pertained to the learned professions of law and medicine, where academic degrees were seldom if ever necessary for professional practice. The college in this era, then, was but one means of finding one's place in adult society and economy.

The Dartmouth College Case: The Debate over "Private" and "Public" Colleges

No account of government relations and landmark developments in the first half of the nineteenth century can exclude the famous 1819 case of *Dartmouth College v. Woodward*. The gist of the reinterpretation offered here is that the implications of the case have been misunderstood, especially the claim that John Marshall's ruling helped to "create" and protect the "private college sector" of American higher education.

A labyrinth of historical events led to the famous Dartmouth College case and its travails through the appellate courts up to the Supreme Court. Briefly, after the creation of the new United States, charters were subject to review by the new state legislatures. In New Hampshire, political rivalries between the legislature and the Dartmouth College board evidently led to aggressive attempts to wrest control of the college from its board and from its founding family, the Wheelocks. The incumbent Dartmouth officials protested that this was a capricious political act, and that the legislature's alteration of the charter was a violation of contract law. After a lower court ruled against the college, Dartmouth officials appealed the ruling to the Supreme Court. In a decision that has become legendary, Chief Justice John Marshall ruled in favor of Dartmouth, leaving its charter protected from state meddling.

The standard interpretation of the ruling is that "the Dartmouth College case stands in history as the Magna Carta for private colleges in the United States."[34] However, a reconstruction of events suggests that this claim is less a valid conclusion than a piece of rhetoric that calls for careful reconsideration. Not the least matter of concern is the fuzziness of the ruling by Chief Justice Marshall—a fact that suggests the ruling's limited applicability to American higher education.

The claim about the "Magna Carta of the private colleges" deflates upon close inspection. First, the case had far more importance for contracts associated with business and commercial corporations than it did for colleges and universities. Second, Chief Justice John Marshall and Dartmouth attorney Daniel Webster relied on a peculiar definition of "eleemosynary institutions" to categorize a college. The term refers more to charitable trusts, foundations, scholarship societies, and agencies whose purpose is to gather and then distribute donated funds, as distinct from a college or university whose primary function is to teach and confer degrees. Most important, to celebrate the Dartmouth decision for allegedly creating and strengthening "private colleges" in the United States is to overstate the case. Such a claim attaches a contemporary name to an institution of an earlier era, and so runs the risk of committing the historical sin of anachronism. For starters, if this court ruling gave special designation to "private" colleges, by implication there must also have existed "state" or "public" colleges.

Certainly this was not the case in New Hampshire. Dartmouth was its only college. Does it hold for other states? Again, remember that even such a "state" institution as the University of Georgia was originally called Franklin College when chartered by the Georgia legislature in 1785 and was called by that name for almost a half-century. The institution we now know as Indiana University, a state university, grew out of what in the 1820s was Indiana Seminary in Bloomington. Its reliance on a "state" affiliation was in one sense a public policy answer to Philip Lindsley's complaints about the debilitating impact of denominational squabbling on colleges. The Indiana approach was intended to assure that no single sect would dominate admissions or the curriculum, but apart from that safeguard, it included little on state control or support.

The fusion of "public" and "private" concepts within the same institution was standard practice in the early nineteenth century. It is illustrated in the remarks by the president of Bowdoin College in 1802: "It always ought be remembered that literary institutions are founded and endowed for the common good and not for the private advantage of those who resort to them for education. . . . [Every] man who has been aided by a public institution to acquire an education and to qualify himself for usefulness, is under peculiar obligations to exert his talents for the public good."[35] In other words, there is reasonable doubt that anyone in the early nineteenth century made a substantive distinction between "public" and "private" colleges in the United States. Indeed, the more customary practice in the late eighteenth and early nineteenth centuries was for church-related colleges to petition a state legislature for some funding on the basis that it was a "public" college—a chameleonic strategy that was shifted when the same college officer sought private donations.

Why belabor this point? Despite the presumption that state governments wanted to maintain control over colleges, there is evidence of the opposite inclination. State legislatures wanted to reduce their responsibility for oversight and support of higher education. When colleges within a state petitioned for financial support, governors and legislatures often complied reluctantly and marginally by donating what was thought at the time to be worthless land or perhaps proceeds from an occasional lottery. Systematic annual appropriations simply were not part of the political vocabulary of the era. John Whitehead's *The Separation of College and State* provides the most compelling explanation.[36] Whitehead argued that the terms *public* and *private* were first used in their current sense in the 1870s. The terms were used to distinguish voluntary efforts (e.g., the Red Cross) from the corrupt and inefficient federal programs for health and medical services during the Civil War. The terminology was later picked up by college and university presidents, especially in New England. Eventually it made its way to such Midwestern states as Illinois, where it was used by disgruntled church-related colleges who had lost out in contests for legislative subsidies.

Does this mean that the Dartmouth case was inconsequential? Hardly—but its delineation of clear, strong powers for the academic corporation of Dartmouth College was a "victory" for *all* colleges and universities, whether they are what we would today call "private" or "public." Most "state universities" have charters and boards, and although a governor or legislature can influence or reward and punish, it must be done in accordance with the ground rules of the charter. And one can always find enormous exceptions in the public-private dichotomy. Any feature we think is unique to a "private" college and its board probably has at least one close match in what we loosely call higher education's "public sector."

Conversely, the idea that a "private" college board is exempt from scrutiny and control by its state government is inaccurate. The charter a state grants to a private college can be revoked, although this happens rarely and only with good reason. The state of New York stands as exhibit A. Even today its regents have some ultimate authority over all the institutions chartered in the state. The most recent example that comes to mind is Adelphi University, where in 1997 the New York State Board of Regents intervened by voting to remove eighteen of nineteen Adelphi trustees after having investigated allegations of misconduct by both the president and "his" board.[37] Through its regents, the state had the power to oversee charges that institutional board members had violated public trust. All colleges and universities are—and have always been—"public" institutions in that they are obliged to adhere to their charter and abide by laws, rules, and codes ranging from safety requirements in the workplace to the larger issues of mission and malfeasance. Most conventional accounts of governance in American higher education make the implicit assumption that academic corporations are both distinctive and good because the arrangement protects them against the threat of state government intrusion. There also is a reverse twist: does the "academic corporation" give too much authority to external boards who have little accountability?

Perhaps the most peculiar dimension of the traditional interpretation of the Dartmouth College case is the argument that the court decision had the effect of promoting private college-building. This is unconvincing because there is little evidence that state governments were thwarting college-building initiatives of any sort. In the late eighteenth century some journalists and commentators remarked upon the phenomenon of "College Enthusiasm," the widespread interest in college-building. By 1860, about seventy-five years later, that interest not only had continued but also had increased. At a time when private giving emphasized charitable deeds and public works, ranging from the endowing of asylums to the building of orphanages, the college attracted substantial and enduring support from a wide range of American constituencies. This was the era of the "college-building boom."

3   Diversity and Adversity

Resilience in American Higher Education, 1860 to 1890

National Themes and Local Initiatives

Making sense out of American higher education in terms of the great national social and political events of the 1860s pulls toward two landmarks: the Civil War (1861–65) looms as a pervasive influence on the entire life of the nation, and the Morrill Act of 1862 stands out as pathbreaking legislation that signaled the entrance of the federal government into public policy dealing with creation of the land-grant colleges. Both foci are justified. However, exclusive attention to these "national" events can also obscure important local, state, and regional developments that were perhaps less conspicuous yet more influential in shaping higher education. So although the Civil War and the Morrill Act warrant historical headlines, their influences on higher education are best understood as highly visible products that were a response to innovations and trends at colleges within locales and states. In other words, for higher education in mid-nineteenth-century America, the "national" trends took their lead from an interesting array of state and local initiatives.

The conventional view is to suggest that a major war disrupts business as usual. Colleges are often summarily described as putting new programs on hold or even suspending normal operations. In the case of the Civil War, however, the Civil War also provided some opportunities to initiate new higher-education programs. True, in many colleges in the South students and faculty rushed either to enlist or to take officers' commissions in the Confederate Army, actions that collectively depleted the student body and even the faculty ranks. By 1865, most colleges in the South had abandoned instruction. Many campuses suffered physical damage from battles and shelling or were transformed into shelters and hospitals, for both Union and Confederate forces. This theme permeates the saga of such institutions as the University of Mississippi, whose entire student body enlisted in the Confederate forces; the Virginia Military Institute, whose cadets entered into the battle of Newmarket and whose former instructor, Thomas "Stonewall" Jackson, was a leader and martyr of the Confederate Army; and the Citadel in Charleston, South Carolina, where to this day citizens hold annual ceremonies to commemorate the young cadets who abandoned their formal studies for military service, including defense of their home city.

This heroic profile is, however, an incomplete portrait of how institutions behaved during the Civil War. Some evidence suggests that in the United States — apart from the seceding states — the Civil War provided a political opportunity to push through legislation that had been stalled for several years. Such was the case with the 1862 Morrill Land Grant Act, which had been vetoed in 1859 by President James Buchanan in deference to political pressures from senators and congressmen from the Southern states who resisted extension of federal programs. And the period from about 1860 to 1890 showed a continuation of many of the innovations started in the preceding half-century. Nowhere was this more true than in the proliferation of opportunities for women and in the diversification of curricula offered by colleges and related institutions, especially in the fields of teacher education, applied sciences, engineering, and agriculture.

The Land-Grant Legacy

The 1862 Morrill Land Grant Act is conventionally described as an influential piece of federal legislation that fostered access to useful public higher education. Some historians have hailed this legislation as the genesis of "democracy's colleges" — sources of affordable, practical higher education offered by state colleges and universities. In fact, it was not the first time "land grants" had been used by national or state government to stimulate school- and college-building. Provisions in the Northwest Ordinance (1787) had set aside township lands for schools. Congressional land grants for higher education were made to seventeen states between 1796 and 1861. This largesse included 100,000 acres to Tennessee and 46,080 acres each to the new states of Louisiana, Indiana, Mississippi, Illinois, Alabama, Missouri, Arkansas, Michigan, Iowa, California, Oregon, and Kansas. Ohio, Florida, Wisconsin, and Minnesota received even larger congressional land grants, ranging from 69,120 acres to 92,160 acres.[1]

In addition to this precedent of some federal support being made available through congressional land grants, state governments followed comparable practices within their domains. Legislatures had long been inclined to give land rather than direct financial appropriations to ambitious college-builders who petitioned for charters. Land, after all, was cheaper and more abundant than money for young state legislatures on the frontier. The town of Oxford, Ohio, for example, was the beneficiary of a direct land grant in the early 1800s that carried with it the condition that resources be devoted to establishing educational institutions. Oxford was true to its word and would become home to an array of academies, colleges, and universities over the next two centuries. In other states and townships, however, the commitment to college-building was erratic.

What was distinctive about the Morrill Act was that the land grants were not literal gifts of land on which a state government would build a college. Rather, the act established a complex partnership in which the federal government provided incentives for each state to sell distant Western lands, with the states being obliged to use the proceeds to fund advanced instructional programs. The program began in 1862 with a generous incentive system whereby each state was allotted by formula a portion of federal lands commensurate with the number of its congressional representatives. The state government was then required to dedicate land sale proceeds to establishing collegiate programs in such "useful arts" as agriculture, mechanics, mining, and military instruction—hence the "A&M" in the name of many land-grant colleges.

The historic act was named in honor of Justin Morrill, its longtime legislative champion, who served in both the House and the Senate as a representative of Vermont. It came to be heralded as an innovation in federal support for higher education as well as a model of federal and state cooperation in domestic programs. Its institutional legacy was the accessible state college and university, characterized by a curriculum that was broad and utilitarian.[2]

But whatever symbolic gains were achieved for higher education by the Morrill Act, its effects, particularly in the early decades after its enactment, have been misunderstood or exaggerated. The first misconception is that the Morrill Act was responsible for creating flourishing state colleges in the mid-nineteenth century.[3] In fact, in many states the historic state university was already in operation by 1862 and had little if any connection with the Morrill Act programs. The University of Wisconsin's interest in practical fields of study and statewide extension preceded the Morrill Act. Indeed, the federal legislation often led to schisms and specialization within states. For example, today in Oregon one finds both the University of Oregon and Oregon State University. In Indiana there is Indiana University and the land-grant institution, Purdue. The University of Michigan is distinct from Michigan State University. In South Carolina the land-grant institution, Clemson University, is not one and the same as the historic flagship institution, the University of South Carolina.

Not only did a state government have latitude in separating its land-grant institution from its state university, it also had flexibility in fulfilling the Morrill Act's provisions. Land-grant programs were often grafted on to existing historic colleges. Before the "A&M" land-grant campus came to be associated with the great state universities of the Midwest and West, land-grant funds were often used first to establish state agricultural programs at what would today be considered "private" institutions. This included Dartmouth in New Hampshire, Yale in Connecticut, and Transylvania University in Kentucky. In Virginia, Blacksburg Seminary was the improbable recipient of land-grant largesse. Even today this practice of private universities relying on state partnerships has important legacies: the Massachusetts legislature opted to use the federal land-grant programs at a new "private" institution, the Massachusetts Institute of Technology—not at the state's agricultural college in Amherst. In New York—one of the most important land-grant states—Cornell University, a privately endowed institution, has been the institutional home of the state's agricultural and engineering programs affiliated with the Morrill Act.

Nor did the language of the Morrill Act explicitly define the courses of study a state was to implement. In addition to the "A&M" fields, the Morrill Act gave states broad encouragement to offer the liberal arts. Some states took advantage of this latitude and used the land-grant resources essentially to create a liberal arts college. Foremost among these was California, where California College of Oakland was transformed into the University of California, with a curriculum that closely approximated the offerings of a New England college. At other land-grant state colleges, the hiring of faculty and the design of academic programs sometimes had only the most incidental connection to agriculture or engineering. In some cases this was a lifesaver for the state colleges in their quest to attract students—especially when professors came to understand that for many rural youths the driving ambition in going to college was to acquire credentials that would enable them to escape the farm. The "military" component of the "A&M" designation often has been given less attention by historians than agriculture, mechanics, and mining. Ironically, required military training for male undergraduates—and, later, connections with such programs as the Reserve Officer Training Corps—was one of the most successful provisions of the Morrill Act.

The Morrill Act did not put the federal government into the business of building colleges. Indeed, there was little federal oversight of the programs at the state level once the initial terms were met. Each state had the responsibility to sell its allotment of Western lands. The extended debate in Congress was not about higher-education programs but rather whether the unsettled lands should be opened to commercial development or subjected to orderly apportionment by the government to promote settlement while simultaneously raising revenues. The Morrill Act was a triumph for the latter approach. Some states (e.g., New York) marketed their properties vigorously to acquire abundant resources for carrying out their statewide higher-education plans. In other states (e.g., Rhode Island), officials sold their land allotment cheap, leaving the state with few resources. In short, there was great state-by-state variation as to how the land-grant act was harnessed.

If there is a legacy of the Morrill Act for higher education as a part of federal government policies, it is that higher education was an afterthought, a secondary beneficiary of a major federal initiative. The Morrill Act was a by-product of extended discussions in Congress over federal land policy. The central question was how to deal with vast expanses of land in the West, and to what end—not whether one should build state colleges or even promote advanced educational programs.[4]

Some historians have observed that Justin Morrill's expertise in Congress pertained more to land policy than to education. He felt strongly that the undeveloped Western lands should be used and had the vague idea that linking the sale of these lands to some kind of educational program might serve as an antidote to commercial exploitation. He relied heavily on the counsel of educational lobbyists like New York's Amos Brown, who came to Washington, D.C., bringing with them the perspective and experience of higher education in their home states. The home-grown educational policies of such states as New York, Ohio, and Illinois thus provided the blueprints for federal policy and the ultimately "national" trends in American higher education. To understand what this entailed, it is worthwhile to resurrect the local educational innovations of some of these states.

Agricultural and Technical Education

The 1862 Morrill Act gained energy from activities taking place in several states. Perhaps the most significant source was New York. The appeal of higher education as a popular enterprise was so great that by 1845 the regents of the state of New York had authorized operation of 145 educational institutions designated as "seminaries." Offering a range of advanced instruction, many of these institutions would eventually gain official standing as a "college" or "university." But in the state of New York in the mid-nineteenth century they were defined apart from such chartered colleges and universities as Columbia, Union, Hamilton, Rensselaer, Rochester, and St. John's.

The names and categories of some of the institutions make little sense today. Categories were fluid, and today's clear distinctions between secondary and higher education were not in place. One important example was Genesee College, an institution that grew out of Genesee Wesleyan Seminary.[5] It offered a variety of educational programs, ranging from elementary and secondary education to collegiate instruction. Under the auspices of the Methodists, the academy and college attracted students from a variety of denominations in the region. This regional constituency, combined with the strong support of Methodists throughout the state as a source of donors, subscribers, and paying students, gave Genesee a reasonably strong and diverse base. Prompted by success, in 1848 the Genesee delegation petitioned the state legislature for a "university charter" that would combine the original seminary along with a degree-granting college and other affiliated schools. Central to this proposal was the inclusion in the curriculum of applied sciences as well as agriculture and technical education. Although the legislature denied the request for "university" status, it did approve the creation of "Genesee College." The college was granted the right to confer academic degrees, and it would have professorships in natural history and agricultural sciences. By 1860, Genesee College was a successful institution with diverse programs. It was a serious contender for designation as one of the New

York State institutions eligible for the anticipated federal land-grant funds.

Genesee was not, however, the only aspirant. Another ambitious, innovative New York organization was the "People's College," an innovative institution headed by the indefatigable Amos Brown—a theologian from New Hampshire who had found a career in educational reform. Brown had in mind the establishment of a mechanics institute that offered advanced studies involving technology—subjects we would today call engineering.[6] The cornerstone of the college was laid in 1858. Over the next several years, in the course of his institutional presidency, Brown visited Washington, D.C., and became involved in discussions with Senator Justin Morrill. According to Brown's memoirs, Morrill was sufficiently impressed by Brown's educational views that he enlisted him in the land-grant effort. Brown proceeded to lobby members of Congress to vote in favor of the emerging federal land-grant proposal. It is in this way that New York's higher-education advocates came to have a direct influence on national legislation.

Elsewhere in the state there was also a group that worked to found a "New York Agricultural College." In 1853, after several years of fund-raising and lobbying for state support of agricultural education, they obtained a college charter. The remaining cast member in this drama was Cornell University—or rather its founder and principal donor, Ezra Cornell. Cornell had at one time given some support to the nascent New York Agricultural College, but he eventually abandoned this project. Instead, he shifted his energies to creating a new university bearing his name. Between 1860 and 1865 several institutions and interest groups within the state committed themselves to intense negotiation. Cornell himself strengthened his position with the legislature by putting up massive amounts of capital to supplement any state land grant. He also made donations to Genesee College, probably to appease its administrators' concerns and to suggest that with some division of labor and mission, New York could accommodate a range of institutions.

After 1862 the odd man out in these quests for individual and institutional favor in New York was Amos Brown, who previously had been influential in gaining support in Washington for the land-grant act. For a while Brown's People's College was considered the leading contender for New York's land-grant designation. It was a hollow victory, however, because the state legislature's terms were so stringent as to be impossible to meet. They required Brown to show evidence of large amounts of capital, a condition it was unlikely he could satisfy. Brown accepted the terms but then reluctantly acknowledged that the constraints he faced forced him to capitulate. His new hope was that his lobbying on the Morrill Act could be parlayed into a position at the new Cornell University. He was wrong. Andrew Dickinson White, Ezra Cornell's longtime colleague and educational advisor, was named as the first president when Cornell University finally opened in 1868.

Meanwhile, Genesee College's representatives changed their strategy. They realized that their political clout would ultimately be insufficient to offset the huge donations and capital Ezra Cornell could offer if his new university was awarded New York's land-grant designation. Hence they abandoned their original academic plan. However, in 1870 this same group of Methodist educators and leaders regrouped to found Syracuse University.

Cornell University, then, ultimately claimed victory in the New York land-grant sweepstakes. This triumph for Cornell was the capstone to a serious competition in academic enterprise and educational innovation that had been unfolding for several years. The dynamics of these collegiate enterprises, including agricultural and technical education, were in place long before the prospect of federal land-grant funding came into play.

Competition and Cooperation in Scientific and Technical Education

Serious commitment to "useful education" reached its apex in such Northern states as New York, Ohio, and Massachusetts. Planning for the founding of the Massachusetts Institute of Technology started in 1851, the same year the Cincinnati College of Agriculture opened for instruction. Investment in advanced technical education also attracted attention in the South, even though Southern congressmen led the opposition to federal involvement. Their objections pertained not so much to scientific and technical education as to the precedent of federal projects intruding on state's rights. A good example of the generation of educational innovation in the South was the University of North Carolina, where in 1851 a faculty delegation made an extended summer tour of technical and scientific programs in New York, Connecticut, Massachusetts, and Rhode Island. Two years later, thanks to the report of that group, the University of North Carolina opened its own college of applied science.[7]

Whether one looks at New York or North Carolina, the interesting story is that there was substantial yet scattered support for technical education. This groundswell of curiosity elicited diverse recommendations and often complicated proposals to fund programs. Lack of consensus on educational form and function, not lack of interest, was the ironic obstacle to local and state institution-building. One insight provided by the touring North Carolina delegation was that the new programs being established in one locale were usually not informed about innovations in neighboring cities or states. The result was that throughout the Northeast, developments in applied science took place without coordination among sites, even though new programs at one institution might coincidentally be fairly similar to those at one in another nearby state.

Within this maze of program-building, a curricular issue that surfaced time and time again dealt with connecting new and old courses of study. Where should practical education stand in relation to the liberal arts of the established colleges? Should it be a strand within the bachelor of arts curriculum? Would a college be well advised to add a new degree track, such as the Ph.B. (bachelor of philosophy), that reduced emphasis on the classics while increasing the number of new fields? Another appealing model was simply to create a new "scientific school" within the historic institution. The California legislature made a provision in the state constitution for a Mechanics Institute distinct from the University of California. Once again there was no consensus among the participants and advocates. To add to the fractured character of events, although the "A&M" designation linked agriculture and mechanics, to the participants and principal figures of the mid-nineteenth century the two fields of study were distinct, and often in conflict.

Representatives of skilled workers had mixed thoughts about the academic ventures that incorporated practical and applied fields. One of their main reservations stemmed from the question, To what extent were proposals for mechanical education an attempt to usurp the role of established craftsmen? Their concerns were warranted. For example, one champion of practical education programs in New York State argued that such programs would allow employers to replace skilled workers with prison labor. Not surprisingly, proposals like this were resisted by craft guilds.

In agricultural education, there were strong disagreements between traditional agrarians—grangers, yeomen, and small farmers—and advocates of an industrialized approach to large-scale production. Added to that conflict, many farmers doubted whether taxpayer subsidies of agricultural education would have much influence on crop production. They also viewed scientists and scholars as being unqualified to give advice on farming. On the one hand, the variety of philosophies and strategies over practical education created a fertile educational environment. On the other hand, disagreements and tensions between institutions and groups impeded consensus in the drafting of state or federal policies.

Fragmentation continued even after passage of the Morrill Act in 1862. The new influx of federal resources prompted some states to make substantial alterations in their plans. Local rivalries often shaped state strategies. In Kentucky, for example, religious denominational disputes caused Transylvania University (also known as Kentucky University) to fall from favor in the state legislature, leading to the dissolution of the land-grant program at that institution and, soon thereafter, to the creation of a new state institution across town, Kentucky State College (later renamed the University of Kentucky). Likewise, in New Hampshire the state land-grant program was eventually taken away from historic Dartmouth and transferred to the new State Agricultural College at Durham. This pattern was repeated in Connecticut. The state legislature initially identified Yale's Sheffield Scientific School as the land-grant recipient. Later this role was transferred to the new state college at Storrs.

With the exception of the promising energy at the Universities of Wisconsin and Michigan, great land-grant institutions were scarce in the Midwest in the 1870s and 1880s. In Illinois, debate over the location of the state college veered toward outright opposition. Residents of Champaign-Urbana thought that a reform school or prison would be a greater advantage to their community than a state industrial college would be. In many instances civil engineering and mining engineering attracted more interest from students and employers than agriculture did. These shortfalls in the new programs of the land-grant colleges suggest that the most dramatic changes in American higher education around midcentury could be found in other initiatives, including the numerous attempts to provide for the higher education of women.

Women and Higher Education

By 1860 at least forty-five institutions offered collegiate degrees to women. They had a variety of institutional names, including "college," "academy," "female seminary," and "literary institute." Their curricula ranged from vocational training to genteel finishing-school programs, from professional education to the liberal arts. Overriding this variation was the fact that higher education for women had a presence at midcentury that would have been unthinkable two decades earlier. It was simultaneously unpopular with most Americans and increasingly attractive to a significant minority. The research of Margaret A. Nash has revealed some of the complexity in higher education for women during this period. In the college town of Oxford, Ohio, for example, one finds no fewer than three women's colleges in the 1850s and 1860s.[8] Each institution carved out a curricular emphasis and a student constituency, usually based on social class.

Expanding access to higher education for women, usually seen as an extremist activity, received an unexpected boost from the fears of conservative constituencies. In the South, traditional groups that usually opposed education for women sometimes decided to fight fire with fire.[9] Their logic was that it was better to build a women's college close to home that inculcated traditional religious and regional values than to risk having young Southern women attend a renegade Northern college. A comparable rationale operated with Catholic families in all regions of the country. It was safer to send a daughter or niece to a local Catholic women's college than to a Methodist institution far from home.[10] Thanks to this mix of motives and sponsors, the growth and diversity of women's colleges emerged as one of the most distinguishing features of American higher education after 1850.

Normal Schools

Any discussion of the advanced education of women in the nineteenth century ultimately overlaps with the subject of teacher education. So much attention goes to the proposals for adding instruction in engineering and agriculture that historians have often overlooked another area of exceptional growth: the professional education and certification of teachers. Over time these institutions attracted a succession of names, including "normal schools" and "teachers' colleges." They often conferred a certificate or a license of instruction rather than a bachelor's degree. Many eventually became comprehensive colleges. The field of professional teacher education was sufficiently attractive that it generated a number of private institutions. Later, as public schooling was expanded, state government created state normal schools and, later, state teachers' colleges. After the Civil War the most ambitious private venture was Alfred Holbrook's National Normal University. The son of Josiah Holbrook, a successful promoter of the American lyceum movement, Alfred envisioned his National Normal University as the center of a growing enterprise. As part of the preparation of future teachers, Holbrook and his colleagues took great interest in curricular development and pedagogy as a science.

Normal schools reflected the diversity of their constituencies. Some were created for women only. Others were coeducational. And in some coeducational institutions, women came to be a majority.[11] The history of the normal schools is confusing because it is not always clear how they were classified in the education taxonomy. At times they were lumped with secondary schools. At other times they were considered a distinct category within higher education. Finally, at some universities they were seen as one of the academic tracks.

The College of William and Mary in Virginia provides a good illustration of this state of flux. The historic college had suspended instruction during the Civil War and had barely managed to survive financially into the 1870s. Without much support from the Episcopal Church, the college faced the prospect of relying on student tuition payments—a bleak prospect, because in the impoverished Virginia state economy, few could afford to pay for college. William and Mary's only hope was to pursue support from both federal and state governments. In each case the institutional leadership invoked the historic character of the college. The college petitioned Congress for war reparations to rebuild the colonial institution. The petition was denied. Within Virginia, the college lobbied the legislature to support renovation of the Old Dominion's historic college, which had emphasized liberal arts education for future leaders. This effort too met with little enthusiasm. The one proposal that did gain state legislative approval was that William and Mary should receive an annual state subsidy for providing advanced instruction for white males who would agree to teach in the state's young, expanding public school system. This was especially appealing to the legislature because it meant that the all-male College of William and Mary, although not a public institution, would then become a kind of counterpart to the women's normal school. The college's annual appropriation from the state legislature provided more than 90 percent of its operating budget for over two decades.

This case illustrates a trend that was taking place in most states: the growing appeal of compulsory public schooling and the subsequent demand for educated, certified public school teachers. Whereas advocates of the Morrill Act in 1862 estimated that agriculture and applied sciences would be the locus of expansion in higher education, the professional field that enjoyed the most growth, first in student enrollments and then in employment, was education.

Commerce in the Collegiate Curriculum

The place of such utilitarian fields as agriculture and engineering in higher education was a matter of great concern to the educational reformers of the late nineteenth century. Given this practical emphasis, one curious omission in the public discussions of the time was the apparent lack of interest in bringing business into higher learning. Even though by midcentury the United States had complex business organizations—especially railroad companies and steel manufacturers—there was little inclination to look to colleges for training or certification for such careers. Banking remained almost exclusively a self-determined career based on apprenticeship or family connections.

Running counter to this dominant trend, there is some fragmentary evidence that commerce did have a place in the higher-education visions of the mid-nineteenth century. One determined benefactor had plans for a school of commerce at the University of Louisiana, but the project was abandoned in 1857. Although no distinct business school emerged, some compilations show that in the 1850s there were 160 or so commercial courses on offer throughout the country. In some cases it was a relatively short course of six weeks devoted to the rudiments of bookkeeping and business correspondence. Yet the range was vast, the best example being the experiment associated with the Wharton School at the University of Pennsylvania.[12] Joseph Wharton's school at the University of Pennsylvania, founded in 1881, was committed to presenting a broad, liberal course of study for the education of future leaders in business. An interesting side note to curricular history is that when the liberal arts faculty at the University of Pennsylvania rejected proposals to add departments of history, government, and economics, these new fields were rescued from orphanage by being adopted by the Wharton School.

The Wharton School was one of many examples in which the lines between liberal and professional education were blurred. It was, how-

ever, exceptional. Universities' commitment to creating schools of business administration did not gain momentum for a few decades. The
collegiate legacy by 1890 was that presidents and professors understood
that even—or especially—future businessmen were a growing constituency for the bachelor of arts course of study.

Discussions and Debates about the Character of a Modern University

It is hard to sort out the exact connections between ideas and institution-
building in the mid-nineteenth century. Magazines such as *The Nation,
Atlantic Monthly,* and *Harper's,* as well as daily newspapers, regularly
printed articles about the future of higher education. These articles
tended to promote the creation of a truly modern American university.
Their authors had in many cases studied in Europe and returned to the
United States full of praise for the advanced scholarship and academic
freedom of the German universities. For example, Lincoln Steffen, an
influential editor, wrote thoughtfully about the semester he spent at
Heidelberg. Numerous scholars who had pursued advanced studies on
the Continent argued that the seriousness of purpose associated with
advanced scholarship at German universities was essential for national
development and ought be transplanted to the United States.

One contributor to this public forum in the mid-nineteenth century
was Francis Wayland, president of Brown University. Wayland was not
only an influential campus leader but a nationally known author who
sounded the alarm for American higher education in the 1850s. In his
articles he depicted the typical American college as obsolete because it
was out of touch with the demands of an energetic, industrial society.[13]
He, along with F. A. P. Barnard, cited demographic statistics on college
enrollments to make the case that the traditional college was of declining
appeal in a democratic, capitalistic nation. Wayland's views were shaped
by the problems he faced as president of Brown, where his numerous
attempts at innovation were thwarted by a stubborn faculty. Despite
Brown's location in a highly populated industrial area, enrollments were
disappointing. Wayland's attempts at curricular innovation repeatedly
failed to attract large numbers of eager, paying students. This frustration
was the impetus behind his nationally circulated articles on the need for
a utilitarian curriculum housed within a modern university.

Another strand in the discussion of the prospects for American higher education involved examples from abroad. A customary approach in dealing with higher education in this era has been to invoke Cardinal Newman's *Idea of a University*, based on his inaugural lectures as rector at the Catholic University of Dublin in 1852.[14] Intoxicating in their grace and allusions, these lectures were often reprinted, but there is scant evidence that Newman's ideas were actually implemented at his own university, let alone at any in the United States. One is forced to the conclusion that his ideas were not especially compelling to his contemporaries. The lecture series was cut short for lack of interest in Dublin. Publication of the lectures was delayed for years, and when they finally did appear, it was in condensed form. Newman's plans for curricular reform were rejected in his own university, where professional education and a medical school prevailed. Newman's classic lectures were more celebrated in anthologies published in the mid-twentieth century than they were actually read or heeded by contemporary advocates of higher education.

Newman personified the plight of the philosopher as administrator. According to Lytton Strachey's insightful 1918 profile, his initial hopes for Catholic University quickly faded: "For the next five years, Newman, unaided and ignored, struggled desperately, like a man in a bog, with the over-mastering difficulties of his task. . . . His mind whose native haunt was among the far aerial boundaries of fancy and philosophy, was now clamped down under the fetters of petty detail and fed upon the mean diet of compromise." The struggling advocates of university reform in the United States between 1870 and 1890 would have found a kindred spirit in Newman, who as rector of Catholic University "had to force himself to scrape together money, to write articles for the students' Gazette, to make plans for medical laboratories, to be ingratiating with the City Council." Strachey suggested a fitting epitaph for this visionary university-builder, one that Brown's Francis Wayland would have empathized with: he was a "thorough-bred harnessed to a four-wheeled cab; and he knew it."[15]

In addition to the little-heeded essays of Cardinal Newman, there was a persistent flow of provocative articles in American journals about the future of the incipient American university.[16] They were widely read and well written, but again there is little evidence that they directly shaped institution-building or curricular reform. The so-called university-builders who wrote so prolifically in the 1870s and 1880s in such periodicals as *Harper's Magazine* and *Atlantic Monthly* noted correctly that the "college" was a vague entity, with great variations in the quality and kind of academic preparations a student brought to the campus. As a solution they proposed that a new "university" structure be implemented in the United States to elevate the inconsistent, uneven system of collegiate education into something more demanding and academically selective. These arguments were intriguing and compelling, but they did not address the root problem that caused colleges to be so undemanding: American secondary schools were few in number and uneven in their offerings. Even if one were able to carve out an advanced program that dissolved the historic college in favor of a new university, from whence would the students come? Unfortunately, few American institutions could seriously consider implementing such a rigorous course of study because most did not have the luxury of being selective in their admission of students, many of whom were not well prepared academically. How best to encourage serious academic work was the preoccupation of a generation of national commentators on American higher education.

The articles about the future of the American university increasingly shifted from analysis to advocacy. In 1884 John Burgess published a book that gave extended answers to the series of questions posed in its title, *The American University: When Shall It Be? Where Shall It Be? What Shall It Be?* After a lengthy tour of the issues, Burgess concluded that the truly great modern university ought to be urban in location, privately controlled, and characterized by advanced studies in the arts and sciences. This conclusion was both intriguing and plausible, yet discerning readers noted a remarkable coincidence: the features Burgess advocated matched closely those of his own institution, Columbia University in New York City, where he was dean of the faculty and professor of political sciences.

Columbia had made great gains, thanks to Burgess and his colleagues, in evolving from a college to a university. Advanced degree programs made headway elsewhere in the country as well between 1860 and 1890. For example, Yale conferred the first Ph.D. in the United States in 1863, acknowledging the advanced work of Josiah Willard Gibbs of the Scientific School. Yet this achievement was exceptional even at Yale and did not spark much emulation elsewhere. According to Roger Geiger, statistics appearing to show a proliferation of doctoral degrees in the 1880s are misleading.[17] Most of these degrees were conferred by diploma mills:

colleges that accepted fees and conferred a Ph.D. without offering much in the way of scholarly supervision or advanced facilities such as libraries or laboratories.

An important exception to such opportunistic ventures was the Johns Hopkins University, founded in Baltimore in 1876. It was the most impressive example of the German university's ideals of advanced scholarship and Ph.D. programs being transplanted to the United States. But this remarkable institution was an exceptional feature of the American higher-education landscape. Although it would inspire future generations of academic leaders as a model of graduate study, Johns Hopkins was so far ahead of most colleges and universities that aspiring competitors fell drastically short of its example until well into the twentieth century.

Premature Obituaries for the Liberal Arts Colleges

An undercurrent in the proposals for utilitarian studies and a modern university was the notion that the historic liberal arts colleges were inadequate—and, as a fitting punishment, were floundering in matters of enrollments and finances. But was this so? Probing the condition of "colleges" and "universities" around 1880, James Axtell found that only twenty-six institutions (seventeen of them formally called "colleges") had enrollments surpassing two hundred students. According to Axtell, "Amherst was as large as Wisconsin and Virginia. Williams was larger than Cornell and Indiana, and Bowdoin was the near equal of Johns Hopkins and Minnesota. Yale with 687 students was much larger than Michigan, Missouri, or the City College of New York."[18] Nor did the "modern universities" often surpass the established colleges in terms of such scholarly resources as libraries or laboratories. Graduate studies, especially Ph.D. programs, were at most a marginal part of university offerings in the late nineteenth century.

The historic colleges in fact proved reasonably capable of providing new fields of study without transforming themselves into "universities." Far from being in decline, the liberal arts colleges displayed considerable resilience in the post–Civil War decades. Dartmouth College is a good example. According to Marilyn Tobias's reconstruction of the academic life of the college, by the 1880s Dartmouth had become a remarkably vital center of learning. Its professors pursued research and conducted original experiments and fieldwork in a variety of areas. They wrote for scholarly journals and participated in scholarly organizations. Such activities did not conflict with their commitment to teaching and collegiate education. Students, meanwhile, had initiated projects in a variety of new disciplines and topics. Recent alumni who had prospered in Boston, New York, and Chicago returned to their alma mater to make certain that it was preparing students appropriately for the dynamic conditions of the American economy. A striking exception to the overall vitality of the institution was its longtime president, Samuel Colcord Bartlett. In 1881 a group of Dartmouth faculty, students, alumni, and trustees aligned to bring Bartlett to trial, on the charge that he had thwarted inquiry and innovation on all fronts. "Old Dartmouth" was literally put on trial, and the curmudgeon Bartlett was removed as president of the college.[19]

Reform did not mean that the college was turned into a university. Rather, the new president, William Jewett Tucker, ensured that additions to the curriculum and course of study—including professional schools—supplemented rather than replaced the institution's collegiate identity and mission. Over the next twenty-five years Dartmouth's invigorated collegiate model, emphasizing liberal education for Christian character, had great appeal, and enrollments went from about three hundred to over two thousand during the period.

The Dartmouth "trial" was exceptional, but it was also symptomatic of adaptations taking place at historic colleges in other regions. As George Peterson has demonstrated, comparable patterns held true for such small New England colleges as Amherst, Williams, and Wesleyan.[20] And Bruce Leslie's historical study of liberal arts colleges in Pennsylvania and New Jersey around 1870 confirms this picture of institutional vigor and prosperity.[21] Close historical analysis of Bucknell, Franklin and Marshall, Princeton, and Swarthmore College casts doubt on the conventional view that the historic colleges were unwanted in the "age of the university." Colleges were highly respected within their locale. Professors at the liberal arts colleges enjoyed both high income and high status within the community. Religious affiliations were not necessarily rigid. The colleges were financially stable and growing, with increasing appeal to the children of upper-middle-class Protestant families. Families, faculty, and students themselves subscribed to the notion of collegiate education as the crucible for the nurturing of "gentleman scholars." Far from being a period of stagnation that marked the "death of the liberal arts college," for many institutions the period 1870 to 1890 was an era in which the college campus was transforming itself into an increasingly attractive academic community.

Bruce Leslie opted not to look at colleges in the South after the Civil War because he felt that the depleted state economies and the preponderance of small, marginally funded church-related colleges made the region an unlikely place to expect college vitality. Surprisingly, later scholarship suggests that the resilience Leslie found among the Middle Atlantic private religious colleges also characterized some Baptist colleges in the South during the 1870s and 1880s. This phenomenon was due to the efforts of educational reformers who had worked together at Southern Baptist Seminary in South Carolina. After the Civil War their progressive reform work took them to Baptist colleges in Kentucky, Virginia, and Texas. For example, Georgetown College in Kentucky chose as its president Basil Manly, Sr. — previously the president of the University of Alabama and a leader at Southern Seminary in South Carolina. To top off his credentials as a conservative leader, Manly was also a former Confederate chaplain who had led the prayer at Jefferson Davis's inauguration as president of the Confederate States of America. Surprisingly, these past affiliations were poor predictors of Manly's approach to higher education in the South after the Civil War.

Manly and a close circle of Southern Baptist educators recognized that their effort to connect religion and higher education was destined to fail unless they adapted to the harsh new environment of the postwar South. Although Manly had been a partisan Confederate, he was also a realist who saw the need to put aside old animosities in order to focus on educational reform and economic development. His work in Southern Baptist education was cross-fertilized with advanced ideas he brought from other regions, namely, from the experience of having been educated at Newton Theological Institution in Massachusetts and Princeton Theological Seminary. At Georgetown College, Manly initiated an elective system that included such new fields as English literature (in this he had sought advice from Noah Porter, the president of Yale). He also emphasized liberal education for lay Baptists, as distinguished from focusing on a Baptist seminary devoted to educating future clergy. According to Christopher Beckham, Georgetown College and other Southern Baptist colleges, "while distinctively Southern and strongly Christian in character and focus, were not slavishly sectarian."[22]

At Richmond College in Virginia, one of Manly's colleagues, John A.

Broadus, carried out comparable reforms. As president he made it clear in the 1868 – 69 catalogue that prospective students would find "no sectarian bias in instruction" but rather a commitment to the education of Christian gentlemen. He recruited students from an increasingly varied background and encouraged them to study diverse subjects. Their liberal arts course was advertised as being practical and appropriate to any future profession, including business. Broadus also added a "commercial course" to the formal curriculum.

These Baptist educators also advanced progressive views on the education of Southern women. Richmond Female Seminary, an institution exclusively for women affiliated with Richmond College, reflected Broadus's interest in the examples set by New England women's colleges. And the president of Baylor, a Baptist institution in Texas, was a champion of coeducation. These three colleges demonstrated that a campus in the South could be conservative and denominational without being stagnant or indifferent to social and pedagogical changes.

Student Life: Lyman Bagg and *Four Years at Yale*

Advocates of a "new modern American university" complained that college was no longer very appealing to energetic young American men. When one looks at student memoirs rather than the polemical articles by university reformers, however, a markedly different picture of the American college emerges. A good example of the student perspective comes from Lyman Bagg, who entered Yale College as an undergraduate a year after the Civil War and graduated in 1869. Bagg was a pack rat who saved mementos and artifacts of his student days and then spent three years organizing the material into a book. He explained his project as follows: "The erroneous and absurd ideas which very many intelligent people who have not chanced to experience it, entertain upon the subject of college life, have led me to believe that a minute account of affairs as they exist today at one of the chief American colleges would not be without value to the general public, nor without interest to the alumni and undergraduates of other colleges as well as the one described."[23] Bagg then proceeded to provide a thorough 713-page guide through the highly organized activities, customs, and rituals of undergraduate life at Yale. Eating clubs, honor societies, varsity sports, literary groups, debating teams, initiation rites, college songs, and codes of conduct all were explained in clinical detail.

Bagg's *Four Years at Yale* reveals that undergraduates had created an intricate, compelling world within the official campus structures. A great deal of emphasis was placed on the ability to hold one's own within the rough-and-tumble student culture. Many of the student activities showed considerable signs of creativity and pragmatism. "Eating clubs," an entity that later would be regarded as a highly formal organization, had a very different character around 1870. According to Bagg, they were created by groups of students who banded together each year to pool resources; one student would be placed in charge of collecting dues and then negotiating with landlords to rent a dining space and to hire a cook. An eating club usually dissolved at the end of the college term. Other activities demonstrated comparable initiative. If American collegiate life immediately after the Civil War was in decline, there was little evidence of it at Yale.

Yale is an important illustration of this point. Recall that in 1824 it had been singled out as the foremost proponent of a classical curriculum—a commitment that champions of a modern university criticized as reactionary and part of the reason American youth were losing interest in going to college. Moreover, Yale had maintained its commitment to main-line Congregational theology, including daily chapel and an unapologetic commitment to a curriculum that emphasized piety and character-building as well as intellect. This should have been a formula for disaster. But contrary to the predictions of critics, Yale had flourished and by 1870 was the largest college in the country. Its conservatism was not synonymous with stagnation. In terms of curricular offerings, Yale had added a land-grant program, a scientific school, and a law school. Above all, its student life was robust—a matter of national interest and aspiration.

The central feature of undergraduate life was that it was intricately organized by and for students, with a system of rewards and punishments that persisted regardless of the college administration's attitudes. The vitality of the extracurriculum served as a buffer to the demands of coursework and examinations. By 1870, collegiate life at Yale and elsewhere was set in the mold of a four-year curriculum in which students affiliated with their entering class as freshmen, sophomores, juniors, and seniors. The most conspicuous additions to the undergraduate cosmos were Greek-letter fraternities and intercollegiate varsity teams, especially in crew, track and field, baseball, and football.

The significance of Lyman Bagg's account in *Four Years at Yale* is that the model associated with Yale College was emulated across the country. Bruce Leslie's study of four colleges in the Middle Atlantic states between 1870 and 1890 suggests that this model of collegiate life flourished at Bucknell, Princeton, Swarthmore, and Franklin and Marshall.[24] The same was true of institutions in Ohio, Iowa, and California. This is not to say that some institutions did not try new arrangements for undergraduate life. Coeducation, new fields of study, and new constituencies were also part of the story. Cornell University stood out as an exciting institution whose early classes included Civil War veterans as well as women. Its motto projected a distinctively American optimism: "I would found an institution where any one could study any thing." True to this spirit, its curriculum included such daring new fields as American history, Romance languages, and modern literature as well as civil engineering and applied sciences.

How might one reconcile the dire portraits of colleges in decline with student accounts of dynamic campus life? The disparity can be attributed in part to the interpretation of statistics. Attempts at nationwide data collection in the late nineteenth century seemed to indicate a decline in the popularity of college. But this interpretation does not take into account either the uncertainties in the statistical categories involved or the larger demographic trends of the day. For example, the appearance of declining college enrollments was sometimes due to changes in the taxonomy of American education. When a college added a scientific school, a normal school, or an agricultural program, students enrolled in these new fields may not have been counted as being enrolled in the historic college. Ironically, those colleges that did add modern, useful fields experienced at best a mixed response to their curricular innovations. Between 1865 and 1890, enrollments in agricultural departments faltered. At times in the 1870s and 1880s, farmers and their agricultural societies lobbied strongly against extending agricultural courses. Civil engineering probably fared the best of any of the kinds of useful arts encouraged by the Morrill Act. Given the slow start of agriculture and applied sciences as part of the undergraduate college, one has to appreciate the enduring appeal of the oft-maligned classical curriculum associated with the bachelor of arts degree.

A second factor that must be considered in analyzing the demographics of college enrollments was the massive wave of immigration into the United States that occurred in the late nineteenth century. This influx quickly swelled the total population base against which estimates of college enrollment percentages were made. Immigration of diverse ethnic groups worked another influence on American higher education: new groups founded new colleges that emulated the existing historic colleges while making accommodations for their constituents' distinctive religious or national origins. One finds in the period after 1870 a proliferation of new colleges founded under church auspices. Catholic and Lutheran institutions now joined the older Protestant denominational colleges founded by Methodists, Baptists, Presbyterians, and Congregationalists. The religious affiliation of a college was often a sign of ethnicity. Lutheran colleges in the Midwest, for example, were intended to provide access to higher education for the sons and daughters of German and Scandinavian immigrants. Likewise, Catholic colleges overwhelmingly enrolled students whose families were from Ireland and, later, Italy and parts of Eastern Europe. Most revealing, however, is that the new colleges tended to imitate the forms of college life pioneered by Yale and the established colleges. The net result was that each interest group tended to create its own institutions, instead of trying to gain admission to established colleges operated by rival religious or ethnic groups. Hence American higher education in the late nineteenth century was on the whole reasonably diverse, though characterized by segregation.

The statistical signs of college-going losing favor in American life also were exacerbated by the unevenness of the American educational system. Most colleges and universities could not afford the luxury of selective admissions. A paying student, however weak his or her secondary-school preparation, was unlikely to be turned away. Despite the publication of formal entrance requirements, most college admissions exams were flexibly graded. When applicants were woefully underprepared for college-level studies, colleges and universities responded by providing auxiliary courses. Hence most American colleges dedicated a sizable proportion of their curricula to preparatory or remedial courses that would (for a price) help bring students up to par for "college work." Even such prestigious and financially well endowed campuses as Vassar devoted a great deal of their resources to students who had enrolled in the preparatory department.

Although the colleges and their undergraduate extracurricula were predicated on the ideal of a four-year experience, in practice there was a great deal of deviation from this ideal. The completion of a bachelor's degree was hardly a universal accomplishment, nor was it expected to be so. What emerges is a highly diverse and often inconsistent pattern of college attendance, with dropping out or transferring being ordinary activities that got little mention in the annual reports of presidents and deans. At the College of William and Mary in Virginia, for example, the course of study and arrangements for student activities reflected a commitment to the four-year bachelor of arts experience. In practice, however, well over 90 percent of the college's students between 1880 and 1900 opted to end their studies after two years. This was not indicative of academic failure. Rather, pragmatic students, primarily those from impoverished backgrounds, stayed just long enough to complete their L. I. (license of instruction) certificate, which would allow them to gain immediate employment as public school teachers, even without the bachelor of arts degree.

Furthermore, the definition of the college experience, as a formal entity distinct from secondary education and from graduate studies, remained unclear. The American system of public high schools was still very uneven, resulting in a shortage of well-prepared applicants. But at the other extreme, the late-nineteenth-century institutions known as "academies" were not merely secondary schools. They often described themselves as advanced or even terminal educational institutions. Many of them came to be known as "preparatory schools." In the twentieth century this phrase connotes an institution intended to prepare a student for college admission. In the 1870s and 1880s, however, the term would have connoted an institution designed to provide a preparation for life, not merely a preparation for admission to Harvard, Yale, or Princeton.[25]

Coeducation and Women

One of the major changes associated with the academic community in the years after the Civil War was the allowance for coeducation of women and men. Oberlin had pioneered this practice several decades earlier. Among the new institutions, Cornell University is usually cited as exemplary, with the trend following at state universities and colleges in the Midwest and West. In New England and in the South, single-gender education remained the norm.

However much the new approach was publicly celebrated, coeducation in practice achieved at best a mixed record. Women at Cornell and the University of California, for example, were not treated equally or even well. Admission into the college or university hardly precluded segregation within the walls. Tracking into particular courses and majors, discouragement from some fields, and, above all, exclusion from extracurricular organizations and activities were the disappointing realities of coeducation.[26]

There were two corollaries to the mistreatment of women within the coeducational structure. First, women took the initiative to organize their own formal and informal extracurricular activities in defiance of the college administration and the dominant extracurriculum led and controlled by the college men. Second, the new women's colleges inherited an opportunity to provide a distinctive structure and organizational culture for the higher education of women. This included abundant opportunities to participate in journalism, athletics, music, and literary groups. The women's colleges also provided an unprecedented opportunity for both students and faculty to pursue advanced studies and serious academics. One result of this was that an inordinate number of alumnae from the women's colleges of the 1880s went on to pursue advanced studies in law, medicine, and Ph.D. programs. The women's colleges profited from a windfall of timing. The period between 1870 and 1890 was an ideal time for outfitting a new campus because it coincided with the new availability of scientific equipment and apparatus. A well-funded new women's college could swiftly match and surpass the laboratories and libraries of the established men's institutions. One historian has described the community of scholars in the early decades of such women's colleges as Wellesley as an "Adamless Eden."[27] Whether or not one accepts that characterization, accounts of the academics and campus life at Wellesley, Vassar, Bryn Mawr, Mount Holyoke, and Smith indicate that women's colleges were distinctive and effective. Furthermore, by 1890 the impetus for founding and endowing women's colleges was gaining, not losing, momentum.[28]

College Administration and Finances: The Roots of Large-Scale Philanthropy

One of the most perplexing historical riddles in American higher education is how colleges planned and then implemented their annual operating budgets. The published tuition charges were low, and even if they had been collected from a full student enrollment they would have been inadequate to pay for salaries and services, let alone construction. When enrollments fell short, as they often did, finances were even tighter. Even those colleges that were the beneficiaries of substantial gifts were still tuition dependent and often short of cash.

According to Frances Wayland, the president of Brown University, colleges commonly engaged in a peculiar form of consumerism in their pricing strategies. Students who registered early were charged full tuition. However, if a college had not met its enrollment quota as the start of the academic year approached, it might offer discounts in a last-ditch effort to fill empty seats with paying customers.[29] Wayland took this practice as evidence of the classical collegiate curriculum's lack of appeal. He argued that colleges would do better to offer a modern curriculum and charge a fair price for it. The flaw in this argument was that there was no consistent link between an institution's curriculum and its popular appeal. Some of the most modern institutions, such as Cornell University in New York, had difficulty filling their classes. Yale, meanwhile, one of the country's most conservative and tradition-bound institutions, had the largest enrollment of any campus in the nation.

Tuition charges did vary from place to place, with tuition at the New England and Middle Atlantic colleges being the highest. Yet as a general rule, tuition charges were not prohibitive anywhere. If a student was excluded from a particular college, it was more likely due to social, gender, ethnic, racial, or religious discrimination than to the price of attendance. Most colleges were not turning away applicants. To the contrary, colleges struggled to persuade young Americans to go to college rather than pursue other adventures. Also, the economic environment between 1860 and 1890 was such that college attendance, let alone a bachelor's degree, was hardly a prerequisite for most professional pursuits. Given this fact, it is remarkable that colleges remained as appealing to prospective students as they did.

Limited resources at most colleges meant that the administrative structure was lean, with the college president serving as the primary academic officer. Although presidents were the principal fund-raisers, most institutions also depended on a paid "college agent" for the combined external activities of recruiting students and enlisting donors and promoting college subscriptions.[30] Some colleges added a "catchall" administrator who might serve as bursar, registrar, and librarian. College faculty continued to have some responsibility for monitoring student conduct, although there were signs of specialization, with a dean sometimes taking over student discipline.

Most colleges continued to be dependent on unspectacular but essential small gifts from the community. Many communities viewed their local college as indispensable, so citizens and town governments were a popular target for solicitations by college officials. Thanks to the appeal of the local college to merchants and real estate developers, the indefatigable fund-raising by mid-nineteenth-century college presidents and their agents was reasonably successful.

After 1850, religion transformed the role of philanthropy in higher education. Instead of devout individuals making large donations to help found a denominationally based college, religious groups such as the American Missionary Association, a group with strong connections to the Congregationalist church, used highly organized methods to raise and distribute money for college-building across the nation. Such efforts resulted in the diffusion of the New England collegiate model to the Midwest (Cornell and Grinnell in Iowa, Lawrence in Wisconsin, Carleton in Minnesota) and all the way to California (Pomona College).

An important, relatively quiet change in American higher education between 1850 and 1890 was the increasing influence of substantial philanthropy. Large gifts, often in the form of foundations, trusts, and estates, became a potent vehicle for innovation. Abbott Lawrence of Boston, for example, gave substantially to Harvard College, endowing facilities that ranged from a scientific school to a museum. Outside the metropolitan areas, in western Massachusetts, bequests from prosperous manufacturers endowed an academy and also transformed Amherst and Williams into financially sound institutions.

Women's colleges were major beneficiaries of the new philanthropy. Ironically, these colleges often enjoyed fund-raising success precisely because they were outside the mainstream. Because women's education did not enjoy popular support, it relied instead on the intense commitment of maverick donors. The wealthy brewer Matthew Vassar, for example, used his fortune to start a women's college in Poughkeepsie, New York, relishing the idea that his unusual gift would make a difference. His devotion was such that he continued to contribute to the college's projects long after its founding. Vassar's gifts of $1.25 million (more than $16 million in 2000 dollars) marked a turning point, the transition from the "subscription and small gifts era to the period of donations of six and seven figures."[31]

Massachusetts was a fertile source of support for the higher education of women. Major gifts from the Durant family led to the founding of

Wellesley College. Sophia Smith, troubled by the good fortune of a large, unexpected inheritance, relieved herself of the financial burden by founding Smith College in Northampton, about five miles from pioneering Mount Holyoke. In the South, Josephine Louise Newcomb gave a series of gifts starting in 1886 that provided an endowment for the women's college associated with Louisiana University, later known as Tulane. Merle Curti and Roderick Nash estimate that the Newcomb family gifts eventually totaled over $3.5 million (about $70 million in 2000 dollars).[32]

The crucial coincidence for the transformation of philanthropy in American higher education was the coming together of industry and religion in what has been termed the "Protestant work ethic." For a growing number of prosperous Americans, hard work and good works came to be seen as necessary partners. Colleges benefited from the world-view of wealthy entrepreneurs who acknowledged their obligation to be stewards of important educational endeavors. This was the margin of wealth that enabled some colleges to get started with excellent facilities.[33] A good example of such philanthropists was Samuel Williston of western Massachusetts, a trustee of Amherst College. Williston came from a farming family but had made a fortune in button manufacturing. He took his role as college trustee seriously. Between 1845 and 1874 he gave Amherst $150,000 ($2.4 million in 2000 dollars). Boston merchants who were college graduates started by the 1850s to demonstrate sustained, substantial support with gifts as high as $175,000 ($3.6 million in 2000 dollars). According to Curti and Nash, William Johnson Walker, who over the course of his adult life gave over $1 million to colleges, personified this new philanthropy.[34]

These new forms philanthropy included another variation: foundations and funds whose emphasis was on issues and constituencies, not just individual institutions. Equally important was the notion of long-distance philanthropy, especially Northern wealth that was looking South. Berea College in Kentucky, an innovative institution committed to coeducation of the races, was one example of such philanthropy. Two others were the Peabody Education Fund of $3 million ($36.8 million in 2000 dollars) for educational assistance to the South and the 1882 John F. Slater Fund for the Education of Freedmen. All three were cases of interregional philanthropy, with money from New England and other parts of the North being directed to the Reconstruction-era South.[35]

Interregional Philanthropy and the Black Colleges

Protestant groups such as the American Missionary Association, associated with the founding of liberal arts colleges in the West, also displayed great commitment to the education of African Americans. The AMA was central to the founding of Hampton Institute, Fisk University, Howard University in Washington, D.C., Atlanta University, and Talledega College in Alabama.[36] The rapid increase in funding for the education of African-American students via the AMA as well as through the Slater and Peabody foundations was accompanied by debate regarding the black colleges' emphasis on the liberal arts relative to the industrial arts and applied fields. Although their contribution has often been overlooked, black church and community associations were deeply committed to founding and funding their own local colleges. Michael Dennis has found that these indigenous attempts at college-building tended to insist that liberal education was crucial to preparing a future black leadership, and that this primary commitment must not be usurped by industrial training.[37] This position would later be reiterated by W. E. B. DuBois in his call for a truly "higher" education for what he called the "talented tenth" of the black population. The debates between 1860 and 1890 over liberal versus practical education in the black colleges were a variation on the theme of the curricular debates that permeated all American higher education in that era.

One difference, however, was that for the black colleges, "practical education" usually carried with it the baggage of race combined with socioeconomic tracking within an increasingly industrialized economy. In other words, black higher education was not preparing alumni for professions and fields associated with leadership and genuine power. Ultimately, large-scale philanthropy from the North tended to favor segregated black institutes and colleges whose curricula offered preparation for skilled crafts and trades, all designed to make education for African Americans part of a plan for regional economic development within the confines of a conservative, racially segregated social and political structure.[38] There was less emphasis on bachelor's degree programs in the arts and sciences, on preparation for the learned professions of law and medicine, or on training for future political leaders. In terms of the education of a black leadership elite, the clergy remained the single most influential profession.

Hampton Institute in Virginia was, along with Tuskegee in Alabama, one of the most celebrated and well-supported institutions for black higher education as a practical curriculum. It was both successful and controversial.[39] Its overt emphasis on industrial and agricultural programs tended to mask its latent function as a normal school that educated African Americans to teach in a variety of fields. Its commitment was to economic development rather than, for example, the deliberate education of a black intelligentsia or preparation for political leadership. Buoyed by private donations and federal funding, Hampton Institute's grand architecture was combined with a self-sustaining institutional economy complete with a farm, dairy, machine shop, home economics, and shoe repair. The host city of Hampton would over time come to be known for its concentration of educated professionals, a black middle class.

Hampton Institute is usually associated with its African-American heritage, although its original commitment and enrollment included substantial provision for the education of Native Americans. About a third of its initial students were drawn from the displaced tribes of the Southwest. To this day there are scholarship funds dedicated to Native American students. Hampton Institute was not alone in this commitment. The Carlisle School for Indians in Pennsylvania and other similar institutions were founded during the late nineteenth century.

An Overlooked Contribution: The Comprehensive American University

New fields and expanding constituencies are the keys to understanding higher education in the three decades after the Civil War. The principal transformation of the American campus between 1860 and 1890 was, nominally and superficially, the change from "college" to "university." That generalization requires qualification. True, the term *university* was used to identify an increasing number of institutions, and, as noted before, the opening of the Johns Hopkins University in 1876 brought to fruition the quest for a genuine modern American university. Nevertheless, the American "university" remained more a matter of aspiration and terminology than of nationwide achievement.

If there was a prototype American "university" between 1860 and 1890, it was created through a process of expansion and annexation by a college so as to create a configuration of colleges. This is to be distinguished from an essential shift in mission to dissolve the "college" core and become a "modern university." In other words, by 1890 the German ideal of advanced scholarship, professors as experts, doctoral programs with graduate students, and a hierarchy of study had few adherents in the United States outside of Johns Hopkins. Rather, the American university that surfaced around 1890 typically was the historic college, internally renovated and then supplemented by new programs and departments. Often this was a parallel development. That is, the historic college was not necessarily a hub that newer programs radiated out from and deferred to. It was more of a smorgasbord for student choice. As in the 1830s and 1840s, few professional schools required a bachelor's degree for admission. Even at such prestigious universities as Harvard and Columbia, the professional schools of law and medicine were fairly autonomous and not connected in any meaningful succession with the collegiate curriculum.

If the Morrill Act of 1862 made a contribution to American higher education, it was that it helped expand the state college into this "university" model of federated units. The act had not yet had much effect in the creation of "research universities" defined by doctoral programs. Faculty teaching loads remained heavy, with only token allowances for graduate courses and seminars. Most of the curricular offerings associated with land-grant funding were for undergraduates. The Morrill Act did enhance professional education by connecting it to bachelor's degree programs, as distinguished from licenses, diplomas, and certificates. The proliferation of new academic units resulted in a relatively flat structure, with almost all programs being confined to the undergraduate level. Prior to 1890 the federal land-grant act had few provisions for advanced programs, extension sites, or research centers. It did enable a number of institutions to hire faculty in a range of fields, especially in the sciences. If these new professors brought to the campus an increased interest in original research and scientific inquiry, it was to a varied extent, usually determined by individual initiative. The natural and physical sciences were the primary beneficiaries of this movement. There also were signs that the emerging disciplines of the social and behavioral sciences — economics, history, political science, and psychology — staked a claim to faculty positions and course offerings.

This American hybrid model seems to have evolved without much central planning. Contrary to the hopes and claims of the university-builders whose manifestos and proposals were widely published, the American university of the era was not the product of an inspired, overarching vision. Yet it was surprisingly pervasive. Examples of the arrangement were found in every region, despite the lack of an articulated philosophy or coherent campaign. In New England, for example, Dartmouth College added the state's land-grant agricultural program to its collegiate core, along with a law school, a medical school, and a scientific school. In the South, Transylvania (also known as Kentucky University) had at one time a liberal arts college, a normal school, a commercial course, a medical school in Louisville, and a theology school. Almost a century before the University of California's Clark Kerr wrote about the "multi-versity," Transylvania and its late-nineteenth-century counterparts already embodied this loose, decentralized alliance of "schools." It is a pattern that explains Columbia in New York City, with its original college, its School of Mining, its Teachers' College, and eventually its affiliated College of Physicians and Surgeons.

Despite the incentives offered by the infusion of funds from the federal Morrill Act of 1862, by 1890 state support for higher education was uneven at best and usually uncertain. In the South, following the Reconstruction-era legislatures, state governments were especially frugal—and outright wary about taxing citizens for regular, generous support of public school systems, let alone state colleges and universities. In the Midwest and West the rhetoric of Progressivism as a political movement for social reform made some headway toward persuading legislators and citizens of the value of sustained investment in public higher education. Yet even these proposals met with opposition, dilution, even outright rejection. The surprising result as of 1890 was that the great expectations for the "age of the public university" had been fulfilled by the extension and expansion of the American college.

Contrary to the bold pronouncements of academic writers in the national journals of the 1870s and 1880s, the American college displayed unexpected appeal and utility, and the cultivation of truly strong universities would not be completed for several decades. Even the public institutions that gained support via the Morrill Act looked and behaved more like the allegedly archaic "private colleges" than like modern state universities. And those university presidents—such as Charles Eliot at MIT and, later, Harvard—who were in the best position to pioneer graduate programs actually devoted most of their administrative attention and writing to the reform of undergraduate education.

The lack of a widespread research structure and resources for doctoral programs did not rule out the possibility of changes in how collegiate faculty defined their roles and went about their work. Charles Eliot gained national fame (and notoriety) for his bold innovations in bringing an elective system to Harvard College. The extent to which his Harvard model then diffused to other institutions was uneven. Some colleges made provisions for electives in student curricula, while others retained a fixed course of study. There is evidence of increasing provisions for specialized departments, although it was unusual for a student to "major" in a particular field. The biggest impact of this evolution toward a university as a conglomeration of colleges was in faculty identification. Whether at an Amherst College or a University of California, by 1890 many professors had, on their own initiative, become "men of science" or "men of letters." They set up their own laboratories, collected their own books and journals, conducted botanical fieldwork, wrote books and tracts, and gathered specimens and artifacts for museums of natural history. In many cases this activity was a "bootleg" operation that did not show up in official catalogues. With the exception of certain major projects, such as the museum of natural history at Harvard, endowed by Abbott Lawrence, these scholarly endeavors usually had to be pursued by professors on a piecemeal basis. These incremental gains in the scope of scholarly pursuits and expanded notions of research and teaching laid the groundwork for later, larger battles in the faculty's campaign for academic freedom.

The relative silence of state and federal governments on matters of campus enhancement in the 1880s did not necessarily mean a lack of government interest in technology, applied science, or research. There was no imperative that colleges or universities would be the institutional site for large-scale government projects. However, the federal government had created its own scientific infrastructure, with such components as the U.S. Coast and Geodetic Survey and the U.S. Geological Survey, along with the Department of Agriculture's Weather Bureau. The Geological Survey enjoyed international praise for the quality of its scientific work. Its budget was substantial: $500,000 a year for the period 1881– 84 ($8.9 million to $9.6 million in 2000 dollars). Federal scientists faced continual scrutiny from impatient members of Congress who favored research that had practical, predictive value.[40] Nevertheless, the federal government's investments in scientific surveys and research remained strong. The groundwork for funding federally sponsored projects to be carried out at colleges and universities may have been put into place by the Morrill Act of 1862, but in 1890 it was still only starting to percolate as a serious, enduring national policy.

Access and Exclusion

The quality that most strongly characterized the varied institutions within American higher education in the late nineteenth century was localism — the essential quality of that source of civic, religious, or racial pride that Daniel Boorstin has called the "booster college."[41] Whether the institution was a state university, a women's college, a church-related campus, or a black college, the support of the immediate local community as a source of both students and donors was essential. Each college continually experimented with different ways of attracting enrollments and gifts. For example, Wesleyan University in Connecticut held firm to its commitment to liberal arts education while casting off its identity as a local men's college and redefining itself as a Methodist institution serving a broad geographical region. Later Wesleyan turned to coeducation as a strategy, only to abandon the plan after a few years and resume being a men's college.[42]

Such vacillations were common at many institutions. Seldom did a college or university have the luxury of carrying out a coherent philosophy of higher education without at least considering concessions that would favor institutional survival. What was operating across the country was an increase in access to higher education achieved through some broadening of the curriculum combined with specialization as to clientele. On balance, colleges provided more increase in access than in choice to the individual student. In other words, a young man or woman considering going to college in 1880 or 1890 could be reasonably certain of finding an affordable institution that provided a bachelor's degree curriculum. But depending on the personal characteristics of the student, the choices would often be confined to a narrow range of institutional types. Most colleges enrolled students who lived nearby. Few were heterogeneous in the composition of their student bodies. Some rough demarcation, usually along the lines of gender, religion, or race, combined with geography to define a particular college's central constituency. As a result, colleges were segregated and often practiced unabashed discrimination as to whom they chose to admit. Yet on the whole, an increased number of constituencies and special interest groups found some accommodation, often by creating their own campuses. The advent of co-education of men and women at some colleges and universities, of course, was an important departure from the tendency toward segregation. But coeducation was not a pervasive feature of the post–Civil War campus. Rather, it was one of several institutional variants available to students as consumers.

Institutional differences were often magnified in the public arena. Today, for example, Harvard, Yale, and Princeton tend to be regarded as birds of a feather, individually and collectively illustrative of an Ivy League type. This was not the situation in 1890, when each of the three historic institutions claimed a distinctive tradition and educational commitment. At regional gatherings of New England college presidents, Charles Eliot of Harvard and Noah Porter of Yale disagreed vehemently on what the undergraduate experience ought to be, with meetings sometimes ending as shouting matches.

Between 1860 and 1890, American institutions of higher education responded pragmatically, albeit imperfectly, to the challenge of competing with the attractions of a commercial and industrial economy. They did so by adding new curricula that were intended to attract new kinds of students—all as a supplement to their historical missions and traditional audiences. Most college presidents recognized that they had to consider making changes, even though it was not always clear which specific combination of changes would be most appropriate and effective. The church-related colleges tended to maintain a denominational affiliation while reducing their strict sectarian emphases. A philosophy of higher education whose traditional emphasis was on piety henceforth had to acknowledge the growing importance of intellect. Often the compromise was to fuse piety and intellect. A modern liberal education was to be concerned with building character as well as saving souls.

This cautious yet continual exploration on the margins enabled American higher education to elbow a place for itself and even generate magnetism in an increasingly industrial economy. The challenge for college presidents was to convince American families that an undergraduate education was worthwhile and affordable while maintaining the college's essential commitment to education for character. This commitment by the college and investment by a student's family would be a passport into a professional group, an American middle class. All this ferment among the historic colleges and the new state institutions took place at a time of abundant opportunities and risks in the American economy. This confluence left numerous hungry, underfunded colleges trying to define both a mission and a market. Most institutional soul-searching and jockeying for position focused on undergraduate education. State colleges that were linked to the 1862 Morrill Act remained underdeveloped for several decades. And for all of American higher education, the halcyon era of university-building characterized by advanced scholarship and specialized research was yet to come.

4 Captains of Industry and Erudition
University-Builders, 1880 to 1910

The Quest for the Great American University

Between 1880 and 1890 only a handful of institutions in the United States had legitimate claim to being a "real university." Apart from Johns Hopkins, Cornell, Harvard, Clark, and Columbia, the list of serious contenders was slim. Although building the American university attracted a great deal of attention, most articles at the time dealt with the aspirations for what the future American university might be rather than reporting on what it actually was. All this changed dramatically over the next three decades. A landmark event occurred in 1900, when the presidents of fourteen institutions met to form the Association of American Universities—an act that would have been premature a decade earlier.[1] The charter members were:

- Harvard University
- Johns Hopkins University
- Columbia University
- University of Chicago
- University of California
- Clark University
- Cornell University
- Catholic University
- University of Michigan
- Leland Stanford, Jr., University
- University of Wisconsin
- University of Pennsylvania
- Princeton University
- Yale University

Another sign of maturation came in 1910 when Edwin Slosson, editor of the magazine *The Independent,* observed that one now could identify a cluster of "great American universities." Slosson was an influential journalist who held a Ph.D. in chemistry from the University of Chicago. His focus on the national importance of American universities as a novel entity was no whim. He spent two years visiting institutions and then devoted over five hundred pages to scrutinizing fourteen institutions that he selected for a series of monthly articles. The series was so successful that the collected profiles were then published as a complete book, *Great American Universities.* Slosson's selections overlapped closely with the charter membership of the Association of American Universities, with a few notable changes that illustrated how quickly institutional reputations could rise or fall. Clark University of Worcester, Massachusetts, and the Catholic University in Washington, D.C.—both members of the original AAU—were absent from Slosson's elite group. In their place he included two state universities from the Midwest: the University of Illinois and the University of Minnesota. Slosson's selections also depicted the continuity in campus prestige. Apart from these alterations, twelve of the original AAU members of 1900 retained their high standing, at least according to Slosson's criteria.

As a corollary to the handful of "great" universities, according to Slosson, by 1910 there was also a discernible entity he called the "S.A.U."—shorthand for the "standard American university." This "S.A.U." embodied similarities of form, structure, mission, and vocabulary to represent maturity and crystallization. How, given the flux and lack of advanced scholarship in American institutions around 1880, had this evolution taken place? And what were the distinguishing features of the "standard American university"? Before describing these institutional components of 1910, let us consider the dynamics of university-building in the formative decades between 1880 and 1910.

Growth and success characterized the era of the "university-builders" between 1880 and 1910. The wealth and energy of the period made for an exciting time in higher education. It was not, however, a smooth evolution. Accounts of the university-builders—a mix of donors and presidents—indicate that the risks and rivalries that defined American business competition of the era were replicated on the American campus. The similarities prompted Thorstein Veblen to coin the satirical term "captains of erudition," echoing the popular phrase "captains of industry," to characterize the university-builders' approach to academic affairs.[2] Among the university-builders there was distrust, contempt, chicanery, and sabotage. Fortunes fell fast. Between 1893 and 1896 a sustained economic depression drove down the stock market value of several university endowments, and with it some of the grandiose plans of university presidents.[3] Most of all, there were no ground rules about propriety, nor was there any blueprint for what a "university" ought to include — or omit.

Philosophical arguments and extravagant designs were the order of the day, but it was an open forum that had no expert jury to impose standards. Donors and presidents at one university had little knowledge of or concern about what was going on elsewhere — unless, of course, it was seen as a threat to their own work. Given this environment of ambition and wealth without order or rules, between 1880 and 1910 there was a high shakeout rate among ambitious institutions. Competing for talent, raiding the faculty of rival institutions, and building lavish facilities were common practices. This phenomenon was hinted at by Clark University and the Catholic University dropping out of the top rank between 1900 and 1910. In the case of Clark University, its distinctive plan for emphasis on graduate studies and advanced work in the behavioral sciences fell victim to an inadequate operating budget. Public knowledge of this weakened financial position left Clark vulnerable to rival institutions. A faculty raid led by President Harper of the University of Chicago sealed Clark's descent from the top rank of universities. The Catholic University in Washington, D.C., failed to fulfill its promise of providing a national locus for advanced scholarship with a distinctive Catholic perspective. Each institution had its own saga of great expectations followed by disappointments and derailments.

One factor contributing to the emergence of many universities during these decades was industry — the discretionary wealth generated by American corporations and enterprises in the late nineteenth century. The $7 million gift for the founding of the Johns Hopkins University and its hospital in Baltimore in 1876 was the largest philanthropic bequest ever seen in the United States at that time. Indexed for inflation, the gift would have been worth $112.8 million in 2000. Beyond the philanthropy made possible by business fortunes, industrial organization provided models for academic structure. Foremost among these influences was the approximation on the campus of a corporate model of hierarchy and offices for faculty and staff. Second was the growing numerical presence of industrial leaders as trustees on university boards, eventually leading to the rhetorical slogan, "Why can't a college be run like a business?"

Religion played a central (though often overlooked) role in this institutional evolution, in both substance and style. Even though some commentators at the time described religion as waning in influence and often out of touch with the new trends of commerce and science, there is intriguing evidence that it was a driving force in the industrial and corporate ethos of the era. This influence carried over directly to the shaping and subsidizing of American higher education. John D. Rockefeller's gift of $12 million (about $229 million in 2000 dollars) to found the University of Chicago was offered in cooperation with the American Baptist Education Society to create an eminent Baptist institution in the Midwest. Vanderbilt University carried out the vision of a great Methodist university. Elsewhere in the South, Benjamin Duke drew from his fortune in tobacco, railroads, cotton, and utilities to give over $2 million between 1898 and 1925 ($29.5 million in 2000 dollars) to help revive Trinity College, a struggling Methodist institution.

In addition to these direct ties between denominations and university-building, large-scale philanthropy for higher education was fueled by a hybrid doctrine that came to be known as the "gospel of wealth." At about the same time, Dwight Moody gained a following in the American business community with his nondenominational doctrine of giving, a "stewardship of wealth." It was a doctrine that was timely for university fund-raisers because Moody provided the rationale for connecting this "good works" dimension of Protestantism and prosperity to the cause of supporting higher education through generous donations. From time to time, donors and founders representing other religious groups followed suit. Perhaps the best testimony to religion as a central force in creating the modern American university came in 1884, when an alliance of heiresses and wealthy businessmen from New York, Philadelphia, and New Orleans provided the endowment for founding the Catholic University of America—strategically located in the nation's capital—to assure that advanced American scholarship in philosophy and theology would include a Catholic perspective.

Religion, then, was hardly a negligible force in the shaping of higher education at the end of the nineteenth century. Rather than focusing exclusively on the alleged conflict between religion and the university ideal of science, we should note how the two forces enhanced one another. "Science" as it was invoked in American institutions — government, business, and education — was less a value system at odds with religion than an organizational ethos that prized order and efficiency. Whether reforming public schools, businesses, or higher education, the Progressives had confidence that their reliance on expertise and analysis could promote the "one best system" in American institutions.[4] For an endeavor or an organization to be "scientific" meant that it was disciplined, ordered, and systematic — in other words, that it adhered to the principles of "scientific management." *Science* used in this sense connoted efficiency, effectiveness, and accountability, the very principles that were the source of the ideological conflict that pitted the industrial entrepreneurs against the experts and engineers in their markedly different attempts to shape the character and tenor of organizational life.

The emergence of American universities between 1880 and 1910 was due in part to the good fortune of optimal timing. Along with the unprecedented industrial wealth, there was a new level of philanthropic generosity.[5] One analysis of American giving between 1893 and 1916 revealed two important coincidences: first, gifts and bequests in general increased dramatically — more than fivefold — in that quarter-century; and second, the proportion of those gifts going to colleges jumped from about 47 percent to around 75 percent in those decades. As beneficiaries of giving, colleges ranked very high, surpassing museums, charities, libraries, public improvements, parks, and religious organizations.[6] Trinity College in North Carolina, for example, was the beneficiary of Benjamin Duke's generosity mainly because Duke diverged from his original plan to provide funding for a Methodist orphanage. When Commodore Vanderbilt became enamored of the idea of a university as his memorial, he scuttled such projects as a retirement home for railroad workers. When museums and observatories were endowed, they were often part of a university. All charitable endeavors benefited during this period of prosperity and generosity, but colleges and universities were the boat most favored by the rising tide.

Philanthropic generosity toward higher education enjoyed a multiplier effect in its connections to public relations, thanks to a technological revolution in graphics.[7] It was the golden age of illustrated national magazines. Monthly and weekly periodicals, including *Century, The Independent, The Outlook, Harper's, The Nation, Munsey's,* and *McClure's,* became the preferred reading of a nationwide educated middle

class. Profiles of new, expanding buildings and refurbished historic campuses came to be a staple feature.[8] Simultaneously, biographies of donors and presidents created and projected popular images of both the
captains of industry and the captains of erudition. Even when the magazine biographies were critical, the new generation of large donors and
ambitious presidents gained fame through the visibility of notoriety, if
not adulation.

Campus Architecture and the University Spirit

The new visibility of the emerging university was most evident literally
in its architecture. The architectural paradox of the American university
of this period is that the newer the campus was, the older it appeared
to be. Thanks once again to the unprecedented wealth (and egos) of
donors, the new universities were magnificent memorials that relied on
historical revival forms to connect the present to the past.[9] Improvements in technology, including reinforced concrete and eventually I-
beam construction, made possible the erection of tall office buildings
clothed in Gothic stone or colonial brick. Whether for municipal buildings or lecture halls, Americans took planning seriously. The task of the
university-builders was comparable to designing a complete city. For
example, in 1900 Phoebe Apperson Hearst pledged $80,000 (about $1.6
million in 2000 dollars) to sponsor an international contest to find an
architect worthy of designing a campus for the new University of California that would make it the "Athens of the West."[10] One of the designs,
submitted by Emile Bernard of France, included an ornate classical gymnasium and stadium. Soon thereafter it was expanded to include a Greek
theater and a campanile. Mrs. Hearst was so enthusiastic about the initial
buildings that eventually she made generous contributions to fund the
design and construction of Hearst family monuments — including architect John Galen Howard's mining and engineering building and a
women's gymnasium and swimming pool, all with exquisite classical
motifs. Elsewhere other universities caught the fever of the "campus
beautiful," sponsoring competitions to match Berkeley's classical vision.[11] Not only did the competitions attract the leading architects of the
day, they also fostered a new expertise in landscape design. Beatrix Farrand, whose career spanned almost a half-century, was among the first
to persuade the boards and officials of institutions ranging from the

University of Chicago to Princeton to invest in planning and purchasing such details as campus benches, gardens, walkways, groves, grottoes, and ornamentation.[12]

Gothic-revival architecture was both nostalgic and functional. Its large spaces were especially well suited to housing the unprecedented new libraries, laboratories, gymnasia, and observatories. In Palo Alto, California, the Stanford family opted for a Mediterranean style. Even Egyptian-revival architecture enjoyed a spurt of popularity. The period of heroic university-building served as a reminder of two crucial features of campus life: prior to 1890, American colleges had been small in size and simple in their mission and functions. To the American public, the grand turn-of-the-century colleges and universities, with their magnificent buildings and exquisite landscaping, were the equivalent of today's theme parks. Even the academics reveled in this architectural boosterism. This zeal continued well after World War I. The University of Pittsburgh's magnificent "Cathedral of Learning," a product of community and academic fund-raising that was completed in 1929, was a prime example of "girder Gothic" and civic pride. The American university had captured the popular imagination both as a tourist destination and as a source of inspiration. The nation's journalists knew this and responded with regular articles on the American campus as architecture's showplace.[13]

Structural Changes in Historical Perspective

The structural changes symbolized by the dynamic campus architecture of the period were the backdrop to essential changes in the American universities' administrative and intellectual structures. Any historian tackling universities of this era must acknowledge a debt to Laurence Veysey's *The Emergence of the American University*.[14] According to Veysey, during the period between 1865 and 1910 the American university evolved and ultimately congealed into forms familiar to us today. In terms of intellectual and curricular movements, several conceptions of higher learning coexisted with varying degrees of conflict and cooperation. "Piety and discipline," "liberal culture," "utility," and "research" were some of the traditions invoked by academic visionaries and entrepreneurs. Within each emergent university, these disparate, often conflicting, notions took on varying configurations.

At the same time, the formal institutions started to display some common structural and administrative characteristics—a patchwork arrangement usually marked by pragmatic responses rather than coherent master plans. Veysey described this crystallization as the "price of structure."[15] At times the absence of a major donor obsessed with a particular philosophy or vision had the benefit of leaving academic planning to academics. Commodore Vanderbilt admitted, "If it was to build a railroad, I would know what to do, but I know nothing about a University."[16] In a similar vein, Daniel Coit Gilman gratefully recalled Johns Hopkins and his generous founding gift:

> The founder made no effort to unfold a plan. He simply used one word,—UNIVERSITY,—and he left it to his successors to declare its meaning in the light of the past, in the hope of the future. There is no indication that he was interested in one branch of knowledge more than in another. He had no educational "fad." There is no evidence that he had read the writings of Cardinal Newman or of Mark Pattison, and none that the great parliamentary reports had come under his eye. He was a large-minded man, who knew that the success of the foundation would depend upon the wisdom of those to whom its development was entrusted.[17]

In contrast to Hopkins's restraint, the university presidents usually had elaborate schemes in mind for their academic projects. Cornell's first president, Andrew White, recalled how the "Cornell Idea" had first formed in his mind, with inspiration from Oxford and Cambridge:

> Every feature of the little American college seemed all the more sordid. But gradually I began consoling myself by building air-castles. These took the form of structures suited to a great university:—with distinguished professors in every field, with libraries as rich as the Bodleian, halls as lordly as that of Christ Church or of Trinity, chapels as inspiring as that of King's, towers as dignified as those of Magdalene and Merton, quadrangles as beautiful as those of Jesus and St. John's. In the midst of all other occupations, I was constantly rearing these structures on that queenly site above the finest of the New York lakes, and dreaming of a university worthy of the commonwealth and of the nation.

White acknowledged, "This dream became sort of an obsession. It came upon me during my working hours, in the class-rooms, in rambles along the lakeshore in the evenings, when I paced up and down the walks in front of the college buildings, and saw rising in their place and extending to the pretty knoll behind them, the worthy home of a great university."[18]

Neither Andrew White nor his fellow university-builders were content to let the inspiration of an Oxford or a Cambridge wholly shape their plans. They recreated the beauty and dignity of the established international universities but put together their own curricular schemes, adding modern history to the faculty or incorporating engineering and agriculture into the arts and sciences, along with hundreds of other permutations. The case of Andrew White and his vision of Oxford and Cambridge transplanted to upstate New York suggests that even the reflective academic visionaries were inconsistent, or at least heterodox, in their combining of England's historic architecture with an American curriculum that would have made little sense to an Oxford don.

According to Laurence Veysey, this combination of intellectual and organizational churning was such that prior to World War I the ground rules and forms of university prestige and practice in the United States had been staked out and pretty much filled in. Although professors wrote profusely about the ideal American university, the donors and presidents who were the major builders were often silent on the matter. It's hard to decipher the extent to which the new great universities were the embodiment of a clear philosophical view or were the product of idiosyncratic notions borrowed belatedly and selectively from the clear ideas presented by scholars. The university-founders, those whom Veblen dubbed the "captains of erudition," were energetic, ruthless pioneers who sometimes operated with little regard for government or public opinion. They were comparable to today's major league baseball team owners: wealthy, indulged, and able to put into motion pet ideas about how an organization should be staffed and operated. Leland and Jane Stanford, for example, were focused on building a campus that would be a memorial to their late teenaged son. Mrs. Stanford showed no restraint in tending to the big issues as well as the myriad details of the magnificent campus plan. The university-builders often thought themselves to be above the law. However, it was not a period of illegal activity; rather, there were few rules or laws to break. Between 1880 and 1900, higher education was the ultimate unregulated industry.

A Profile of Campus and Community: Chicago in 1893

Events in Chicago in the 1890s illustrate how these social, economic, and political trends converged to help foster America's great new universities. Even Chicago's most loyal supporters acknowledged its unattractive location and unappealing climate. Dwight Moody, a businessman turned religious reformer—and one of the most influential Americans of the late nineteenth century—summed up the Chicago mood: bustling with commerce and an energy that overrode the barren landscape, harsh winters, and lack of amenities.[19] To anyone who thrived on commerce, Chicago was an exhilarating place. And with commercial wealth came city-building—an activity that would include campus-building. The funding and founding of the University of Chicago was a broad-based venture. In addition to the unprecedented generosity of John D. Rockefeller's gift of $12 million in the early 1890s (about $229 million in 2000 dollars), the project attracted strong civic support from Marshall Field and other successful local merchants. Field, for example, donated the large land tract on the Midway for the campus. Another trustee gave generously to subsidize a well-equipped physics laboratory; others provided an observatory, a graduate school of science, and endowments for twenty-nine professorships. The tradition of matching funds and reciprocation continued—and impressed the founder, Rockefeller, so much that by the early 1900s his total support reached about $35 million (more than $660 million in 2000 dollars). Although the new university had a Baptist affiliation, it was embraced across all constituencies as the city's favored campus.

Indicative of this civic pride kindled by prosperity was Chicago's hosting of the Columbian Exposition of 1893, at the time the largest tourist event in the history of the nation. It brought twenty-seven million visitors along with international publicity to this relatively young, provincial city. The Columbian Exposition—its setup and opening—coincided with the construction and opening of the new University of Chicago. The two literally were neighbors on the Midway, and both attracted visitors, each enhancing curiosity about the other. As Jean Block recalled, "The Gray City of the University of Chicago and the White City of the World's Columbian Exposition were twin progeny of youthful Chicago, created by ardent, ambitious businessmen eager to change the city's image from one of barbarous materialism to one of refinement and culture."[20] In another bit of good timing, the Columbian Exposition took place just as the picture-postcard industry was tooling up in the United States. For the photographers and postcard manufacturers, Chicago's architectural wonders—the ornate buildings of the Columbian Exposition and the Gothic spires of the University of Chicago—provided ideal subject matter. So in addition to the many visitors who enjoyed Chicago's magnificent and unprecedented vistas, hundreds of thousands of friends and family members received a vicarious glimpse via high-quality, mass-produced postcards. The opportunity was not lost on the University of Chicago leadership. They broke ranks with academic tradition and sought, rather than shunned, publicity ranging from ribbon-cutting ceremonies and elaborate academic processions to daily contact with newspaper reporters.

Public relations and community relations personified a new type of American university president. Chicago's William Rainey Harper stands out even in an era of heroic leaders. He became a local hero of sorts, dubbed Chicago's "young man in a hurry."[21] The University of Chicago came to be known locally and nationally as "Harper's Bazaar." Understanding his biography is essential for understanding the modern American university. As the first president of the University of Chicago, he was a leading figure in the development of the modern university in the United States. An academic prodigy, he enrolled at age ten as a freshman at Muskingum College, where he studied languages and music and graduated at age fourteen. He went to Yale and earned a Ph.D. in philology in three years, before his nineteenth birthday. While in graduate school he married the daughter of the president of his undergraduate alma mater.

After Harper completed his Ph.D. at Yale, he worked as a teacher and school principal in Tennessee and Ohio before accepting an instructorship in Hebrew theology at the original University of Chicago. He was a full professor of divinity by 1880. He was named president in 1886, the last year before the institution closed. He then went to Yale as a professor of Semitic languages in the graduate department and as an instructor in the divinity school. He taught Hebrew, Assyrian, Arabic, Aramaic, and Syrian. He continued to oversee summer schools, journals, a correspondence school, and the printing office. Soon he branched out into lecturing and began giving public courses on the Bible, finding a new means by which he could expound on the origins of the Bible.

Harper's reputation as a prodigious scholar of religion, and his Baptist affiliation, attracted the attention of John D. Rockefeller, who was making plans and donating generous amounts of money for the founding of a university. In 1891 Harper accepted Rockefeller's invitation to be the first president of the new University of Chicago, and he served for fourteen years, until his death in 1906 at age forty-nine. Although Harper was impressive as a scholar, he made his enduring contribution to American higher education as an organizational genius and innovative leader. He was gregarious and worked well with civic leaders and donors in Chicago. Harper was unabashedly ambitious in his plans for the new University of Chicago and channeled that zeal into the ruthless recruitment of talented faculty, students, and administrators. He gained the envy and scorn of college presidents across the nation when he raided the faculty of Clark University in order to enhance the behavioral sciences at Chicago. In concert with Professor Albion Small of sociology, whom he appointed dean, Harper introduced a number of pioneering changes at the University of Chicago, including an elaborate bureaucracy of academic departments. He built a modern, innovative university amid the historic motifs of a monumental Gothic-revival campus that was the pride of the city.

Harper understood and thrived in the setting of a complex, multipurpose institution. He added such new features as a two-year junior college and an extensive summer school. From its founding, the University of Chicago's charter distinctly emphasized educational opportunities for women. Harper adhered to this provision, and Chicago was coeducational from the start. Harper obtained generous funding for scientific laboratories, an observatory, a university press, and a graduate school with numerous Ph.D. programs, professional schools, research institutes, and a library. At the same time he also emphasized intercollegiate football with a magnificent stadium designed to draw spectators from throughout the city. His hiring of Yale's Amos Alonzo Stagg as football coach and athletic director was instrumental in making the University of Chicago Maroons the dominant champions of the Western (later known as the "Big Ten") conference. And, with Harper's approval, Stagg created the prototype for the highly commercial athletic department that had direct access to the president and the board of trustees, with little accountability to normal channels of faculty governance.

Harper paid no deference to academic conventions, whether in admissions examinations or degree requirements. He endorsed the coeducation of men and women. He relied on advertising, billboards, and mass mailings to promote all facets of campus activities. He was committed to systematic public relations and fund-raising. He served on numerous boards and committees in the city and nation. The University of Chicago was to be a modern university that was central to a dynamic metropolitan area and that created the national prototype for a truly great American university. Ironically, Harper's energy and ambition left a mixed impression on benefactor John D. Rockefeller. Rockefeller clearly admired Harper's talent and wanted him as the university's president. But he was also wary of Harper's penchant for spending, especially when it pertained to Rockefeller's money, so he relied on Frederick Gates to act as an intermediary to screen and monitor campus projects.

Harper personified the indefatigable university president. In 1905, while hospitalized with terminal cancer, he published a book about education, revised two scriptural articles, published a biblical text, and finished writing a major scholarly work. In a final expression of the zeal he brought to the university presidency, on his deathbed he was busy making plans for his elaborate funeral procession, including detailed instructions for Chicago faculty to march wearing full academic regalia.[22]

Large-Scale Philanthropy: The Gospel of Giving as the Religion of Higher Education

Commerce in the United States of the late nineteenth century was characterized by a lack of federal regulation or intervention. This laissez-faire environment, combined with technological breakthroughs in manufacturing and mining, coincided with a nationwide demand for new products and services. Oil refining, railroads, shipping, coal mining, and steel production were at the heart of the economic boom. The same lack of regulation that stimulated daring enterprise also, not surprisingly, made for high-stakes gains and losses—a remarkably inefficient economic system. We are most fascinated by those corporate leaders who triumphed—the "captains of industry"—and emerged as both heroes and villains: Andrew Carnegie in steel, John D. Rockefeller, Sr., in oil refining, Cornelius Vanderbilt in shipping and railroads, Ezra Cornell in telegraph and communications, the Armour family in meatpacking, and Leland Stanford in railroads. Philanthropy also drew from mercantile wealth, as evidenced by Marshall Field in Chicago, Paul Tulane in New Orleans, and William Marsh Rice in Houston. All these names would become familiar in their association with the founding and funding of ascending universities.

The largest benefactors justifiably attracted the most attention, both from journalists in their own time and from historians later. They are not the whole story, however, and are best understood as the crest of a large, diverse wave of support for colleges and universities in this era. For example, although the Morrill Act of 1862 first comes to mind as the source of support for scientific and technical education, generous support and serious commitment for these fields also came about via new private institutions endorsed by individual donors. The array of new institutions testifies to business leaders' sustained commitment to practical education at a high level. Cooper Union in New York City, Lehigh in Pennsylvania, Renssellaer in upstate New York, Drexel in Philadelphia, Rice Institute in Houston, Worcester Polytechnic Institute in Massachusetts, Armour Institute in Chicago, and, of course, the Massachusetts Institute of Technology were part of the groundswell. Even maverick enterprises became a source of generous support for colleges and universities. Tufts University near Boston acknowledged the gifts of circus impresario P. T. Barnum by selecting as its campus mascot Jumbo, the star elephant of Barnum's "Greatest Show on Earth." Russell T. Conway, the peripatetic inspirational speaker who thrilled ambitious crowds with his "Acres of Diamonds" speech on the fusion of wealth and virtue, helped endow the Philadelphia campus that came to be Temple University.

What is most fascinating about higher education in this period is the devotion and financial support new endeavors received from individuals who were not alumni or even college graduates. As Merle Curti and Roderick Nash note, it was the "friends" of higher education who, often with little fanfare, helped higher education in the United States diversify its curricula and operate from a reasonably solid financial base.[23] Civic pride brought together disparate groups who worked in a united front to assure that, one way or another, a city got its own university. In Los Angeles a deliberately ecumenical group of civic leaders that included Jews and Catholics accepted the invitation of Methodists to found the University of Southern California—a private university that served the metropolitan area that had been neglected by the governor and by the University of California.

Along with the friends and benefactors, there was another important set of actors in the synergy of university-building: the fund-raisers, whose nickname at the time was the "honorable beggars." These were the catalysts of higher-education philanthropy who served as middlemen between donors and campus presidents. They had a rare talent for gaining access to business leaders. Most of the innovators in this field had been Protestant clergy or had been active in organized church work before devoting themselves full time to professional fund-raising. During this period the fund-raisers' work of getting and giving money for campus projects was elevated to a sophisticated endeavor.[24]

A central figure between 1880 and 1910 was Frederick Gates, who represented the connections between the old-time religion and the modern philanthropy of university-building. Gates was secretary of the Baptist Education Board and the son of a Baptist minister. Among his early successes in fund-raising was having persuaded the Pillsbury family of Minnesota to donate some of their agricultural and milling wealth in support of a Baptist academy in Minneapolis — predictably renamed Pillsbury Academy. As administrative director for the Baptist group, Gates worked patiently with William Rainey Harper and Thomas Goodspeed to persuade John D. Rockefeller, Sr., to consider providing ample funding for a new University of Chicago.

Gates and his colleagues described their work in colorful terms. In their conversations they called soliciting for funds "fishing expeditions" and prospective donors "trout." A prospective donor who was on the brink of committing a substantial sum was "big with gift." At other times they called benefactors, with some apology, "victims." Gates's 1890 memorandum on the "Rules of Procedure" for fund-raising captures the combination of serious business and relish for the hunt that characterized what he and his colleagues called "canvassing" for gifts. Gates started out his memorandum with straightforward advice on grooming and deportment. Since the solicitor would be dealing with "busy men," he was advised, "On entering, go straight to your subject without palaver." Canvassing should be systematic and deliberate: "Work continuously, rapidly and at a hot pace. . . . Canvass every day and all day, moving rapidly from man to man, rain or shine. Read nothing, write of nothing, think of nothing, so long as your canvass continues, but the canvass."[25]

Gates knew whereof he wrote, as he had used these principles himself, first in Minneapolis in courting the Pillsbury family, and then with Goodspeed in the initial fund-raising for the new University of Chicago. Serious purpose, however, required sensitivity, as he elaborated:

> I said in my second point that you must keep good natured. I now wish to say that you must also keep your victim, if I may so call him, also good natured and this throughout. Constantly endeavor to make the interview continuously pleasant for him. If you find him embarrassed at any point relieve that embarrassment. For illustration: He may be embarrassed by the smallness of the amount, which he can give. The best class of men are. Reassure him on this if you find he needs it and on any other point of embarrassment. . . . If you find him big with gift do not rush him too eagerly to the birth. Let him take his time with genial encouragement. Make him

feel that *he* is making the gift, not that it is being taken from him with violence. . . . Appeal only to the noblest motives.[26]

Gates's approach evidently worked well. The key, according to businessmen who explained why they had responded generously to a Frederick Gates or a Dwight L. Moody, was that these middlemen spoke the language of real businessmen: "They are one of us."[27]

Another pioneer in the era of large gifts for higher education was Holland N. McTyeire, a Methodist minister who combined his clerical calling with philanthropic "fishing expeditions." McTyeire's prize "trout" was Cornelius Vanderbilt. Vanderbilt was notorious for turning away fund-raisers. To rid himself of one bothersome solicitor, he presented the fund-raiser with a one-way ticket—presumably on Vanderbilt's own steamship line—to Central America. McTyeire, who by this time had been named bishop of the Methodists in the South, met Vanderbilt by chance in New York, thanks to his in-laws' connections. After much patient listening and many conversations with the commodore, McTyeire eventually won his interest and respect—so much so that Vanderbilt lamented that McTyeire had not opted to be a lawyer for the railroads.

The gradual progression of McTyeire's fund-raising efforts with Vanderbilt brought together several threads. First, McTyeire advanced the notion that building a church-related educational institution was preferable to building a church. Second, he gently convinced Vanderbilt that a complete university would be a more fitting memorial than a freestanding seminary. Third, he argued convincingly that the founding of a Methodist university in the South would be an effective gesture toward healing the intersectional wounds that had been left by the Civil War. Vanderbilt liked the man and his ideas. The result was that the commodore endorsed the idea of funding in Nashville a truly distinguished university with a Methodist affiliation, including a seminary along with an undergraduate college, graduate schools, and professional schools. Vanderbilt's one stipulation was that McTyeire, who had been the middleman, must also be the chancellor of the new university. In an interesting display of reserve, Vanderbilt did not meddle into the operation of the university; in fact, he never once visited the campus.[28]

University Presidents as Entrepreneurs

The generation of university presidents at the turn of the century came to be called giants—sometimes only by themselves, in self-congratulatory moments, but also by admiring contemporaries and later historians. Some of the memorable presidents were also superb fund-raisers: William Rainey Harper, although short in height, stands out in their ranks. Other notables include Charles Eliot of Harvard, Benjamin Ide Wheeler of the University of California, Daniel Coit Gilman of Johns Hopkins University, David Starr Jordan of Stanford, G. Stanley Hall of Clark University, Holland McTyeire of Vanderbilt, Andrew White of Cornell, and Seth Low and then Nicholas Murray Butler of Columbia.

One important characteristic of these pioneering presidents was that they served for a long time. Another is that they were public figures whose influence extended beyond the campus into local, state, and national affairs. For university presidents in major cities, it was typical to serve on the local school board—a model established by Eliot of Harvard for Boston's schools and Columbia University's Nicholas Murray Butler for New York City's public schools. Eliot had also been instrumental in supporting the expansion of the American Red Cross, an effort that included an extended campaign to expose graft and corruption in U.S. government services. In effect, Eliot and his presidential colleagues were integral to the advancement of a vigorous private sector for varied social and humanitarian services. Seth Low exemplified the fusion of family and business wealth with university leadership—a combination that was especially potent in New York City's commercial culture. In his successful tenure at Columbia University he also used the power of his office to extend philanthropy to higher education elsewhere. He was, for example, a leader and donor in support of black colleges in South Carolina and other Southern states.

Much of the publicity went to the newly founded universities, whose massive construction projects and heroic architecture were conspicuous. Less obvious was the philanthropic work of refurbishing historic institutions. Charles Eliot of Harvard did not seek the publicity of Chicago's William Rainey Harper. Quietly and effectively, in his four decades as Harvard's president he transformed and solidified Harvard's financial and academic position. Eliot worked closely with leaders and established families in Boston to transform Harvard. According to historians Merle Curti and Roderick Nash, "Eliot emphasized Harvard's contributions to public service, making clear what was wanted and why it was needed. Gifts flowed in, with the result that endowment funds tripled between 1869 and 1878 and tripled again in the next twenty years."[29] In the two decades after 1869, Harvard's gifts for current uses increased 150-fold.

Between 1889 and 1909, this figure then doubled. Harvard's endowment in 1909, at the time of Eliot's retirement, was a little over $22 million (over $420 million in 2000 dollars).

The great university presidents of the era also wrote emphatically and often on current events in national periodicals. They were involved in national politics. When Theodore Roosevelt was president of the United States, he found time in his Western hunting expeditions to visit his close friend, Benjamin Ide Wheeler, president of the University of California. Roosevelt used the university's Charter Day ceremonies as an opportunity for a major address and extended his visit in order to meet with Wheeler and California's governor-senator Hiram Johnson to plan his election platform. For some university presidents, involvement in current events led to visibility—and trouble. Benjamin Andrew of Brown, drawing on his expertise as an economist, angered his own board of trustees. Win or lose, the university presidents were in the thick of public affairs. Their universities were nationally important.

Taking Stock: Characteristics of the Great Modern American University

Culling from each of the "great" universities examples of their best practices, one can construct a composite profile of the turn-of-the-century American university at its zenith:

Philanthropy on a large scale. Universities for the first time had a permanent financial base—so much so that a new descriptive phrase came to be used: the "privately endowed university." In addition to defining Harvard, Stanford, Chicago, and Columbia, the phrase also referred to an emerging subset of state universities—for example, the University of Wisconsin, the University of Michigan, and the University of California, whose endowments and gifts from generous friends allowed them to transcend meager and erratic state appropriations.

Presidential presence. A university president was expected to be enterprising and able to interact with the external political and industrial world as well as to move in academic circles.

Professors as professional experts. The professionalization of the faculty was a conspicuous and important trend, with professors increasingly known as experts in a field. This expertise included membership and participation in disciplinary groups and publications—national associations and journals, such as the American Historical Association, the

American Economics Association, and the American Psychological Association. (Sociologists initially used a slightly different nomenclature, calling their group the American Sociological Society. However, in view of the public impression the resulting acronym might create, they soon changed the name to the American Sociological Association.) Each group sponsored a national conference and a national journal. One sign of institutional prestige was for a university to be the host institution of a scholarly journal, with a distinguished scholar from the faculty serving as editor. The price was that the university would have to provide office space and staff assistance. Two universities — the Johns Hopkins University and the University of Chicago — stood out in their willingness to host and subsidize numerous journals.

A new conception of academic professionalism was essential to the creation of a university professoriate. The gradations of rank and promotion — instructor, assistant professor, associate professor, and full professor — became conventional. Most important, the ranks were tied to the institution conferring tenure and the privileges of academic freedom to professors who had gained promotion and passed muster. Academic freedom was institutionalized beyond the individual campus with the creation of the American Association of University Professors, intended to provide assurance and redress for faculty members who claimed to have had their academic rights violated by irate presidents or cantankerous board members.

The new faculty ethos was personified in Thorstein Veblen. He angered trustees and presidents alike with his brilliant, witty writings about the "theory of the leisure class" and "conspicuous consumption." His satirical profiles of university trustees as misplaced businessmen earned Veblen both praise and scorn. He created professional problems for himself with his conduct. When students complained that he had mumbled during the opening lecture of the semester, he agreed and recommended that they transfer to another course. When called onto the carpet by the president about rumors of his affairs with women students and faculty wives, Veblen did not deny the charges but shrugged his shoulders as if to say he was powerless to change his ways. Not surprisingly, Veblen was hired and fired by several leading universities. Fortunately, late in his career he found a succession of visiting appointments, thanks to the influence of his former graduate students, who themselves had become established professors across the country.

Veblen was atypical, in both his brilliance and his conspicuous personal misconduct. He stands out because he tested the patience and principles of even supportive presidents and professors. His reform agenda leaned toward advocacy of a technocracy—a planned society guided by expert engineers and characterized by efficiency. Ironically, his personal habits guaranteed that he would have had trouble fitting into the very scheme he proposed.

Pedagogy. In place of the traditional obligatory "daily recitation," university coursework featured two innovations that pulled in completely opposite directions. The first was the lecture, with a large audience and little discussion—a forum for the professor as expert. The second was the opposite, complementary vehicle, the seminar, in which a small group of advanced students met with a professor to discuss original research on a specialized theme or topic. Teaching and learning at the university also took place outside the formal classroom, by means of well-stocked libraries as well as museums, observatories, fieldwork, and research expeditions.

Professional schools. Following the pioneering example of the Johns Hopkins University in 1876, the modern American university brought professional schools into its structure and organized them with sequencing and connection with academic units. Over time this meant that some universities also added entrance requirements—for example, one had to have completed two years of undergraduate study before being admitted to professional school. The Johns Hopkins University set a high standard when it required medical school applicants to have completed a bachelor's degree. The net result was a sequential curriculum, a hierarchy of instruction and certification whose capstone was the Ph.D.

Curriculum. Professors tried to exert a strong academic influence on the undergraduate course of instruction, with emphasis on research in their own work. Science and utility were fused to a varying degree with liberal culture and piety. According to E. L. Godkin, editor of *The Nation*, in 1881 Yale and Harvard stood at opposite poles in the debate over curriculum and mission. Harvard's elective system, deemphasis on patrolling student life, and its secular character pitted it against Yale with its fixed curriculum, cohesive student life, and Congregationalist tradition. Closely related to the elective system of choice was the simultaneous obligation of focus. The university-builders leaned toward a curriculum that progressed toward specialization, with juniors and seniors opting for a "major" field. This extended into graduate studies, where a master's or doctoral candidate declared for a particular field.

Within each institution one also finds intense battles for curricular primacy. The seriousness of this competition is depicted in Robert Mc-Cormack's novel *Night Thoughts of a Classical Physicist*. When a professor ends up on the losing side of a departmental skirmish, the result is humiliation: he is "like Professor Victor Jakob, who while teaching Newtonian physics in the German university early in this century . . . realizes his status when the custodian stops cleaning his chalkboard."[30] The curricular disputes were particularly bitter in the field of psychology, where advocates of laboratory research and experimental design were at loggerheads with those who envisioned psychology as an armchair discipline, akin to philosophy.

Professionalization of students. A key feature in the modern American university was the recruitment and sponsorship of graduate students — master's degree and Ph.D. candidates. Serious and well prepared, most had already completed a bachelor's degree and perhaps other requirements set by their field by the time they began their doctoral studies.

Facilities. To carry out modern scholarship, the campus was enhanced with large, complex facilities. The advent of serious scientific inquiry in the late nineteenth century pointed out dramatically how under-equipped the older colleges had been. Whereas the early-nineteenth-century campus library was tantamount to a museum, with limited circulation and short hours, the university library was a scholarly dynamo. Journal subscriptions, acquisition budgets, rare-book rooms, archives, reference services, and study carrels transformed the expectations for the library's physical plant and professional staff. Likewise, an observatory or laboratory came to be seen as a necessary workplace, subject to constant upgrading. Storage requirements for specimens and data in all fields rendered the existing campus facilities obsolete.

The dynamics of the academic enterprise. Bringing the "university movement" to life involved not just the expenses of constructing a new library or stocking a laboratory but also the orchestration of administration, faculty, and students according to a specific script. This included a great deal of obscure tedium devoted to creating a scholarly infrastructure in the United States. As articulated by influential professors at the Johns Hopkins University, the strategy was to build a base over several generations. The graduate seminar was a crucial incubator. Doctoral students worked on individual projects under the guidance of a senior professor. Later, after completing the Ph.D., these former graduate students would write documented articles and monographs, which in turn would be published in academic journals sponsored by national scholarly associations.

J. Franklin Jameson, who had left Brown University to join the history faculty at Johns Hopkins, was the influential director of the American Historical Association. He used the association as a forum in which to express his hopes for American scholarship. His strategy was to build a strong base of scholarship over time, and he laid out the procedure when he pronounced that America needed good third-rate scholarship. The remark was neither sarcastic nor mean-spirited but was rather a response to the voids in scholarly activity.[31] Jameson was acknowledging the fact that most professors, at colleges as well as universities, had not earned a Ph.D. Nor did many professors spend much time doing research and writing articles. Teaching loads were typically heavy. Research was an exceptional activity, marginal except at a few institutions.

Analyzing the Great American Universities

Edwin Slosson's 1910 anthology of fourteen great American universities ended up raising as many questions as it answered. It is clear, for example, that academic disciplines and departments had come to be recognized across institutions, and each discipline had spawned its own national organizations. Faculty at the great universities were increasingly expected to have earned the Ph.D. — and, in turn, to serve as chairs and advisors for a new generation of Ph.D. students. Advanced scholarship, laboratory research, fieldwork, libraries, scholarly journals — all were the academic tools of the trade.

Yet even within the mature universities there were substantial variations in scope. This variation is evident in the vital statistics regarding the Ph.D. programs as a central feature of a university. Between 1898 and 1909, commitment to doctoral programs was uneven. Seven institutions — Chicago, Columbia, Harvard, Pennsylvania, Yale, Johns Hopkins, and Cornell — conferred two hundred or more Ph.D.'s each in a little more than a decade. Some of the "great" universities had scant doctoral productivity. For example, Illinois, Stanford, Minnesota, Princeton, California, and Michigan each granted fewer than one hundred Ph.D.'s in a ten-year period. For the state universities of the Midwest and West, this low figure probably represented immaturity associated with a lack of both resources and qualified graduate students. Princeton, however, was markedly different. It had students, prestige, and resources. What it lacked was the inclination to embrace the university ideal of graduate studies. For years it had strenuously avoided moving into doctoral studies, preferring to have its Ph.D. be an honorary rather than an earned degree.

Slosson's list was conspicuous for its omissions. Clark University and the Catholic University, both of which had been charter members of the Association of American Universities in 1900, had evidently abandoned emphasis on graduate studies and advanced scholarship — illustrative of the fallout in institutional aspiration. Brown University and Dartmouth were not included, although both were thriving, had graduate and professional schools, and competed for faculty and students with the institutions in Slosson's circle. Indicative of the slow emergence of the Midwestern state universities as full players was the absence of such universities as Indiana, Iowa, Northwestern, Purdue, and Ohio State from the top tier. Although the Johns Hopkins University was included in the roster, its condition in 1910 was markedly depressed when contrasted to its confidence and vitality from 1876 to 1900. The foremost embodiment of a continental university nurtured in the United States was at low ebb. Among the fourteen institutions, Johns Hopkins had the lowest annual income, the lowest number of students, and the lowest number of instructors. Princeton was included among the "great" universities even though it had little inclination toward offering Ph.D. programs. In other words, Slosson himself had to hedge on his selections because no list of "great" American institutions could afford to leave out Johns Hopkins and Princeton, regardless of their statistical profiles.

When one looks closely at Slosson's compilations of institutional charts, the most surprising trends pertain to the professional schools. Although the university-builders had talked a great deal about transforming law, medicine, and theology into "learned professions" beyond the bachelor's degree, few universities had followed through. The biggest curricular disappointment of the university-building era was that it elicited little evidence of coherence between undergraduate liberal arts education — the "college" — and professional education. In 1910 the University of Michigan, for example, had two medical schools — medicine and homeopathy — both of which competed for high school graduates. Most universities failed to integrate their medical schools into the advanced scholarship of the life sciences. Perhaps the biggest shortfall was that university-affiliated medical education persisted as an exceptional, optional route to professional licensure and practice.

Most state universities spread their enrollments across a range of un-selective professional curricula, few of which required a bachelor's degree for admission or advanced scholarship for completion. Even the prestigious private universities succumbed to this trend. The University of Chicago, for example, extended its programs to include education and pedagogy simply by annexing the existing Cook County Normal School. Enrollments in graduate courses were minuscule. One reason the memoirs about faculty work with doctoral students conveyed such a leisurely, highly personal tone was that there were so few doctoral students. University-builders may have cited Ph.D. programs as a distinguishing feature of the modern university, but even at many of the "great" American universities, doctoral studies remained marginal, both for students and for faculty. Clearly, the rhetoric was well ahead of reality.

The "great" universities varied in size and mission. The largest student enrollment—based on head counts for all programs, including summer sessions—was at Columbia, with 6,232, followed by Harvard, Chicago, Michigan, Penn, Cornell, Wisconsin, and Illinois, each of which had enrollments of between 4,000 and 5,500. Stanford, Princeton, and Johns Hopkins were each below two thousand. By standards of the mid-twentieth century, when flagship state universities typically enrolled between twenty thousand and sixty thousand students, the "great" universities were not necessarily "large." In 1910, however, when hundreds of colleges had enrollments of fewer than three hundred students, a university enrollment of four thousand or more was gargantuan. Two of the smaller "great" universities—Princeton and Johns Hopkins—had for decades made deliberate decisions to avoid becoming large. Both succeeded, but for different reasons. Princeton was faithful to its collegiate character. In contrast, the Johns Hopkins University of 1910 actually had enrollment shortfalls and was struggling with strategies to increase both undergraduate and graduate matriculation.

The uncertain condition of Johns Hopkins was the most troubling account in Slosson's anthology. Four decades earlier, Johns Hopkins had set the pace and the tone for a university committed to graduate studies and advanced scholarship. President Daniel Coit Gilman had been universally praised by faculty, graduate students, and trustees for having animated the institution with a unique spirit of scholarship. By 1910, however, its financial profile indicated an institution in dubious health. At a time when some newer universities were ascending, Johns Hopkins was showing serious signs of strain. Had its architects and leaders overestimated the commitment or ability of the United States to support the apparatus of serious advanced scholarship?

The university-builders had certainly underestimated their dependence on a base of primary and secondary education. The health of the American university was directly intertwined with the availability of the American public high school, an institution that was not yet universally accessible. Efforts by the University of Michigan to work with state government and local communities in certifying public high schools represented a major step forward in this extended partnership, but Michigan remained exceptional rather than typical. Most universities, state and private, continued to operate preparatory departments for students who could not pass the college entrance exam. And, as the land-grant university presidents learned in the 1890s, most state legislatures had yet to convince taxpayers that strong, recurring subsidies for public higher education ought be a role for state government.

By 1910, presidents and boards had learned firsthand that they had underestimated the difficulty of funding the annual operating budget of an ambitious university. Only eight universities reported an annual operating budget of $1 million per year (about $18 million in 2000 dollars), with Harvard, Columbia, and Chicago pulling far ahead of the pack, at around $1.6 million to $1.8 million each for 1910 (about $29 million to $33 million in 2000 dollars). Even allowing for inflation, the "great" university of 1910 was small when surveyed against its counterpart at the end of the twentieth century. In 2000 a typical university with doctoral programs and a research emphasis probably had an operating budget of over $1 billion per year (about $54 million in 1910 dollars). Even the largest American universities of 1910 were lean and had to stretch to cover their annual operations.

Several ascending universities were strapped for cash. In the case of two—Stanford University in California and Rice Institute in Houston, Texas—the generous founding gifts were of little use because the donors' wills were tied up in contested probate cases. At Stanford, where the founders had championed a policy of not charging students any tuition, the situation was so dire that only the personal stewardship of the widow of Leland Stanford, Jane Stanford, enabled the university to meet its payroll and pay its bills for several years. Slosson's financial summaries indicate little capacity for any of the universities to attract outside funding for research projects. Prospects for a second wave of major gifts were slim after 1900. The pioneering industrialists had already indulged their whims of funding a campus that would be an architectural memorial. There was less glamour associated with gifts for the prosaic functions of running a campus.

Land-Grant Universities: The Second Wave of Funding and Legislation

By 1880 there were signs of stagnation among the colleges and universities that had been designated as land-grant institutions as part of the 1862 Morrill Act. George Atherton, a political economist who left a faculty position at Rutgers in New Jersey to become president of Pennsylvania State College, rescued them from the doldrums of state indifference and uninspired mission. Atherton got in touch with fellow land-grant presidents in several states and persuaded them to align for purposes of lobbying in Washington, D.C. Atherton's strategy was effective. His first strategic coup was to work with fellow presidents, Congress, and the U.S. Department of Agriculture to promote passage of the 1887 Hatch Act for the funding of agricultural experiment stations at the land-grant colleges. The second land-grant act, the Morrill Act of 1890, replenished federal funding for the land-grant programs and authorized the founding of additional land-grant colleges. In sum, between 1887 and 1914 Congress passed a succession of major pieces of legislation that expanded and consolidated federal interest in such fields as agriculture, military training, and engineering. The second wave of legislation included provisions for research experiment stations, without which the state colleges had neither the facilities, the personnel, nor the extraordinary funding necessary to build an enduring applied research base. The internal leadership of Atherton and his colleagues combined with the external resources of these supplementary federal programs laid the groundwork for the emergence of the great land-grant universities of the Midwest and West. The most successful state universities enrolled between three thousand and four thousand students each in 1910.

The proliferation of federal programs had another impact on the growth of public higher education. It also made possible the extension of the land-grant program to two heretofore excluded groups: black colleges in the Southern states, and the historic state colleges in the Southern states that had not been eligible for land-grant program participation during the Civil War. The establishment of the black land-grant colleges illustrated both the gains and the limits of higher education in the Progressive era: it extended access and services to blacks yet did so only within the framework of racial separation. This concession to Southern states actually anticipated rather than followed the Jim Crow ethos that the Supreme Court would affirm a few years later in the *Plessy v. Ferguson* decision. Even though all land-grant institutions of the decade were underfunded, the seventeen black institutions were dispro-portionately neglected with respect to facilities, salaries, and staffing. They were ill equipped to conduct advanced, original research. Often overlooked in the land-grant saga is the fact that the black land-grant colleges pioneered a feature that would eventually diffuse to the entire Morrill Act legacy: the extension program of providing direct advice on crops and home economics to local farm families.

By 1900 the state land-grant colleges and universities had started to demonstrate the ability to deliver kinds of practical instruction and ser-vices long advocated by populists. The partnership between land-grant applied research and government regulation coincided in Kentucky to produce a "New Fertilizer Law" in which state college agents were autho-rized to undertake quality control. This meant setting up checkpoint stations where farmers brought fertilizer to be analyzed for content of nitrogen and other essential chemicals. Such prosaic responsibilities ac-tually increased the legitimacy of the state colleges in farmers' eyes be-cause it erased doubt that a state land-grant college was getting carried away with abstract esoteric studies. It demonstrated that the scientific tools of the campus could be applied to everyday problems.

Agriculture was not the only success story. Civil engineering, mining, and military training were popular choices among students and domi-nated enrollments in this era. Furthermore, the land-grant mission was interpreted to include teaching and home economics, a decision that made the state colleges attractive to women. Home economics, some-times offered as a part of the agriculture units, was one of the most suc-cessful new fields. It ranged from basic outreach services on household maintenance to advanced scientific research on nutrition. Its complex legacy was both to bring women into higher education as teachers and students and at the same time to quarantine them to a "women's sphere."

Throughout the new land-grant state colleges, professors often devel-oped a "bootleg" curriculum. A botanist from Germany hired to study plant pathology and crop yield might bend his courses and seminars to include pure research as well as applied science. Specialties and subfields sprouted within the interstices of the formal catalogue. The federal programs thus provided both direct utility and the seed money and time for genuine academic innovation.

The legacy of the second wave of land-grant legislation was to consolidate the public image of land-grant colleges as a collective idea. It also brought three federal units into a close working partnership with state higher education: the Departments of Agriculture, Interior, and War, each of which would bring both resources and accountability to the land-grant campus. The legislation also perpetuated some tensions within land-grant colleges, as each president dealt with issues of governance and control between the campus and the agricultural experiment station or officer-training programs. Who, for example, would bear the expense of uniforms and weapons for cadet training? The question weighed heavily on college presidents with lean budgets. When the agricultural experiment station directors talked among themselves about leaving the state universities in order to form a federal alliance, governors and state legislators finally started to consider regular and adequate annual state appropriations.

Land-grant institutions were not the whole story of developments in state higher education. In some states there emerged rivalries between land-grant institutions and those state universities that were independent of the Morrill Act programs. In addition to these broad contours, there were interesting regional differences within public higher education.

Midwestern State Universities

One result of the collective lobbying of the land-grant association was that many of the state universities in the Midwest started to catch up to—or, rather, to catch—the spirit of the University of Wisconsin. Thanks to a progressive state government and the effectiveness of its longtime president, Charles Van Hiise, Wisconsin had developed its statewide extension service independently, quite apart from federal programs. One magazine article in the early 1900s hailed the "Wisconsin idea" as a way to "send a state to college."[32] The University of Wisconsin gained early on from its sponsorship of applied research, as some of its faculty innovations—namely, a procedure for measuring butterfat content in milk—revolutionized American agriculture and brought respect as well as royalties to the university. Wisconsin also distinguished itself in developing highly respected Ph.D. programs, especially in economics and history.[33] One measure of Wisconsin's prestige was the election of

Frederick Jackson Turner, a professor at the university and a recipient of a Ph.D. from Johns Hopkins, to the presidency of the American Historical Association. Turner used his inaugural address on the "frontier thesis" to serve notice to the established East Coast institutions that serious scholarship also had a home in the West.

Also central to the "Wisconsin idea" of higher education was the notion that campus and capital ought to cooperate. Since both were located in Madison, the setting was right. The university was a model system for providing educated, responsible experts to fill the state's civil service in a range of fields, including accounting, public health, geography, medicine, law, and engineering. Wisconsin's state civil service in turn was hailed as a model of the Progressives' "good government" by educated, responsible elites. This did not necessarily assure the University of Wisconsin freedom from legislative tensions. What President Van Hiise did accomplish, however, was a sustained record of building academic excellence within the state university framework.

Along with the University of Wisconsin, the University of Michigan hinted at the potential the state universities of the upper Midwest possessed to gain national stature as full-fledged modern universities. Whereas Wisconsin had a tradition of support and appreciation within its host state, the University of Michigan survived years of neglect from its state legislature and made great gains in the latter decades of the nineteenth century. Perhaps more than any other state university, it initiated a program that made the campus the coordinating center of the entire state public school system. This program included an elaborate procedure whereby University of Michigan professors systematically traveled to and inspected high schools throughout the state. Any high school that passed faculty muster received university certification. The linchpin of this "certificate system" was that any graduate of a certified high school was guaranteed admission to the University of Michigan.[34]

The "California Idea" in Higher Education

California provides a good example of the connections between a political reform ideology and a state system of higher education. The greater San Francisco Bay area had the luxury of two ascending universities — Stanford and California — along with the College of the Pacific in Stockton, a normal school in San Jose, Catholic colleges in San Francisco and Moraga, and Mills College for Women in Oakland. In fact, higher education was overbuilt—and maldistributed, with no state university presence in the growing Los Angeles area.

The University of California, located in Berkeley, became the fulcrum for a distinctively Western version of Progressivism. As noted earlier, California's leaders in state government and education enjoyed remarkable national influence. Governor and Senator Hiram Johnson and the University of California's president, Benjamin Ide Wheeler, gained national recognition for their statewide plans. They could also count on endorsements from President Theodore Roosevelt, who visited Berkeley and was the featured speaker at the university's Charter Day ceremonies. The philosophical base of this Progressive plan for higher education was the premise that a sound, affordable state university was a good way to educate future generations of enlightened, capable state leaders and citizens. In practical terms this meant that the University of California charged no tuition. This policy, combined with a statewide public elementary- and secondary-school system, would nurture an educated, informed state citizenry that would be an antidote to the abuses and corruption of the "trusts" associated with the Southern Pacific Railroad and the oil companies. Hence statewide coordination and student recruitment characterized the "California idea" in higher education during the early 1900s.[35]

Ironically, the University of California and Stanford continued to attract generous support from the very families and industries associated with the abuses they were trying to reform. The Stanford family estate, administered by Jane Stanford, was the only source of funding that enabled Stanford to keep operating. The University of California in Berkeley became the favored charity of Phoebe Apperson Hearst, heir to the Hearst newspaper fortune. The most bizarre twist in the "California idea" of a state university as a source of responsible citizens was the case of Abraham Reuf, an 1887 graduate of the University of California. Reuf was the longtime political boss of San Francisco whose graft and corruption on city contracts for utilities and gas lines were responsible for fires after the earthquake of 1904. After his conviction on bribery charges he was sent to prison, where he gained fame by establishing the first University of California Alumni Chapter of San Quentin. This was probably not the model of education and public service the university-builders had in mind.

The distinguishing feature of the "California idea" in higher education was that utility was to be fused with educating for character and public service. This principle underlay the success California and Stanford enjoyed early on in the education of engineers and civil servants. Herbert Hoover, for example, was a member of the first graduating class at Stanford. A mining engineer, he made a fortune in Latin America and then turned to public service, ultimately being elected president of the United States. It is less well known that he had astounded international as well as national leaders after World War I with his effective systematic coordination of food relief for European countries—a feat accomplished by bringing the principles of engineering problem-solving to the social project of mass distribution and administration.

State Universities in the South

No universities in the South showed up in the historical lists of great universities in the early 1900s. Even Thomas Jefferson's "academical village" of the University of Virginia had fallen on hard times, with problems ranging from lack of operating funds to devastating fires. In the post–Civil War Reconstruction era, the historic state universities struggled to find a role that combined funding with legitimacy.

Typical of this groping and drift was the University of South Carolina, an institution that enrolled both "colored" and white students during the years of radical Reconstruction in the 1870s. After that venture was abandoned, the university in 1880 briefly tried to reconstitute itself as the state's land-grant college to gain eligibility for federal funds by taking on the name South Carolina Agricultural and Mechanical College.[36] The experiment was short-lived. For most of the South during this era, the usual picture of higher education is the one associated with "Pitchfork Ben" Tillman, the populist legislator who wanted to close down the University of South Carolina. Some of the caricatures of his populist anti-intellectualism are misleading because they present his ideas out of context. Tillman was in fact not at all opposed to higher education. He just wanted to emphasize utility and to move public higher education away from the historic privilege that had been reserved for the sons of wealthy planter families. Although he shifted support away from the historic University of South Carolina, he also worked to found and support the state's new land-grant campus, Clemson College, named after the grandson of John C. Calhoun.[37]

Tillman's support for useful studies at Clemson helped stimulate a move throughout the South to revitalize historic state universities. Between 1880 and 1920 a generation of presidents set aside the "moonlight and magnolias" campus ideal. Instead they embraced Progressivism and its emphasis on utility and accountability. They shared a vision that economic development and public service offered a way to build statewide educational systems. This was the experience of such presidents as Charles Dabney of the University of Tennessee, Edwin Alderman of the University of Virginia, Walter Barnard Hill of the University of Georgia, and Samuel C. Mitchell of the University of South Carolina. The University of North Carolina, probably the most prosperous and prestigious of the state universities in the South, benefited from large alumni gifts and was able to chart a more ambitious, advanced path than its counterparts in adjacent states.

The Southern state universities did not have the luxury of pursuing advanced scholarship or doctoral programs. Rather, they focused on building a foundation of useful fields, primarily at the undergraduate level. A generation of presidents at state universities embraced the elements of Progressivism in a concerted effort to make their institutions part of a process of state and regional economic recovery.[38] Eventually the all-white state flagship universities—especially the University of North Carolina at Chapel Hill—received a windfall benefit from Northern philanthropists. For years the New York City–based charities had donated substantial monies to black schools and colleges in the South. But the state university-builders now cautioned against that strategy, on two counts. First, they warned the Northern foundations that if they limited their investments to black educational programs, they would increase rather than reduce racial tensions within the South; foundation support should be extended to projects involving both races. Second, they argued that if the aim was overall state and regional economic development, then resources simply had to be concentrated in the institutions that could do the most good—that is, the all-white flagship state universities. Their logic was compelling, and by 1910 foundation policies had undergone a substantive shift, much to the advantage of the all-white state universities.[39]

Catholic Colleges and Universities

Most state universities were located in small, rural towns—deliberately placed away from a state's major urban center. Since most recent Catholic immigrant groups—namely, Irish, Italians, and Slavs—tended to settle in cities, the rural state universities whose students were primarily

from Protestant families had the formidable buffer of geographical distance to maintain homogeneity of both religion and ethnicity.
Hence the combination of geographical and religious differences tended
to make the urban Catholic universities institutions geared to serve
the first generation of urban college-goers. This urban mission of the
Catholic colleges was evident in their names, which often included the
name of their host city: Boston College, Providence College, University
of Seattle, University of San Francisco, Seattle University, and St. Louis
University. Jesuit institutions, including Loyola Universities in Chicago,
New Orleans, and Los Angeles, were another staple of higher education in
cities. The hallmarks of the urban Catholic colleges were utility and upward mobility, especially for the sons of first-generation immigrants.

One case involving higher education and social mobility played out
in a dispute about the "Latin question" between St. Mary's College and
the Jesuits in California. When the Christian Brothers proposed to offer
the bachelor of arts degree and instruction in Latin at St. Mary's College
in San Francisco, the Jesuits from Santa Clara and the University of San
Francisco objected on the grounds that the proposal violated the order's
charter. The Christian Brothers were supposed to be devoted to vocational training; this had been their assigned role in France and other
European countries. Latin and the arts and sciences were the domain of
the Jesuits. The Christian Brothers argued that Europe was an unsuitable
model for interpreting the mission of higher education in the United
States. In America, the most useful education was, ironically, the most
useless one. Studying Latin and earning a bachelor's degree might not
confer distinct job skills, but a bachelor's degree was the prized passport
to social mobility for ambitious young Americans. The Christian Brothers prevailed and were allowed to continue teaching Latin.[40]

The Academic Kitchen: Women as University Scholars

The "university movement," with its professed commitment to academic excellence, provided a bittersweet environment for women. Several
of the highly publicized new universities—namely, Stanford and the
Uni-versity of Chicago—shared with the state universities of the Midwest and West a commitment to coeducation. At first there were signs of
earnest commitment. Alice Palmer Freeman, former president of Wellesley College, was recruited by William Rainey Harper to be the first dean
of women at the University of Chicago.[41] Chicago in its early years was

renowned for the opportunities it offered to women as students, faculty, and staff. This commitment, however, was exceptional.

Women were certainly welcome as students. Indeed, their share of undergraduate enrollments was high, ranging from 33 percent to 50 percent in many cases. This high participation rate extended into graduate programs, especially at the University of Chicago. The early generation of alumnae from the flourishing women's colleges constituted a large percentage of the women enrolling in coeducational university graduate programs. Bryn Mawr College in Pennsylvania worked out arrangements for its alumnae to pursue doctoral studies at the Johns Hopkins University—arrangements so successful that Bryn Mawr came to be nicknamed "Jane Hopkins."

Unfortunately, these statistical gains in university access for women were offset by two recurring patterns: women students were often pigeonholed and thwarted in the curriculum and in campus life; and, most invidiously, those who completed advanced degrees encountered blatant discrimination in the academic job market. Those women who pursued a life of professional scholarship in coeducational institutions between 1890 and 1910 were at times called "pioneers." According to recent research by Geraldine Joncich Clifford, their journals and autobiographies reveal that they also described themselves as "lone voyagers"—isolated within the university faculty culture.[42] Maresi Nerad's structural metaphor for the marginalization of women on campus is that they were confined to the "academic kitchen" of the emerging American university.[43]

The gallery of "lone voyagers" included such professors as Marion Talbot of the University of Chicago, Maria Louise Sanford of Swarthmore and the University of Minnesota, Lucy Diggs Slowe of Howard University, and Grace Raymond Hebard of the University of Wyoming. Agnes Faye Morgan of the University of California is a particularly important figure. She came to Berkeley with a Ph.D. in chemistry from the University of Chicago. Her charge was to build home economics as a substantive, scientific field. Although her own research gained credibility and honor via publications, Morgan never succeeded in building a home economics program that was adequately funded or acknowledged on her home campus. This failure was not due to lack of effort or merit. Rather, Morgan was impeded time and time again by evasion, obstruction, and even sabotage from a succession of deans and presidents. Her proposals to raise admissions standards and degree requirements so as to emphasize sciences and mathematics were rejected. False promises from deans and presidents over the years led to false hopes. The disparity between the success of her research on vitamins and nutrition and the disrespect and meager funding her program received expanded rather than shrank over time. The irony is that in 1962, seven years after the University of California faculty had voted to close out the program at Berkeley and move it to the Davis campus, they named a Berkeley building in honor of Agnes Faye Morgan. Postretirement honors in bricks and mortar were a pleasant symbolic gesture, but a more fitting tribute would have been to provide Professor Morgan with a decent departmental operating budget.[44]

Women academics in the coeducational university faced marginalization at every turn. They were expected to be simultaneously a part of and apart from the faculty culture. Custom, for example, often dictated that they were not allowed to enter the faculty club or to march in academic processions. A women professor might be singled out for the array of supplementary administrative duties that came with being dean of women, usually at the expense of her own teaching and research.[45] Appointments were often odd combinations of special arrangements, usually without tenure and at substandard salary. According to Margaret W. Rossiter, women scientists in the early twentieth century relied on two strategies. First, the inhospitality of universities in hiring women as professors prompted women to look for employment elsewhere—in federal agencies and in museums and laboratories. Second, several generations of women scientists, many of whom had been students and teachers together, formed "protegee chains" in which senior women scientists sponsored and mentored younger scholars.[46] Linda Eisenmann's research elaborates on Rossiter's observation to emphasize the importance of the women's colleges in this era as employers of women professors and also as advanced centers for scientific research. Eisenmann reports, "Vassar College led in astronomy (especially through the long tenure of Maria Mitchell, the first U.S. woman to discover a comet), Bryn Mawr College in mathematics and geology, and Mount Holyoke College in chemistry and zoology."[47]

Sarah Blanding provides one example of the sacrifices an academic woman had to make in order to succeed. Blanding was an assistant professor of political science and dean of women at the University of Kentucky. In order to advance her scholarship, she left Kentucky to serve as dean of home economics at Cornell University, and she was later named president of Vassar College.[48] She was one of only two women who served on President Truman's 1947 Commission on Higher Education. In an era when insularity was considered an institutional virtue, recruitment and promotion by men for men was acceptable for alumni, but evidently not for alumnae. From time to time a woman with strong scholarly credentials might secure a campus appointment because her husband was an established professor. Lucy Sprague Mitchell enjoyed this uncertain advantage at the University of California and at Columbia, and as founder of the Bank Street School.[49] For one's professional life to be dependent on a marital relationship was small consolation and long odds for an aspiring academic.

Women scholars sought their own solutions to the isolation imposed and tolerated by university officials. According to Linda Eisenmann, foremost among these efforts was the creation of the Association of Collegiate Alumnae in 1881, an organization that would eventually evolve into the Association of American University Women.[50] By 1900 it had a membership of two thousand. On campus, the relatively few women who were professors and administrators formed their own women's faculty clubs, often as a response to their exclusion from generic (i.e., male) faculty clubs.

From Vertical History to Horizontal History: The Great Foundations

After 1900, major donors became less inclined to undertake the building of a new campus. This shift in interest had multiple causes. First, donors got tired of fending off requests from a growing number of petitioners. Second, there was the recurrent worry that American higher education had become overextended, with too many immature institutions. Gradually the focus shifted to new strategies for influencing education.

The most attractive vehicle was the philanthropic foundation — a source of horizontal influence across the institutional landscape. This included the vision that advanced scholarship in selected topics might best be promoted by establishing special institutes that would attract scholars from across the nation. One example was the Carnegie Institute in Washington, D.C. Between 1907 and 1928 its focus was the nationwide support of history as a discipline. After that, the emphasis shifted to archaeology. In addition to horizontal support for funding academic disciplines, another major innovation in the philanthropic foundations was the deliberate decision to attempt to steer higher education at the level of fundamental policies—what Ellen Condliffe Lagemann has called a commitment of "private power for the public good."[51] Demonstration projects, seed money, commissioned reports, and incentive funding became the tools with which a foundation would try to shape the course of institutions and educational systems.

The major players in this policy drama include the Carnegie Foundation for the Advancement of Teaching, the Rockefeller Foundation and its General Education Board, and the Rosenwald Fund. Although the foundations created after 1900 provided a new way for a philanthropist to carry out a vision, there was a latent, even dysfunctional, unintended effect. Chartering the foundation created a structure that took on a life of its own, with diminishing control by the benefactor whose name it carried.[52] From Andrew Carnegie's biography and other accounts, it is not at all evident that the various pursuits of the Carnegie Foundation for the Advancement of Teaching were precisely what Andrew Carnegie had in mind.[53] A powerful new figure had entered higher education: the foundation director. One such was Frederick Gates, who, having first succeeded in persuading John D. Rockefeller to give money to Gates's favored projects, became Rockefeller's confidant and gatekeeper. One of the most influential foundations was the Carnegie Foundation for the Advancement of Teaching, headed by Henry Pritchett, an engineer who had been president of the Massachusetts Institute of Technology. It is fair to say that the CFAT primarily carried out Pritchett's vision rather than Carnegie's.

From Heroic Chaos to Coordination and Standards

The common commitment of the foundations, most of which were headquartered in the Northeast, was to shift American education, including its colleges and universities, away from uncertainty and sprawl toward coherence and efficiency. Implicit in this approach was the confidence that such mechanisms would also reward talent and promote merit, whether in college admissions or in faculty hiring.[54]

The great foundations, then, are best understood as a part of the larger reform movement designated as Progressivism. When fourteen university presidents met in 1900 to found the Association of American Universities, the event heralded success and maturity. It also signaled grave concerns over quality. In response to the complaints of American professors who had strong ties with European universities, the AAU's exclusionary tone sent a message of reassurance to European scholars and of warning to universities in the United States that most so-called universities were not up to par. The AAU represented a formal response to concerns about standards and standardization. Soon thereafter the College Entrance Examination Board was founded, a private voluntary association committed to creating reliable, standardized college admissions tests. In the absence of any federal ministry of education, it was left to private voluntary associations to become arbiters of standards. Philanthropy was central to this effort—especially organized, large-scale philanthropy. Instead of building new universities, henceforth wealth from Carnegie, Rockefeller, and Rosenwald would focus on chartering and staffing "foundations" that would be overseers.[55]

Such initiatives and institutions were part of the important strand of American Progressivism that Robert Wiebe has called the "search for order."[56] Ratings, rankings, and reputations were the new "three R's."[57] Not only were these ratings a source of pride; they also worked as a tool of coercion and coordination. One initiative of the early CFAT was to use the incentive of a faculty pension plan to induce American colleges to move in particular directions. Colleges were invited to participate on the condition that they standardize their admissions requirements, purge the bachelor's degree curriculum of denominational emphasis, and demonstrate that they had attained some threshold in minimum enrollments. This project introduced the so-called Carnegie unit into American high schools as a way of coding course transcripts as having met thresholds of substance and duration. Although this articulation between secondary schools and colleges gained wide acceptance, the Carnegie Foundation's ultimate plan of providing college faculty pensions was a victim of overpopularity. Eventually the generous terms of the invitation had to be pulled back, simply because they were too expensive for the foundation to bear. Nonetheless, the plan endured in modified form, eventually becoming TIAA-CREF, today one of the largest pension funds in the world.

As mentioned earlier, one condition of a college's eligibility for the Carnegie Foundation faculty pension plan was that the curriculum be free of denominational orthodoxy. What, then, of the place of religion in the university ideal? Many of the "great" universities, whether state or privately endowed, retained some loose religious affiliation. Harvard was exceptional in that its president, Charles Eliot, refused a major gift whose condition was that Harvard reinstate a daily chapel requirement. Indeed, daily chapel was standard practice at many state universities. In fact, most state universities were heavily Protestant in admissions and in the tenor of campus life. There were numerous cases of attempts by presidents and boards to purge biologists and other scientists whose teaching about evolution was in conflict with church doctrine. From time to time certain professors proclaimed their atheism in class lectures, giving rise to predictable furors on and off the campus. Ironically, however, most of the controversies involving religion and science took place in the social and behavioral sciences. Sociologists and anthropologists who examined religious practices across numerous cultures and historical periods were usually more subject to censorship than biologists and physicists were. A further corollary is that most of the highly publicized academic-freedom cases centered on faculty members' errant political views rather than their religious beliefs.

Clergy and college board members who felt that Christian orthodoxy was endangered by the university ideal probably overestimated the academic threat while underestimating the growing appeal of secularism in American life. Ministers expressed alarm about declining church attendance among youthful parishioners. Leisure activities, city life, cigarettes, movies, vaudeville, and a thousand other elements of American popular culture were probably more threatening to piety and religious conformity than the university was. Even the adamantly church-related colleges struggled in vain to hold the attention of their students. Daily chapel, for example, might have persisted on some campuses that prided themselves on their fidelity to traditional religious practice, but the content of daily chapel changed over time. Ministers and presidents gradually came to share the pulpit with successful alumni giving inspirational talks. The secularization of American life in general, rather than aca-demic atheism, altered the place of religion on the American campus. Financial pragmatism and the lure of a Carnegie pension plan did indeed prompt many presidents and boards to reconsider precisely how important a denominational influence was to the character of their campus.

In addition to financial incentives, a foundation might use commissioned reports as a policy tool. The strategy was for a project investigator to analyze some issue or theme that cut across the nation. Foremost among such ventures was Abraham Flexner's 1910 report on medical education in the United States and Canada.[58] This report demonstrated the power of systematic analysis to bring reform issues into the public domain. It provided in narrative form the equivalent of Thomas Eakins's painting *The Gross Clinic*, which graphically depicted surgeons who took pride in their unwashed hands and whose prestige was measured by the amount of dried blood on their black frock coats. Flexner was a man with a mission — namely, to set the Johns Hopkins University model of medical education up as the standard by which all medical schools should be evaluated and reshaped. This model required that medical practice be linked to advanced scholarship in the biological sciences. It insisted that medical schools be affiliated with and integrated into a university structure. It was a model to which relatively few of the hundreds of medical schools could adhere.

Flexner's critical study would appear to have been effective, because about 30 percent of the medical schools in the United States closed in the year or two following the report's release. The report's exposé of shoddy practices and institutional shame was not, however, the sole cause. In fact, most of the freestanding medical schools that closed did so because of financial problems that had been problematic for years, rather than as a response to Flexner's report.[59] Medicine enjoyed some local prestige as a learned profession. Nonetheless, it was a competitive, hardscrabble job dependent on patient fees and, for medical faculty, direct student payments. For a 1910 medical school that had a small endowment and was essentially proprietary in its operations, substantial investment in laboratory equipment and advanced instruction would have been the exception rather than the rule. Flexner's report expressed no sympathy for financial adversity at an institution. He was especially critical of the black medical colleges for their lack of standards and inadequate physical plant. He wanted marginal medical schools to suspend operations, and they did. One consequence of his exposé was to decrease consumer options in the short run by reducing the supply of medical doctors.

Later, Flexner would head up comparable studies of education in other fields, including law. These did not achieve the spectacular coverage or even the appearance of reform that his first study of medical education achieved. Flexner championed what might be termed the Johns Hopkins ideal of professional education: full-time study beyond the bachelor of arts degree, with strong ties between scholarship and practice. But when he used the CFAT-commissioned study to excoriate the numerous evening and part-time law schools, he failed. Flexner simply underestimated the political influence the evening law school advocates and alumni had in the legal community and among bar associations.

Despite a mixed record of reform success, the Carnegie Foundation continued to rely on research as a means of exposing weaknesses in American education at all levels. It was not a completely disinterested research agenda. When the CFAT's endowment started to dwindle, fees from commissioned reports came to be the foundation's staple activity and essential for its annual operations. Furthermore, the CFAT reports on a variety of topics were advocacy vehicles to promote the foundation's message of rationalization as reform.

Reform in higher education, then, embodied both the vision and the myopia of Progressivism. From the perspective of the late twentieth century, these early attempts to improve colleges and universities were incomplete because they were inconsistent with modern notions of social justice. Reforms between 1880 and 1910, for example, championed the expansion of higher education but with no apology for discrimination on the basis of race, gender, and class. When Progressives, whether in higher education or politics, pinned their hopes on the "best men" or talked about recruiting "men of science," they meant it literally, with no intention of including women and no remorse for excluding them. Those women who were academic pioneers as early graduates of the prestigious "Seven Sisters" colleges of the Northeast did represent some gains for women but did so without showing much concern about social class inequities among women. Likewise, the federal legislation of 1890 that helped to create the black land-grant colleges expanded access to higher education for an underserved racial minority but gave no consideration to the issue of racial integration on the campus.[60]

Conclusion

In Laurence Veysey's landmark 1965 historical study, *The Emergence of the American University,* and in Edwin Slosson's 1910 anthology, *Great American Universities,* the tendency was to focus on a structural and curricular pattern exhibited by a predictable cluster of familiar, prestigious institutions. This focus may have led Veysey and Slosson to ignore innovations elsewhere. In particular, they overlooked attempts at university-building in the South. This regional bias calls for correction because some of the institutional ventures outside the fourteen "great" American universities may have had considerable influence. Innovations at Transylvania University in Lexington, Kentucky, did not put that institution into the top ranks of doctoral research programs, but they did perhaps

represent an early structural prototype for a comprehensive, multipurpose campus. Around 1890, for example, Transylvania University—
which by then had changed its name to Kentucky University—included
a historic liberal arts college along with a normal school, a law school, a
medical college in Louisville, a theological seminary, a music department, and a commercial course. It was even the original institutional
host for the state's land-grant program until the state legislature shifted
it across town as a new, separate Kentucky State College. Virtually every
issue and innovation heralded among the more conspicuous institutions
of the Northeast were also in evidence here. The federation of diverse
programs that Transylvania University pragmatically pieced together
in the 1890s anticipated what Clark Kerr in 1963 would call the "multiversity." Kerr, however, relied on historical evidence from Berkeley, Harvard, Chicago, and Wisconsin, with no reference to institutional patterns
below the Mason-Dixon line.[61]

A recent generation of historians has called into question Slosson's
claim that by 1910 the American university had hardened into set forms.
Richard Angelo's study of campuses in the Philadelphia area and Paul
Mattingly's essay on "structures over time" advance the revisionist argument that the neat crystallization of higher education into "universities"
versus "colleges" imposed a simplistic typology upon a range of institutional developments.[62] Rather, fluidity, uncertainty, and diversity were
the foremost qualities of the institutions of this era. Angelo found, for
example, that in Philadelphia, students were consumers who opted for
one program over another on the basis of varied, pragmatic reasons.
They did not see the city's array of institutions as clearly defined in terms
of a hierarchy of prestige, with the bachelor of arts degree as the pin-
nacle. This interpretation of fluidity and choice differs from the image
of collegiate prestige Laurence Veysey argued in *The Emergence of the
American University*. There was a great deal of interinstitutional transfer,
with few prerequisites for admission to such professional programs as
law, dentistry, pharmacy, or medicine. Angelo used comprehensive data
on both the University of Pennsylvania and Temple to argue that the
notion of the liberal arts college and its bachelor of arts degree as the
heart or foundation of the university did not really take hold until after
World War I.

One could argue that the University of Pennsylvania was exceptional
because it had always, since the eighteenth century, had a tradition of
emphasizing professional education; its bachelor of arts curriculum

never approached the heritage and stature of Harvard College within Harvard University. Angelo's reinterpretation is attractive, however, when tested across other regions of the United States. If one focuses not on the historic universities of the Northeast but instead on the urban universities of the South—for example, Tulane in New Orleans, Vanderbilt in Nashville, and the University of Louisville in Kentucky—one finds that the center of the emerging university was a local medical school, with peripheral provision for the undergraduate college of arts and sciences. In many American cities, according to recent research by Dorothy E. Finnegan and Brian Cullaty, one of the major success stories in higher education after 1866 was the founding of more than two dozen "YMCA universities"—open-access, affordable urban institutions that did not adhere to the prototype of the "great" university.[63]

Paul Mattingly has contended that even as late as 1910 there was no agreement in the United States as to what constituted a "university."[64] Indeed, even Slosson's *Great American Universities* is inconclusive in this respect. For Slosson, the distinguishing feature of a university was that it offered graduate work—a test that left unresolved a host of other questions about how to define an American university. For others, it was a vague but undeniable commitment to science that characterized the modern American university. Consider the following account of Brown University's transformation in 1889 when it hired Elisha Benjamin Andrews as its new president. Andrews was a Brown alumnus who had studied philosophy and political economy in Germany. Later he served as president of Denison University and then as a professor of history at Cornell University before returning to his alma mater:

> Over the course of his ten-year presidency, he doubled the size of the faculty and student body and quadrupled the University's course offerings, with additions primarily in the natural and applied sciences. The influences of modern science in Brown's rapid growth could hardly be overstated. Riding the high tide of industrial prosperity in the 1880s, Brown, along with countless other universities throughout the United States, experienced a sort of scientific renaissance in the 1890s. As Professor of English Walter Bronson noted in a 1914 history of Brown, "the scientific spirit was permeating every department of thought."[65]

Unfortunately, the phrase "the scientific spirit" conveys nothing about the particulars of forms and structures that set the "university" apart. Partisan reformers such as Henry Pritchett and Abraham Flexner of the

Carnegie Foundation for the Advancement of Teaching were conspicuous and influential, but hardly the sole determinants of the university
form.

Perhaps the best estimate is that the university-builders as visionaries
anticipated a modern American university whose curricular structure
corresponded to the magnificent spires of neo-Gothic architecture: an
ascension in rigor and prestige, well marked by course credits, degrees,
and certification. By 1910, however, at all but a few places, the curricular
function did not follow this architectural form. Instead of a sequential
progression of ascending programs, the American university offered a
linear array of fields, most of which were readily open to all comers. New
students could choose the bachelor of arts course, usually characterized
by classical languages. There was also the bachelor of philosophy track,
offering a general education but without Latin and Greek. Students
could also opt for any number of other programs: medicine, law, engineering, business, theology, or agriculture. Indeed, the success story of
the American university was the emergence of the so-called new professions—business, engineering, forestry, home economics, social work,
and agriculture—as citizens in the campus community.[66] In some
cases—foremost being the agricultural station at the University of Minnesota in the 1890s—the popularity of agriculture and engineering led
to serious discussion among deans as to whether these land-grant units
ought to secede from their struggling state university. Ultimately the
agricultural experiment stations did not break away from their home
states and discontinued their plans to align as a national association
linked to the Department of Agriculture in Washington, D.C. Furthermore, the appeal of freestanding professional schools continued to diminish. However, one is hard pressed to find many programs, whether
the liberal arts colleges or the professional schools, that were rigorous in
their admissions standards or coordinated with other segments of the
campus. Academic planners who had envisioned undergraduate arts and
sciences and the bachelor of arts degree as the heart of advanced studies
had to settle for a smorgasbord.

The American university of 1910 was an adolescent—gangly, energetic, and enigmatic. The almost total lack of federal involvement in
colleges and universities, with the important exception of the Morrill Act
and related land-grant legislation, left a mixed legacy. On the one hand,
the lack of a federal ministry of education probably deprived colleges
and universities of both government funding and a source of substantive

regulation. On the other hand, colleges and universities—and their donors—were spared government intrusion and allowed to innovate. Indeed, such antitrust legislation as the Sherman Act specifically exempted
colleges and universities from its purview, reinforcing a precedent of
government restraint and institutional autonomy that campus presidents would invoke over the next century.[67] This government restraint
also left the door open for the leverage of voluntary associations, including foundations and accrediting groups, to put standard practices into
widespread academic use. As standards and standardization approved by
the Carnegie Foundation for the Advancement of Teaching and the College Entrance Examination Board took hold, some of the pioneering
faculty lamented what they believed to be a decline in the initial spirit of
academic pioneers who had been unrestricted by convention and regulation.

One development that was probably unavoidable was that growth and
specialization created a need for an academic bureaucracy—a structure
characterized by departments and deans, supplemented by regional and
national structures. Yet the paradox of the complexity that characterized
the maturing American university was that faculty were treated as labor.
Professors were expected to be beholden to management and the board
at the very time that they were ascending in professional stature as experts exercising self-determination, participating in national associations, and enjoying such rights as tenure and academic freedom.[68]

The relative gains in new activities, advanced studies, and serious
scholarship were significant. Nonetheless, these innovations did not sup-
plant the essential commitment to undergraduate education. The interesting riddle of American higher education between 1890 and 1910 that
the university-builders overlooked was how the "age of the university"
was at the same time the golden age of collegiate life.[69]

5 Alma Mater
America Goes to College, 1890 to 1920

The "Collegiate Ideal" in the Age of the University

"The essential difference between a college and university is how they look. A university looks forward and a college looks backwards." So wrote Edwin Slosson in 1910.[1] The weakness of his dichotomy was that the American campus of the time was a hybrid that resembled Janus of Greek mythology. It looked in both directions simultaneously. The campus was complex, characterized by multiple personalities. The irony of American higher education from 1890 to 1920 was that the age of university-building also was the golden age of the college. How to explain this coincidence?

A clue is found in the experience of Henry Adams, the brooding Boston patrician and Harvard history professor who was puzzled by American popular culture. In 1876 an undergraduate matter-of-factly told Adams that "a degree from Harvard was worth money in Chicago."[2] Although Adams was bothered by this observation, most Americans were not. College-going was rising in popularity, for several reasons. It was a means of socioeconomic mobility and hence an experience coveted by an increasing number of adolescents. In addition to increasing earning power, a bachelor's degree was perceived as a way for a nouveau riche family to gain social standing. An education at a prestigious college was most likely to be prized by a father who had made a fortune but had not gone to college himself. The self-made man wanted his sons to have the shared campus experience that would position them to associate with young men from established, educated families.

This combination of aspirations connected to higher education was a windfall for college presidents. Whereas in 1870 campus officials fretted over sluggish college enrollments and the demographic data that indicated a shrinking percentage of young men applying to college, by the turn of the century the collegiate situation and morale were markedly different. Along with the grand new campus architecture, the "college man"—and, eventually, the "college woman"—was becoming an imposing figure in American commercial culture. The single most important change in American higher education at the end of the nineteenth century was that college-going became fashionable and prestigious. This meant that the historic institutions had some leverage in the decades when modernization and industrialization were a high priority, and it explains why the undergraduate college associated with the bachelor of arts degree did not wither, despite the dire predictions by the university-builders.

Although the university-builders' public pronouncements tended to disparage the historic college as obsolete, in private conversations they acknowledged that their universities were dependent on the colleges' resurgence. The most pragmatic, obvious reason was that graduate programs needed a pool of educated students from which to recruit their master's and doctoral candidates. Second, as the administrators of the Johns Hopkins University had discovered the hard way, no university could operate without the tuition payments provided by students in the undergraduate college. Finally, the liberal arts college provided the real and symbolic core within the university structure that fostered the loyalty of alumni and donors. As Harvard philosopher George Santayana wrote in explaining why the "university model" had not swallowed up the traditional college at his own institution, "To Harvard College belong the social and athletic traditions of the place, without which, of course, there would be no essential difference between Harvard and Clark University."[3] This phenomenon provided the glue that connected the new modern university with the collegiate tradition so that both flourished.

One characteristic of the collegiate boom was that age, not modernity, bestowed prestige. Henry Seidel Canby, an alumnus of Yale University, called this period the "Gothic age of the American college," an allusion to the dark, often somber campus architecture that was the fertile ground for a lively undergraduate culture just prior to the advent of modernism in American life. Looking back on the decade before the turn of the century, Canby recalled that the "younger colleges, whether they were 'state' or 'privately endowed' institutions, modeled their life and aspirations upon the older colleges."[4] In 1900 the editor of Brown University's alumni magazine expressed the same sentiment: "There is no college in New England that does not need more money, but is it not easy to create the impression that money is the one essential to the building up of a university and to put too high a value on mere college wealth? California and Stanford, fine and strong as they are, cannot buy the history or the elms of Harvard, Yale, and Brown."[5]

Collegiate Celebrations: Photojournalism and Campus Imagery

Despite all the journalistic coverage given to the emergence of the serious scholarship heralded by the emergence of the modern university, an important social development between 1890 and 1910 was that the American public became fascinated with undergraduate collegiate life. Furthermore, this fascination kept growing over several decades. For evidence of this transformation one must go beyond the official course catalogues and also look at clothing advertisements, popular magazines, pulp fiction, college songs, and intercollegiate athletics as the core elements in the connections between the campus culture and the nation's popular culture.[6]

This fascination with collegiate life was evident in the titles of feature articles in national-circulation magazines. In addition to the photojournalism about magnificent new university architecture, editors discovered that readers delighted in articles that gave a glimpse of student life at the prestigious colleges. Writers and photographers provided at least a partial answer to the public's curiosity about what was going on behind the campus walls. Titles in such national periodicals as *The Independent, Atlantic Monthly, The Century, Scribner's, McClure's,* and *The Outlook* between 1880 and 1910 included "The American Undergraduate" (a multiple-episode series by Sedgewick Cooper), "Life at a Girls College," "College Life at Princeton—Old and New," and "On Knowing College Men."[7]

This genre of popular literature was the outcome of the combination of pride on the part of insiders (students, alumni, faculty, and presidents) with the curiosity of outsiders. In keeping abreast of campus developments, journalists acted as interpreters who explained to laymen the unique vocabulary and customs of a given college. Writers recognized that public interest in these institutions was not confined to forms and functions but also involved curiosity about the elusive institutional spirit. As one author explained, "Besides the systematic instruction and research which go on in all colleges and universities, there is a life and atmosphere which is characteristic to each, and which has much to do with the making of the 'whole man.'"[8]

College students were described with metaphors suggesting a congenial collective experience: "colts romping in a pasture," "fellow voyagers in a row boat." In contrast, professors and their families were either invisible or an object of curious pity. Hamilton Holt of *The Independent* wrote a series on the miseries of the lives of coal miners, meatpacking-plant "knackers," sweatshop girls in the garment industry, oppressed black workers in the South, and abused immigrant laborers. He also included a "professor's wife" in his gallery of "undistinguished Americans." According to the profile, a professor at a small Midwestern college made about $1,100 per year in 1905 (about $21,000 in 2000 dollars). The money went quickly. Renting a modest house cost $216 ($4,126 in 2000 dollars) per year, groceries $300 ($5,731), clothing $150 ($2,865), and insurance $100 ($1,910); household incidentals exhausted almost all the rest. A professor's family relied on cheap cuts from the butcher and a vegetable garden to make ends meet. A professor's teaching load was heavy, four to five courses per semester, with additional responsibilities of advising students and hosting guest speakers and visitors to the campus.[9] Given the bleakness of faculty life, it is not surprising that American readers preferred to hear about the activities and antics of undergraduates.

Even though the "collegiate way" converged on a common model, audiences at the turn of the century were fascinated by real and imagined differences between campuses along with "partisan" claims of uniqueness. As Henry Seidel Canby recalled, "The most ardent believer in standardization would not dare assert that college life among the lakes of Wisconsin was identical with experiences in a Princeton dormitory or upon a Southern campus."[10] In this spirit, Pomona College in California tried to persuade prospective students that going to college "out West" was as compelling an experience as "Going Back East." In an "open letter" to a fictional high school senior named Bill, the Pomona College representative reasoned, "When you come to Pomona, Bill, you will be coming to a democratic college, one with the Western stir and enthusiasm, and one where men are rated on their qualities and ability, and not on their blue blood."[11]

This brand of loyalty to one's own campus prompted students to create distinguishing institutional symbols. The period 1890 to 1910 were when colleges adopted institutional colors and mascots. Harvard's Crimson and Dartmouth's Green became familiar symbols both to students and to football fans. For some institutions the choices were obvious. Brown naturally opted for brown and white as its colors and the Brown Bear as the mascot for its football team, the Bruins. Elsewhere, selecting a distinctive set of college colors became more difficult the longer a campus waited, as evidenced by Tufts' belated and unusual choice of powder blue and brown. Who knows what rationale led Georgetown College of Kentucky to imagine itself in pink and gray, with the peculiar nickname of "The Flying Parsons"? Princeton's famous black and orange color scheme was respectfully imitated by numerous Presbyterian colleges elsewhere in the country. In some cases unexpected events influenced the choice of campus colors. At the University of Virginia, for example, students thoughtfully selected gray and red as appropriate colors to honor shed Confederate blood. However, when the manufacturer of the university's athletics uniforms announced that a dye shortage would delay delivery of jerseys and sweaters in the official colors, students opted to use blue and orange as temporary substitutes. Over a century later, Virginia was still using the temporary colors.

Along with college colors, each campus staked a claim to a mascot whose attributes personified the virtues of its varsity athletics teams. Ferocity was the order of the day, as suggested by the Princeton Tigers, the California Golden Bears, Columbia's Lions, Michigan's Wolverines, Wisconsin's Badgers, and Yale's Bulldogs. At times this emphasis led to some illogical combinations, including the University of Pennsylvania's Fighting Quakers and Whittier College's Fighting Poets. Baptist-affiliated Wake Forest College reconciled good and evil by presenting its athletes as the Demon Deacons. Sometimes a mascot was inspired by a sportswriter who reported, for example, that the University of Southern California's team "fought like Trojans" or that the University of Kentucky's team "fought like Wildcats." At times the teams' names conveyed state pride, as with the Indiana University Hoosiers, the Ohio State Buckeyes, the Ole Miss Rebels, and the Virginia Cavaliers. South Carolina College chose the Gamecock as its mascot, to suggest both fighting prowess and its own sporting heritage. Less obviously logical was the choice of Pomona College in California, whose mascot was the Sagehen. Williams College of Massachusetts disconcerted its athletic opponents with the unusual mascot of the Purple Cow. Some emblems and campus mascots suggest that college sports were regarded as what William James called the "moral equivalent of war": the Washington and Lee Generals and the Michigan State Agricultural College Spartans. Teams at engineering schools boasted of their curricula, with Purdue taking the field as the Boiler Makers and the Massachusetts Institute of Technology proclaiming itself home to the Engineers.

In addition to devising mascots, students and recent graduates wrote alma maters and college hymns. They also devised special songs and cheers designed to make one feel part of a campus tribe at athletic events and reunions. One sign of this phenomenon was the flourishing college-songbook industry. The Alumni Council of Amherst College, for example, in 1926 published a 146-page hardback devoted exclusively to Amherst college songs, including the no-nonsense football march "Old Amherst's out for Business" and such sentimental verses as "In the Evening by the Moonlight." College songs were a preoccupation of undergraduates nationwide. By 1903 Hinds and Noble Publishers of New York City had distributed the fourth edition of *Songs of All the Colleges: Including Many New Songs*. The big news, conveyed by a special flyer, was that the publishers had finally obtained permission to publish "The Famous Yale Boola Song." Readers were alerted, "This song is admitted to be one of the most popular ever written—the melody is so 'catchy' that the Orchestras and Bands have taken it up and are playing it everywhere. The chorus fairly 'takes you off your feet'—just try it on the piano. We have printed both the athletic and the sentimental words."[12]

Numerous other publishers sought to mine the thriving college song market. The Intercollegiate Music League headquartered in Boston arranged with Amsco Music Publishers to market to a national audience a 255-page book, *Officially Approved Songs of the American Colleges*. Packed within these hefty anthologies were college songs literally for each and all, ranging from "Ten Thousand Men of Harvard" to Michigan State College's alma mater, "Close Beside the Winding Cedars." Even famous donors were honored in college songs. The University of Chicago was famous for its distinctive song, "John D. Rockefeller." The song starts out with obligatory odes to the university's commitment to wisdom and learning and then in the chorus gets down to serious, specific praise:

John D. Rockefeller, Wonderful man is he,
Gives all his spare change to the U. of C.
He keeps the ball a rolling
In our Great Varsity

He pays Dr. Harper
To Help us Grow Sharper
To the Glory of U. of C.!

These decades were also the golden age of campus music groups such as the Whiffenpoofs and the Krokodiloes, not to mention marching bands and mandolin clubs, whose serenades and concerts marked the annual round of campus events large and small.

These campus events included official processions, including one at the start of the academic year, perhaps a "Founder's Day," and then commencement in June. Students often added their own formal events. At Brown University, for example, "Spring Day" was a chance for seniors to wear their academic robes and present humorous orations and satirical skits that lampooned the faculty and president. At the University of California, "Labor Day" and "Arbor Day" were devoted to campus improvements and celebrations. Stanford's student parades were called "Jamborinos," elaborate events involving floats, marching bands, and renditions of the traditional Stanford song, "Son of a Gambolier."

Autumn football games, especially "homecoming," brought together undergraduates and alumni. And as alumni associations grew, colleges started to sponsor elaborate reunion parades during commencement week. Contrary to the public image of academic life as a solemn affair, the alumni events were carefree gatherings that allowed an "old grad" to be an "old boy," giving some support to the observation that the collegiate life fostered perpetual adolescence. It became customary for a class to settle on some humorous theme for its reunion costumes, with choices ranging from the characters of *Alice in Wonderland* to convicts in striped prison garb. All these details lent an air of pageantry to the proceedings, as if a medieval spirit of festivals and saints' days had breezed through the modern university.

Novelists as well as campus songwriters were alert to the ceremonies and themes of collegiate life. Amory Blaine, one of F. Scott Fitzgerald's fictional characters, provided a prep school student's account of the alleged differences among the elite East Coast colleges:

> "I want to go to Princeton," said Amory, "I don't know why, but I think of all Harvard men as sissies, like I used to be, and all Yale men as wearing big blue sweaters and smoking pipes . . . I think of Princeton as being lazy and good-looking and aristocratic—you know, like a Spring Day. Harvard seems sort of indoors—"

"And Yale is November, crisp and energetic," finished Monsignor.
"That's it!"[13]

College applicants were not the only ones who engaged in institutional comparisons. George Santayana, who had known Harvard as both
a student and a professor, wrote in 1894 that "Harvard was scientific, that
it was complex, and that it was reserved."[14] William Sloane explained
that Princeton stood for discipline and grace.[15] A less erudite but more
enthusiastic appraisal was provided by a turn-of-the-century Dartmouth
student song:

> I'll sing you a song of colleges and tell you where to go;
> Johns Hopkins for your knowledge, Cornell to learn to row,
> Amherst for your high-toned fops, Dartmouth for your men,
> For riches go to Williamstown, or muckers, Brown, amen![16]

The lyrics made sense only if one spoke the esoteric language of the
"college man." *Muckers,* for example, was an undergraduate slang term
referring to brawny lads with bogus academic credentials who were lured
away from foundries and then hired by coaches to play football for a
college. *Row* referred to the members of the varsity crew team. Williams-
town was the home of Williams College in Massachusetts. These were
the kinds of colorful allusions that popular audiences relished.

As the student editors of the *Harvard Advocate* noted, "For some un-
explained reason the general public seems to find the college man fascinating. It takes a deep concern in all his affairs—his athletics, his literary
and social attainments, his pranks and follies. Consequently college fiction is becoming a popular kind of literature."[17] The older colleges, particularly Yale, usually provided the setting and protagonists. Probably the
most pervasive fictional image of college life was the "Frank Merriwell
at Yale" series, published between 1896 and 1915 in the *Tip-Top Weekly,*
with average weekly sales of 1.5 million copies. Often the stories were
romanticized accounts of undergraduate adventures, of highly varying
degrees of authenticity. After the decline in popularity of the Frank Merriwell series, a later generation of serious novelists focused on the dramatic crises of college life. Alert publishers took advantage of the growing interest in college among girls and quickly developed series of juvenile
novels dealing with women's colleges. The common denominator over
the decades was that the American campus had broad audience appeal.

Undergraduates in the Gothic Age of the American College, 1890 to 1910

Public interest in colleges gained momentum around 1890 and soared up to the United States' entrance into World War I. The photojournalism and popular fiction of the era provided a view of the campus from the outside in. But it is equally important to try to reconstruct the college world from the inside out—from the point of view of the undergraduates.

Many of the serious curricular debates among faculty members and philosophers were like badminton games whose volleys went over the heads or beyond the focus of undergraduates. A popular banner found in student dormitory rooms of the 1890s proclaimed, "Don't Let Your Studies Interfere with Your Education!" The intricate social system that undergraduates created attests to how well they heeded this admonition. Courses were seen as a necessary evil, a price to be paid for admission to the greatest show on earth, campus life.

This indifference to serious academic study did not mean that undergraduate life was undemanding. To the contrary, it was excruciatingly stern in its evaluations, rewards, and punishments. Nor did it mean that no students immersed themselves in academic readings and ideas. Those who chose to focus on studies were tolerated within certain boundaries, usually with the clear message that these were not the priorities of the dominant collegiate culture. From time to time a student broke ranks with the campus code and ventured a serious comment in response to a professor's question. Soon fellow classmates responded with smirks, coughing, squeaking chairs, and other reminders that enough was enough. Undergraduates were skilled at defusing earnest intellectual discussions in class. According to Laurence Veysey, this was the golden age of student pranks, most of which served to reinforce the antiacademic norms of the "college system."

The schism between undergraduates and the college administration is best illustrated by the difference between the official catalogue and the student yearbook. The former was a terse, straightforward presentation of requirements and regulations, with no illustrations. Its closest approximation to literary energy came perhaps in a brief historical profile of the campus or a welcoming note from the president and dean. In contrast, the latter was a lavishly bound collection of memorable events, inside jokes, light verse, fond recollections, and elaborate cartoons and caricatures. The student yearbooks had colorful titles, like the Johns Hopkins University's *Hullabaloo*, West Point's *Howitzer*, California's *Tabula Rasa*, Virginia's *Cork and Curls*, Brown's *Liber Brunensis*, and the University of Southern California's *El Rodeo*. The overwhelming impression of turn-of-the-century college life conveyed by yearbooks is that every campus event was captured for posterity in a stylized group photograph. Memories of "Bright College Years" were preserved in a succession of formal portraits of athletic teams, glee clubs, editorial boards, eating clubs, and honor societies, each posed at such familiar campus sites as the steps of College Hall or the old fence (figure 4). The common denominator across institutions and groups is the students' air of self-confident worldliness. These undergraduates in late adolescence appeared to be more mature than their elders. With this affected group persona, it is not surprising that from the perspective of an adventurous, ambitious young white man, going to college was less about degree requirements and organizational charts and more about the initiation into an appealing, intoxicating world. The campus was an American "city state," run by and for students.

Numerous commentators, ranging from Henry Seidel Canby to George Santayana and a later generation of historians, noted that the undergraduates had pretty much created a world on their own terms. Canby described the composite experience of freshmen who stepped off the train at a college town, crossed the town green, and, immediately upon setting foot on campus, noticed the peculiar appeal of citizenship in student life. Despite nondescript campus architecture and rather "dingy halls, boxes ornamented with pseudo-Gothic or Byzantine," the newcomer found the student world so attractive "that in a second of time, between Green and campus," he "dropped, with the easy consequentiality of youth, all illusions of architectural grandeur for the real thing, college life." Canby went on to explain:

> Close at hand or described from memory, it seemed more like a haven for American youth, a little space of time in which energy had its outlet, and where the young made a world to suit themselves, which, for a while at least, the adult world was to accept at surprisingly near the college estimate.

Going to college was a rite of initiation that bonded students and alumni:

> Thousands like myself (so I felt as I tossed the Green) had been there before me in a life which was to become my experience. At home most of us, cer-

Figure 4. Seniors singing on the college fence, Amherst College, ca. 1926 (Amherst College Archives and Special Collections)

tainly I myself, had life in one dimension, with at most a family extension toward an American past. Overnight we were to step through an opening door into tradition—a usable, sympathetic tradition of youth. It was to be our privilege to be born again, painlessly, and without introspection.

The undergraduate culture of the 1890s as recalled by Canby included distinctive dress, argot, symbols, and affiliations, and subscription to a collegiate code—often implicit yet clearly understood:

> Therefore, like all that confident generation, I accepted the college as I found it, and believed in its life and its spirit with a fanatic devotion. I saw that the boys who were strolling that day in the later nineties down the autumn streets were as easily distinguishable among the town crowds as being from another world. . . . There was an arrogant and enchanting irresponsibility in their behavior which was intoxicating. I longed to get rid of my suitcase with its irrelevant books, and into a sweater which I saw to be obligatory—to dress like them, to be like them.

"To dress like them, to be like them"—that was the magnetism that brought together a new American aristocracy and that held the attention of a curious, even indulgent generation of American adults.[18]

Figure 5. Class of 1898 wearing "plug ugly" hats, University of California (The University of California, Berkeley, Bancroft Library)

Student garb varied from campus to campus. At the University of Virginia, any newcomer who dared to wear a bright necktie was hazed. Stanford undergraduates wore sombreros and baggy corduroy trousers. Across the bay at Berkeley, University of California students were easily recognized by their "plug ugly" top hats, each of them autographed by classmates (figure 5). On each campus, special deference was given to those who wore the varsity letter sweaters. Eventually national magazines and clothing manufacturers targeted undergraduates across the country as trendsetters and purchasers for "collegiate" styles of shirts, suits, hats, and shoes. Most conspicuous was the "Arrow Shirt Man," whose stiff collars and handsome features came to typify the strong, confident, and well-tailored college gentleman.

This American collegiate ethos radiated from the influential core at Yale. The key to the "college system" was "Yale's democracy"—the proposition that campus activities provided a free forum in which students might demonstrate their talents and be judged on their merits by student peers. Visitors to Yale described the campus as a "dynamo," energetic and intense in all student pursuits. The important nuance was that the "Yale system" harnessed individual ambition and effort into team efforts for the greater good and honor of one's academic class and the college. This was what made Yale famous as a training ground for future leaders: it provided the critical formula whereby American individualism could be reconciled with cooperation. Yale was America's college. Not all prestigious colleges followed the Yale model. At Harvard, for example, there was a robust "collegiate culture" and related activities. However, its network of "final clubs" based their self-perpetuating membership on sociability, with no pretense at rewarding merit, as was the case with the "college system" in place at Yale and elsewhere.

When the "college system" worked at its best, it was supposed to be impervious to the advantages of wealth and social class. Henry Seidel Canby, for example, claimed, "But we were not impressed by the Great Names of plutocracy—by Vanderbilts, Astors, Rockefellers as such—since we saw them at first hand."[19] The crucial criterion in judging a student was, "What does he *do?*" Accomplishments that brought honor to the college were supposed to be the coin of the campus realm. A student who subscribed to this value system faced a succession of trials. First, one had to demonstrate the talent to make the football squad, to be selected for the editorial board of the literary magazine, or to pass the audition for the glee club. Second, leadership could be demonstrated within each formal activity—for example, as captain of the squad or as editor-in-chief of the newspaper. A third level that usually escaped the notice of outside observers was that high prestige within the campus often went to those who served as managers of student organizations. They came to be known as the "Big Men," the astute decision-makers who "ran things"—identified by their hats, topcoats, and air of serious resolve as they mulled strategies. To a later generation of American undergraduates such a student would be designated by the universally understood acronym BMOC, the proverbial "Big Man on Campus."

In whichever endeavor a student chose to make his mark, the ultimate test was whether class leaders recognized a particular accomplishment as making him worthy of selection for honor groups. Yale, for example, had an elaborate hierarchy of "sophomore societies" and then prestigious secret "senior societies," including Skull and Bones and Wolf's Heads. These organizations varied from campus to campus, but the underlying principles were often modeled on the Yale system. Although undergraduates may have been indifferent about final examinations for courses, they were serious about the solemn "Tap Day," when senior members of the honor groups went through elaborate rituals to identify the chosen few new initiates. At Princeton the fateful day for selection to the prestigious eating clubs was known as "Bicker." The "tapping" procedures for the senior societies appeared to the casual outsider to be comparable to the "rushes" conducted by college fraternities and sororities. This was true in a sense, with one crucial difference. Whereas one was "rushed" by a fraternity as a freshman, "tapping" for membership in a senior society came toward the end of one's college career, because it was a reward for an accumulation of contributions to campus life.

A fundamental plank of the internal rewards platform at Yale and many other colleges at the turn of the century was that it was unabashedly selective. Membership was ultimately based on talent, as judged by incumbent senior society members. Although many students were probably disappointed when they were not chosen for an honor society, so long as most students believed that selections were made fairly, on the strict basis of genuine talent rather than favoritism or connections, the "college system" thrived and the "chosen few" were admired. What one finds in student memoirs and in faculty commentaries after 1900, however, is growing doubt that the collegiate rewards were being distributed according to the avowed criteria. A second line of criticism about the "college system" of the undergraduate world was its presumption that American colleges were truly open to a wide range of talented youth. If the "college life" model was supposed to be an effective mechanism for nurturing future national leaders, what safeguards were in place to assure that it was a fair, open contest? Finally, since the "college system" prided itself on evaluations about student activities apart from the formal course of study, was there a danger of students being systematically steered away from important ideas and developments in the academic curriculum? To test the glorified picture of the "college life" of 1890 to 1910, it's useful to draw on historical data to probe its claims with regard to these areas of concern.

Access and Affordability

The American celebration of the "collegiate ideal" was more than a mere popular fascination with campus life; it was a matter of serious social implications. The artifacts and symbols of college life, although sometimes seemingly frivolous, were in fact symptomatic of serious issues about social mobility and obtaining prestige in American life. Between

1910 and 1920, higher education paid a "price of popularity": problems of propriety accompanied the colleges' growth and increasing prestige.

The first, most obvious limit of the "collegiate ideal" was that it was almost wholly restricted to white males. Moreover, not even all talented white males had a reasonable chance of going to college. College enrollments represented less than 5 percent of the American population of eighteen- to twenty-two-year-olds. Most grating was that within that relatively small group who did enroll in college, not all who sought to become part of this internal collegiate world were allowed to do so. Even though going to college conferred elite status on an individual, not every undergraduate enjoyed first-class citizenship in the campus community.

It was one thing for college to capture Americans' fancy. It was another matter to parlay that dreamy imagery into the reality of matriculating. To gain some sense of just who was going to college, it is useful to consider access as a function of affordability. Tuition and official charges were not outlandish. There were no massive annual increases in expenses between 1890 and 1910. Yet college remained relatively expensive to most American families.

This was true for the family of Alexander Meiklejohn — eventually famous as a college professor and dean, president, and philosopher. The son of skilled industrial artisans who had immigrated to Rhode Island from Scotland, Meiklejohn was bright and a very good high school student; in fact, he graduated first in his class. In 1899, going to high school was still a relatively privileged experience in the United States. But the public high schools of that era were academically strong, especially in the urban northeastern section of the country. Meiklejohn's course of study at the senior high school in Pawtucket — hardly an elite locale — included classes in grammar, penmanship, arithmetic, algebra, Latin, Greek, drawing, and music and culminated with geometry, physics, chemistry, astronomy, French, and ancient history.[20]

Meiklejohn's educational path illustrates the tradeoffs and decisions that faced an education-minded family with modest income. His parents made a deliberate decision to groom Alexander, the youngest of their eight sons, for college; his brothers all forewent college and worked in the Pawtucket mills. Going to college was considered prestigious, but it still usually involved a very local orbit. Although young Meiklejohn and his parents had considered his applying to Yale, they ultimately chose Brown University in nearby Providence.

Brown's tuition was typical of New England institutions: $105 per year for tuition plus $48 for mandatory incidental fees. This total of $153 would have been worth about $3,100 a century later, in 2000. The academic year from mid-September to late June was divided into three sessions, with a summer vacation free for part-time jobs or avocations. This was not particularly expensive for a middle-class family in New England, with an annual income of about $600 to $2,000 (about $12,000 to $41,000 in 2000 dollars). But it was probably unaffordable for most working-class families. In 1890 a skilled industrial worker made about $460 per year ($8,700 in 2000 dollars). Hence any expenditure on college was an extreme demand on the income of even a reasonably well paid skilled industrial worker. In Meiklejohn's case, family members, including the seven brothers, chipped in so that one son—the promising scholar—could afford to pay college bills. For part of his undergraduate years, Alexander Meiklejohn was what we would call a "commuter student"; he lived at home and walked the three miles to the Brown campus. (As a sidenote, this money-saving measure illustrates that even the prestigious historic campuses did not have a completely residential student body.)

As a follow-up to the rough estimate of Meiklejohn's expenses in 1889, it's illuminating to examine the continuity and changes in college prices over the next two decades. In 1907–8, Brown's administration described a "moderate" annual budget as follows:

Tuition	$105
Incidental fees	$48
Room rent	$60
Board	$150
Books and labs	$30
Total	$393

Translated into currency for 2000, this $393 in annual expenses would have been the equivalent of about $7,300 per year. However, for a "liberal" (i.e., expensive) lifestyle, room and board options could make a budget soar to $655 per academic year ($12,200 in 2000 dollars). Tuition charges showed little increase over a decade. The figure of $105 for tuition is a bit misleading because the $48 "incidental" fee—pertaining to various university services, processing charges, and so on—was mandatory. And, as we shall examine in more detail later, even the $655 estimate for "liberal spenders" tended to understate the bills of several thousand dollars per year that a significant number of wealthy students accumulated.

The colleges, including the most elite colleges, did provide some financial aid and campus jobs for modest-income students. Such provisions for undergraduates like Alexander Meiklejohn elevated the "self-help" student to the status of folk hero, the campus equivalent of the self-made man. At best, these provisions meant that a character in a Horatio Alger novel could probably have found a way to go to college in 1900, although he would have been in the minority. Although the American college at the turn of the century was within the reach of some ambitious, hardworking students from modest backgrounds, access was primarily open to a growing middle and upper-middle class of young white men between the ages of seventeen and twenty-one.

One gap in our historical knowledge is a sense of how different tuition charges precisely influenced the socioeconomic composition of student bodies at institutions across the country. In California, for example, both Stanford University and the University of California adhered to a policy of no charge for tuition. It's not clear, however, that such policies opened the floodgates of access and made their student bodies any less skewed toward prosperous families than student bodies in the East or Midwest. Similarly, some memoirs about enrollments at the University of Nebraska in the early 1900s suggest that the student body was drawn overwhelmingly from a prosperous business class.[21] Yet more than tuition expenses, the largest obstacle to college enrollment still remained the uneven availability of academically oriented high schools in sparsely populated regions.

In the South, the economic devastation of the post–Civil War period meant that charges for tuition and living expenses, however low, were beyond the means of most young men. Accounts of Tulane University indicate that even the established families of New Orleans were impoverished. The College of William and Mary in Virginia dealt with the regional economic adversity and billed itself as the "Oldest and Cheapest College in the South"—a two-pronged pitch that fused heritage and affordability. But even low prices fell short as a recruiting device. Analysis of the college's financial records indicate that the bursar often neglected to collect student tuition payments for the simple reason that students had no money. The eventual solution the college came up with was to rely on an annual state subsidy that provided funding for undergraduates who pledged to teach someday in the state's public schools.

Across the nation, most colleges depended on secondary schools in their immediate locale for the bulk of their students. At Brown University, for example, in the 1907–8 academic year, slightly over 40 percent of its students came from the greater Providence area and adjacent Rhode Island towns. The localism is even more pronounced when one includes Brown students who hailed from those Massachusetts towns that were immediately over the state line. Amherst College, one of the most prestigious liberal arts institutions in the Northeast, drew over 60 percent of its undergraduates from two sources: the western section of its home state of Massachusetts and adjacent New York. Amherst drew relatively few students from the highly populated Boston area, even though it was only about a hundred miles away.

Another trend in enrollment patterns by 1900, especially for the most prestigious colleges in the Northeast, was increasing reliance on private boarding schools rather than public high schools for their pool of applicants. This led to the development of "feeder" relations with selected preparatory schools. According to this custom, headmasters and deans of admissions acquired mutual trust in the "fit" of students from the secondary school to a particular college. Lawrenceville School in New Jersey was a feeder to Princeton. Phillips Academy of Andover had strong ties with Yale. Phillips Academy of Exeter and Groton sent large numbers of students each year to Harvard. Deerfield Academy groomed students for Amherst.

Yale was probably the most geographically diverse college, followed by Harvard and Dartmouth. Each had the name recognition, fueled in part by winning athletics teams, to generate interest from students across the country. Yet even these "national" institutions did not stray far from the norm of reliance on applicants close to home. Between 1890 and 1910 there is little evidence of deliberate exclusion in college admissions on the basis of religion, ethnicity, or social class, but there was in operation a system of self-selection whereby high school students matched themselves with an institution that made sense in terms of proximity, affordability, and homogeneity. A campus that had traditionally enrolled young men from white Anglo-Saxon Protestant families relied on that momentum to shape its continuing appeal.

There was a significant minority of crossover applications. One such was Joseph Kennedy, who disregarded the promptings of his family that he go to either Holy Cross or Boston College and opted instead to be in a minority as an Irish Catholic at Harvard. The urban universities— namely, Columbia, Pennsylvania, and Harvard—each had a relatively diverse student clientele, a reflection of massive immigration into their metropolitan areas. Despite this diversity, they remained essentially "lo- cal" institutions in terms of geographical range. The University of Penn- sylvania and its host city of Philadelphia, for example, were sufficiently heterogeneous and diffuse that one journalist observed that it had the "democracy of the street car."[22]

Prior to 1900, official anti-Semitism in admissions was far less than the discrimination a Jewish student would face from fellow students within the campus culture. Exclusion on the basis of race and gender was another matter. An institution declared unequivocally for or against co- education. As a general rule, coeducation of men and women had greater appeal in the Midwest and West than in the Northeast and Southeast. Colleges in New England and the Northeast tended to be gender exclu- sive (i.e., either men's colleges or women's colleges). One concession was the emergence of the "coordinate college"—a college for women that was part of an otherwise all-male university structure. Colleges in the South adhered to racial separation, due to a combination of institutional tradition and state law. Yet even in the Northeast, where racial segrega- tion was not mandated by law, the enrollment of a black student at a historically white college was unusual. President Charles W. Eliot of Harvard, for example, was candid in his public statements about the inadvisability of enrolling more than a few black students at the college. He was also sympathetic to college deans and presidents in the South, who carried out strict policies of racial segregation.[23]

At Harvard and other universities in the Northeast, race was a less volatile issue than religion and ethnicity—not so much as a matter of principle but by default. Eliot at Harvard and Nicholas Murray Butler at Columbia were influential among university presidents, and they often stated their concerns that an influx of the children of immigrants from Ireland and Eastern Europe would infringe on the cultural stature and demographic composition of their historic institutions. Token accom- modation of diverse groups was the rule of thumb at the established colleges of the Northeast and Middle Atlantic regions, as presidents and boards became increasingly preoccupied with the xenophobia associ- ated with retaining or regaining "racial purity."

Another notable characteristic of college admissions practices between 1890 and 1910 was the lack of coherent planning. Most colleges adjusted to the growing interest in college attendance simply by admitting more students. The only sign of institutional concern was the attempt to administer some basic screening on academic preparation, by means of either an entrance examination or a certificate arrangement with a particular high school. Eventually, after 1910, this combination of enrollment growth and lack of systematic admissions plans would catch up with those prestigious colleges whose pool of applicants stretched the limits of the campus's ability to accommodate large numbers.

At times the curriculum provided some clues to the social tracking and schisms of "college life." At Yale, for example, students who enrolled in the Sheffield Scientific School were required to sit at the back of the college chapel. Elsewhere, students in engineering or other applied sciences were regarded as "grinds," a designation denoting second-class campus citizenship. This fragmentation suggests that the "college system" was not achieving the institutional cohesion it purported to promote.

Academic leaders and undergraduates alike often praised the "college system" for its emphasis on trying to bring together a group of students who then would spend four years together and in so doing form a life-long bond as members of a graduating class. A prescribed curriculum, in combination with the initiations and shared experiences of "college life," reinforced this experience. Friendly intramural rivalries included contests that pitted, for example, the class of 1898 against the class of 1899 during freshman week—and for the next four years. Hazing included being made to wear class "beanies" (often known as "ducs") and to adhere to various rules of conduct, all of which promoted the collective "class experience." But did all this effort work? Was the American college truly a cohesive institution for its students?

The cohesiveness of the "college system" has been exaggerated, for several reasons. First, the preponderance of campus songs and college stories leaned more toward nostalgia or aspiration than reality. Second, the enrollment data collected by college officials were often misleading. The usual practice for a president or dean preparing an annual report on enrollments was simply to publish the head count of students enrolled in each class for the year—a procedure comparable to relying on a box-office count of a theater audience from one performance to the next, or to a minister's keeping a week-to-week tally of church attendance. So

long as the concern was merely to sell tickets or fill pews, such gross summaries were adequate. But it is inadequate for analyzing the "college
system" because it did not accurately track the year-to-year retention of
a particular group of students that was supposed to enter as a class and
then bond as a cohesive group or "cohort" for the entire college career.

To illustrate why this methodological distinction is crucial to evaluating the colleges' cohesiveness, it is useful to look at catalogue data. Consider the case of Kentucky State College (later renamed the University of
Kentucky). In the fall 1903, 124 freshmen entered to create the class of
1907. According to the president's official reports, the enrollment pattern
of this class over four years, culminating with the award of bachelor's
degrees, was as follows:

Freshman	124	(100 percent)
Sophomore	115	(93 percent)
Junior	81	(65 percent)
Senior	67	(54 percent)
Bachelor's degrees	64	(52 percent)

The data suggest very high retention of students, as 93 percent returned
for their sophomore year. The dropout rate at the end of the sophomore
year is substantial, but to have more than half of the entering freshmen
persist for a four-year bachelor's degree suggests a reasonably cohesive
cohort. This impression, however, is misleading. If the 124 entering freshmen of 1903 are carefully tracked over four years—something the college did not do—a markedly different attrition pattern emerges:

Freshman	124	(100 percent)
Sophomore	68	(59 percent)
Junior	41	(36 percent)
Senior	34	(30 percent)
Bachelor's degrees	34	(30 percent)

The implications are twofold. First, even at an institution where students enthusiastically embraced the "college life" model, the attempts at
creating a cohesive, enduring class lagged behind the image of college as
a "shared brotherhood." In fact, the attrition rate was formidable, with
only 30 percent of the original group who entered as freshmen staying
on for four years to complete their bachelor's degrees. Second, if one

refers back to the annual enrollment counts published by the university, there had to be some substantial influx of new students each year who had not entered as new freshmen. Who were the added sophomores, juniors, and seniors to explain why total enrollment levels remained relatively high, even though so many of the original freshman students were dropping out? For example, the university records indicate that the sophomore enrollment for the fall of 1904 was 115 students, yet only 68 of that total were freshmen who had entered one year earlier. In other words, the healthy total sophomore enrollment of 115 students was achieved only by adding 47 students from various sources other than the original class.

Evidently college enrollments included a significant number of transfer students each year. These latecomers had lost out on the bonding experience of the important freshman year, an additional source of weakness in the "college class" affiliation. How could they possibly have been integrated into the "class-conscious" network of college life? This revised profile runs contrary to the college's self-portrayals of the time and raises serious questions about both the efficiency and the effectiveness of the "collegiate way." If "going to college" was comparable to a "voyage with shipmates," the American college was a rather leaky boat whose passenger list was substantially depleted by the time it reached shore after four years.

The case of the class of 1907 at Kentucky State College was not atypical for colleges nationwide. Detailed historical analysis of student-by-student enrollment and retention patterns between 1890 and 1910 at a range of institutions — including Brown, Harvard, Amherst, Transylvania, and William and Mary — indicates that during this "golden era," colleges experienced high dropout rates and relatively low levels of bachelor's degree completion. At Amherst College, for example, the graduation rate for entering freshmen between 1880 and 1900 was about 75 percent to 90 percent. In contrast, between 1905 and 1910 the graduation rate fell significantly, to around 50 percent to 60 percent. Transylvania University consistently had a freshman dropout rate of about 50 percent, with seldom more than 10 percent of an entering freshman class persisting to receive bachelor's degrees four years later. Harvard College dared for some years to break the "Bright College Years" model by offering its students the option to graduate in three rather than four years. Also contrary to the image of the cohesive, shared experience as characteristic of the "college system," there is evidence that many undergraduates transferred in and out of institutions.[24]

These enrollment trends and attrition rates must have meant headaches for various college constituencies. For the student leaders, this pattern meant that many of their classmates were "letting the team down" by not maintaining at least a modest academic record. A high dropout rate thinned the ranks of students eligible for college teams and organizations. As for those students who left college for nonacademic reasons, the attrition suggests that the appeal of college life was not as widespread as the popular portrayals claimed. College presidents and boards tended to avoid mentioning these trends in their public messages. Yet in their administrative circles, they faced the problem of finding new, paying students to help them meet the college budget. Faculty morale undoubtedly suffered in the light of such persistently weak academic records, and frequent departures, among students. For an institutional culture that depended on loyalty and affiliation, the high dropout rate was problematic, and certainly at odds with the image of cohesion and continuity.

Resourceful officers in the college alumni associations devised a partial solution. To be counted for life as a college alumnus, one merely had to have enrolled. Completing a degree was not a requirement. Even those who dropped out of college could still claim connection with their alma mater and return for homecoming and other class reunions. And alumni office staff members were free to exploit this sense of campus connection by including all alumni, degree recipients and dropouts alike, on mailing lists for soliciting donations.

Intercollegiate Sports

Since the "collegiate ideal" emphasized character and teamwork, varsity sports flourished as a visible, highly valued component of that ideal. From the start, intercollegiate athletics had been a source of intense enjoyment and rivalry among students. Over time, the games also soared as a matter of public interest, in terms of both paying spectators and news coverage. The early crew races between Harvard and Yale were often weeklong events, complete with newspaper reporters and onlookers watching from private railroad cars that ran along the course route.[25] Later, baseball gained great popularity, especially during commencement week, with college teams playing before large crowds of alumni. By 1880 these activities had been eclipsed by what Frederick Rudolph has called "the rise of football."[26] Most stadiums located on campus were fairly limited as to seating capacity. Hence major rivalries such as the Yale-Princeton game on Thanksgiving Day were played in metropolitan arenas, such as the Polo Grounds in New York City. According to William Oriad, college football and the newspapers mutually enhanced one another. The varsity football teams became the object of extended coverage by eager reporters, commanding front-page headlines day after day. Football also inspired a new journalistic vocabulary and inflated prose style. In exchange for providing dramatic subject matter, the college teams gained local and national publicity, which increased interest among alumni, paying readers, and the general population.[27]

As noted in the preceding chapter, intercollegiate sports shared with other extracurricular activities the characteristic of originally having been run by and for students. Attempts by faculty and administration to gain control were usually derailed by determined undergraduates. Logistics of travel, scheduling, and maintenance of facilities and equipment were coordinated by student managers. The student captain acted as a "playing coach." Alumni who were former players often volunteered to help with training and practices. At the colleges and universities where sports were serious and strong, the typical governance arrangement was the "athletic association"—a formal organization loosely affiliated with the campus but controlled by student officers and financed by student fees and other donations. Between 1890 and 1910 the prototypical athletic association underwent a transformation: professionalization of the staff, namely, the hiring of an athletic director and coaching staff.

On the one hand, this organizational evolution helped undergraduates in their campaign to create their own activities free from faculty and presidential control. It required, however, reliance of sorts on other adults who were coaches and athletic directors and who were paid by the student association, funded by student dues. It also often entailed alliance with such new groups as alumni associations. At its best, the alliance between a student organization and an alumni group provided both power and money that made intercollegiate sports impregnable to reform efforts on the part of the academic leadership.

On the other hand, this formalization of the athletic association usually meant that decision making and budgetary control drifted from the

students to the adults who were paid athletic officers. At Yale, home of
the most successful and well-known football program in the nation for
over three decades, power flowed to alumnus and athletics director Walter Camp. Over time, Camp diverted an increasing quantity of association monies into football, to the detriment of such sports as swimming,
track and field, hockey, and gymnastics. Camp also wielded national influence as the author of a syndicated football column and the originator
of the annual "All American" team selections.[28] It was an entrepreneurial
strategy that allowed a coach and athletics director to gain leverage over
both student groups and academic officials.

Camp's model of intercollegiate athletics administration at Yale
spread along with Yale's football system to other universities. Camp's
foremost disciple was Amos Alonzo Stagg, who gave up his position as
assistant coach at Yale to become head football coach and athletics director at the new University of Chicago in 1892. Stagg held both positions
for forty years at Chicago and perfected the athletics department machinery. He sensed that the university's president, William Rainey Harper, subscribed to the proposition that a winning football team could
bring many benefits to a new university. Hence Stagg negotiated a remarkable contract with the president. For example, he received a tenured
faculty position as well as an administrative appointment as athletics
director and football coach. His departmental budget was exempted
from the customary internal review, and he reported directly to the president—and in some cases directly to the board of trustees. In particular,
one board member, an heir to the Armour meatpacking fortune, took a
special liking to Stagg's athletics program and assured him access to
funds and to the board. Although the university paid his salary and operating expenses, he was allowed to develop various enterprises involving campus sports and to keep the proceeds. Stagg thrived in this enterprising environment. He sponsored the state high school track meet,
charged user fees for campus tennis courts, put up billboards for the
university football team schedule throughout the city, and organized a
host of fund-raising and promotional activities. His team, the Chicago
Maroons, were frequent champions of the Western Conference (later
known as the Big Ten) whose home games routinely sold out to an ap-
preciative metropolitan audience.[29]

Few campus athletics programs could match Stagg's success at the
University of Chicago or Walter Camp's at Yale. Still, many coaches and

athletics directors emulated their model. The result was the emergence as a permanent fixture of the football coach and athletics director as public celebrities and campus czars.

College sports were inextricably linked with commercialism and often with insinuations of corruption. Most attempts by groups of professors to regulate intercollegiate sports were not enduring. The excesses of college sports were not exactly illegal, because there were in fact few rules or governing associations in place. But as Ronald Smith has demonstrated, the distinctive ethos of American collegiate sports plainly diverged from the code of sportsmanship associated with Oxford and Cambridge. In the late nineteenth century the historic American universities — Harvard, Princeton, and Yale — dominated intercollegiate sports in the United States, including selections to the "All American" teams. They also gained fame and support for their spirited contests in crew and in "athletics" (track and field) against Oxford and Cambridge. According to Smith, even in the early years of this international competition, there were marked differences in sportsmanship. For the Oxford and Cambridge student athletes, the emphasis was on following the spirit of play, even at the expense of the letter of the law as spelled out in the rulebooks. The American student athletes inverted the ethos: for them, so long as one technically obeyed the formal rules, it was acceptable to ignore the spirit of the game. "Gaining an edge" over an opponent was considered "fair play."[30]

Inevitably, then, subsequent attempts to bring order and sanity to American college sports were destined to fail. Whether university officials were trying to regulate academic eligibility requirements for student athletes or to eliminate brutality on the playing field, student ingenuity coupled with alumni support usually prevailed. The phenomenon fostered a distinctively American ethos of collegiate sportsmanship.

Women's Colleges

Women's colleges and especially the undergraduate "college woman" were among the most conspicuous and successful features of American higher education between 1880 and 1920. These institutions included those that would later be known as the "Seven Sisters" — Wellesley, Radcliffe, Mount Holyoke, Smith, Vassar, Barnard, and Bryn Mawr — as well as the coordinate colleges of Pembroke at Brown, Jackson at Tufts, and

Sophie Newcomb at Tulane. Most of these colleges enjoyed two advantages: good facilities due to robust endowments, and a clientele of young women from prosperous families. A third common element was a sense of being social and academic pioneers, creating a shared commitment to a strong educational mission.

According to Helen Lefkowitz Horowitz, the original base of these colleges changed during the early 1900s. Students at the women's colleges became immersed in the elaborate internal student culture of organizations and honors known as "The Life." The student groups that set the tone and dominated the activities of the campus were known more for hewing to the tenets of "The Life" than for their commitment to serious study as prelude to a profession or graduate school. The elite women's colleges did not imitate the men's colleges. Rather, they developed an institutional structure and culture that were a variation on some of the themes associated with the men's colleges.[31]

Key players in "The Life" were the "swells"—confident, affluent, poised young women who brought to the women's college all the advantages of wealth, academic preparation, and social graces. They set the tone for conduct and were architects of and major actors in an elaborate series of ceremonies, rituals, festivals, and events that marked the academic calendar. Costumes, ranging from academic regalia to Greek gowns, accentuated the high fashion of daily apparel. Student organizations, ranging from student government to yearbooks and literary magazines, were an object of energy and commitment. Although historians of higher education have often overlooked the fact, athletics were central to the campus culture. The highly competitive activities field days and basketball increased cohesion and affiliation. To the casual outside observer, the dances, dramas, and rituals of the women's colleges suggested an idyllic, leisurely life and lent themselves to caricature. In fact, to the participants the women's college life was demanding in its emphasis on participation, form, conduct, and conformity.

Several of the women's colleges had started out with distinctive living arrangements (e.g., cottages, suites, and quadrangles) designed to combine the curriculum with a residential scheme traditionally associated with the "collegiate way." By 1900 an important additional development was that within the women's colleges, where one lived on campus demonstrated one's place in the campus hierarchy. When Wellesley officials tried to make their college affordable to modest-income women by offering low-priced rooms, the effect was to split the student body according to income, thus accentuating rather than dissolving socioeconomic differences.

Just as the men's colleges of the Northeast set the standard to be emulated nationwide, so did the women's colleges. Vassar, Wellesley, Smith, and Bryn Mawr were the models that founders invoked when creating such women's colleges as Mills College in Oakland, California, Sophie Newcomb College in New Orleans, and Agnes Scott College in Decatur, Georgia. According to Lynn Gordon, the women's colleges in the South — Sophie Newcomb and Agnes Scott being foremost among them — were intended to be "safe" institutions geared toward educating "dutiful daughters and future mothers," with a strong Christian emphasis. Between 1890 and 1910, however, students at these two colleges took the initiative to create associations and organizations that would go beyond the colleges' original mission and provide activities appropriate for the education of "new women." Literary societies, dramatic groups, newspapers, and athletics teams were among the many flourishing extracurricular activities that were not part of the original plan devised by presidents and donors. The students at these colleges wanted options for professional work as an alternative to marriage. They looked more to recent alumnae than to their professors and parents for role models. Sophie Newcomb graduates established a reputation for undertaking urban reform initiatives in New Orleans.[32]

Women and Coeducation

How did the "college system" accommodate gender in those institutions that opted to enroll both men and women? The coeducation of undergraduate women and men was a widespread innovation, especially in colleges and universities of the Midwest and West. The reformers' ideal was to provide equal educational opportunities to young women and men and to offer them the experience of studying and working together. The improvements in access for women, however, were frequently offset by unequal treatment on campus and in the curriculum.

At the University of California, for example, men students called women students "pelicans," a pejorative comment on their personal appearance. Although all students paid the same mandatory activity fees, women were excluded from most campus organizations, including the student newspaper and student government. The university administration endorsed and supported a robust fraternity system but had no comparable provisions for sororities. The faculty discouraged women from enrolling in certain fields of study. The student publications edited by men delighted in ridiculing the women students, constantly warning that their enrollment at the university destined them to becoming physically worn out and altogether unsuited for romance, let alone marriage. At every turn the women students learned the same lesson as women faculty: they were second-class citizens in the campus community. The university administration refused to intervene when male students prohibited women from being members in the Associated Students of the University of California. Women retaliated by forming their own organization, the Association of Women Students.[33] Variations on this theme echoed at Cornell University and other coeducational universities. At Stanford, men students jeered when women dared take to the playing fields with their own athletics teams. In response, the women formed their own alliances and created their own organizations. The larger lessons in development and survival were learned in spite of, not because of, benign neglect and overt discrimination on the part of male students and university officials.

The ridicule served up by men students hardly went unnoticed by the women undergraduates. A humorous counter to the men's taunts is found in the college song "A Model College Girl," written by a woman student:

Never broke a regulation
Never told a lie
Never want to have a vacation
When I don't know why
Always love to go to sections
Love to go to bed
Never nibble sweet confections
When I am not fed

After several similar verses in which the Model College Girl details her adherence to college regulations ("Never take a step imprudent / When I do not walk"), she concludes with a measure of proud independence:

You may gather from these data
Just how good I be!
I'm as proud of Alma Mater
As she is of me![34]

Some universities, including Harvard, Columbia, and Brown, resisted coeducation in favor of what were called coordinate colleges for women. "Harvard Annex," a remarkably apt name, in view of the side-door accommodation of women, later became Radcliffe College. Columbia University did not admit women to Columbia College, opting instead to incorporate Barnard College for women as part of the university structure. In 1891 Brown University acknowledged the College for Women in Brown University—a designation that in 1928 would be changed to Pembroke College.

The experience of women at Brown University was interesting because it reversed the conventional logic about college-educated women and initiatives to influence civic and regional change. Alumnae of many of the first women's colleges distinguished themselves by later creating a variety of civic and reform associations. In Providence, Rhode Island, the opposite sequence held true: a confederation of women's civic clubs and social organizations banded together to raise money and set out a systematic agenda to create a bona fide degree-granting women's college. Led by educated, prosperous women from prominent Providence families, such as Sarah Doyle, the Rhode Island Society for the Collegiate Education of Women was persistent, organized, and effective.[35] Its members worked with the presidents of Brown University, constructed an impressive building for women, and raised necessary funds for programs and for the hiring of faculty and staff. Brown's College for Women admitted its first students in 1891 and received a surge of energy and vision from the newly hired dean, Ann Crosby Emery, a distinguished scholar and Ph.D.

For women undergraduates at Brown University, less proved to be more. In other words, they acknowledged up front the limits they faced. They lacked the land, lavish facilities, and endowments of a Smith College, a Wellesley, or a Vassar. Hence they embraced their mission as an urban institution whose constituency was overwhelmingly from Providence and nearby towns. This proved to be an appropriate, ample market of heretofore underserved women who had completed secondary school. Since the College for Women had to work within the confines of an essentially all-male institution, its faculty and dean emphasized academic parity for women, so that they would be able to take classes taught by Brown faculty and attended by Brown's male undergraduates. At the same time they retained (and relished) the distinct identity of a true women's college within the university structure. This distinction was borne out in the temper of their collegiate activities. Whereas Brown's men followed the conventional pattern of the "college system," the students in the women's college emphasized social and civic change in their choices of clubs and guest speakers. Maintaining a separate women's college provided an antidote to the predictable, pervasive objections of Brown students.[36]

Coeducation worked best at the University of Chicago, thanks largely to the strategies mapped out by Dean Marion Talbot. According to Lynn Gordon, Talbot synthesized a program for women students at Chicago that created what was simultaneously a "Western Yale" and "Western Wellesley." According to this arrangement, instruction and classes were coeducational, with women and men enrolling together and studying the same subjects with the same professors. Talbot made a strong distinction, however, in negotiating arrangements for social life. Her concern was that in a gender-neutral extracurriculum, women would have less than full citizenship. She therefore made certain that the women had their own housing quadrangles and their own elaborate system of clubs, literary groups, and other activities. Since many women students did not live on campus, they were urged to affiliate with "neighborhood clubs" representing students from their home sectors of Chicago. Women undergraduates at Chicago were encouraged to participate in groups dealing with urban issues. They also had the benefit of proximity to a large number of women who were in graduate school, pursuing either master's degrees or the Ph.D. The result was that women flourished at Chicago, academically and in their extracurricular pursuits. Above all, they were at ease with the men in the classroom and indeed surpassed their male counterparts with respect to such academic honors as election to Phi Beta Kappa.

The only problem was brought by success. In 1902, there were 242 women students, representing 48 percent of the University of Chicago's enrollment. Evidently President Harper had growing concerns about the disproportionate numerical and cultural influence women students were bringing to the university. Led by a group of discontented faculty who complained that coeducation in the classroom was harmful to the men students, the faculty senate formally approved a new policy of instructional segregation. For a while the policy had little effect on the campus culture, having apparently been more a priority of the administration than of Chicago's undergraduates. Yet by about 1910, student culture at the University of Chicago had drifted from its original model of integration of women and men to resemble the more typical male-dominated "collegiate culture" of intercollegiate sports and exclusively male groups. Once again the "college system" had demonstrated its incompatibility with genuine coeducation.

The most curious aspect of the academic attack on coeducation was its logical shift. Whereas in 1880 or 1890 the concern of parents, educators, and psychologists was that collegiate coeducation was harmful to women, linked to such dangers as brain fever, physical fatigue, and the risk of becoming aesthetically "unfeminine," by 1910 the reasons for opposition had changed dramatically. Women seemed to have handled the burdens of serious study and campus life quite well. The new insight was that their presence was harmful—or rather threatening—to college men.

The "Collegiate Ideal" and Black Colleges

The participation of black students in the inner workings and rewards of "collegiate life" was negligible even at colleges that had no formal policy of racial exclusion. It was standard practice to exclude the black colleges from the national media, whether major newspapers or other publications about college life. For example, the anthologies of college songbooks published between 1900 and 1920 claimed to be all-inclusive, but the black colleges were not among the hundreds of institutions from all over the country that were represented. Racial segregation being the norm in both the North and the South, did a variation of the "college system" develop in the black colleges?

The first obstacle was that almost all the so-called colleges for black students around 1900 in fact offered little in the way of college-level instruction. Most were confined to elementary and secondary studies. Second, the best-endowed colleges for African Americans—namely, Hampton Institute and Tuskegee—favored agricultural and industrial education to the neglect of collegiate studies. Not surprisingly, black college and professional school enrollments in the South were limited. According to a report by the U.S. Commissioner of Education, black college and professional school enrollments in the Southern states and Washington, D.C., totaled 3,880 in 1900. As a further indication of the paucity of educational opportunity, only 364 African Americans had earned college degrees in the Southern states and the District of Columbia.[37]

Two institutions were conspicuous for offering a liberal arts college education to black students: Howard University in Washington, D.C., and Fisk University in Nashville. These distinctive institutions were characterized by high morale and a strong commitment on the part of students and alumni to providing a highly educated leadership. Lacking endowments and dependent primarily on the contributions of black missionary groups and church associations, Howard and Fisk deliberately set themselves apart from the industrial-vocational model of Hampton and Tuskegee. Yet they paid a high price for this high purpose: they did not become objects of support from Northern foundations or what was called industrial philanthropy. Accounts of student life at these institutions are scant, but most indicate a seriousness of purpose among faculty and students, with little time or money available for the activities associated with the self-indulgent "collegiate way" of Yale and Dartmouth.

Gradually, however, Fisk and Howard forfeited some of their autonomy and mission as their boards came to be filled by candidates championed by the national foundations and the Rockefeller General Education Board. This change brought substantial endowments and resources to the underfunded colleges. It also brought Fisk and Howard increasingly into the fold of emulating the "college system" from elsewhere. As W. E. B. DuBois concluded in a commencement address at Howard University in 1930, "Our college man today is, on the average, a man untouched by real culture. He deliberately surrenders to selfish and even silly ideals, swarming into semiprofessional athletics and Greek letter societies, and affecting to despise scholarship and the hard grind of study and research. The greatest meetings of the Negro college year like those of the white college year have become vulgar exhibitions of liquor, extravagance, and fur coats. We have in our colleges a growing mass of stupidity and indifference."[38]

From Petty Larceny to Grand Theft: The Excesses of College Life

The "collegiate ideal" at the turn of the century brought together disparate individuals and conferred rewards for talent and loyalty, especially upon those who worked for the overall good and honor of the alma mater. As suggested earlier, proponents of the "college system" claimed that the collegiate world was essentially democratic in that it paid little deference to the advantages of family lineage or wealth. What mattered most in the collegiate world was what one could do, what one could contribute to the various activities that honored the college. Henry Seidel Canby was correct in pointing out that there were numerous instances in which the sons of a wealthy family could not prove their mettle in the action-oriented culture of the campus.[39] So when the collegiate ideal was realized, it theoretically brought out the best in an American tradition.

At its best, the "collegiate ideal" was embodied in such public figures as Theodore Roosevelt and Woodrow Wilson. Both were statesman scholars, famous as presidents of the United States. Both had also relished undergraduate life—Roosevelt at Harvard, Wilson at Princeton. Roosevelt took great pride in having been a standout member of Harvard's boxing team. Wilson found time to coach football while he was a professor of political science at Wesleyan. Both manifested the ideal of "muscular Christianity" whereby intelligence was combined with character and action.

Unfortunately, there is strong evidence that the implementation of the celebrated "collegiate ideal" began to fall short after 1900. Roosevelt and Wilson were products of the "college system" of the late nineteenth century, and they were troubled by what they saw in the colleges in the years prior to World War I. The complaints that surfaced after 1900 were indicative not of occasional slips but of systemic problems. The recurrent concern was that collegiate rewards were not, as promised, based primarily on talent and merit but had become a matter of favoritism and nepotism. Princeton had come to be known as the nation's "most pleasant country club." The dean of Harvard College was forced to take the time to write an article for a national publication dispelling allegations that Harvard had come to be dominated by a "Fast Set." Princeton's president, Woodrow Wilson, acknowledged that the faculty and administration had lost control of campus life: "So far as the colleges go, the sideshows have swallowed up the circus and we in the main tent do not know what is going on."[40]

Wilson's political career—first as governor of New Jersey and later as president of the United States—gained impetus from his failure as president of Princeton to reform the social snobbery of the powerful college eating clubs. Wilson learned the hard way that a coalition of alumni and undergraduates could present formidable opposition to a college president trying to alter campus traditions. Having lost his campus battles, he shifted his energies to the more congenial foes of the statehouse and capital. But not even the president of the United States could solve the growing problems of college life. In 1904 President Theodore Roosevelt was so upset by newspaper photographs of brutality on the college football field that he summoned leading college and university presidents to the White House to discuss reforms in college sports. To his great disappointment, representatives from his own alma mater, Harvard, joined with Yale and Princeton in refusing to attend.[41]

The presidents of Harvard, Yale, and Princeton later got a taste of their own medicine when undergraduates ignored their calls for summit meetings to bring order to the collegiate organizations. Defiance of academic leadership was widespread, but especially so at the prestigious East Coast colleges. At Yale, for example, student groups deliberately ignored President Arthur Hadley's prohibition of off-campus activities. They defied his order by hosting expensive banquets and dances at hotels in New York City. In the undergraduate world of Yale, prestige was inversely related to academic performance. Each class vied for the honor of having the lowest academic rating. In one yearbook the class of 1904 boasted "more gentlemen and fewer scholars than any other class in the memory of man." Not to be outdone, the class of 1905 countered with the self-congratulatory claim:

> Never since the Heavenly Host
> With all the Titans fought
> Saw they a class whose scholarship
> Approached so close to naught.[42]

The 1912 novel by Owen Johnson, *Stover at Yale,* offers a vivid portrayal of the "college system" gone awry. Whereas many college novels were either romanticized accounts or the efforts of outsiders who had little firsthand knowledge of campus life, *Stover at Yale* is the critical account of an insider. Johnson graduated from Yale in 1900 and had been editor of the literary magazine. His novel starts out as a predictable account of freshman Dink Stover's initiation into the celebrated college life, with all the typical challenges and triumphs. But then Johnson departs from the formula. His hero finds that election to honor societies is not always based on talent but rather is a matter of connections with the "right crowd." A student's place in the campus hierarchy is determined by his prep school affiliation, not his performance in sports or extracurricular activities. There is a pronounced chasm between wealthy and low-income students. This three-hundred-page novel spanning four years of undergraduate life makes virtually no mention of academics. References to classroom work come up only when a student must reluctantly turn down an invitation to some activity in order to "bone up" for, say, a Latin class recitation.

According to Johnson, the "Yale system" was on the brink of implosion because its intricate system of rewards and honor societies had failed to accommodate both the growth and the diversity of the Yale student body. Johnson's novel also alludes to some serious changes in the connection of a college education to the life of the nation. One rebellious student editor tells a group of critical classmates, "We are a business college purely and simply because we as a nation have only one ideal — the business ideal." The tragedy of the historic "collegiate ideal" was that its rising popularity had been accompanied by a fall from its original values: "Twenty years ago we had the ideal of the lawyer, of the doctor, of the statesman, of the gentleman, of the man of letters, of the soldier. . . . Now everything has conformed to business, everything has been made to pay."[43] At the conclusion of the novel, genuinely talented students are selected for the honor societies, suggesting that the "college system" had regained its appropriate, virtuous course.

Shifting from fiction to fact, we find that the excesses of the "college system" at Yale and elsewhere resulted in persistent, serious problems. Even President Eliot of Harvard confided toward the end of his academic career that his commitment to educational ideals had produced disappointing results. Under his watch, he lamented, Harvard had been so overtaken by a preoccupation with "lands, buildings, collections, money and thousands of students, that I have sometimes feared that to the next generation I should appear as nothing but a successful Philistine."[44]

One failure of the "college system" was its weak record in preparing students for roles in national politics. One searches in vain for signs of serious student interest in the major political issues of the day. In what was one of the most politically dynamic periods of American history, ambitious undergraduates ignored national events and ideas and were preoccupied with the insular world of campus rewards. The competition for places in clubs and honor societies may have been a good rehearsal for getting ahead in American business life, but it was counterproductive for anyone who aspired to be a senator or governor or to be elected to any other office requiring political skills. Whereas the careers of Theodore Roosevelt, William Howard Taft, and Woodrow Wilson exemplified the success of the "collegiate way" of the 1870s and 1880s as prelude to public life, the elite East Coast colleges of the period 1900 to 1920 did a poor job of grooming students to be candidates in national elections. Calvin Coolidge (Amherst class of 1895), elected president of the United States immediately following World War I, was a prime example of the lackluster, staid style of "college man" being turned out by the colleges of the era.

Franklin Delano Roosevelt, elected to four terms as president of the United States, seems to contradict this trend. He was, after all, a Harvard graduate from a wealthy, patrician New York family. On closer inspection, however, one finds that Roosevelt was an exceptional character. He rejected the customary college life of the Harvard "club men," becoming an activist maverick who immersed himself with zeal in newspaper writing and numerous other projects. Years later, during his presidency, he was considered a "traitor to his class." His "New Deal" social and tax policies were seen as a betrayal of the upper class in general and Republicans in particular. And, as became evident at Harvard College reunions, he was openly criticized by most of his fellow alumni as a traitor to his college class of 1904.

The "college system" appears to have worked more effectively as preparation for future political leaders at the young universities of the Midwest and West than at the historic private colleges of the Northeast. By the 1920s, one starts to see young alumni of the state universities running successfully for governor, for state office, and for Congress. The careers of Earl Warren and Robert Sproul typify the "old grad" connections of the young state universities. Warren and Sproul had been close friends at the University of California from 1910 to 1912. Classmates and members of the marching band, they remained in close step during the 1930s, with Warren being elected governor of California and Sproul becoming president of the University of California. Being an alumnus of a state college was often a liability for a candidate trying to woo populist voters, who tended to distrust a college education. Herbert Hoover, who had been a diligent engineering student at Stanford and a member of the first graduating class (1895), was a conspicuous success who combined the Midwestern values of his Iowa childhood with a West Coast sense of adventure and thrift to create a political image that was extremely appealing to American voters. He was a "college man," but more precisely he was a self-made man rather than a "club man."

Perhaps the biggest disappointment of the celebrated "college life" was its emphasis on conformity and its discouragement of imagination. Singing groups and dramatic clubs gave some outlet for creative impulses, but students' dedication to artistic performance was distinctly amateur, secondary to "getting along" with classmates. Nor were the scientific breakthroughs made by professors and students in college laboratories incorporated into the system of campus honors. Accounts of Princeton seniors prior to World War I indicate that many left blank the sections of their graduation questionnaires that asked them to summarize their political interests or professional plans. George Anthony Weller's 1932 novel about life at Harvard, *Not to Eat, Not for Love,* captures the limits of the "college system" between 1890 and 1920 in what would have been a fitting epitaph: "Remember this: the great in college are the near-great afterward, and sometimes they are even less than that."[45]

Other novels of the era reinforce this impression of deficiency. According to F. Scott Fitzgerald, for example, recent Princeton graduates seldom had clear plans for their future. Many drifted into indifferent jobs with brokerage firms obtained through connections with fellow Princetonians. There was no passion, no commitment in their career moves. They made their choices by default, reasoning that the brokerage houses could most likely accommodate a few more close friends.[46] Where was the energy and vision that "college life" was supposed to have instilled in its acolytes? The irony of the Gothic age of the American college was that many of the most interesting students, and student pursuits, were to be found outside the prestige of "college life."

Student Groups and Activities Outside the Dominant Collegiate Culture

The "collegiate culture" was both conspicuous and dominant. Its visibility, however, was disproportionate to the actual number of people involved. In other words, its leaders and proponents were a minority. Large numbers of students were excluded from full citizenship in the culture, and as student bodies increased in size and diversity, the number of outsiders increased as well.

The architectural legacy of the expanded student body in the early 1900s was the student union (figure 6). This building provided an alternative to the eating clubs and secret societies. It acknowledged that the campus was not a cohesive residential entity but rather was characterized by diverse living arrangements, including the arrangements of commuter students. It also represented an attempt by college administrators to exert some influence, perhaps control, over the patterns of student life. The student union movement was a truly nationwide phenomenon. It was the first means by which college officials sought to reduce the dispersion of students into residential cliques, such as the one on Mt. Auburn Street near Harvard Square that was known as the "Gold Coast" because of the expensive private dormitories, favored by wealthy undergraduates, to be found there. Although the elaborate student unions represented a substantial gain for commuter students and other outsiders, it did not diminish the segregation of the various student factions' living arrangements. The wealthier students merely avoided using the student union facilities. From time to time presidents and deans considered building mandatory campus housing for undergraduates, but this was an outrageously expensive proposition that did not come to fruition, even at the most well endowed universities, before 1920.

The Curriculum

Another limitation of the dominant "college system" was that its autonomy from college officialdom (including faculty) caused it to underestimate the significance of changes in the curriculum. The "college system" evidently made few intellectual demands, except perhaps in the acquisition of the ingenuity necessary to evade serious study. Hinds and Noble, the same New York City publisher whose college songbooks enjoyed such brisk sales, made additional forays into the college publishing market. One of its best-sellers among undergraduates in the early 1900s was *College Men's 3-Minute Declamations,* a collection of "up-to-date selections from live men like Chauncey Depew, Hewitt, Gladstone, Cleveland, Presidents Elliot [sic] (Harvard), and Carter (Williams) and others." It promised "new material with vitality in it for prize speaking." The book's success prompted the publishers to offer a companion piece for women students, *College Maids' 3-Minute Readings.* Works like these, along with the flourishing contingent of "cram schools" adjacent to a university campus, allowed students to get ahead without a great deal of effort.

Although most publicity justifiably focused on the "Big Men on Campus," the stars of the athletics teams and social clubs, the American campus had become sufficiently large and complex that it was being transformed on the margins, away from the core of "college life." The

Figure 6. *Postcards of new student union buildings, ca. 1900–1920: (clockwise from top) Stanford University; Indiana University; University of California, Berkeley; Harvard University (The University of South Carolina, Museum of Education, Hawley Postcard Collection)*

proponents of "college life" might have been justified in their indifference to the formal curriculum if, for example, the teaching had been stultifying and course of studies uninteresting. However, the curriculum was being energized and diversified. Unfortunately, such curricular changes were largely unappreciated by the advocates of "college life." The tragedy of the system perpetuated by student leaders was that it kept them from noticing the exciting curricular innovations that were taking place. Ironically, the very success of the "college system" set in motion a counterrevolution—a series of thoughtful, spirited reform movements initiated in the 1920s and 1930s.

Exclusion and Selective Admissions: The Irony of Administrative Reform

For years the increasing popularity of college-going meant that deans and faculties simply expanded enrollments to meet the demand. Given that most colleges had for years had trouble filling their classes, enrollment growth was hardly seen as a problem. Eventually, however, such facilities as lecture halls, laboratories, libraries, and dining halls became saturated.

Colleges used various criteria in deciding which applicants to admit. The main task was to document that an applicant could do college-level work. Options included the College Entrance Examination, usually offered in June, as well as "certificate" arrangements with approved high schools. The University of Michigan was most famous for its statewide school certification program, but the practice was used elsewhere. Brown University, for example, advised applicants to check with their headmaster or principal to see if Brown had certified their secondary school. Finally, each college continued to offer its own battery of entrance examinations, usually in early September before the start of classes.

With a rising number of applicants, however, some colleges ultimately had the luxury of choice in using selective admissions to determine the size and social composition of the student body. In a word, they could be "discriminating" as gatekeepers to the college. This meant that social exclusion was shifted to the admissions office, instead of taking place within the world of student activities and organizations. Perhaps the biggest irony of the advent of selective admissions was that the greatest abuses of intolerance and religious and ethnic discrimination within campus life had taken place at those institutions that were most diverse in the composition of their entering classes. Most conspicuous were the large private urban universities—Harvard, Columbia, and the University of Pennsylvania, as parts, respectively, of the Boston, New York, and Philadelphia metropolitan areas. When serious problems surfaced and factions within the campus clashed, the customary response of college officials was, ironically, to side with the "college system" and reinforce the exclusionary tendencies of the dominant student organizations.

The introduction of "selective admissions" is a case in point. During the 1920s two alumni of New England colleges attempted to persuade college presidents to limit the size of entering freshmen classes. They explained the plan: "It may be said that this method produces an aristocracy of culture. But we must have an aristocracy, if we would have the highest culture, and it will be no less, rather a gain, to the nation and to the world if some of the colleges will be content to remain small, to drop the unworthy and the hopeless, and devote themselves to training for scholarship and leadership."[47] This approach had the potential for both good and ill. If indeed it caused deans of admissions to give priority to applicants with strong academic records and scholarly inclinations, then the approach favored merit. Unfortunately, there is no compelling evidence that selective procedures always rewarded talent. Often as not, the selective-admissions machinery was used to increase the social homogeneity of a campus by rejecting applicants from religious and ethnic minority groups. President Abbott Lawrence Lowell of Harvard and Dean Frederick P. Keppel of Columbia, for example, expressed open concern about the "Jewish problem" at their institutions when estimates of Jewish enrollment reached between 15 percent and 40 percent. Their fear was that such imbalances would scare away applicants from established white Protestant families. Their solution was to impose admissions quotas, both overt and covert. The implications of admissions policies had become more complicated by 1910. Thanks in large measure to the success of the American public high school, college admissions offices had to take seriously the strong academic records presented by a growing number of applicants from cities and schools outside the college's familiar orbit of nearby boarding schools. The nationwide improvements in the college preparatory studies that public high schools provided also raised the question of what was the actual aim of selective-admissions reform. Was it to raise academic standards by identifying talent? Or, rather, was it to use testing as a transparent social screening mechanism whose ultimate accomplishment was to reduce the friction caused by diversity in the student body? As Marcia G. Synnott documented in her 1979 study of admissions policies at Harvard, Yale, and Princeton, the implementation of selective admissions was a peculiar "half-opened door" for talented newcomers from minority backgrounds.[48]

Even if a college opted for admissions policies that made the college student body smaller and more homogeneous, college presidents were still left with the growing problems of an unruly, autonomous student culture. The result at most colleges after 1900 was an expansion of the administrative bureaucracy to include a growing number of deans and assistant deans whose main responsibility was policing student conduct. At the larger universities, mutual avoidance had increased the gulf between students and faculty. Into that void entered the new student-affairs officials who acted as both mediators and enforcers.

The problems spawned by the gregarious "college life" of undergraduates brought about another administrative change. Colleges and universities increasingly recognized that they had to make formal provisions for curbing if not controlling alumni affairs. When alumni associations and clubs first sprouted in the 1890s, college presidents had no precedent for synchronizing their own agendas with these groups' activities. And as alumni and booster groups put more and more energy and money into supporting such student activities as sports, college officials were caught in a curious bind. Presidents had missed their timing: the crucial moment at which they could have exerted authority over external affairs had passed, and now they could no longer afford to alienate alumni as donors. The administrative compromise was to encourage alumni activities and to concede to their involvement in college sports, in the vague hope that this distraction would keep them from meddling in serious academic business. Best of all, this compact might even turn out to stimulate generous support of other university projects.

It was wishful thinking. The typical university president of 1920 had essentially mortgaged his tenure in office in such a way that educational policies had to coexist, and even compete, with the sideshows of college life. Henceforth he would have to cooperate with a coalition that included a board of trustees, an athletics association, and an alumni office that were often all enthusiastic products of the same undergraduate "college system" the academic administration wanted to bring to heel. For the president of a state university, successful alumni were now occupying seats in the state general assembly or even the governor's office, and they all wanted prime seats at the homecoming game. Faculty, probably the least organized campus constituency, were already wary of authoritarian presidents who had little regard for academic freedom. Now that university presidents had to make substantial concessions to alumni groups, professors felt even more distance from campus priorities and decision making.

What presidents discovered was that the same organizational skills and tenacity that undergraduates had brought to "college life" ten or twenty years earlier now resurfaced in highly organized alumni groups and even on boards of trustees. Student leaders might not have excelled in their studies, but they had learned well the lessons of how to control the priorities of the campus.

World War I and the Colleges

Although the United States made a relatively late entrance into World War I, its commitment was extensive. College presidents were supportive of the national war effort. At the same time, they worried that enlistments and a military draft would cut drastically into college enrollments and normal operations. Most student yearbooks dedicated elaborate graphics to patriotic depictions of students devoting themselves to the war effort.

Student enlistments in the armed services varied greatly from campus to campus. According to Lynn Gordon, student participation in the military was especially strong on the East Coast. At Harvard and Yale, for example, enrollments dropped by 40 percent in a single year, with Princeton and Cornell showing declines of 35 percent and 27 percent respectively. On the West Coast, however, only about 10 percent of the students at Stanford left school for military service.[49] Gordon's findings conflict with an anecdotal account in a 1937 Stanford alumni publication, which described how twenty students formed the first Stanford Ambulance Unit in 1918 and reported that eventually "more than half the undergraduates saw service and practically all of those who remained behind prepared themselves in some way or another for participation." Once again college songs play a prominent role in the activities, with Stanford hosting a chorus of ten thousand Student Army Training Corps cadets and soldiers on the university football field in June 1918 to join with Madame Schumann-Heink for what was described as the "world's largest musical event."[50]

Despite the varying degrees of campus military participation, all college presidents expressed a mixture of public support for the war effort and private concern about its impact on their institutions' survival. Given the dependence on enrollments and tuition payments, their fears were warranted. President Woodrow Wilson offered a mutually beneficial solution with the creation of the Student Army Training Corps in July 1917. The SATC quickly established on-campus training programs for cadets and officers that were funded by the federal government and provided generous per capita compensation to the cooperating colleges.[51]

According to Jonathan Frankel, 540 colleges and universities across the United States "turned themselves into training campuses, and roughly 125,000 men were inducted into the Students' Army Training Corps.... Participating institutions received much-needed funds to house, feed and instruct student trainees; in return the government would receive a mentally and physically trained body of fighting men."[52] The significance of the SATC was that it smoothly connected the campus to the larger national war effort. In so doing, according to David O. Levine, it transformed how the American public viewed the campus, and how the campus positioned itself with respect to events unfolding outside the college walls.[53] College and university presidents scored a remarkable coup by persuading national leaders and the public that a comprehensive, effective war commitment required college-trained leaders and also many kinds of civilian expertise that the resilient American campus was best suited to provide. The colleges benefited from having Woodrow Wilson as president of the United States, for he shared with the academic leaders an expanded notion of leadership and national service.

Wilson's support and the colleges' public relations efforts meant that college students would not be subjected to a wholesale conscription into the infantry. In fact, the opposite occurred. Hundreds of thousands of young men were brought onto campuses as part of the SATC. Colleges had to amend their admissions requirements in order to comply with federal guidelines for officer recruitment. Dormitories and gymnasia were converted so as to house military exercises. Uniformed cadets were the typical college students, at least for a few years. Some colleges actually gained both new federally subsidized construction projects and student enrollments, thanks to the SATC. Frankel's case study of the SATC at Harvard illustrates the program's impact.[54] Between the 1916–17 academic year and 1917–18, Harvard's enrollment had declined from 4,976 to 2,998 — representing a decline of $400,000 in tuition income (more than $5.3 million in 2000 dollars). Harvard and other universities, however, paid a price for this militarization of the curriculum. Instruction was predictably slanted toward support of military policies. Customary courses in, for example, history were suspended in favor of more focused, practical studies. By late 1918, reviews of the SATC by university administrators and faculty had concluded that the program had intruded on regular college studies to a troubling degree. What had begun as a good-faith attempt at national service, a promising partnership that would fuse military training with liberal education and simultaneously keep colleges operating financially, turned into yet another necessary evil for academics.

The armed services and the various federal agencies involved in science and technology initiatives did not rely systematically on colleges and universities for expertise during World War I. The standard assumption was that industry, not higher education, was the more reliable source of experience in product development. There were important exceptions, however. Chemist James Conant of Harvard, for example, gained fame for experiments that led to refinements in the use of mustard gas as a weapon. Another sign of change came in 1916 with the formation of the National Research Council and the Naval Research Laboratory, mechanisms for identifying and coordinating talent among industrial, university, and government scientists. But on balance, the major role campus played during World War I was to serve as a convenient site for the training of military personnel. (One notable by-product of this role was the innovative contributions made to the science of large-scale psychological and aptitude testing by university-based psychologists, who developed the tests to be used for military recruits, not college applicants.) Despite the federal government's limited utilization of faculty expertise, the positive example of cooperation during World War I set the stage both for greater public awareness of the campus as a useful resource and for future academic-government partnerships.

World War I did provide a dramatic opportunity for an extension of the "collegiate hero" role: students were serving as ambulance drivers or "ace" fighter pilots for expeditionary forces even before the United States entered the war. Hobey Baker of Princeton, the most famous college figure of the immediate pre–World War I era, personified the gentleman athlete.[55] A graduate of exclusive St. Paul's School, at Princeton he was

CALIFORNIA MEMORIAL STADIUM, UNIVERSITY OF CALIFORNIA 5703

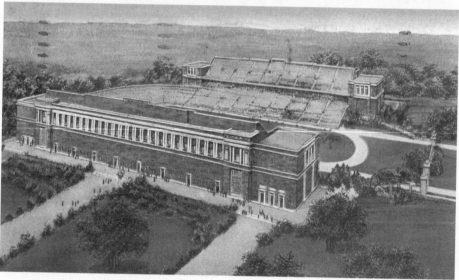

Figure 7. Postcards of new "Memorial Stadiums" for college football, ca. 1904–25: (clockwise from top) Memorial Stadium, University of California, Berkeley; Memorial Stadium, University of Minnesota; Soldier's Field, Harvard University; Memorial Stadium, University of Illinois (The University of South Carolina, Museum of Education, Hawley Postcard Collection)

an All-American player in football and hockey. Most of all, he was famous for his code of sportsmanship, his gentlemanly behavior, and his
good looks. He was the inspiration for the fictional college heroes con-
jured up by his admiring Princeton classmate, F. Scott Fitzgerald. After
graduating in 1914, Baker floundered in his search for a suitable job or
activity. Along with a number of other former college athletes, he joined
the famous Lafayette Escadrille as a pilot. Here was the action and drama,
comparable to that of the college gridiron or hockey rink, that had been
so disappointingly absent from adult life. Soon Baker had become one
of the most celebrated American aces of World War I. His Spad airplane
sported Princeton's black and orange colors, and he earned the respect
of fellow pilots. When he received his discharge at the end of the war,
Baker took off on the ritual farewell maneuvers, saluted by fellow pilots.
But his engine failed, and this heroic veteran of many combat missions
died in the crash. News of Hobey Baker's death and reviews of his flamboyant college accomplishments made headlines in virtually every newspaper in the United States. Princeton honored him by naming its hockey
facility Baker Rink. To this day, each year the outstanding collegiate
hockey player is awarded the Hobey Baker Cup.

Public mourning for the deaths of Hobey Baker and other collegians
who died in World War I underlay another contribution of the Gothic
age of the American college to the national landscape and memory. Perhaps the most visible legacy of World War I on the American campus is
the architectural monuments of the 1920s. Most colleges received abundant donations from alumni and citizens to pay for the construction of
elaborate facilities named in honor of students who had served in World
War I. The most popular monument was the huge football facility, often
called Memorial Stadium, with seating capacities of between thirty
thousand and seventy thousand (figure 7). The proliferation of such
monuments attests that the popular appeal of student extracurricular
life, especially college football as a spectator sport for mass audiences,
was increasing its hold.

6 Success and Excess

Expansion and Reforms
in Higher Education, 1920 to 1945

Building the American Campus: The Commitment
to Mass Higher Education

The impulse to build large football stadiums at colleges and universities across the United States after World War I indicated that the American public was becoming more, not less, interested in higher education, especially its extracurricular activities. Stadium construction was symptomatic of a larger movement to create a monumental campus. The movement had begun between 1890 and 1910 at the historic colleges and was now being extended to underserved regions and cities.

This wave of campus-building signaled a transformation in access to American higher education — a shift away from being a scarce commodity and an elite experience. The nation was edging toward a commitment to mass higher education, a goal that was fueled by the expansion of public secondary schools. Predictably, the increased number of high school graduates created a large new pool of college aspirants. The result was that between World War I and World War II, enrollment in colleges and universities increased more than fivefold, from 250,000 to 1.3 million. Whereas fewer than 5 percent of Americans between the ages of eighteen and twenty attended college in 1917, over the next two decades that figure increased to 15 percent. In 1937 the editors of *Life* magazine, a new national-circulation publication, summarized this demographic and architectural transformation as follows:

> This growth has moved the centre of educational gravity from the Atlantic seaboard to the Middle West. It has made 80% of higher education coeducation. It has changed the campus from a scholarly retreat to a new and fabulous design for four years' living. It has caused colleges to expand and multiply until their mere bricks and stone is worth two billion dollars [$23.9

billion 2000 dollars]. Behind this vast investment is tremendous faith in the benefits of higher education. This faith is a cornerstone of any democratic philosophy, the pith and kernel of what writers since Jefferson have called the American Dream.

Presently the colleges will turn out their annual product—150,000 members of the Class of 1937. These boys and girls—and the others like them who will make up the Classes of 1938, 1939, and 1940—will in 20 years occupy the seats of authority. Only then will the historian be able to tell how far mass higher education has advanced the American Dream.[1]

During this era, the last vestiges of large-scale philanthropy from great industrial fortunes were used to construct startling new campuses. Foremost was a gift of $20 million ($200 million in 2000 dollars) that transformed struggling Trinity College into the imposing medieval-revival spires of Duke University in Durham, North Carolina.[2] Whereas Duke's physical plant was made possible by the tobacco and utilities fortunes of its namesake family, elsewhere the money necessary for campus construction came from a combination of private donations and local fundraising initiatives spread across an entire metropolitan area. The new wealth from Coca-Cola soft drink profits allowed the Candler and Woodruff families in Atlanta to energize Emory University.[3] A similar civic effort went into resurrecting the University of Pittsburgh's campus with its magnificent new "Cathedral of Learning" that housed modern functions amid the medieval motifs of a hybrid form hailed as "girder Gothic."

Duke, Emory, and Pittsburgh, of course, represented the continued popularity of the "university" model. At the same time, other institutional types—including new technical institutes, junior colleges, teachers' colleges, business schools, municipal colleges, women's colleges, labor colleges, Catholic colleges, and regional state colleges—flourished. The "booster college" came of age in the period between the world wars, thanks to the generous support of state legislators, taxpayers, and alumni donors. The period also saw the development of an indigenous American institution, the two-year "junior college," especially in the West and Midwest.[4]

This groundswell of institutional pride and alumni loyalty enabled relatively new state universities to claim a share of the prestige that was once the domain of such institutions as Columbia, Harvard, Chicago, Yale, and Princeton. In the Los Angeles area, donors committed funds to support land acquisition in Westwood, an area of bean fields near Hollywood, in order to create a University of California at Los Angeles out of what had been the modest Southern Branch of the "real" University of California at Berkeley. By 1920, local enthusiasm for the project had raised funds for ornate Mediterranean-style academic buildings, with an attention to detail that extended to importing a large boulder so that UCLA could have its own "Founders Rock" to provide a source of instant heritage. It was the sort of finishing touch that would help many a new campus along in its quest for legitimacy. The founding of UCLA also marked an important structural innovation in the governance of higher education: the multicampus statewide university system.

UCLA's founders were not alone in their attention to campus details. In Louisiana, populist governor Huey Long insisted that marble imported from Italy be used for both the new football stadium and the academic buildings that defined Louisiana State University as the "people's college" in Baton Rouge. One widespread sign of state pride in higher education was found in the WPA Guides published by each state in the mid-1930s, in which colleges and universities were featured as prominent points of interest for tourists and locals alike.

The support for campus construction continued throughout the Great Depression. The *Life* magazine editors noted in 1937:

> There is scarcely an institution of higher learning in the U.S. which does not subscribe to the belief that it is not complete until it has a row of columns somewhere on its campus. On this page are three Ionic proofs that the belief is countrywide. What these columns signify is not a love of classic architecture but an overwhelming respect for the physical entity of a university commonly called its plant. More than $2,250,000,000 [$27 billion in 2000 dollars] is invested in U.S. university plants. It is the plant that the philanthropist thinks of first when giving money to a college. He vastly prefers to construct a building than endow a professor's chair.[5]

Evidence of this passion for building included the columns of the University of Nebraska's Social Science Hall, the main building of the Massachusetts Institute of Technology, and the administration headquarters of Texas A&M College.

At the University of California at Berkeley, the growing power and prestige of the relatively new professional schools were reflected in the classical-revival design of Hilgard Hall, home of the School of Agriculture. Greek-revival columns and a marble bas-relief depicting heroically proportioned cattle heads and shocks of wheat provided the base for the inscription in granite, "TO RESCUE FOR HUMAN SOCIETY THE NATIVE VALUES OF RURAL LIFE." That inspiring bit of public relations was misleading, because the schools of agriculture at Berkeley and elsewhere were actually undermining traditional rural values with the research and development on technology and crop production that they undertook, often at the bidding of powerful associations of growers.[6] Elsewhere on the American campus, new scientific facilities were built that went beyond Spartan functionality and aspired to grandeur. Universities spared no expense in the design of new facilities, whether astronomy observatories and physics laboratories, dormitories and student centers, or sports arenas.

College Sports

Not only did colleges build large football stadiums, they also filled them with paying customers. Intercollegiate athletics soared as a major source of campus public relations. The University of Southern California and Notre Dame scheduled annual games, alternating between Los Angeles and Chicago. At both sites crowds often surpassed 100,000, with a record attendance of over 120,000 achieved in 1929 at Chicago's Soldier Field. Few other games could match such numbers, but many came close. Traditional rivalries, including such annual games as Harvard versus Yale, Michigan versus Ohio State, Stanford versus California, and Texas versus Texas A&M, were usually played out to sellout crowds ranging from sixty thousand to seventy-five thousand. Intersectional football games and the dedication of a sparkling new stadium became a symbolic rite of passage for an ambitious university claiming newfound stature. Such was the case when the University of Georgia hosted the famous Yale football team at the dedication of Georgia's new Sanford Stadium in 1929. (The University of Georgia, founded by Yale alumni in 1785, had long invoked its Yale ties. This even extended to its having the same mascot as Yale teams: the Bulldog.) This event marked the first time that Yale had allowed its football team to travel outside the Northeast for a game. To crown this landmark in the University of Georgia's saga, the university hosted a weeklong celebration in honor of its Yale guests, and then for the first time defeated the Yale football team.[7]

Across the nation, the enthusiasm for football extended to such other intercollegiate sports as basketball, track and field, crew, and swimming. The regional trends in attendance and national championships signaled a redistribution of college sports success. According to *Life* magazine in 1937, the persistent trend was that "sports records move West":

> In the past two decades, athletic reputation has largely moved West and South. A host of high-school athletes, graduating in the elaborate sports arenas of the State universities, have rudely trampled the belief of an older generation that Harvard, Yale, Princeton, Cornell and Pennsylvania symbolized greatness at football, crew and track. Today Minnesota dominates the $30,000,000 [in 2000 dollars, $360 million] football business that draws 20,000,000 people into stadiums each autumn. Today, Washington rules the rivers and its graduates coach the Eastern crew. For the past decade a handful of Stanford and University of Southern California track men have monotonously beaten the East whenever their teams chanced to meet. In specialized sports, the University of California is tops in tennis; and Michigan, having wrested swimming supremacy from Yale, now vies with Yale at golf.[8]

This is not to say that the historic East Coast colleges had declined in either emphasis or ability. Rather, varsity sports talent had become distributed nationwide. Coaches at Harvard and Yale, for example, could still boast of outstanding football teams. They also had to acknowledge that the innovative, adventurous passing attacks and talented players who graduated from public high schools in Texas and California were not intimidated by the historic records that the Ivy League institutions had established decades earlier. The growing strength and regional pride of the Midwest were perhaps best exemplified by Governor Harold Stassen of Minnesota, whose speeches often cited the connection between the state's greatness and the success of the University of Minnesota's national-championship football teams of the 1930s.

The downside to the nationwide popularity of intercollegiate sports was that athletics directors and ambitious coaches continually stretched the limits of acceptable practice. Abuses became so rampant that the Carnegie Foundation for the Advancement of Teaching (CFAT) undertook a detailed, systematic three-year study of the condition of college sports. Howard Savage's report for the CFAT was released in October 1929 and received headline coverage in newspapers nationwide.[9] Numerous presidents and athletics directors fussed and fumed that the report was inaccurate. But it was not, and Howard Savage and the Carnegie Foundation's board provided elaborate documentation for their claims. The report's finding was that college officials, including presidents and professors, had forfeited control of the public spectacles. En-

terprising coaches had emerged as influential, prosperous, and sometimes corrupt public figures. Furthermore, local business interests (which
the report called the "downtown group") pushed hard to increase the
commercial potential of intercollegiate football. The CFAT recommended
that presidents take back control of the campus sports programs.[10]

In the years immediately following the release of Savage's 1929 study,
intercollegiate athletics experienced some decline in revenues and spectator attendance. This was not due to any popular saturation with college
sports (as the Carnegie Foundation's representatives had hoped would
take place). Rather, nationwide economic problems associated with the
unemployment of the Great Depression simply meant that Americans
had fewer discretionary dollars to spend on sports tickets than they had
in the 1920s. Even after the stock market crash of 1929 had caused university resources to dwindle, university officials continued to accommodate alumni and public zeal for the building of football stadiums. At
Southern Methodist University in Dallas, for example, the board of
trustees garnisheed faculty wages in 1931 to pay off debts for the new
football stadium whose plans had originally been approved during the
boom years of 1927–28.[11]

By 1935, college football game attendance had recovered from its temporary decline and proceeded to surpass all previous records. As for the
kinds of structural reforms advocated by the Carnegie Foundation, some
presidents and athletics directors worked to strengthen accountability by
forming conferences, many of which included the new position of commissioner. These measures were not especially effective, and college
sports officials — with the blessings of their presidents and boards of
trustees — devoted more attention (and resources) to promoting big-
time sports than to curbing its excesses. For example, as Murray Sperber
has documented, athletics directors increasingly relied on the services of
high-powered Madison Avenue advertising agencies for publicizing varsity games. The Don Spencer Agency of New York City energized college
sports promotions nationwide with high-quality programs and posters.
The advertising agencies increasingly viewed intercollegiate athletics
and its spectators as a media market to be exploited. Newspaper publishers also cashed in on this lucrative market in a variety of ways, ranging
from daily coverage to more elaborate campaigns to promote trophy
winners and ticket sales. Athletics directors, coaches, presidents, trustees,
and alumni association officials were informed, willing participants in
the various efforts mounted in press rooms, radio network offices, movie

studios, and public relations firms. At the same time, academic leaders showed little commitment to establishing a national organization devoted to regulating the business of college sports.[12]

Trouble in Paradise: Popular Images of Campus Life

If the colleges became famous between the world wars for their magnificent architecture and big-time sports, they also became notorious for the hedonistic behavior of their students and alumni. Whereas the "college man" of 1890–1900 had been portrayed as a gentleman, the image changed between 1920 and 1930. Homecoming celebrations, commencement week reunions, proms, year-round fraternity gatherings—all were associated with alcohol. Bathtub gin, speakeasies, gambling on college sports, and the other stereotyped activities that characterized the roaring twenties had now ceased to be the exclusive province of Chicago gangsters and New York racketeers; they dominated the popular image of campus life as well. College life also came to be associated with distinctive clothing and accessories—during the 1920s, yellow rain slickers, corduroy trousers, and baggy sweaters. A decade later, saddle shoes for women and tweed jackets and oxford-cloth button-down-collar shirts for men had become the collegiate conventions. National magazines regularly featured articles and advertisements with "back to college" themes in their September issues. In 1936, Macy's Department Store of New York City jumped on the college bandwagon, marketing styles for the "Champion of the Ivy League" with the following prospect for autumn fashions: "Our college traveler reports from every stage of his tour of the New England seats of learning that undergraduates are tally-hoeing like mad after covert—the hardy and handsome fabric so long identified with the hardy and smart English fox-hunting man. Now its popularity is spreading to the university club in the city."[13]

A preoccupation with undergraduate life surfaced in serious literature as well as articles and advertisements. F. Scott Fitzgerald and Percy Marks were the most prominent practitioners of this genre, in such novels as *The Far Side of Paradise* and *The Plastic Age*. Profiles of campus life, ranging from the elitism of Yale to the rough-and-tumble culture of medical students at the University of Minnesota, surfaced in the novels of Sinclair Lewis. Fiction was only one medium for the distribution of collegiate imagery. It was also projected weekly in the nationally syndicated cartoons of John Held in the 1920s, and it extended to the Hollywood movies of the 1930s, including such box-office hits as the Marx Brothers' *Horse Feathers*. The anti-intellectualism of the era was captured in the ethos of the "gentleman's C" as the exalted standard of minimal scholastic performance.

The popular imagery of higher education cut across gender lines. The archetypal "college woman" of the period between the world wars shared in the celebration of misbehavior associated with the flapper and the "new woman." Whether in movies or magazines, audiences were titillated by hints of promiscuity on the campus. Dorothy Parker of the *New Yorker* wrote sarcastically about misbehavior at the Yale prom. In 1921 the headlines for one Boston tabloid announced in bold print, " 'Petting Parties' of Love Hungry Girls Shock College Boys." The subheadline elaborated, "Astonishing Things the Society Buds Do at Brown University Dances Bring Sharp Scoldings in the College Newspaper."[14] Graphic commentary that would not have been tolerated in print at the turn of the century had come to be accepted with a wink and a nod by a new generation of sophisticated readers who expected, even relished, tales of collegiate excess.

The college woman as socialite was a phenomenon that spread to all regions of the country. By the 1930s, magazine coverage of Midwestern state universities, such as the University of Missouri in Columbia, included photographs of women enjoying the leisurely life of debutantes and sorority members. Stephens College — a private two-year college for women, also in Columbia — gained distinction for its Georgian campus that provided a riding academy, stables for thirty-six horses, and a country club. Its curriculum included the "world's largest Bible class" and a "grooming clinic" (for students, not horses) offered by a New York cosmetics expert. As one journalist noted in 1937, "Surpassing in swank even such swank Eastern schools as Bennington and Sarah Lawrence, Stephens takes a long midyear outing. This year President Wood took his girls to New Orleans, commandeered 262 Tulane men for a dance, came on to New York, commandeered West Point for another dance."[15]

Humorous depictions of higher education became a recurrent theme of the full-colored covers and feature articles of the *Saturday Evening Post*. Even the extended economic crisis of the Great Depression could not dampen the American public's fascination with the subject. Perhaps the most conspicuous evidence of this enduring appeal was the attention higher education received in the pages of *Life* magazine. Its issue of 7

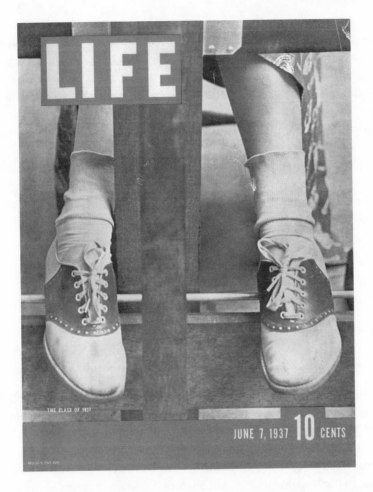

Figure 8.   Cover of Life *magazine, 7 June 1937 (TimePix, Inc.)*

June 1937 was entirely devoted to all facets of the American campus (figure 8).

Why was the American public so fascinated by, and tolerant of, the antics of college students? According to David O. Levine, "going to college" had become sufficiently entrenched in the American "culture of aspiration" between the world wars that youthful indiscretions were tolerated and even encouraged as part of the process of upward social mobility that the college facilitated.[16] If an undergraduate made "good contacts" and associated with the "right crowd," unrestrained parties and the spectacles of football weekends were a small price to pay. Indeed, the high jinks of campus social life were often seen as a sign that a son or daughter had become part of a secular elect. Just as England's shopkeepers of the early nineteenth century expected elite young military officers *not* to pay their extravagant tailoring bills, so the American public expected a new elite of college students to prove their status by misbehaving in ritualized ways.

If there were complaints about such accounts of student life, they often came from envious colleges whose activities were not being covered in the press. The undergraduate editor of Ohio State University's *Daily Lantern* complained to the editor of *Life* about the regional bias of the allegedly "national" photojournalism:

> We college students out here in the Midwest have a complaint to register concerning your magazine. Ever since you began publishing you have on occasions, carried pictures showing college life in American universities—but so far you have apparently assumed that there are no American universities this side of the Alleghenies.
>
> We, out here in the educational hinterland have enjoyed your pictures of eastern schools—but darn it, we do things out here too.[17]

Students and alumni from numerous colleges and universities throughout the country echoed this refrain. A Cornell alumnus was especially miffed that the phrase "Harvard, Yale, and Princeton . . . and perhaps Cornell" dominated most discussions about great American universities. He countered by listing all the innovations Cornell had contributed to American higher education, and concluded that discussions about campus greatness should begin with the words "Cornell . . . and perhaps Harvard, Yale, and Princeton."[18]

The Media and Higher Education: Popular Images of the American Campus

For decades, print media had allowed Americans to read about the prestigious colleges and to study the images of campus life captured in photographs. And now, radio broadcasts enabled listeners to be part of the live events of a big football game. Indeed, the nationwide radio broadcasts of Notre Dame's football games created an entirely new constituency: the "subway alumni" who had never set foot on the Notre Dame campus in South Bend, Indiana, yet who listened to every game and sent in donations. Thanks to these broadcasts, priests in such distant places as Brooklyn regularly reminded parishioners to root and pray for the "Fighting Irish." Nuns teaching in Catholic elementary schools in Cleveland or Seattle would mention Notre Dame's games to their students. Notre Dame was the biggest beneficiary of such broadcasts. Other institutions enjoyed smaller (though still considerable) increases in the number of their faithful fans through the help of radio.

If the sounds of campus life as broadcast on radio were compelling to the American public, moving images were even more irresistible. Movies, especially talking movies, with campus settings were an attractive draw for viewing audiences, who flocked to theaters nationwide to view a succession of Hollywood productions. For the price of a matinee ticket one could watch privileged undergraduates without actually setting foot on a college campus or sitting in a university lecture hall. Even though only a small percentage of Americans actually attended college, now anyone could become a vicarious alumnus.

A classic example of this genre is the Marx Brothers' *Horse Feathers* (figure 9). Released in 1932, at the height of the Great Depression, the movie drew on the experiences and events of earlier decades, presenting the vaudeville stage humor of turn-of-the-century immigrant groups amid the props and stages of the 1920s. Set at fictional Huxley College, archrival to Darwin University, the loose plot revolves around Groucho Marx's inauguration as President Wagstaff. The college is in financial trouble, has indifferent students, and has suffered several years of losing football teams. Wagstaff, a businessman, has been recruited to rescue the sinking college. The audience is treated to a cast of familiar stereotypes: dawdling professors, fawning deans who agree with everything the president says, and well-tailored students who sit good-naturedly through dull lectures. Although the classroom is featured in numerous scenes, the main events revolve around football. Alumni and local businessmen bet on the games, and college administrators obsess about recruiting brawny working-class lads for the team. Presidents, gamblers, and boosters have a common meeting ground in the town's speakeasy.

There are some accurate elements among the caricatures. The student body is coeducational, made up of good-natured young men and women, all of them white and prosperous. The "tramp athletes" are Irish — "Mullins" and "Molloy." The only black character in the movie is a hotel maid.

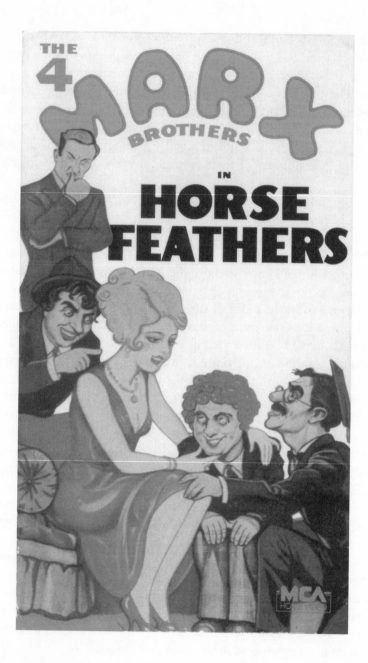

Figure 9. Poster for the Marx Brothers movie Horse Feathers, *1932 (MCA Home Video, Inc.)*

Two of the Marx Brothers step outside their Jewish immigrant identity to portray Italian immigrants who work as street vendors.

Horse Feathers was one of many popular movies that dealt with college life. At the end of the interwar period, the 1941 Hollywood biography of the legendary Notre Dame football coach Knute Rockne reinforced the collegiate celebration and was the top box-office movie of the year.

Reconstructing Campus Life: Student Memoirs

Media depictions of undergraduate life were understandably slanted toward extracurricular activities and flamboyant behavior. The distortion did not go unnoticed by the university community of the day. In 1923 a famed Harvard historian lectured at Brown University on the difficulty of reconstructing the character of student life at medieval universities. To emphasize his point he cited his own times, noting, "The studious lad of today never breaks into the headlines as such, and no one has seen fit to produce a play or film 'featuring the good student.' Yet everyone familiar with contemporary universities knows that the serious student exists in large numbers."[19] According to a report on undergraduate life at Dartmouth, "to those of a conservative temper, it quite naturally seems that Dartmouth, founded to Christianize the heathen, has now degenerated into heathenizing Christians."[20] Even Lucius Beebe—famous in adult life as a wealthy man of sport and leisure and holder of the dubious distinction of being the only student to have been expelled for misconduct from both Harvard and Yale—thought press coverage of the elite colleges was off the mark. He believed that editors and writers treated the campus merely as an "inexhaustible source of gratifying upper-class tumults."[21] Undergraduates were amused by the superficiality of popular "college novels." The student editors of the *Harvard Lampoon* ridiculed the genre by composing a formula for aspiring authors:

> It is well to begin by spending at least half a day at the University, jotting down the names of streets and buildings. You will depend on these for local color.
>
> Make your characters extravagant, financially and otherwise. Make them appear several times stretched in lounging robes before a blazing fire while the rain patters on the window panes—at least once in the front row at the Tremont.
>
> Make them drink frequently and variously, and smoke on every possible

pretext. Put a bull pup in each chapter and a Morris chair on every page. Talk familiarly of the Regent, Gore Hall, and clubs. . . . Introduce a girl who is innocuous and one or two who are not.[22]

In contrast to the popular images of an exhilarating campus life, many accounts by students suggest that the American campus was a sober, even somber place in the late 1920 and 1930s. A wealth of information can be drawn from the literary legacy of students and recent alumni who took the time to set down their experiences in memoirs, short stories, and novels. This was the golden age of student journalism and student writing. The campus newspaper, edited and published by student associations, came into its own. Another enterprise was the student humor magazine—an enduring source of insights and satire as well as a training ground for a future generation of American authors.

Undergraduates had customarily been at odds with their elders, whether parents, professors, or deans. The student hero often was the nimble classmate who could hold his own in debates with faculty and administrators. Students admired those of their fellows who could navigate the organization well enough to fulfill minimal degree requirements while pursuing maximal extracurricular activities. The ultimate administrative rule at Harvard was that a student should maintain three Cs and a D and keep his name out of the newspaper.

Such was the administrative arena in which undergraduates lived and learned. At Princeton in the early 1930s one freshman attained legendary status when a history professor stopped his lecture to scold him for having his eyes closed. Having been reprimanded for failure to pay attention, the student—Edward Prichard—proceeded, without opening his eyes, to summarize the professor's remarks, even correcting some factual inaccuracies.[23] Prichard was bright but not a "grind." These qualities served him well not only as a folk hero among Princeton undergraduates. Later, at Harvard Law School, he was editor of the *Law Review* and was selected to clerk for a justice of the Supreme Court. Yet his law school courses were secondary to his participation in various political campaigns. After law school he went to Washington, D.C. A member of Franklin Delano Roosevelt's "Brain Trust," he was considered the ultimate wit. His brilliant legal briefs won him respect. His impersonations of public figures—a skill acquired at Princeton—made him a favorite of President Roosevelt.

Prichard, a bright boy from Kentucky, had made an impressive ascent.

Another self-made collegiate "All American" of the 1930s was Byron White of the University of Colorado. The son of a poor Colorado farming and mining family, White graduated first in his undergraduate class and also won national honors as a star football halfback. He played professional football to earn money for law school. Later he was appointed a justice of the Supreme Court. The success of such collegiate heroes as Ed Prichard and Byron "Whizzer" White — a nickname he deplored — reinforced the American belief in college as a vehicle for upward mobility based on talent and perseverance.

There was, of course, some truth to the mythology. On balance, however, the intricacies and rewards of the collegiate social system introduced students to the realities rather than to the ideals of American society. Talent alone was seldom sufficient to get ahead. Hence one legacy of the "golden age of college life" that diffused into the 1920s and 1930s was a tendency for students at all the campuses to be split into haves and have-nots — usually along the lines of the Greek-letter system of fraternities and sororities versus the ranks of the "Independents." Power and prestige went disproportionately to the self-perpetuating social organizations. Despite this schism, all students endured — and recalled — the shared experience of trying to make sense of the curriculum's elective system and to find their way around a large campus.

James Thurber, most famous for his decades of humorous writing at the *New Yorker,* wrote memorably about his freshman year at Ohio State University. The essay confirms that while presidents and professors may have been exhilarated by the new elective system and the expanded mission of the university during the interwar years, most entering freshmen had little knowledge of or interest in this grand institutional design. The elective system was more often than not a shared experience in surviving such obligations as passing a swimming examination, completing a course in a life science, or fulfilling an ROTC drilling obligation with rifles left over from the Civil War.[24]

Thurber's bemused recollection of mass higher education at a Midwestern state university was similar in tone to Robert Benchley's recollection of Harvard. In recalling "What College Did to Me," Benchley left a guidebook to assist future generations of undergraduates in navigating the curriculum. He noted with mock gravity:

> My college education was no haphazard affair. My courses were all selected with a very definite aim in view, with a serious purpose in mind — no class

before eleven in the morning or after two-thirty in the afternoon—and nothing on Saturday at all. That was my slogan. On that rock was my education built.

As what is known as the Classical Course involved practically no afternoon laboratory work, whereas in the Scientific Course a man's time was never his own until four p.m. anyway, I went in for the classics. But only such classics as allowed for a good sleep in the morning. Man has his health to think of. There is such a thing as being a studying fool.

For Benchley, the elective system meant enrolling in such courses as Fine Arts 6 ("Doric Columns: Their Uses, History and Various Heights") on Tuesdays and Thursdays at 1:30, and in Music 9 ("History and Appreciation of the Clavichord") on Wednesdays and Fridays at noon. He fulfilled his foreign language requirement with German 12b ("Early Minnesingers—Walter von Vogelweider, Ulric Glannsdorf and Freimann von Stremhofen: Their Songs and Times"). When confronted with an exam question dealing with maritime relations between the United States and Newfoundland, Benchley tried to distract the instructor with the rhetorical question, "Has any one considered this from the point of view of the fish?"[25]

Given the rigor of his courses, Benchley devised a study system that was "no less strict." He recalled, "In lecture courses I had my notebooks so arranged that one-half page could be devoted to drawings of five-pointed stars (exquisitely shaded), girls' heads, and tick-tack-toe. Some of the drawings in my economics notebook in the course on Early English Trade Winds were the finest things I have ever done. One of them was a whole tree (an oak) with every leaf in perfect detail. Several instructors commented on my work in this field." At his dormitory, an evening "seminar" just happened to include a poker hand, dealt in front of a vacant chair. When a student said, "I'll open for fifty cents," the seminar would be on. Benchley concluded, "At the end of the seminar, I would go back to my desk, pile the notes and books on top of each other, put the light out, and go to bed, tired but happy in the realization that I had not only spent the evening busily but had helped put four of my friends through college."[26]

Thurber recalled an exasperated drill instructor once telling him, "You are the main trouble with this university!" But as Thurber understood, the problem was not himself literally or singularly, but rather students like himself.[27] To deal with the growing size of entering classes, full of such indifferent or independent-thinking undergraduates as

Thurber and Benchley, university administrators started to add the machinery of student-affairs officers. George Anthony Weller described the
"young dean" at Harvard as follows:

> He was a slim middle-sized man of twenty-eight who was usually dressed
> in dark blue, with brown hair smoothly parted in the middle and a decent
> oval face. He had been a baseball manager and third marshall of his class,
> and there was a place waiting for him in the Dean's office when he came
> back from his year at Cambridge. They had made him Dean of Records,
> which meant days of writing letters like: "I regret to inform you that the
> Committee has not found it possible to grant your petition to retake the
> midyear examination in Geography 12." . . . Sometimes he said, "Please feel
> free to call at my office," or, "If at any time I can be . . ." And he always said,
> "It has not been found possible," because there was still for him in the word
> "impossible" something too much like a knell. He knew the Catalogue and
> the past decisions of the committee. . . . When queries came to him he did
> not answer directly if he could help it. He reached for the Catalogue of
> Courses, and with a lean hand, he passed over the book, opening at the
> solving page.[28]

The student-affairs staff emphasized the enforcement of regulations.
Most likely, college administrators had an uneasy sense that the expanded
numbers of students had put the institution in a precarious situation—namely, one of increased responsibility for student conduct and
decreased ability to control it. Institutions devoted little expertise and
few resources to retention or to counseling. Many professors regarded
the requirement of serving as a faculty advisor to large numbers of marginal students as a necessary evil, to be fulfilled in a perfunctory manner.
Students who were either indifferent or bewildered were equally bored
by the required meetings with an assigned advisor. As a result, the dropout rate, especially at state universities, was high. In fact, undergraduate
education between the world wars was characterized by high attrition
even at prestigious institutions. Consider the profile of the class of 1929
at Harvard College. It was relatively large by national standards, with
about one thousand having entered as freshmen. Four years later, 356 had
either dropped out, transferred, or failed to complete degree requirements. Indicative of increasing geographic and socioeconomic diversity
was that 130 were from public high schools in the Midwest and West and
135 were from East Coast public high schools. About three-fourths came
from various New England private schools.[29]

The undergraduate preoccupation with the cat-and-mouse game of the "hidden curriculum" was neither entirely surprising nor unwarranted. Despite the bold pronouncements and hopes for the "great American university" of 1910, the American campus of the 1920s and 1930s was a grim, isolated place. A good account of this situation is provided in Edward Shils's matter-of-fact recollection of his undergraduate days at the University of Pennsylvania in the 1930s. According to Shils, in the 1930s the American professorate saw itself—and was seen— as comparable to a "priesthood, rather uneven in their merits but uniform in their bearing; they never referred to anything personal. Some read from old lecture notes. . . . Others lectured from cards that had served for years, to judge by the worn and furry edges which were visible to students who like myself sat in the front of the lecture room. The teachers began on time, ended on time, and left the room without saying a word more to their students, very seldom being detained by questioners." Shils went on to recall, "The classes were not large, yet there was no discussion. No questions were raised in class, and there were no office hours."[30] Professors possessed expertise, as documented by their holding of a Ph.D., but seldom were public figures or celebrity experts interviewed by reporters or asked to be guests on radio shows. Their pull was inward. The university was a citadel or haven, not a publicity-minded entity.

Shils was not alone in invoking the priesthood metaphor for faculty. Brendan Gill, longtime editor of the *New Yorker,* recalled his undergraduate days at Yale, where students noticed that many of their professors did not marry and lived in rented apartments near campus. According to Gill, salaries were sufficiently low that many Yale professors could not afford to support families, settling instead for a bachelor life of books and scholarship.[31]

Teaching at the University of Pennsylvania and elsewhere was dominated by the lecture format, not only for high-enrollment introductory courses but also for most upper-division work as well. The professor typically lectured while students quietly took notes. There was little discussion. Both students and professors were wary of any faculty member who drifted into fraternization with students or who brought personal asides into classroom teaching. Even at such universities as Penn or Brown, research and writing for publication remained curiously marginal activities. Professors squirmed uncomfortably if a president hinted that published scholarship ought to be a job requirement.

Although Shils's classes at the University of Pennsylvania may have been reasonably small, many universities accommodated expanding enrollments by increasing the number of lecture seats. At the University of Wisconsin, for example, an introductory course in economics enrolled over 840 students. The standard procedure was to have the lectures—taught by a senior professor—divided into smaller discussion groups led by a graduate student, known as "the section man" in undergraduate parlance. The large classes at Wisconsin and Berkeley were extreme. The lecture format, however, was pervasive.

For parents, alumni, and legislators, higher education overwhelmingly meant undergraduate education. The quiet transformation that was taking place outside the public purview was the gradual expansion of graduate studies, including master's and doctoral programs. The authors of college novels of the era noted the increasing appeal of professional schools such as law and medicine. However, their observations are not altogether flattering. At Harvard, undergraduates considered law school students to be second-class citizens, grinds who were wholly separated from campus life.[32] The towering figure in the system was the stern, charismatic lecturer who was simultaneously demanding and aloof. From the perspective of formal institutional history, Harvard Law School was hailed for having shored up its curriculum with its distinctive case-study method. But what did this mean for the law student? The Harvard Law School of the 1920s and 1930s did not employ selective admissions. Rather, the approach was to allow most applicants to enter and then to subject first-year students (known as "One L's") to a demanding, highly impersonal experience characterized by strict grading on course examinations. The result was that the entering class was large—from six hundred to seven hundred students—but the attrition rate was high, often approaching 40 percent.[33]

Ph.D. programs of study were highly specialized. Graduate students usually worked on very specific topics, often as apprentices to senior faculty members. They occupied a marginal position in the campus world. There were some important exceptions. When Edwin Shils finished his bachelor's degree at Pennsylvania, he entered a Ph.D. program at the University of Chicago, where he found a distinctive institutional environment of lively debate, intense scholarly energy, and give-and-take between graduate students and professors. This was not, however, the typical experience of graduate students at most universities. Economist John Kenneth Galbraith, recalling his doctoral studies in agricultural economics at Berkeley in the 1930s, noted that, like most graduate students, he stayed late at the library each night. At midnight closing, he walked back to his cheap apartment, passing through fraternity row, where he heard singing and carefree laughter, punctuated by "what Evelyn Waugh correctly described as the most evocative and nostalgic of all the sounds of an aristocracy at play, the crash of breaking glass. Here were men with a secure position in society and who knew it and who were content."[34] Galbraith and his fellow graduate students knew that this was a collegiate world of which they would never be a part. They accepted this in a matter-of-fact way and proceeded to carve out their own groups and activities within the university world.

Accounts of graduate student life at Harvard paint a similar picture. Undergraduates either ignored graduate students or viewed them with a combination of pity, contempt, and transient curiosity. A Harvard undergraduate walking around Cambridge one night saw the "long silent hall of the fifth floor in Perkins, where burnt late the desk lamps of graduate students in zoology, mathematics, Slavic languages." At an art history lecture, "only the graduate students at the front of the room were listening, it seemed"—and one of them, the fashionable undergraduate noted, was wearing white socks. Only the lonely graduate students remained around the campus during Christmas vacation. Commuters, whether undergraduates or graduate students, were also despised for being unrefined "grinds": "The commuting students, carrying briefcases, many wearing tortoise shell glasses with extra lenses of power, are coming up out of the subway, talking examinations. Unlike those who live in the dormitories, who are now ordering breakfast in the restaurants in the Square, they will be too early for nine o'clock lectures. . . . While they wait they put the time to advantage by rereading their notes." The wealthy students' disdain for the commuters was a mixture of anti-intellectualism and anti-Semitism. A typical commuter student was one "Abraham Eckstein, who lives in a Dorchester threedecker and whose father did piece-work in Brooklyn, but now owns his own little shop." Members of the Princeton eating clubs and the Harvard "final clubs" occasionally offered admission to a few "good natured Irishmen who were athletes" as a concession to democracy—a transparent gesture that fooled no one.[35]

Generous donations by the Rockefeller Foundation allowed a small number of prestigious universities to establish remarkable International Houses. The University of California, the University of Chicago, Harvard, and Cornell were among those that benefited from such philanthropy. Although the composition of their undergraduate student bodies reflected the overwhelming localism that characterized virtually all American campuses, these institutions were able to attract a number of foreign students, suggesting at least a slim commitment to transcending provincialism in the student experience. Several American colleges and universities also gained an international perspective in their faculty as a result of war and dislocations in Europe. Refugee scholars from German universities, purged from their academic appointments by the Nazi administration, fled to the United States and often accepted teaching appointments at institutions that previously would never have been able to recruit such talent. However, the impact of such newcomers on the tenor of undergraduate life was minimal, or at best uneven.

Despite the emphasis on conformity and the tendency to give conspicuous rewards to a closed social elite, the American campus between 1920 and 1940 had one saving grace: its complexity. The same labyrinth of course requirements and campus offices that bewildered students as freshmen ultimately provided the nooks and crannies wherein students could explore and demonstrate diverse talents. To be an honors student and departmental undergraduate assistant in physics, for example, hardly brought a junior or senior the adulation associated with being elected president of the interfraternity council. But it did provide opportunities for specialized scholarship, and prospects for graduate study and a career path that would have been unheard of a decade earlier. Similar scenarios existed for the fine arts, performing arts, and other new fields. Whether or not one gained membership in a Greek-letter fraternity or sorority, the typical campus provided ample clubs, libraries, museums, and special collections that allowed serious students to immerse themselves in the academic life.

From time to time at major universities graduate students and senior professors built strong networks that made the campus the home of a substantial academic experience. In this era before low airfare and routine travel to distant national conferences, established and aspiring scholars alike had to rely on colleagues in the local setting. According to John Kenneth Galbraith, Berkeley professors sought out discussions, even arguments, with doctoral students over coffee or beer. Hubert Humphrey, later a senator and vice president of the United States, recalled his days as a professor of political science at the University of Minnesota, where the high point of the week was having waffles for dinner with graduate students who talked for hours about scholarly trends and contemporary politics.[36] Comparable scenarios were reenacted at every campus, although they have rarely worked their way into the official histories of colleges and universities because these incidents and alliances were seldom included in such conspicuous records as senior yearbooks and campus newspaper articles.

The New Women's Colleges

Women had a strong numerical presence in higher education between the world wars, constituting about 40 percent of the undergraduate enrollment in 1940—a substantial increase, considering that sixty years earlier, few women had even been permitted to work toward a bachelor's degree. This dramatic gain was due in large measure to the appeal of the new women's colleges as well as the policies of coeducation at many institutions. The statistical record, however, tends to mask the essential tensions that persisted in discussions as to what the educational options for American women should be.

One perplexing issue raised by the statistical summary is whether women were indeed gaining increased access. According to David O. Levine, the largest proportional gains for women as undergraduates took place between 1890 and 1910, at which time women represented more than 40 percent of college enrollments. As a percentage of total enrollments, then, women's share actually declined slightly between the world wars. However, the huge increases in total enrollments for all students between the wars meant that far more women had access to college in 1940 than in 1910. The number of women undergraduates increased from about three hundred thousand just prior to World War I to about six hundred thousand on the eve of World War II.[37]

A second, more subtle source of concern is that between 1910 and 1940 the historic women's colleges seem to have lost the clarity of purpose and energy that had characterized their pioneering years. As was true of American higher education in general, there was no consensus among the women's colleges as to what the undergraduate experience ought to be. Smith College, for example, drifted away from its commitment to building a great women's university. By the 1930s Vassar offered a rigorous academic undergraduate curriculum, yet with an emphasis on preparing young women for roles as wives and civic volunteers. Such new institutions as Sarah Lawrence College in New York, Scripps College in California, and Bennington College in Vermont were part of a new generation of women's colleges that came of age in the 1930s. The new spirit of what has been called Progressive education was expressed in the Scripps College motto, "Incipit vita nova" (A new life begins). Each of the new women's colleges made good on this curricular promise by shaping a distinctive course of study and hiring faculty according to innovative criteria. There is little doubt that the prestigious women's colleges were special places. Nonetheless, the sense was that women were still being segregated within the curriculum.

The commitment to increasing educational opportunities for women did not entail a commitment to reducing discrimination according to class, ethnicity, or race. Sarah Lawrence College, for example, relied on a strict quota system in the 1930s that discreetly (and effectively) limited the number of Jewish women admitted.[38] Bennington College gained renown of sorts as the most expensive college in the nation, with annual tuition charges of $1,650 ($20,500 in 2000 dollars). To add to the price of the undergraduate experience, Bennington's students were expected to experience "metropolitan life" and live at their own expense in such places as New York City during the generous breaks from the academic term. Whether intentional or not, such expectations tended to put a private women's college beyond the financial (as opposed to intellectual) grasp of talented young women.

By the 1930s the historic women's colleges known as the Seven Sisters — Wellesley, Radcliffe, Smith, Mount Holyoke, Vassar, Barnard, and Bryn Mawr — had acquired a collective reputation as the alma maters of a talented, privileged elite of American women. It was an identity that gave little attention to social justice in matters of race or economic class. According to Linda M. Perkins, prior to World War II these seven women's colleges had graduated only a few hundred black women, although their total alumnae ranks numbered over ten thousand.[39] Within their circle, there were some significant differences in policies and practices. Wellesley and Smith, for example, had a heritage of access, having admitted black women applicants since the late nineteenth century. In contrast, Vassar, Barnard, and Bryn Mawr showed little evidence of even modest accommodation. M. Carey Thomas, the founding and longtime president of Bryn Mawr, was an outspoken advocate of Anglo-Saxon superiority and purity and explicitly refused to consider black women as candidates for admission during her tenure. In many cases the admission of a black woman to the elite colleges was the result of an oversight, evidently due to her having a light complexion that allowed her to "pass." When such mistakes were belatedly uncovered, it often kindled controversy on the campus and in newspapers.

Even at those women's colleges that admitted black women, there were serious limits in their educational practices. Students were drawn almost entirely from established professional families in Cambridge (Massachusetts), Baltimore, Washington, and New York City. There was little sign of commitment to geographical outreach to the South. Black students either were forbidden to live in campus housing or, later, were sequestered in separate dormitories. Wellesley College was exceptional in asserting the right of a black student to dine at commons. On balance, the memoirs of black alumnae suggest that their academic experience was strong, they were proud of having attended and graduated from a distinguished college, and they were devoted alumnae. Within this numerically small group, the black women who graduated from the Seven Sisters colleges showed disproportionately high postgraduate achievement in completing advanced degrees and in practicing as medical doctors, lawyers, and judges.

The prototype of the "all women's campus" was not the exclusive province of the private or independent sector. Several states, especially in the South, established public women's colleges. The roster included North Carolina College for Women in Greensboro, Florida Women's College in Tallahassee, Mississippi College for Women, Texas Women's University, and Longwood College and Mary Washington College in Virginia. The extension of opportunity was once again incomplete, each of these institutions being racially restricted to white women.

Coeducation, the fastest-growing model, provided both access and exclusion to women. In the typical comprehensive campus, women tended to be steered into particular academic programs and discouraged from others. Although women enjoyed numerous, diverse opportunities within campus life, they were unlikely to attain positions of leadership such as editor of the student newspaper or president of the student body. Women did achieve parity of sorts in the flourishing Greek-letter sorority system that mirrored the men's fraternities as a source of privilege and power. Women had groups of their own—Delta Delta Delta, Pi Beta Phi, and so on. However, even though a state university in the Midwest might have as many as twenty-three Greek sororities, achievement was often defined in terms of the men's Greek fraternities with rituals such as serenades and "pinning." A sorority woman aspired to be the "Sweetheart of Sigma Chi."

The rise of the sororities in university social life had another consequence for women as coeducational students: it provided a conduit to
other kinds of campus recognition. Homecoming events had originally
been intended to bring alumni back to the alma mater, but between the
world wars the focus shifted to the incumbent undergraduates, and specifically to the selection of a homecoming queen and her court from
among the sororities' members. Coeducational institutions also hosted
an array of beauty pageants and festivals throughout the academic year,
all part of a complex ritual of competition and selection. One example
of this development was the "Illio Beauties" of the University of Illinois,
showcased each year in the campus yearbook, *The Illio* (figure 10). The
editors announced:

> JUST HOLD YOUR BREATH . . . !
> Prepare to be dazzled! For months you've been eagerly waiting to find
> out who are the fourteen most beautiful women on the Illini campus.
> You've watched the contest starting with 236 beauties, representing each
> house on the campus, narrow down to 56 in the first elimination and down
> to 26 in the second elimination.
> You've envied the faculty judges their job of picking the final twenty-six
> queens whose pictures were sent to Hollywood.
> You gasped when you found that Cecil B. DeMille was to judge the final
> twenty-six pictures.
> You have waited a long time, but this is it. Prepare yourself! Here are our
> queens![40]

What the yearbook editors portrayed as a source of common interest
and bonding among the members of the university community was in
fact indicative of the schisms among the institutional subcultures identified by sociologists Burton Clark and Martin Trow—what historian
Helen Lefkowitz Horowitz has called the "insiders" versus the "outsiders."[41] At the same time that women were achieving a presence in the
Panhellenic sororities and campus beauty competitions, there is nationwide evidence of changes in their academic plans. Compared with the
women undergraduates of 1890, the "co-eds" of 1920, 1930, or 1940 were
less likely to pursue an advanced degree, especially in the learned professions of medicine or law. Allocation of student fees for programs was
skewed, with support for men's varsity intercollegiate athletics dwarfing
the token provision for women's teams. When evaluated by the composite student opinion, it was a social system that appeared to work reasonably well. However, for a student—male or female—who wished to

Figure 10. The "Illio Beauties" of the University of Illinois, 1946 (Illio, yearbook of the University of Illinois)

pursue an unconventional route of academic concentration or extra-curricular activity, the American campus could be surprisingly difficult to navigate.

The biggest change for women students between the world wars was their shrinking opportunities to pursue advanced degrees and graduate studies. Few women were admitted to law or medical school. The new master's of business administration programs were almost exclusively male. This tracking away from certain fields also took place at the under-graduate level. Even though business administration was the most pop-ular field of study in this era, few undergraduate women studied for the

"B.B.A." Business education for collegiate women was markedly different from the education of future corporate managers and executives. One sign of the changing professional and cultural climate for college-educated women was the popularity of the Katharine Gibbs School in New York City—popularly nicknamed "Katy Gibbs." Its market niche was to provide entry-level secretarial skills to young women—in particular the alumnae of prestigious women's colleges—who sought jobs in New York City and other metropolitan areas. In Chicago the Gregg College advertised itself in university yearbooks as providing "secretarial training for college students." In the early 1940s it claimed to have enrolled students from 137 colleges and 31 states. Its aim was to provide an intense four-month course for "opening the door to business"—evidently something that a young woman's completion of a bachelor's degree could not assure.

The uncertain prospects for academic and professional advancement that faced women at all institutions were perhaps of less concern to parents and families in a conservative American culture than other issues associated with higher education and gender. For decades, parents had been worried that college posed two threats to their daughters, both of which rendered them unfit for marriage. First was the fear that highly educated women were unappealing as potential spouses. Second was that tightly knit communities of women undergraduates promoted lesbian relations. By 1940, the "good news" for cultural conservatives from both the coeducational and all-women's campuses was that the American college woman appeared not to have forfeited her prospects for marriage and motherhood. Whether or not the price for this accomplishment was worth the decrease in professional options available to a generation of educated American women made only small ripples in public discussions between the world wars.

African Americans and Higher Education

Most journalists reporting on American higher education were color-blind in the sense that they paid little if any attention to black college students. For example, the 1937 issue of *Life* magazine devoted exclusively to the American college includes no mention of a black college. Nor is a black student featured in any photograph in the issue. This example underscored the majority culture's presumption of segregation and indifference to racial integration.

Although racial exclusion was a matter of both law and custom at state universities in the South, its expression was often implicit rather than explicit. In the Louisiana State University catalogue of 1936, for example, the official information on "Admission to the University" merely states, "Graduates of high schools of Louisiana, public and private, approved by the State Department of Education, are eligible for admission to the Lower Division of the University on presentation of a diploma or certification of graduation." Moreover, graduates "of high schools outside of Louisiana which have been accredited by proper regional or State authority may be admitted to the Lower Division upon presentation of a diploma or certificate of graduation." The only reference to African Americans in the Louisiana State University catalogue of 1936 appears in the section on the College of Agriculture's "Farm and Home Demonstration Work." Black workers employed to work with the university's demonstration services were designated as "local agents." Seventeen such agents were assigned to provide outreach in thirty-eight parishes that had a high percentage of black residents. The catalogue notes, "All of these workers are under the immediate supervision of the district agents (White)."[42]

Enrollment prospects for black students remained limited, not only in the segregated states but nationwide. Even though such vocal black leaders as Marcus Garvey praised universities in the North for admitting black students, the statistics suggest that the impact of such gestures was marginal. Estimates of total black undergraduate enrollment at colleges and universities apart from the segregated black campuses ranged from about fifteen hundred to two thousand per year in the mid-1930s. Enrollment in black colleges increased after World War I from slightly more than two thousand to about fourteen thousand in 1930. Despite this percentage growth, access to higher education for black students lagged far behind that for whites. Just prior to World War II a white between the ages of eighteen and twenty was four times more likely than a black of the same age group to enroll in college.

One consequence of segregated undergraduate education was that it provided some increased access for black students who wished to pursue graduate degrees at prestigious universities in the North. This came about when state governments in the South attempted to demonstrate some measure of compliance with the "separate but equal" dictum by establishing state scholarship funds for black students to pursue graduate studies and professional degrees outside the state. Kentucky, for example, established the Anderson Mayer State Aid Act of 1936.[43] No fewer than sixteen other states set up comparable programs. Columbia University, the University of Chicago, Indiana University, the University of Michigan, and Howard University were the major beneficiaries of these portable state scholarships.

Racial exclusion in higher education was a national rather than a regional phenomenon. In the 1920s even such socially progressive schools as Antioch in Ohio refused to admit black applicants. Odious as the legal segregation of the universities and colleges of the South was, the actual behavior of the allegedly integrated campuses in the North warrants little commendation. In 1940 the University of Michigan's administration forbade black students to live in campus housing. Comparable practices were evidently in place at other state universities in the Midwest and North. Consider the case of Jesse Owens, the gold medallist in four track and field events at the 1936 Berlin Olympics. Owens, an African American, was admitted to the Ohio State University. His scholarship for track and field covered only a small portion of his tuition and living expenses. He was not allowed to live in any of the campus dormitories. He supported himself by running a dry-cleaning and pressing business and living in an off-campus rooming house. According to the research of David O. Levine, only a few American campuses deviated from a strict policy of racially segregated dormitories.[44]

From time to time newspapers featured profiles of outstanding black collegians such as Paul Robeson of Rutgers University in New Jersey or Jackie Robinson of the University of California at Los Angeles. Robeson, later to become a world-famous baritone and actor, was an honors student at Rutgers and a star football player on the same team as future television star, bandleader, and producer Ozzie Nelson (of "Ozzie and Harriet" fame). Even though he was a presence in the undergraduate life at Rutgers, Robeson faced social exclusion within the campus. College sports, often hailed for its egalitarian character, seldom achieved this ideal. Coaches from Northern schools would agree to keep their black student athletes out of games played against teams from Southern states that forbade racial integration.

Despite the slights and slurs of racial segregation, few black students could resist the lure of the accolades and forms of "college life." The Greek-letter system of fraternities and sororities was one such attraction. At black colleges such as Fisk in the 1920s, undergraduates chartered their own fraternities. In racially integrated institutions, such as the state

Figure 11. Black sorority, University of Illinois: Delta Sigma Theta, 1946 (Illio, yearbook of the University of Illinois)

universities of the Midwest, black students came to terms with the Greek system not by achieving racial integration but rather by creating their own exclusively black fraternities and sororities that were sequestered within the Greek system. At the University of Illinois, for example, Delta Sigma Theta was the black sorority within the Panhellenic circuit (figure 11). The two black fraternities were Alpha Phi Alpha and Kappa Alpha Psi (figure 12). The result was inclusion without integration.

Rescuing the Collegiate Curriculum

The collegiate excesses and successes that pervaded media coverage of higher education provided fertile ground and a common foe for critics and reformers. First, the extreme hedonism of campus activities gave critics the justification they needed to devise numerous reform proposals to correct the conspicuous problems. A second unexpected windfall for reformers was that while newspaper and magazine coverage focused on sports and campus social life, reform groups were free to go about their planning for educational innovation without intrusion or publicity. The multiple reform contingents were comparable to teams of termites, each working industriously beneath the surface of campus life to topple the dominant structures.

   The common foe that united academic reformers was well characterized in the following call for change made by Robert Maynard Hutchins

Figure 12. Black fraternities, University of Illinois: Alpha Phi Alpha (top) *and Kappa Alpha Psi, 1946* (Illio, *yearbook of the University of Illinois*)

in his 1931 announcement of the creation of a "New College" at the University of Chicago shortly after his inauguration as president: "College is *not* a great athletic association and social club in which provision is made, merely incidentally, for intellectual activity on the part of the physically and socially unfit. College *is* an association of scholars in which provision is made for the development of traits and powers which must be cultivated, in addition to those which are purely intellectual, if one is to become a well-balanced and useful member of any community."[45] The commonality among the diverse reform initiatives was that undergraduate studies were amorphous and gave little attention to the serious study of significant matters. According to Burton R. Clark, the key to institutional transformation and the creation of a "distinctive college" in this era was the convergence of an educational crisis with a visionary, charismatic leader—usually a new president. Such was the broad contour of resurrection at such institutions as Antioch College in Ohio, Reed College in Oregon, and Swarthmore College in Pennsylvania.[46]

The proposed antidotes to the general problem of incoherent, indifferent undergraduate education were diverse and often conflicting. One recurring ingredient was a commitment and passion for reform that bonded presidents, board members, faculty, staff, and students.[47] At the University of Chicago, President Hutchins relied on a "great books" curriculum as the core of a revitalized undergraduate experience. In Annapolis, Maryland, Scott Buchanan relied on classical languages, original texts, and a "great books" curriculum to bring rigor as well as good students to a floundering St. John's College. For Frank Aydelotte, the new president of Swarthmore College near Philadelphia, a notion inspired by Oxford University was the tonic for the American college's malaise. Specifically, Aydelotte introduced an "honors program" that simultaneously rewarded and demanded much of serious students. It included intensive seminars, special courses, and a senior thesis to be evaluated by an outside examiner.

For several reformers the credo was that function and character followed form. They emphasized architectural change, whereby the large campus was broken down into small units that offered a special educational arrangement. Examples of this line of argument included President Abbott Lawrence Lowell's endorsement of a new "house" system at Harvard. Thanks to a generous gift from Yale alumnus Edwin Harkness, Lowell had the resources to begin construction of an elaborate, expensive system of "houses," complete with student lounges, libraries, game rooms, athletic facilities, and faculty apartments for resident advisors. Yale then reconsidered its original reluctance to respond to Harkness's overtures and enthusiastically accepted a large gift that enabled the university to establish its system of residential "colleges." Most universities, however, did not have the luxury of donors like Harkness. For them, the building of elaborate residential quadrangles was out of the question.

Another variation on the structural approach to institutional reform took place outside Los Angeles, in Claremont, in the 1920s. Pomona College, a thriving liberal arts college founded by New England Congregationalists about a half-century earlier, resisted the standard tendency simply to keep expanding enrollments as applications increased. Instead, under the leadership of James Blaisdell, Pomona's board initiated a plan to put a ceiling on enrollments and then to cooperate with donors, educators, and civic leaders to help found a succession of new liberal arts colleges geographically adjacent to Pomona. The result was an "Oxford plan" tailored to mass education in modern America—a honeycomb of residential colleges that shared some facilities such as a main library and that were chartered as a corporate federation while allowing each college to enjoy autonomy and its own special mission.[48] This blueprint for an academic commonwealth made possible the founding of Scripps College, an autonomous yet cooperating women's college literally up the street from Pomona. It also allowed for the creation of Claremont Graduate School for advanced-degree programs in selected fields. The net contribution of the Claremont plan was to provide for an increasingly populous and education-minded region a trustworthy structure for extending liberal education in a small-campus residential setting to an expanding pool of qualified college applicants.

For academic reformers who wished to make their distinctive mark on American higher education, high hopes often led to disappointment. President Lowell's magnificent (and expensive) "house" plan was lambasted by most Harvard student groups, who considered it to be an administrative infringement on the tradition of student self-determination. Student architectural critics initially ridiculed the plan as a "model village." No reform was guaranteed to be successful or to work as its originator intended. At Amherst College, philosopher Alexander Meiklejohn aimed to introduce a genuine democracy of talent into this prestigious academic community. Motivated in part by his own background as a bright scholar from a family of modest means, Meiklejohn worked to turn the historic liberal arts college away from plutocracy and toward meritocracy. He also asserted the role of the college president as a scholarly leader whose time was devoted more to discussions with students than to fund-raising. These unpopular ideas, along with other tensions and disputes—including outright personality conflicts and individual animosities—caused Meiklejohn to fall from favor with board members and some senior professors. When word of his firing reached students, a large number of graduating seniors boycotted commencement ceremonies and refused to accept their degrees. Meiklejohn's setbacks at Amherst did not extinguish his drive for collegiate reform. He soon accepted an invitation to create an honors residential college organized around a multidisciplinary study of classical civilization that would be an academic enclave at the sprawling University of Wisconsin.

Over time, bits and pieces of the innovations developed at these various campuses worked their way into the curriculum and vocabulary of most colleges and universities. Despite such influences, however, these distinctive colleges shaped by reform-minded academics did not immediately alter the dominant character of American colleges and universities prior to World War II.

Philanthropy and Structural Reform

Whereas the campus critics and reformers mentioned above emphasized renovating a single institution as a model for the future, the major foundations tended to focus on the architecture of the nationwide system of higher education. The most far-reaching plans to reform the structure of American higher education percolated from the private sector of organized American philanthropy. Between 1920 and 1940 a coalition of major foundations accelerated their effort to bring both standards and standardization to American higher education, an initiative started in the early 1890s. The Carnegie Foundation for the Advancement of Teaching and the Rockefeller Foundation's General Education Board worked in tandem with the United States Bureau of Education to collect and analyze data, toward the common goal of rationalizing colleges and universities into effective systems.[49] This partnership was uneven. The private foundations dwarfed the United States Bureau of Education in terms of staff and resources, and the government agency was reduced to a vehicle for testing foundation pilot studies and, later, publishing reports shaped by foundation-generated data and findings.

The foundations' standards were widely implemented. For example, their advocacy of a corporate model for universities was reflected in the changing composition of academic boards and university presidencies. In 1880 the overwhelming majority of presidents and board members were drawn from the ranks of the clergy. By 1930, corporate executives, corporate lawyers, and bankers comprised over 73 percent of board positions at fifteen prominent private colleges and universities. At a sampling of state universities, private universities, and technical institutes, the figure was 65 percent or more — roughly double the representation of these professions on academic boards in 1880.[50]

The foundations changed the strategies of philanthropy. Instead of giving money primarily to found a new campus or providing a pension fund to complying institutions, the CFAT now used the tool of the "survey" to shape the governance of a single campus—or in some cases the systems for a complete state. Henry Pritchett, former president of the Massachusetts Institute of Technology, published pivotal articles in such national publications as *Harper's* to advocate a long-term vision in which American institutions were categorized and then monitored by systematic measures. In advocating the transfer of a "corporate model" to the campus, he emphasized that internal financial controls were intended to define professors and their work in terms of countable (and accountable) units. Boards were henceforth to be filled primarily by corporate executives, natural leaders to whom university presidents would report and respond. In short, American higher education was scheduled to undergo a managerial revolution.

Systemwide efficiency, according to the representatives of the major foundations, demanded that institutional missions be reworked to avoid program duplication. This meant that there was a rough hierarchy in which a relatively small number of private universities in the Northeast became the pacesetters in prestigious undergraduate education combined with Ph.D. programs. As Clyde Barrow points out, the nation's five largest foundations had endowments worth far more than most college and university endowments. The General Education Board alone had assets of $53 million in 1909 (more than $1 billion in 2000 dollars), the equivalent of 20 percent of all college and university endowments of the time. This meant that foundation support had the power to build approved projects at selected universities. They knew this and used their resources to carry out a policy of concentration within American higher education. According to Barrow, "The five largest foundations gave approximately 86 percent of their disbursements to only thirty-six institutions from 1923 to 1929 among a total of over a thousand higher education institutions in the United States."[51]

This extended foundation initiative included attention to the political economy of higher education. For example, the Carnegie Foundation for the Advancement of Teaching would conduct a survey of a state's higher-education situation. The recommendations of its report would, predictably, tend to favor the creation of a strong flagship state university and perhaps a single governing board for all public institutions in the state. Foundation officials then would present these policy recommendations to a governor and legislature. Although the Carnegie Foundation enjoyed considerable success in this multiple-step approach, from time to time its inconsistencies stirred political opposition. In California the creation of a strong state university and statewide network was hailed as a progressive antidote to the power of the Union Pacific Railroad and Standard Oil. The weak spot in this logic was that public higher education was being asked to adopt the same organizational scheme and dynamics as the industrial monopolies they were supposed to counter. In such a case, the best rationale was that the new system of higher education could perhaps fight corporate fire with corporate fire.

Elsewhere, in the states of Washington and Nebraska, populist legislators were not sanguine about the CFAT proposals for reforming their state higher-education institutions. To the foundation officials, the mixing of liberal arts and utilitarian fields within and across institutions sounded an alarm of "inefficiency." Hence they tended to favor strict separation of such "land-grant" fields as agriculture and engineering from the university's traditional liberal arts. Angry state legislators and state university presidents from time to time pointed out that the Morrill Act had always been intended to promote the mix of the liberal arts with the applied fields of study. Just as Western voters and state representatives resented Wall Street bankers, so did they distrust foundation officials from distant, hated New York City.

In the South, according to Clyde Barrow, university trusteeship was dominated by a regional elite. But unlike the boards of a Harvard, Columbia, Chicago, or Yale, the Southern boards were primarily an agricultural rather than industrial elite.[52] Where the Carnegie Foundation campaign eventually did succeed in the South was in its ability to persuade governors and state university presidents that an efficient campus was the key to rescuing a stagnant state and regional economy. The best example of this kind of alliance occurred in North Carolina, where sociologist Howard Odum's Institute at the University of North Carolina became the headquarters of the regional economic gospel. It was a message echoed at such utilitarian institutions as Georgia Institute of Technology, a relatively young campus in downtown Atlanta that enthusiastically embraced its mission to "engineer the New South."

One of the most widely disseminated manifestos of the foundation perspective was the 1930 book by Abraham Flexner, *Universities: American, British, and German*. Buoyed by the success of his earlier report on the waste and low standards of medical schools in the United States and Canada, Flexner now turned his attention to the entire American university. The book, based on a series of lectures he had given at Oxford University in 1929, started out with an overview of exemplary mature universities in England and Germany. Oxford and Cambridge were admirable, according to Flexner, for their excellence but were of limited utility in the twentieth century because of their anachronistic emphasis on liberal education of the cultivated amateur. He singled out for special praise the high-powered German universities, with their emphasis on professionalized scholarship and scientific method and their coordination with state funding and governance. And he ferreted out examples of weak academic programs and dubious degrees that he felt testified to the immaturity of higher education in the United States.[53]

Despite some skirmishes and setbacks, the general contours of the Carnegie Foundation plan gained a widespread audience and even some partial acceptance across the nation. The foundation's plan for standardization and standards was probably the single most ambitious campaign ever mounted to shape American higher education, yet even this concentration of influence and resources was not adequate to create a genuine national "system." The foundation's proposals were rife with inconsistencies and instances of historical illogic that have usually been ignored or explained away. For example, the Carnegie Foundation's leaders, including Henry Pritchett and Abraham Flexner, cited the European universities as models of efficiency that American universities should emulate. But they ignored the fact that the European universities had long favored a governance arrangement featuring a strong, autonomous faculty working in concert with a ministry of education. There was little evidence in European higher education of a corporate model that relied on an external governing board of business leaders. And despite their praise for the European model, the corporate leaders and foundation officials who embraced American higher education as their reform project had little interest in fostering a truly powerful, autonomous, European-style faculty.

Perhaps the main oversight in Flexner's diatribe against the contemporary American university was his failure to see that American business had contributed to the very weaknesses he deplored. At one time he would extol corporate executives as the shepherds who would lead the American campus out of the wilderness of sloth and inefficiency. At another, he would emphasize that it was the hegemony of the "downtown business crowd" that supported and demanded lamentable excesses of big-time college sports. Perhaps the explanation for the apparent inconsistency is that the foundations favored a business elite that was drawn from the boardrooms of a handful of national corporations, as distinguished from the provincial boosterism of local business leaders. It is also puzzling that Flexner took the college and university presidents to task for having added various new professional fields to the curriculum. He singled out home economics, journalism, and business administration for particular criticism, yet these were among the fields that business leaders had championed to ensure that the American economy would have a workforce of college graduates trained in useful fields.

The most puzzling point in Flexner's critique of American higher education is his claim that the university had lost its sense of a central mission. He portrayed his own mechanical solution of standards and standardization as a moral proposition. In fact, it was merely morally self-righteous. One searches in vain for a time when the American campus had the clarity of purpose for which Flexner longed. Certainly his futuristic plan carried with it little that was convincing about values. Indicative of the oversights of Flexner and his colleagues was their praise for the German universities of the late 1920s. They failed to note that for years these prestigious institutions had been purging their student bodies and faculties of politically nonconforming scholars as well as imposing constraints on the genuine pursuit of truth. Control, not inquiry, was the consequence of the foundation-based structural innovations.

Proponents of the corporate ethos as a model for American higher education seldom seemed to be bothered by such inconsistencies. *Efficiency* was their watchword, but the penny-pinching evidently did not extend to corporate largesse used to build an expensive campus that glorified a family name — even though the buildings were not especially useful. For example, when the magnificent new Gothic campus for Duke University was opened, the administrators discovered that preoccupation with the chapel had distracted the architects from other elements. In one aca-demic building, there were no faculty offices. Efficiency of a sort was achieved, however, by assigning the overlooked professors to shared office space in a closet.

Such oversights reinforced the concern of some critical professors across the nation that the foundation's representatives and their corporate partners were either ignorant or contemptuous of strong-minded professors and what was termed "faculty values." In the period between the world wars, professors countered the top-down initiatives of their own, drafting statements and forming organizations to oppose or protest the drift in institutional governance. At Columbia University, for example, such nationally prominent scholars as James McKeen Cattell and Charles Beard spoke out. The expressions of opposition included statements endorsed by the Association of American University Professors. On balance, however, the faculty countermeasures were scattered and ineffective.

The foundation representatives' quest for a corporate model for higher education was not altogether clear in its vision for the American professor. Although they invoked the model of a business corporation, their reform efforts at universities resulted in an organizational ethos reminiscent of a civil service bureaucracy. The professional expertise of professors was simultaneously a source of envy and of distrust; it represented energy to be defused. Ironically, this attitude created an environment that was particularly hostile to those truly bright and self-starting scholars who could have made novel contributions. At worst, the corporate model promoted an accountable "business as usual" operation that was antithetical to inspired teaching and original research.

Most embarrassing to the corporate executives who advocated transplanting their methods and means to the campus was the disastrous example of their model in the national economy. Their obsession with efficient management of factories often left them oblivious to sound economic policies associated with large-scale investments and enterprises. The weaknesses were most evident in the stock market crash of 1929 and the futile efforts by major banks and corporations to rescue the sinking American economy. Did Flexner and Pritchett still believe that industrial efficiency was the key to the national welfare? Evidently so, as numerous college and university boards adamantly spoke in opposition to New Deal policies—overlooking the catastrophic situation into which their own leadership had shepherded the national economy.

On balance, the recommendations of the Carnegie Foundation and the General Education Board had a strong influence on university presidents and board members. It was, nonetheless, an incomplete triumph of the "managerial revolution."

Institutional Profile: Stanford and the Roots of the Entrepreneurial University

How did the universities actually go about implementing reforms and devising survival strategies in the 1930s? One institution that took to heart the ethos of the major foundations and corporations was Stanford

University.[54] In the 1920s it had been a medium-sized campus, known as a pleasant place that showed sporadic signs of scholarship. Its medical school in San Francisco was not distinguished. But it enjoyed the advantages of a mild climate and a beautiful campus, and it was a favored destination for the sons and daughters of prosperous California families. Stanford allowed a great deal of latitude with respect to academic rigor. Most undergraduates considered the ability of Stanford's football team to challenge the University of California and the University of Southern California for selection to the Rose Bowl to be a top institutional priority.

Stanford's academic atmosphere started to change in the early 1930s, under the watchful eye of Provost Frederick Terman. The son of a world-famous psychologist known for intelligence testing, Terman was a professor of engineering. His notable initiative was to promote intense cooperation among engineers and physicists, especially on research projects that involved contracts with industry. To build such partnerships, Terman worked deliberately to purge the physics department of an older generation of professors whose notion of university work did not include applied research. Over time, Terman as provost extended this plan to numerous departments. In an era before substantial federal research grants, Stanford pioneered research and development that connected the campus with corporations. The strategy had the strong support of the Stanford board of trustees, whose influential members included alumnus Herbert Hoover.

Stanford's course as charted by Provost Terman also demonstrated the extremes of the corporate model. Departments, including history and classics, that could not show a record in bringing in research contracts were scrutinized, even punished. A deal would be struck whereby the department would agree to offer large-enrollment survey courses as a means of paying its own way. Even a Nobel Laureate biologist was scolded for his failure to bring in external monies. By 1940, Stanford University typified the multiple personalities and layers of the complex American campus. Its intense support of high-powered, utilitarian studies in the applied sciences coexisted with its traditional indulgence of an idyllic undergraduate social life and varsity sports program. At times this hybrid approach worked far better than expert planners ever imagined. A case in point was the dramatically changing contributions a student could make to the alma mater over time: David Packard, class of 1934, first gained fame at Stanford as a star defensive end on the football team, a member of the famous "Vow Boys" who took Stanford to the Rose

Bowl. A few years later his teamwork with a fellow alumnus in developing electronic circuitry in a rented garage near the Stanford campus provided the basis for the application of electrical engineering to the development of computers. When David Packard and William Hewlett started their work, plums and peaches, not technology, dominated the Santa Clara Valley economy. Thanks in large part to the education and later support provided by Stanford, Hewlett and Packard helped pioneer the development of Northern California's "Silicon Valley" of electronics and information technology.[55] The Stanford model of research focus combined with the university as landlord and commercial catalyst grew and eventually blossomed as the model of an enterprising university.

"Booster Colleges" and the New State University President

The most prominent state universities were in the Midwest and West. The University of California claimed an enrollment of twenty-five thousand students and Ohio State University had nineteen thousand. By 1936 the University of California no longer regarded itself as being in the shadow of the older East Coast universities. It embodied a new model — the extended, multiple-purpose university that had numerous campuses. As the editors of *The Golden Book of California* explained in their profile of "The University of Today":

> Flashing white buildings, cool green trees, warm brown hills — that is the University of California's Berkeley Campus which is remembered by thousands of alumni strung from Capetown to Ceylon, from Berkeley to Bombay. No other university campus in the United States can boast the setting of the Berkeley Campus, and few have had the benefit of the foresight of planning which has been enjoyed at Berkeley.
>
> But when one speaks or writes of the University of California he tells only a part of the story if he refers merely to Berkeley. There is the Westwood campus at Los Angeles blossoming from barrenness into a place of singular beauty. There are the buildings, old and new, of Medical Center in San Francisco, and on the top of Mount Hamilton in Santa Clara County is perched Lick Observatory. Nestled on the shores of the ocean at La Jolla is the University's Scripps Institution of Oceanography, and in a valley near Pomona, the W. K. Kellogg Institute of Animal Husbandry is a place of flowers and meadows. The Riverside Citrus Experiment Station, built on the side of a hill, overlooks miles of orange groves, and the Branch of the College of Agriculture, a large scale farm itself, is set at Davis in the Sacramento Valley.[56]

Central to the surge of the new American state university was an innovative style of presidential leadership, best illustrated by Robert G. Sproul of the University of California and Herman B. Wells of Indiana University. Both were devoted alumni with a background in finance. Neither one claimed or aspired to stature as a scholar. Both had dealings with the business community, but neither was a corporation executive. Furthermore, each represented indigenous talent. Provincial by the standards of the New York–based national foundations, young presidents such as Sproul in California and Wells in Indiana relied on their state and local roots to help them build great state universities.

They were similar in that they combined the loyalty of an alumnus with the shrewd eye of an accountant. Each had keen technical knowledge of state finance as well as the ability and disposition to lobby knowledgeably and effectively in the state capital. They came to budget subcommittee hearings with comprehensive data and worked patiently with legislative and gubernatorial staffs to document their case for state support. They were champions of systematic decision making characterized by annual funding formulae. Sproul and Wells both had credibility with state officials that they had built up over the years before they came to academic administration. Wells, for example, was universally praised in Indiana for having headed the task force that reformed the state's banking regulations—a system whose weaknesses had been exposed during the Great Depression. Sproul had started his career as an accountant and auditor for Oakland's municipal government. In short, each knew public finance from the ground up.

While their approach to relations between campus and statehouse emphasized stability and trust, their enthusiasm as loyal alumni was expressed in large-scale systematic fund-raising. Sproul overcame the problem of chronic underfunding by the California legislature by forming the "Order of the Golden Bear," a prestigious circle of alumni, most of whom were businessmen. Sproul convened this group from time to time for advice, but in fact its main contribution was to serve as an engine for larger-scale fund-raising.

Presidents like Sproul and Wells understood the importance of building a faculty by making the young university attractive to talented rising scholars. A crucial coup for Berkeley, for example, was persuading a young physicist Ernest O. Lawrence to leave Yale for California. Lawrence had felt both professionally underappreciated and socially snubbed in New Haven. At Berkeley he was given both research resources and appreciation—a combination that made the University of California the ideal institutional home where the research and development projects of his Radiation Laboratory revolutionized large-scale university scientific research.

State funding for Indiana University was fairly stable over the years, but austere. Wells good-naturedly accepted the fact that his home state was not wealthy. By avoiding contentious biennial fights with governors and legislators, he was free to devote time to statewide public relations and the quiet building of research programs. He was helped in this endeavor by the university's "IU Foundation"—a privately incorporated entity affiliated with the state university. It served a dual purpose: to seek out prospective donors and funding, and then to turn over its monies to the university for academic programs. It was a strategy that worked. The IU Foundation provided research funding for a struggling young biochemistry professor at a time when no other foundation or federal agency would support his work. Later he showed his gratitude by bequeathing to the IU Foundation the patents and royalties from his work relating to fluoride, the substance that would become a fixture in American life as the cavity-fighting ingredient in Crest toothpaste.

The most obvious success stories of the 1930s were the great state universities of the Midwest and Pacific Coast. However, to understand the pervasive gains of public higher education nationwide, it also is useful to take stock of state universities in the South—a region considered to be an outlier of sorts in that it chronically lagged in funding and access. A good example of the diffusion to the South of the multipurpose state university model was the transformation of Louisiana State University begun under Governor Huey Long. It is interesting to take stock of how, after Long's departure to the United States Senate, LSU's administration attempted to extend the improvements and building that he had set in motion.

LSU had an enrollment of slightly more than four thousand students and offered a vast array of undergraduate courses and degree programs. It had also moved into graduate education, including Ph.D. programs. Despite the state's weak tradition of funding public education, Louisiana State University was able to assert a substantial statewide presence. Between 1925 and 1935 it doubled the number of its faculty from 168 to 394 professors, many of whom were hired as the result of competitive nationwide searches. It undertook publication of such prestigious scholarly journals as the *Southern Review*. Most notable was its extension of the curriculum to embrace a wide array of professional and vocational fields, including field stations and institutes as well as undergraduate instruction.

The main campus at Baton Rouge, three miles from the state capitol, was the jewel in the university's crown. Other facilities included the Northeast Center in Monroe; the Medical Center in New Orleans; numerous state agricultural experiment stations dedicated to agronomy, animal husbandry, animal pathology, dairy husbandry, agricultural economics, entomology, horticulture, parasitology, plant pathology, poultry, sugarcane, truck farming; and additional centers funded by the U.S. Department of Agriculture. The Agricultural and Home Economics Extension Staff included a nineteen-member supervisory force, twenty specialists, two editors, and over one hundred agents assigned to the statewide parishes.

At the main Baton Rouge campus, undergraduates who came from the state's high schools could pick courses and majors from an unprecedented array of departments. The traditional arts and sciences had been joined by a teachers' college, a college of engineering, agriculture, commerce, and pure and applied science, a school of music, a school of library science, a forestry school, and a law school. Louisiana State University also had moved into graduate work, offering numerous programs leading to master's degrees and some provision for Ph.D. studies.

Although the 1936 catalogue presented an overwhelming array of offerings, the extent of the university's innovations had perhaps been exaggerated. True, LSU was, as it claimed to be, a Ph.D.-granting institution, but at commencement in June 1936 it conferred a total of two Ph.D.'s, as against more than a thousand bachelor's degrees. For all the talk of graduate programs, LSU's overwhelming commitment was to undergraduate education.

On paper the emerging state universities were a marvel of comprehensive networks, programs, and services. LSU, for example, expanded beyond its showcase campus at Baton Rouge to include substations for agricultural specialties throughout the state. The size and presence of the ascending state university such as LSU represented a mixed achievement. If one looks beyond the largest campuses, such as the University of California and Ohio State University, one finds that the typical state campus had a total enrollment of undergraduate, graduate, and professional students in the range of twenty-five hundred to seventy-five hundred. The following roster from the 1940 *World Almanac* suggests the typical enrollments and faculty size:[57]

Institution	Enrollments	Faculty
Indiana University	6,492	310
University of Iowa	6,802	649
University of Nebraska	7,210	429
University of Oklahoma	7,236	292
University of Kansas	4,831	255
University of Oregon	3,592	234
University of Virginia	2,895	170
Rutgers University	2,900	470

What is striking about these institutions is their similarity to Louisiana State University in matters of size and curriculum. On the one hand, the creation and growth of these state universities heralded the expansion of stable public higher education. On the other hand, patterns of enrollment and degree completion reinforce the finding that the prototypical American state university was not first and foremost a home for advanced scholarship. Nor is there much evidence that the state university of 1940 was a coherent entity in which numerous professional schools and advanced fields radiated outward from a historic liberal arts core. Instead, one finds a more or less linear arrangement of fields, with the arts and sciences being only one of many seats at the university table.[58] Availability of external funding for advanced projects and special scholarly initiatives remained limited. Patronage in terms of developmental grants and innovative research projects were the exception, not the rule. The ascending state universities enjoyed growing support from generations of alumni and state legislators—but only so long as the campus avoided controversy in politics or losing teams in football. For most, their imperial structure surpassed the substance of their actual course and program offerings. The typical state university remained underfunded and overextended.

Localism and the Growth of the American Junior College

Although state university presidents such as Robert Sproul at Berkeley and Herman G. Wells at Indiana University liked to depict their institutions as "having a statewide presence" and "serving the people of the entire state," the reality was that no single campus could provide any measure of statewide access and service. The consequence was that in hundreds of communities across the United States the local "junior college"—often hailed as a uniquely American invention—emerged as a successful institution. Whether public or private in affiliation, the typical junior college of the 1920s usually offered a liberal arts curriculum that represented the first two years of work toward the bachelor's degree. President William Rainey Harper of the University of Chicago had envisioned the two-year junior college as a vehicle for setting the first two years of undergraduate study apart from upper-division and graduate programs. In the Midwest and West this original notion was fused with the idea of local initiative to create an academic campus whose students would then transfer to a four-year campus to complete the bachelor's degree.

Over time the original two-year academic emphasis was supplemented—and sometimes eclipsed—by the inclusion of a technical or vocational curriculum. Most important is that these institutions were products of genuinely local initiatives. Despite some limits in size, scope, and resources, they were one of the success stories of the period between the world wars because they provided affordable, geographically accessible college studies. By 1940 there were 456 junior colleges, with a total enrollment of 149,584 students.[59] Many of their graduates who received the "associate" degree transferred to four-year colleges to complete the bachelor's degree. The appeal of this new institutional model was exemplified in California, which had forty-nine junior colleges offering instruction in the 1930s. In most cases these were funded through local property taxes, comparable to arrangements for public support of elementary and secondary education. Private junior colleges were almost completely dependent on student tuition payments.

By the 1930s, the popularity of the junior colleges had made them problematic to state university presidents and to representatives of the major national foundations. This was because these local initiatives were outside the system—and control—of the established institutions. The ultimate aim of the system reformers was to shift junior colleges away from the liberal arts (and hence away from their role of providing the first two years of college instruction), and toward terminal vocational programs.[60] Advocates of such reforms also wanted the junior colleges to be synchronized with, and to defer to, the hierarchical statewide system engineered by the established state university.

Access and Affordability: Changes in the Price of Going to College

From 1880 to 1920, college tuition charges at even the most prestigious campuses were both stable and relatively cheap. After 1920 this started to change, with a major escalation of college pricing taking place in the 1930s. According to Claudia Goldin and Lawrence F. Katz, "The average (listed) in-state tuition plus fees for under-graduates at public sectors in 1933 was $61 ($753 in 1997 dollars), as compared with $265 ($3,272 in 1997 dollars) in the private sector."[61] One national survey indicated that tuition fees went from an average of $70 in 1920 to $133 in 1940.[62] Translated into 2000 dollars, this would be the equivalent of an increase from $601 to $1,143. A 1939 survey for the General Education Board showed that 42 percent of American colleges and universities charged more than $200 in tuition fees in 1936 – 37, whereas in 1928 – 29 only 37 percent had charged fees at that level.

By the mid-1930s the prestigious institutions in the Northeast charged about twice as much as established private universities in the Midwest. According to Stuart Stoke's 1937 study published in the *Journal of Higher Education*, "Amherst, Williams, and Wesleyan all charge tuition fees of $400, while women's colleges of comparable type in the same geographical area charge $500. State universities, such as those in Wisconsin, Illinois, and Michigan charge from incidentals to $100 per annum, while large independent universities in the same area tend to charge $300."[63] The University of California continued its tradition of charging no tuition for students who were state residents, although it did assess various student fees. Louisiana State University's pricing structure was similar to that of the University of California. Residents of Louisiana were not charged for tuition but did pay in 1936 a "general university fee" of $30 per semester to cover the costs of various student services and facilities. Undergraduates from outside Louisiana paid $30 tuition per semester ($372 in 2000 dollars).

The increase in tuition charges at private colleges was especially noteworthy because it took place at a time when earned income was declining because of the effects of unemployment and bank closures during the

Great Depression. Furthermore, in 1940 private institutions enrolled a majority of college undergraduates, despite the relative growth of public higher education. Rising prices hit modest-income students especially hard because few colleges or universities provided much in the way of scholarships or other forms of financial aid. Nor was there any program of federal need-based student financial aid to offset the increased charges. The net effect was to put prestigious colleges increasingly out of the reach of all but a small percentage of American families.

Socially prominent women's colleges led the pack. In 1931 Vassar College set its annual fee for tuition and residence at $1,200 ($13,500 in 2000 dollars). As noted earlier, in 1936 Bennington College charged $1,650 per year ($20,500 in 2000 dollars) for tuition and living expenses. To put it into perspective as a consumer item, in 1940 a new Pontiac automobile cost $783 — about half the price of an academic year at an established private college. On balance, those private colleges that calculated that they could attract a prosperous student body raised tuition and living charges substantially. Meanwhile, numerous state universities were able to remain attractive to prospective students thanks to relatively low tuition charges made possible by state subsidies plus attention to economies of scale in institutional budgeting. During the 1930s, however, the overriding trend was that college prices were going up while resources for most college students were going down.

To cope with these impediments, students cut room-and-board expenses by seeking out cooperative living arrangements, by renting rooms in cheap boardinghouses, or by living at home. Jesse Stuart, later famous for his essays and fiction about Appalachia, recalled that financially strapped undergraduates at Vanderbilt University drank a great deal of water to alleviate their hunger. At many universities, students economized by skipping meals, relying on bottles of milk kept cold on windowsills during winter months as an alternative to breakfast or lunch. Within the campus community, a barter economy emerged to replace cash with services. Professors were often paid in scrip — or not paid at all. Despite the inevitable crises, both students and professors tended to carry on with their regular activities. When jobs were scarce and money for salaries was not available elsewhere, the best option seemed to be to continue in one's customary role.

The federal government did provide some relief via work programs as part of the Federal Employment Relief Act, for which many undergraduates were eligible. Colleges also benefited from campus construction projects undertaken as part of such federal work-relief programs as the Works Progress Administration and the Public Works Administration. Such programs were short term, however, and were not designed to bail out struggling colleges and universities. To the contrary, congressmen and cabinet officials emphasized that direct support for higher education was not on their agenda. It just so happened that colleges, along with such other institutions as hospitals and museums, were in the right place at the right time for public works projects. The result was that enrollments in colleges, universities, and other higher-education institutions increased during a period of extended problems in the national economy. This resilience indicated that undergraduate education had consolidated a secure place for itself as a cultural institution, a vague object of faith in prospects for upward mobility in American society.

Even though some boosters emphasized the economic benefits of investment in higher education, a college degree was more a pedigree than a meal ticket. The reality was that completing a college degree in the 1930s provided little assurance that a graduate could get a job. Investment in higher education provided little immediate relief from a depressed job market. Most college graduates in the decade were either underemployed or unemployed. Entry-level salaries reported by alumni of the 1920s were far higher than those for college graduates who entered the job market in the 1930s. But even though the new college graduates were disappointed, even bitter, about their insecure position in the American economy, younger generations of high school graduates continued to apply to and enroll in college in record numbers.

James Conant, the chemist who was selected to succeed Abbott Lawrence Lowell as president of Harvard, introduced an important innovation in 1937. He dedicated substantial financial aid resources to providing Harvard scholarships to applicants from regions outside the Northeast. This strategy planted the seed for extensive future programs in which college admissions at prestigious institutions became a serious hunt for talent, regardless of geography or family income. Its immediate impact at Harvard was to give the president and faculty a systematic tool for shifting undergraduate admissions away from its historical pattern of dominance by affluent students from a small number of private boarding schools.

Conant's innovation was the genesis of need-based financial aid, a tool that would transform college admissions at many institutions in future decades. The significance of this financial aid program was not that it dramatically changed the socioeconomic composition of Harvard or any other university during this era. Rather, its historical importance lay in its novelty. The fact that it was such a conspicuous exception to the rule of institutional and family expectations about how a college education was to be financed demonstrated just how widespread the presumption was that paying for a college education was a burden for the student and family, not the institution, to bear. Even though higher education in the United States was edging toward mass participation, most Americans still saw college as a privilege rather than a right.

End Point: The Conservative Campus

The academic reformers may have been justified in lamenting the waste of "college life." Yet the wild activities associated with undergraduate life were ultimately conservative because they sealed once and for all the popular belief that "going to college" was a rite of passage into the prestige of the American upper-middle class. Fraternity initiations, weekend parties, homecoming extravaganzas, and football bowl games reinforced established norms of getting ahead in American society. They posed no threat to dominant political or economic values. The campus provided a convenient, effective arena for the mating ritual of collegiate men and women. Indeed, one strand of the lore associated with "Betty Co-ed" was the observation that she was a candidate for the "M.R.S." degree as well as for the B.A. Traditionally underserved groups (e.g., the working class) could now aspire to a college education, at least for their children if not themselves.

The social function of college coexisted with an increasingly potent albeit vague economic function. Job applicants took pride in listing "some college" as part of their educational record, even if this had not included completing a four-year course of study. For those students who did persist to commencement, a college degree, particularly in such fields as engineering and business, increased access to entry-level white-collar jobs. Most occupations in the United States, however, did not have a tight connection with academic credentials. In some cases the technical skills acquired through having studied civil engineering, pharmacy, or accounting gave a student an edge in hiring decisions. In other cases the mere social prestige of being a college alumnus conferred leverage in the job market.

One artifact of material culture that captures this consolidated char-

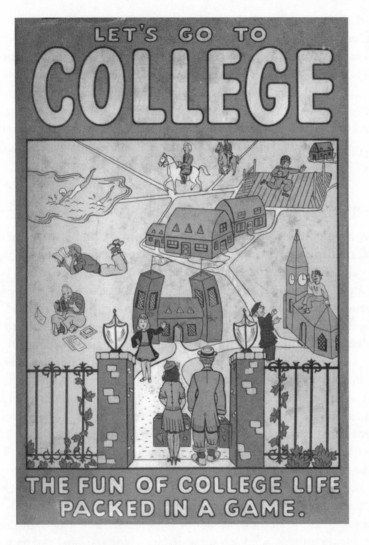

Figure 13. "Let's Go to College" board game, 1944 (The Electric Game Company)

acter of higher education was the popular 1940s board game "Let's Go to College" (figure 13). Players competed with one another to progress through the ranks of "freshmen," "sophomores," "juniors," and "seniors." Activity cards included four categories: "fun," "sports," "re-exams," and "flunk." Penalties included trips to the bursar's office to make payments.

Colorful characters included a dean ("Scrutinize Z. Marks, M.A."), a president ("Dr. O. G. Flunk"), a comptroller ("Roland N. Dough, B.S."), and a football captain ("Lyon Buck, R.A.H."). As in movies and magazine articles, serious study and the curriculum were depicted as obstacles to be avoided as players navigated the campus game board. Marketed as the campus equivalent of "Monopoly," it promised "the fun of college life packed in a game!" It was, of course, simplistic and superficial. Nonetheless, its images and icons were harmonious with the themes conveyed by college and university yearbooks.

Taking Stock of Academic Freedom

The conspicuous glamour of undergraduates and campus extracurricular life tended to obscure the serious business of teaching and learning. Ironically, this tendency to ignore the world of scholarship, among both professors and students, may have been an unexpected blessing. The lack of a spotlight on their activities actually meant that professors and their relatively small number of devoted advanced students were free to explore esoteric fields that would have made little sense to board members or to parents and the general public. That student humor magazines of the era poked fun at the highly specialized course titles and obscure departments was a left-handed tribute to the fertile ground American colleges and universities provided for the expansion of the curriculum. Advanced seminars and doctoral programs remained a thin crust at all but a few universities, but at least it was a durable margin of specialized scholarship. Hence in the informal sense of opportunity to pursue topics and special work, American professors made great gains in the content and character of the academic workplace between the world wars.

Less clear is the status of academic freedom in the formal, structural sense during this era. Scholarly organizations with national and regional chapters continued to grow. The Association of American Universities gained in membership, yet with a mixed record of effectiveness in its confrontations with authoritarian presidents and impatient trustees. Most likely the American professoriate was gaining strength quietly and slowly, especially when specialized expertise might be in demand by some external constituency.

A paradox of the professors in this era was the ability of some to command resources and respect while others—probably the majority—were either resigned to or content with accepting business as usual. This paradox would be illustrated when an ambitious president or provost (such as Terman at Stanford) set out to build a dynamic, high-powered faculty: those with skills in demand enjoyed great bargaining power, while those in departments that had fallen from favor or never experienced prestige would be vulnerable to purges or marginalization. No faculty organization provided much protection from this downside to institutional advancement. With few exceptions, university and college presidents held the crucial cards in the game of faculty hiring, promotion, and firing. Even at such a large university as the University of California, President Robert G. Sproul personally reviewed and deliberated on every faculty appointment. Decades earlier, President Nicholas Murray Butler of Columbia had showed little patience for the impertinence of even the internationally regarded professors who dared to question his decisions. Perhaps the major gain for faculty in terms of campus power was the emergence of the "departmental chair" as a seignorial role—an enduring source of local patronage and power, determined more by immediate campus politics than by national scholarly reputation. Scholarly expertise, however, would become an unexpectedly important source of power and prestige during World War II.

World War II and the Utilitarian Campus, 1941 to 1945

The major foundations of the 1930s were not optimistic about the efficiency or effectiveness of the American campus. Yet for all its duplication, inconsistencies, and sprawl, American higher education proved to be both resilient and useful as part of the national war effort in World War II. In some ways this cooperation extended the precedent set in World War I—namely, the campus reconstituted itself to provide a hospitable setting for a variety of intense military training programs at hundreds of colleges.

Perhaps the best indication that the "college spirit" had conceded priority to the "win-the-war spirit" was the voluntary decision by colleges to reduce and often suspend their varsity athletics programs. Even such high-profile national events as the Rose Bowl game were altered to accommodate the national emergency, with the traditional New Year's Day game being moved out of harm's way from Pasadena, California, to Durham, North Carolina. Further indication of the goodwill between the military and the campuses is that many of the army and navy training bases fielded highly competitive football squads, conveniently stocked with star college players and coaches who had either enlisted or been drafted. A curious abuse that occurred throughout World War II involved the United States Military Academy, whose administration and athletics officials took advantage of the easement that extended draft deferments to its cadets. The academy took advantage of this convenient privilege by obtaining congressional appointments for a prodigious number of athletes whose "national service" was fulfilled on the playing fields of West Point—not on the battlefields of Europe or in the campaigns of the Pacific theater.[64]

The preferential wartime treatment of athletes, whether at West Point or on military bases, was in tune with standard collegiate indulgences of peacetime. It was also an exception to the predominant spirit of wartime cooperation and service demonstrated by hundreds of thousands students, professors, and administrators. Along with the accumulated wartime changes in campus enrollments and operations, the major innovation for American higher education during World War II was that professors in a variety of fields demonstrated both expertise and a willingness to contribute that expertise to unprecedented wartime applications. These projects included advanced instruction in esoteric languages. Whereas the typical American student probably had had only cursory exposure to the obvious foreign languages of French, German, and Latin, their professors became war heroes of sorts through their expertise in languages previously unheard by most citizens. Deep within the departments and electives of the American university there were faculty who could read, write, and teach Japanese, Italian, and Russian. Professors of geography and history promptly provided government agencies with briefings on culture, terrain, and politics as well as customs and language for a host of understudied regions and countries. A biologist who had won little recognition on campus for his research on tropical diseases could become a national hero by contributing his expertise to the war effort. Most prominent in the campus effort to win the war was the involvement of physical-science faculty in defense-related research and development, including the atom- and hydrogen-bomb projects.

The ability of colleges and universities to mobilize on short notice for specialized services defined by numerous federal agencies during World War II would have surprised the critics of an earlier era. In 1930, for example, Abraham Flexner had singled out the University of Chicago and its citywide billboards publicizing the schedule of home varsity football games as a prime example of an undisciplined institution that had drifted into inappropriate activities.[65] Roughly a decade later, Chicago had dropped varsity football and left its campus stadium to deteriorate. The stadium fell into disrepair, its empty seats becoming overgrown with shrubs and weeds. Was this a sign of decline? Appearances are deceptive. By 1942 the stadium had become the secret site of the Manhattan Project, whose research laboratories were located in the old locker rooms underneath the grandstand.[66]

This and related research endeavors signaled the maturity of academic science in the United States. The universities' effectiveness during the crises of World War II had an enduring legacy—namely, the success of academic cooperation in large-scale applied research projects provided the rationale for future partnerships between the federal government and universities. This accomplishment would indelibly transform the missions and funding of American higher education in the period following the end of World War II in 1945.

7 Gilt by Association
Higher Education's "Golden Age," 1945 to 1970

Postwar Policies and Possibilities

Following World War II, American higher education enjoyed a quarter-century of support marked by the "three P's" of prosperity, prestige, and popularity. The unexpected good fortune was so heady that journalists and college administrators as well as historians have called this a "golden age." Success, however, did not provide an exemption from campus problems, many of which were associated with growing pains. Lack of certainty and lack of precedents meant that for the higher-education participants in the thick of events between 1945 and 1970, change and a new set of pressures transformed institutions without benefit of a gyroscope or road map. Most telling was the new phrase "postsecondary education," used by legislators and reporters to describe the diversity and complexity of numerous institutional missions and categories.

The shape of American higher education was simultaneously altered in two contrasting ways. On one front, its base was extended so as to move significantly closer to providing mass access to higher education. On another front, the tip of the pyramid was pushed upward as American colleges and universities showed increasing capacity to add advanced, academically selective programs, from the undergraduate level on up through the professional schools and doctoral programs. During this period the so-called research university emerged as a powerful new entity that earned international respect for American scholarship. During the same years the public junior college (eventually called the community college) flourished as a new, distinctively American institution. And to further complicate the landscape, postwar America was fertile ground for the emergence of a popular for-profit higher-education sector, including vocational institutes and trade schools. These innovations coincided with continued growth and prestige at the well-known established private and public colleges.

Nowhere was the unexpected, uncertain tenor of American higher education more evident than in the new architectural forms that cropped up on campuses as World War II ended. In contrast to the magnificent student-union and stadium construction of the 1920s, between 1945 and 1952 the landmark structure was the hastily built Quonset hut, usually made of corrugated aluminum. It is peculiar that such a modest, unlikely type of building signaled the start of a period of unprecedented campus prosperity. Individually each Quonset hut was unimpressive, usually dismissed as an unsightly makeshift facility. But when multiplied by dozens per campus, they graphically symbolized the growth and innovation that various external groups were coming to expect of the campus. The fact that many of these buildings remained in use for several decades after the war confirms Oscar Wilde's observation that "nothing is so permanent as a temporary appointment."

To put this postwar growth into perspective, it is useful to review enrollment data from the prewar era. In 1939–40, total student enrollment at all colleges and universities was just under 1.5 million. During World War II, regular student enrollments dipped substantially as a result of the military draft. The lack of students (and professors) led the president and faculty at Harvard to consider implementing a moratorium on enrollment and instruction at Harvard Law School and in other advanced graduate programs. All this changed after 1945. By 1949–50, total student enrollments had ballooned to almost 2.7 million—an increase of about 80 percent in one decade. This was no aberration, for the figure increased to about 3.6 million in 1960 and then doubled again over the next decade, reaching over 7.9 million in 1970.[1]

The fundamental historic change that set into motion the dramatic expansion of enrollments as well as numerous curricular innovations was that higher education had come to be a major focus of attention in the formulation of public policies at both the state and federal levels. This was in large measure a sign of recognition by government agencies and the American public that higher education had been effective and engaged during World War II. The corollary was that cooperation between government and higher education would possibly have a place in large-scale planning for the transition to a peacetime society, including a civilian economy, long after the end of the war.

None of these transformations of polices and programs were inevitable. Rather, their incubation represented the convergence of several disparate threads of government explorations that eventually led to some piecemeal initiatives. Ultimately, higher education gained sustained state government support combined with federal commitment to advanced research and to access to higher education. During the same decades, major foundations also provided substantial grants to higher education — provided that participating colleges would take on new tasks. But this hindsight summary runs the risk of imposing a false sense of coherence and unity on what was at the time a number of fractured, uncertain ventures. It would be inaccurate to speak of "public policy" and the transformation of higher education between 1945 and 1970. More precisely, various groups pursued multiple public policies and programs without clear coordination — and without any assurance that these experiments would become permanent fixtures.

Accommodation and Access: The GI Bill

American colleges and universities became unwitting partners in postwar federal policies almost as an accident and afterthought. For President Franklin D. Roosevelt and Congress, the concern was twofold: first, how to adjust wartime production to a peacetime economy, and second, how to avert the civil strife of disgruntled military veterans who arrived home without jobs or good prospects. Roosevelt and Vice President Harry Truman remembered well the government's public-relations nadir: the "Bonus March" to Washington, D.C., by tens of thousands of unemployed World War I veterans who then set up "Hooverville" camps near the White House during the Great Depression. Congress and the cabinet had been giving some thought to postwar recovery plans since as early as 1943. By 1944, when an eventual Allied victory was likely, Congress and government agencies explored possibilities for conversion to a peacetime economy that would maintain social order. It was a discussion, however, that did not yet include colleges or their leaders in any central role.

In 1944, Congress focused its attention on drafting a bill that showcased a program known as the "52-20 Club." It guaranteed each veteran an unemployment benefit of $20 per week ($195 in 2000 dollars) for one year. Known as Public Law 346, the Servicemen's Readjustment Act focused on strategies to suspend returning GIs from the labor market so as to allow factories adequate time to retool for the switch from tank treads to automobile tires. A belated addition to the bill that was pushed by a handful of legislators and the American Legion included some provision for educational benefits. Disagreements between the Senate and House over the mixing of educational programs with medical and employment benefits held up the bill in 1943. The compromise version narrowly passed by one vote in a joint conference.

According to Edwin Kiester, Jr., the 1944 bill guaranteed military personnel "a year of education for 90 days' service, plus one month for each month of active duty, for a maximum of 48 months. Tuition, fees, books and supplies up to $500 a year would be paid directly to the college or university (at a time when private universities charged about $300 per year tuition and state universities considerably less). Single veterans were to receive a subsistence allowance of $50 a month, married veterans $75 a month."[2] Translated into 2000-equivalent dollars, indexed for inflation, this was comparable to $4,800 per year for tuition with a subsistence allowance of $489 per month for a single veteran and $734 per month for a married veteran.

Few expected much of the government's college plan. A feature article in the 18 August 1945 issue of the *Saturday Evening Post* observed that GIs were rejecting educational programs in favor of seeking jobs. Many college officials expressed reservations, even opposition to the act. What they really wanted was "business as usual," with traditional students returning in healthy numbers to resume the "real" college life that had characterized the late 1930s. Even supporters of the GI Bill projected that only about 8–10 percent of veterans would take advantage of the federal government's program that allowed them to enroll in college.

These early verdicts turned out to be off the mark. By the fall of 1945, eighty-eight thousand veterans had applied and been accepted for participation. By 1946, GI Bill college enrollments surpassed one million, and total benefits paid out by the federal government as part of the act exceeded $5.5 billion ($48 billion in 2000 dollars). By 1950, of the fourteen million eligible veterans, more than two million, or 16 percent, had opted to enroll in postsecondary education as part of the GI Bill.

One reason the program gained so much momentum is that some colleges deliberately put into place materials and programs that encouraged veterans to consider college. Harvard, for example, anticipated the postwar changes by initiating a vigorous advertisement and recruitment program among overseas servicemen before the war ended. In preparing brochures that projected an image of Harvard to GIs, the university sought to stimulate interest among talented young men who might be unfamiliar with "going to college." The concise, glossy brochure *What about Harvard?* provided potential applicants with attractive pictures of campus life and encouraging information. The no-nonsense prose encouraged inquiries from servicemen who were "of serious purpose" and who "mean business." Admissions requirements were flexible. Advanced standing was offered for those who could demonstrate achievement in a variety of forms. The brochure emphasized:

> This does not mean that intellectual brilliance is required for admission—or for success after admission. Character, experience, promise, all-around performance are vital.
>
> Harvard recognizes that the veteran of this war will expect something else from education than the ordinary peacetime student. Clearly the man who has been making life and death decisions at sea, in the air, and on the ground has other ideas than the man who comes direct from high school. The University is bending every energy to meet the needs of these men.[3]

The net result of such efforts was that many colleges and universities experienced a doubling in enrollments between 1943 and 1946. According to Kiester, eleven thousand GIs enrolled at the University of Wisconsin, pushing the size of the student body from nine thousand to eighteen thousand. Rutgers went from seven thousand to sixteen thousand by 1948. Stanford's enrollments increased more than twofold, from three thousand to seven thousand.[4]

What was notable about the Servicemen's Readjustment Act was the innovative terms of its educational program. First, it was an entitlement, which meant that all veterans who satisfied the published eligibility criteria were guaranteed the educational benefits. There was, in other words, no limit on the number of participants, nor was there a "first come, first served" constraint. Second, the tuition and benefits payments were portable. They could be "carried" by the veteran to the institution of his or her choice, so long as the institution met criteria for government approval. A GI could choose to apply not only to the undergraduate college at Harvard or to the University of Illinois, but also to junior colleges, trade schools, vocational programs, or graduate professional schools of law, medicine, dentistry, pharmacy, architecture, or engineering.

The catch was that an institution had to be federally approved if monies for tuition and benefits were to be transferred to a campus bursar.

This bureaucratic caution was warranted because veterans who qualified for the GI Bill became prey for a mushrooming industry of diploma mills and opportunistic educational programs that often were little more than a post office box and a brochure. The government charge was simultaneously to protect servicemen and to be a steward for taxpayers' dollars. Yet the federal government really did not want to get into the business of certifying colleges and schools. Nor did college and university officials relish the prospect of the campus being subjected to federal inspection in much the same way as Department of Agriculture representatives scrutinized and then stamped a rating on meat en route to supermarkets. The happy resolution was that the federal government agreed to accept as a proxy the institutional evaluations that colleges and universities themselves rendered as part of voluntary accreditation associations. This was a windfall for such regional accreditation associations as the Southern Association of Colleges and Schools, the Western Association of Schools and Colleges, the North Central Association, and so on. Henceforth, regional accreditation and its cycle of an institutional self-study and team visit every ten years became standard procedure among degree-granting colleges and universities—especially if they wished to be eligible for federal funds.

One legacy of the 1944 GI Bill was that quantitative change prompted qualitative change in the structure and culture of the American campus. The first innovation took place in the ways in which colleges and universities went about evaluating student applicants. Decisions now had to be made quickly, even though the applicant pool was much larger than usual. More problematic was that this new cohort of potential students often did not have traditional transcripts and college preparatory records. Furthermore, since colleges needed to move students through degree programs quickly, so as to free up space, admissions decisions now included evaluations to allow for advanced placement, for waivers of course requirements, and for a host of other complicated decisions. College administrations responded by relying on proxies for secondary-school transcripts, by considering the training and experience acquired by an applicant in the military. And colleges started to make increased use of standardized testing for both admissions and placement decisions.

The swelling of postwar enrollments signaled the need for massive construction of laboratories, classroom buildings, and dormitories. It also meant that college administrators had to accommodate the needs of new kinds of students—students older than the traditional college age of seventeen to twenty-one, students who were married and had children, and students who were disabled veterans. Numerous accounts in memoirs by students and faculty attest to the collision of cultures on campus and in classrooms as an unprecedented type of student cohort enrolled alongside recent high school graduates. GI students were typically depicted as worldly and experienced, impatient with the juvenile features of college life. They were pragmatic, hardworking, and in a hurry to complete their degrees. Above all, many of these students were first-generation college enrollees who came from families that had little experience of or expectation for a college education. The presence of the GI students also prompted traditional college constituents to rethink their activities. How, for example, could the hazing of a fraternity initiation intimidate a twenty-six-year-old army veteran who had been in mortal combat?

At times the large number of veterans absorbed as college students elicited mixed results for a campus. Contrary to some accounts, it is not accurate to say that veterans had no interest in traditional campus activities. In varsity sports, the presence of the veterans meant that there were unprecedented numbers of male students trying out for teams. In 1945 the coach at one naval training base in North Carolina accepted the head football coaching position at the University of Maryland on the condition that he be allowed to bring some members of his navy base service football team with him as undergraduates. The university president agreed enthusiastically and even took the initiative to arrange for a busload of sixty veterans to be picked up at the North Carolina naval base, be granted automatic admission, enroll immediately, and play three varsity games even before the academic year began.[5] Elsewhere, football squads swelled to as many as two hundred players.

The pragmatic, impatient GI collegians shaped curricular enrollments by voting with their feet—that is, by opting for courses and majors in such employable fields as business administration and engineering. At times there was a substantial difference in perspective between professors (especially in the arts and sciences) and GIs. For example, in Irwin Shaw's novel *Rich Man, Poor Man,* a reform-minded economics professor points out to the undergraduates in his 1949 classroom the inequities of the U.S. income tax structure, to the benefit of affluent families and corporations. The undergraduates, many of them students on the GI Bill, heed the lesson. They become inspired—not to try to change the regressive character of the tax code, but to go into business and partake of the tax advantages themselves.[6]

The students on the GI Bill tended to reinforce the conservative nature of the American campus. Nowhere was this more pronounced than in gender as a variable in enrollment patterns. Whereas women represented about 40 percent of the undergraduate enrollment in 1939–40, this participation rate dropped to 32 percent in 1950. The sixty thousand women military veterans enrolled in higher education as participants in the GI Bill represented a high participation rate (about 30 percent, compared with male veterans' 18 percent rate). Women nonetheless constituted a small percentage of total GI Bill enrollments. Hence one consequence of the GI Bill was to masculinize the postwar campus—both in terms of the sheer numbers of new male students matriculating, and by intensifying the split between the typically male fields of study and those now deemed appropriate for women. Although in the aggregate, enrollments in such professional fields as engineering and business soared, the increase was not marked by any gains for women in these fields. To the contrary, women's enrollments in such professions declined substantially in the 1950s. In sum, the social transformation of higher education set into motion by the GI Bill had a differential impact in that it enhanced the opportunities across lines of economic class, but with the opportunities inordinately favoring men rather than women. Not until 1970 would women regain the 40 percent proportion of higher-education enrollments that they had attained in 1940.

While the GI Bill enhanced postsecondary education opportunities for modest-income veterans, it had limited impact on race relations at colleges and universities. Black veterans were eligible for GI benefits and hence the program helped increase the number of black students who enrolled in college. But the terms of the GI Bill carried no requirement that participating institutions demonstrate nondiscrimination. Colleges that had traditionally excluded racial minorities continued to do so, with no penalty from the federal government. Indeed, at the time the GI Bill was being drafted, the U.S. armed services still had policies of racial and ethnic discrimination, especially in the United States Navy. The economic benefits of educational opportunity had yet to be extended to concern for civil rights. At best, the doctrine of "separate but equal" would be the operating principle for race relations in American organizations.

Despite the unexpected appeal and success of the GI Bill, neither its original advocates nor its critics envisioned it as a permanent program. It was large but finite, a temporary accommodation to alleviate a specific problem. Yet it furnished compelling data for advocates who wished to alter American higher education permanently by using government financial aid as a means to promote affordable universal access to undergraduate programs. The GI Bill was both a model for and a prelude to the distinct yet related higher-education policy discussions of the late 1940s. The most notable product of this situation was *Higher Education for American Democracy*, the 1947 report of President Harry Truman's Commission on Higher Education, chaired by a Columbia University professor, George Zook.

Access and Affordability: A Blueprint for Mass Higher Education

On 13 July 1946, President Harry Truman established a Commission on Higher Education whose twenty-eight members were charged with the "task of examining the functions of higher education in our democracy and the means by which they can best be performed." Specifically, Truman asked the commission to concern itself with "ways and means of expanding educational opportunities for all able young people; the adequacy of curricula, particularly in the fields of international affairs and social understanding; the desirability of establishing a series of intermediate technical institutes; the financial structure of higher education with particular reference to the requirements for the rapid expansion of physical facilities."[7] Implicit in this charge was the directive to explore whether the principles of the GI Bill might be extended beyond an intense, short-term program. The question was whether sound future policy ought to include an array of programs that would increase college choices and affordability for an entire generation of American citizens coming through the primary- and secondary-school pipeline.

The significant feature of this endeavor was that it marked the first time a president of the United States deliberately extended federal inquiry into nationwide educational issues; the Tenth Amendment of the United States Constitution customarily reserved the topic for state and local government. Particularly interesting was the rationale that higher education was integral to the national interest, including its international and social roles as well as national defense. Almost all commission reports succumb in part to the blandness of compromise and generic discussion. The Truman Commission Report avoided that syndrome and managed to assert forcefully a number of findings and recommendations that would be the blueprint for subsequent federal policies involving financial aid and the long-term expansion of postsecondary education.

When viewed from the perspective of 1980 or 2000, the report reads like a script for a succession of programs that ultimately became both familiar and famous. It presaged, for example, the tensions of racial segregation in public schools that would play out in the landmark 1954 case of *Brown v. the Board of Education of Topeka, Kansas*. It presented data and commentary on the inequities and injustices of discrimination in higher education on the basis of income and race. Its chapters provided pioneering commentary on the imperative for legislation and programs that a later generation of legislative and institutional reformers would group together under the umbrella term "social justice." And whereas most previous national discussions by foundations and other groups had focused on established colleges and universities, the Truman Commission Report devoted substantial attention to the public community college as an institution crucial to ensuring universally accessible postsecondary education. The foundation of the report's educational proposals was the economic argument that the United States devoted far too little of its gross national product to investment in postsecondary education. The report concluded with detailed plans for capital investment and taxation to make the educational expansion feasible.

The Achilles heel of the report was that it moved too far, too fast, in its suggestions for federal involvement in higher education. Although the president of the United States had established the commission, there was no imperative that its recommendations be linked to legislation either by the president or by Congress. President Truman was a Democrat and yet also a financial conservative. He was reluctant to pursue massive higher-education programs funded by the federal government. The report also suffered from bad timing. Truman was already facing a hostile Congress and an unsupportive press, especially with respect to his international programs and national defense policies. This situation, on top of his existing fiscal caution, made him unwilling to expend political capital pushing for an expanded federal role in higher education. In short, the Truman Commission Report was an intriguing policy program that was all dressed up but with no place to go. It had neither the precedent nor the presidential clout to work its way into congressional subcommittees.

The Truman Commission Report was controversial in that its recommendations ran the risk of encouraging federal intrusion into state and local policies, especially in the matter of state laws that mandated racially segregated public education. To put into context the cautious pace of lobbying for racial integration in colleges and universities, it is useful to note that this was precisely the time that Jackie Robinson had broken the "color line" in major league baseball—a landmark event that was both controversial and divisive. Given the current state of race relations in American institutions (whether baseball or the campus), politicians made certain that at the federal level, the commission report's immediate fate was to be tabled. Its influence would be revived ten to twenty years later during the legislation associated with John F. Kennedy's New Frontier and, later, Lyndon B. Johnson's Great Society civil rights initiatives.

Although the Truman Commission Report brought the federal government into the nationwide discussion about higher education, it was state governments, private foundations, and individual colleges and universities that took the initiative in the late 1940s and early 1950s to carry out its kinds of recommendations. It had been premature, perhaps presumptuous, for the commission to take on a visionary role. After all, governors, legislators, and state university presidents in such states as California, Illinois, Minnesota, and New York were already committing to investments in postsecondary education. State governments had already made a college education reasonably affordable and accessible to a large percentage of the American population, at least within the boundaries of their particular states. Moreover, the idea of federal educational policies was anathema to the presidents and boards of the nation's private colleges and universities, who were justifiably concerned about protecting their prerogatives of institutional autonomy and self-determination. They were also concerned about the relatively reduced role the Truman Commission Report envisioned for private colleges and universities; the report seemed to drift toward the illogical fatalism that federal monies somehow had to go primarily to public (state) institutions.

What American higher education had around 1950, thanks to state-by-state initiatives and new programs initiated by foundations, were nationwide trends without a national policy. And, as Paula Fass found, racial minorities made more gains in literacy and access to educational programs in the military than they did in public schooling during this era. The limitation was that these educational gains in the military had been achieved without racial integration.[8]

The Federal Government as Research Patron: "Big Science" as the "Best Science"

In marked contrast to the Truman Commission's attention to mass higher education, the other major area of federal policy deliberations after World War II focused on prospects for elite, advanced research and development in the sciences. The manifesto for this line of advocacy was Vannevar Bush's 1945 report *Science, the Endless Frontier.*[9] Bush was a physicist and electrical engineer from Massachusetts who had served as president of the Washington, D.C.–based Carnegie Institution. During World War II he headed up the federal government's Office of Scientific Research and Development. Given his success in having brought academic science to the solution of wartime problems, he was well positioned to make the case for extended federal support of research well after warfare had ceased.

Bush's argument had a particular historical and emotional dimension. Responding to the vague popular lament that America had lost the sense of pioneering adventure associated with the frontier and westward expansion, Bush argued that this pioneer spirit could be recaptured by shifting from geography to scientific inquiry as the arena for national exploration. Science was the appropriate and endless frontier. To this end, Bush recommended creation of a permanent and well-funded federal agency (an entity that would become the prototype for the National Science Foundation).

The essential principle that Bush and his colleagues emphasized was that such federal programs were not egalitarian in nature. The watchword was that "Big Science" was the "Best Science," and this meant a system of competitive grants awarded to university scientists who submitted proposals and were then selected by peer review to carry out government projects. The system stood in marked contrast to the practices of the late nineteenth century, when the federal government opted almost exclusively to build its own laboratories, agencies, and research infrastructure. Over time, the federal government would pursue both options. The historical significance of the competitive research grants advocated by Bush was that they were the genesis of what became the permanent support mechanism for a small number of powerful, well-funded research universities. These were the program and policy structures that would define large-scale academic scientific research for decades to come.

For Vannevar Bush and his close scientific colleagues, such as Harvard president and chemist James Conant, this was serious business. Patience was a luxury the campuses could not afford in bringing their underdeveloped science programs up to par. Proven excellence in solving high-level scientific problems was to be the coin of the research-grant realm. In practice this meant that projects would—and should—be awarded to a relatively small circle of established scholars and universities. The scholarly teams assembled for the wartime Manhattan Project provided a good model. "Big Science" as the "Best Science" was the appropriate policy by which to match talent with high priorities and sophisticated problems.

Unlike the 1947 Truman Commission Report, Vannevar Bush's *Science, the Endless Frontier* made a prompt, lasting impact on federal policies and programs. In essence the federal government became a research patron and contractor—not only through the new National Science Foundation (created in 1950) and the enhanced National Institutes of Health, but also through research and development initiatives undertaken in its disparate departments and agencies. The Departments of Defense, Energy, Agriculture, Transportation, and Health increasingly issued requests for proposals from academic experts to compete for specific research assignments. The wrinkle that bothered such advocates as Bush and academic scientists was that the new forms of research support tended to favor the applied projects and immediate payoffs sought by military-related federal agencies. How to promote sustained federal funding for pure science remained problematic.

How did universities respond to this new external environment? Some—including Stanford, MIT, Caltech, Johns Hopkins, and Berkeley—were ideally poised to compete for the growing array of new federal research grants. Furthermore, this relatively small circle of high-powered applied-science institutions was attractive to such federal agencies as the Department of Defense or the Atomic Energy Commission when seeking a permanent campus site for a federal research institute. The Jet Propulsion Laboratory at Caltech and the Research Laboratory of Electronics at MIT exemplified this trend. In the case of Stanford and MIT, most of their previous experience had been in the continual quest for contracts from private industry. For Stanford, the transition to the federal grant arena was a welcome change, for the National Science Foundation and other academic peer-review agencies were actually more cognizant of the preferences and work styles of university scientists than were the highly specific, pragmatic contracts from industry.[10] The University of California's flagship campus at Berkeley was on the vanguard of investment in an applied-science infrastructure that could deliver quickly the kinds of facilities and talent needed for large-scale federal projects, especially in physics and biology.

The unit within the American university that was most transformed by the post–World War II infusion of federal research funding was probably the medical school. Even though such reformers as Abraham Flexner had argued since the early 1900s that medicine needed to be linked to advanced scholarship in the biological sciences, only a few universities had pursued this proposition with much success. The Johns Hopkins University was the leader in fusing academic and professional work, but it remained exceptional, and few institutions were able to emulate its model. Most medical schools drew their entering students from the "pre-med" ranks of biology majors. The limitation of this linkage was that although a student might make connections between an undergraduate biology course and a medical school lecture, there was little assurance that medical school faculty were in touch with the new developments in research by biologists and other natural scientists. This changed in the early 1950s with the increasing availability of major research funding from the National Institutes of Health. Medical schools now increasingly extended their work in the clinical education of future M.D.'s to include research and publication by medical school faculty. One manifestation of this change was the addition of Ph.D.'s in the natural and physical sciences to the medical school faculty and research staff. Eventually, interdisciplinary institutes and research centers connected academic departments to the medical school. This process even led to the development of increasingly sophisticated research departments and rewards within the medical school itself. Medical schools benefited from the extension of pre-paid medical health plans from employers as well as the later growth of federal government plans such as Medicare that provided reimbursements for university teaching-hospital clinics. By 1960, medical schools and their host university medical centers typically stood out as among the most well-funded research institutions.

Harvard University illustrated some of the complications of this new research era. On the one hand, its president, James Bryant Conant, was one of the instrumental figures in the development of working relations between academic science and the federal government during both world wars. Nevertheless, Harvard's administration and faculty had mixed feelings about federal funding and were concerned about the potential for conflict. This was only the first of many institutional debates over whether accepting federal research funds compromised the spirit of academic inquiry. Eventually, however, Harvard and other universities had to face the fact that once the federal government's foundations and agencies became major funding sources in the sciences, it was virtually impossible for any university to maintain a leadership record in those selected fields without federal research funding.

The situation sent shock waves through the academic community because it meant that an external federal agency had the power to alter campus governance and institutional mission, including essential tenets of academic freedom. For once the principal headache facing university presidents was not a shortage of money but rather the political problems created by new monies and their uneven distribution.

Academic Freedom and Politics of Higher Education

When various groups, ranging from Congress to university presidents, agreed on the proposition that higher education was crucial to the national welfare, the rhetoric originally emphasized the positive contributions that colleges and universities could make, either by educating citizens in a democracy or by providing research expertise that contributed to national defense. However, in the years immediately following World War II, the rhetoric acquired a different emphasis—namely, concern that the American campus was a haven for dissidence and disloyalty. The Cold War campaign of Senator Joseph McCarthy's House Un-American Activities Committee and other investigative bodies caught most campus leaders off guard, since their presumption was that they were part of the solution, not the problem, in safeguarding the United States as a potent democracy in the new international order.

One thread that tied this criticism of the universities to the growing

involvement of the federal government in academic science was the controversy over the politics associated with such leading nuclear physicists
as J. Robert Oppenheimer. The premier physicists and chemists of the
day were cosmopolitan intellectuals whose work had allowed them to
move easily in and out of leading university settings, and from there into
federal research projects and back. But their reputations were compromised by vague charges of membership in the Communist party and a
host of related insinuations. Expressions of dissent, including overt support of international cooperation and peace, were was seen as a sign of
national disloyalty. President Robert Maynard Hutchins of the University of Chicago, for example, attracted the wrath of Senator McCarthy
when Hutchins tried (unsuccessfully) to persuade nuclear physicists to
not disseminate their knowledge and techniques and eventually to dis-
continue their research in this field.[11] The campaign against disloyalty
gained momentum in 1951, when the precocious undergraduate editor
of the *Yale Daily News,* William F. Buckley, published *God and Man at
Yale*—a provocative tract that lamented the alleged departure of Yale
and other established colleges from their traditional mission of service
to church and state.[12]

Public episodes like these brought to the fore two questions. Did the
receipt of federal research grant funds obligate a university to submit to
new tests for political compliance? And did such standards infringe on
academic freedom? Ultimately the questions extended beyond specific
research projects to broad inquiries into faculty conduct and the demand that faculty, especially at state universities, be required to sign a
loyalty oath.

Although the highly publicized congressional hearings chaired by
Senator McCarthy have received the most attention, these national episodes were only one part of the story of the postwar politics of higher
education. The investigations conducted by state legislatures and campus administrations showed that local politics were especially important
in shaping academic freedom. Ellen Shrecker, in her exhaustive 1987
study, *No Ivory Tower,* documented a surprising phenomenon: numerous state university presidents took the initiative to subject their faculties
to loyalty oaths and codes of conduct exceeding anything that vigilant
congressional or state officials might have required. Many campus presidents proved to be more interested in defusing external scrutiny than in
defending their professors' traditional rights of academic freedom.[13]
The most conspicuous examples were seen at the University of Califor-

nia, the University of Washington, and the University of Nebraska, yet variations on the theme surfaced at institutions nationwide. The most extreme consequence was the outright firing of some professors. At Berkeley, several senior faculty gained renown for refusing to sign a loyalty oath and then resigning their tenured appointments. Whatever gains President Robert G. Sproul believed he had achieved by purging the University of California of disloyalty were quickly offset by the university's loss of standing in the national academic community. It was uncertain whether Berkeley would still be competitive in attracting world-class scientists. Sproul was surprised to learn that the board of regents was watching him more closely than they were the university faculty.[14]

Less visible than the loyalty oath drama at the University of California were the hundreds of cases nationwide in which presidents and boards of trustees quietly and without due process ended faculty careers. The best depiction of the anti-Communist malaise that spread even to small liberal arts colleges was Mary McCarthy's 1952 novel *The Groves of Academe*.[15] In contrast to the general trend of presidents succumbing to the conformist pressures of legislatures and congressional investigations, a handful of university presidents—namely, Robert Maynard Hutchins of the University of Chicago and Harvard's new president, Nathan Pusey—had the courage to swim against the tide of Cold War hysteria over the real and imagined threats of Communism on campus. Each spoke out effectively for academic freedom. One disappointing development between 1948 and 1953 was the collapse of the Association of American University Professors and its failure to provide faculty members and institutions with reliable representation throughout the assorted skirmishes and major battles.

After the incendiary episodes of the anti-Communism loyalty oaths, by 1954–55 the universities still had to confront the long-term albeit less dramatic issues of reconciling federal research programs with campus autonomy. In addition to matters of principle concerning classified research, censorship, and authority to set a research agenda, academic officials had to try to hammer out mutually acceptable ground rules on the logistics of large-scale research grants. Questions of accountability, for example, ranged from such major policy issues as division of responsibility for research project overhead costs to the seemingly trivial (but problematic) ways in which academic researchers reported their time commitments to federal agencies. The issue over how research overhead costs would be handled and by whom was crucial because presidents and deans wanted to minimize expenditures of their own institutional funds on facilities and personnel necessary to fulfill external grant obligations. And there was always the tempting (but illusory) hope that a major grant had sufficient flexibility that it could be "bootlegged"—that is, diverted in part to subsidize existing university work that was only tangential to the grant specifications.

Transcending all these issues were the warranted concerns of such presidents as A. Whitney Griswold of Yale, who feared that federal agencies, not universities, would henceforth determine the course of "Big Science." Cabinet secretaries and federal agency directors were indifferent to such concerns. After all, their priority was neither to build universities nor to mediate internal campus issues. A university was a convenient locus in which specific academic experts could provide answers to specific applied problems. The universities, however, had far less reason to be sanguine. Sustained involvement in the federal research grant competition meant at the very least investment in such new offices as a vice president for research, including the elaborate staffing necessary to keep abreast of present as well as future research grant possibilities. The unexpressed concern of some academic leaders was that the cost of compliance with federal regulation, combined with the government's intrusion into the rhythm of academic life, would be a perpetual headache. As Roger Geiger discussed in his 1993 work, *Research and Relevant Knowledge*, the American campus—including the universities historically committed to advanced scholarship—was constitutionally ill suited to the kinds of interaction that external grants imposed on what was essentially a teaching institution.[16] Yet by the late 1950s the offerings of federal research grant dollars were so generous, and the truce between government regulators and campus administrators was sufficiently cordial, that most ambitious universities drifted persistently toward the various federal agencies as sources of sponsored research.

The Appearance of the "Federal Grant University," 1950 to 1960

Despite problems of philosophical and administration coordination, by 1960 one could identify a small number of universities who were inordinate beneficiaries of the federal research grant bonanza. President Clark Kerr of the University of California could write about the archetypal "federal grant university" as the apex of American—if not international—higher education. Kerr, in his Godkin Lectures at Harvard (published in 1963 as *The Uses of the University*), noted, "Currently, federal support has become a major factor in the total performance of many universities, and the sums involved are substantial. Higher education in 1960 received about $1.5 billion from the federal government—a hundred fold increase in twenty years."[17] Translated into 2000 dollars, this was the equivalent of about $8.7 billion.

The significant detail of this largesse was its skewed character in two dimensions. First, a small number of federal agencies were the source of virtually all federal research funding. The National Institutes of Health, for example, accounted for 37 percent of the total. Other major patrons included the Department of Defense, the National Science Foundation, the Atomic Energy Commission, the Department of Agriculture, and the National Aeronautics and Space Administration. Not surprisingly, sponsored research projects were concentrated in a few fields, particularly physical and biological sciences, health sciences, and engineering.

The exclusive character of the federally sponsored research enterprise was further intensified by the pattern of grant awards. According to Clark Kerr, in the 1960 federal funding for both project research and large research centers, "six universities received 57 percent of the funds . . . and twenty universities received 79 percent."[18] Within this circle of twenty universities, federal research grant dollars had come to account for a substantial part of a typical annual operating budget, ranging from a low of 20 percent to a high of 80 percent. Not only did this external funding set twenty universities apart, it also changed the internal dynamics of rewards and priorities within this select institutional cluster. It fractured a research university into its "haves" and "have nots." One corollary was the boost in power (and sometimes prestige) the federal funding gave to some professional schools, including engineering, agriculture, public health, and medicine.

The new addition to the higher-education vocabulary was "soft money"—originally meant to distinguish transient external funding from the "hard money" of permanent institutional operating budgets. Over time, however, the distinction became blurred. Base salaries and teaching loads became increasingly incidental for those departments that were positioned to compete successfully for substantial federal research grants. Furthermore, the credo of "Big Science as the Best Science" meant that peer review by external committees established by federal agencies gave strong priority to a research team's track record. The result was that the "rich got richer," with renewal of multiyear projects along with new awards to previous, proven recipients being neither unusual nor unexpected. Hence the question arose: After how many consecutive years of renewed funding did "soft money" become indistinguishable from "hard money"? Yet even in those universities well suited to participate in the federal research grant arena, presidents and deans were vexed by an essential feature of federal policy—namely, that there was little if any grant support directly for teaching and for "normal" institutional operations. This was most acute in university medical centers, where deans and chancellors faced the paradox of abundant funding for new, esoteric research projects while having to scrounge to maintain operating budgets for clinics and teaching programs.

Another of the multiple consequences of federal research investments became apparent in the alliances and orbits within higher education. Although almost all college and university presidents were members of the American Council on Education, campaigns and conversations about government policies increasingly shifted to the Association of American Universities—the Washington, D.C.–based group of leading research universities whose membership was by invitation only. It is important to note that membership in the AAU did not drive a wedge between public and private institutions of higher education. Membership was drawn from both sectors. Nor was it simply a matter of large institutions setting themselves off from smaller ones. Rather, inclusion in the AAU was determined by the prestige of institutional effort in doctoral programs and sponsored research.

One unexpected consequence of the concentration of research power in a relatively small circle of elite universities was that it promoted, rather than discouraged, institutional aspirations across the higher-education landscape. Given the challenge of "up" or "out" in the pursuit of external grants, numerous institutions chose either to stay in the game or to enter it for the first time. In what Clark Kerr called the "frantic race to remain contemporary," each year a growing number of professors and presidents mused about and then explored their own prospects for landing a subsidized project.[19] This "grantsmanship," as it was fashionably termed, was closely connected to the adding on of new degree programs, especially Ph.D. offerings. So whereas the established research universities may have believed that in setting themselves apart they had discouraged outsiders, in fact they had kindled ambition and imitation. The University of California at Los Angeles was probably the best example of a young institution that had the good timing as well as the talent to secure a place in this elite company. Over time, especially between 1960 and 1970, an increasing number of newcomer universities entered the competition for external grants. It was still a risky environment. As Roger Geiger has documented in detail, institutions such as the University of Pittsburgh started in 1955 to make a concerted effort to move into the prestigious research ranks. Despite its investments and planning, the president and his large contingent of vice presidents and academic support staff ran into problems. In focusing on the rapid expansion of advanced graduate programs, they neglected Pitt's traditional base of undergraduates, whose tuition payments had been a central source of annual budgets. The new initiatives also tended to alienate an older generation of alumni. Eventually the innovative university faced compression and was even on the brink of financial collapse.[20]

The first wave of post–World War II federal research funding leveled off in the late 1950s. It was replenished and then surpassed by a new impetus in 1957—namely, the congressional response to the Soviet Union's launching of the Sputnik satellite. The National Defense Education Act injected unprecedented new resources into advanced scientific research. Furthermore, it included provisions for training programs, including doctoral fellowships in such fields as Eastern European languages and other disciplines outside the usual boundaries of the natural and physical sciences. The good news for universities was that opportunities to apply for a broad range of research and development grants expanded throughout the 1960s. To enhance the deal, academic scientists commanded respect and even deference for their expertise that might somehow help the United States surpass scholars in the Soviet Union and other Eastern bloc Communist countries.

The Expansion of Ph.D. and Graduate Degree Programs

One impetus for adding on new research and doctoral programs was that in the late 1940s projections by some economists led to the conclusion that the expansion of American higher education, especially to accommodate mass higher education, would leave the nation with a serious shortage of qualified college and university faculty. In other words, there was a Ph.D. shortage that put the vision of expanded higher education at risk. The alarm was understandable, in view of the enrollment data. The heroic age of university-building at the turn of the century had not generated a stable, fully mature constellation of advanced degree programs nationwide. For example, in 1939–40, enrollment in master's and Ph.D. programs totaled just under 106,000 students—roughly 7 percent of all higher education enrollments. If the United States economy were to depend on the expertise scholars, both as scientists in industry and as professors in all fields, the pipeline was inadequate in terms of both capacity and quality.

One sign of response was that graduate enrollments more than doubled in the next decade, reaching 237,200 in 1950. However, this figure still represented only a minuscule percentage of total college and university enrollments. In a clustering comparable to the concentration of federal research dollars in a small number of institutions, around 1950 the same twenty universities accounted for the preponderance of doctoral degrees awarded. If national commitment to extending mass higher education were to play out in the coming decade, American universities were going to have to increase drastically their ability to educate, and graduate, students with Ph.D.'s in a variety of disciplines—the future professors for a wide variety of institutions, ranging from small colleges to large research universities.

The allure of expansion and ambition, however, was tempered by internal constraints, especially at universities that were relative newcomers to graduate programs. Deans had to deal with faculty requests for more advanced courses and seminars—a proposition that meant small enrollments. The same professors also demanded reduced teaching loads, increased library expenditures, and up-to-date laboratories. Sabbaticals and research leaves were mentioned as standard policies for a research university faculty. Commitment to building a doctoral program drove up salaries in another way: qualifications for chairing doctoral dissertation committees usually meant that a faculty member had to be tenured, and often a full professor. Such senior-level appointments commanded salaries far higher than a dean would have to pay to a new assistant professor just out of graduate school. All of these measures drove up institutional expenditures drastically. The problem was not insurmountable if a graduate program fulfilled two criteria: being at a prestigious university, and being in a field amply supported by federal agencies. Otherwise, it was a tough situation because most state legislatures and tuition-paying families remained concerned with basic provision for undergraduate education.

One fortuitous solution for presidents and deans, if not for undergraduates, was the increasing reliance on the teaching assistant. The advent of the "T. A." meant that a university could accommodate huge increases in the size of its undergraduate student body while simultaneously providing funding and apprenticeship work for an expanded number of doctoral students, especially in fields that had little chance of obtaining research grants. Indicative of the increased attention to Ph.D. programs was that the number of doctorates conferred rose from 6,420 in 1949–50 to 11,622 in 1960–61 and then continued to surge, to just about 30,000 in 1969–70. What the aggregate data do not show is that most universities may have added a large number of doctoral programs that were insubstantial skeletons. The paper gains generated by a proliferation of programs often were not accompanied by ample tuition-paying enrollments or resources. The consequence was that at many aspiring universities, advanced studies remained expensive frosting on the cake.

Starting in the 1950s, the increasingly attractive solution to the problem of scarce research resources was for a university president to identify selected fields as "steeples of excellence." Those designated as having both potential for prestige and the ability to attract external resources enjoyed a multiplier effect of added institutional support. The other departments were precisely that—"other fields," left out and left over.

Philanthropy and the Prospect of External Funding

The entrance of the federal government into sponsored research at universities after World War II seriously altered the ecology of external relations, for two reasons. First, the federal government supplemented and often surpassed private foundations as the major source of incentive funding that colleges and universities could seek. Second, the increase in federal research grants coincided with a relative decline and withdrawal of some historic foundations from sponsored projects. The Carnegie Foundation for the Advancement of Teaching, for example, had been one of the foremost sources of policy influence in higher education in the early twentieth century. Yet by 1950 it had lost the leverage of having funds to distribute and withdrew, at least temporarily, from the stage. In the meantime, the Ford Foundation—a relatively young philanthropic organization that had opened shop in 1936 as a local, family-based operation—began to assert a distinctive identity in higher education after 1947. Given the namesakes of the major foundations—Carnegie, Rockefeller, Rosenwald, and Ford—they were considered bastions of capitalism. To their surprise, however, even they were subjected to charges of subversion by a House committee in 1952 and by a Senate committee in 1954. Evidently their support of some scholarly projects involving folk tales, art, philosophy, and textbook revisions were thought to be un-American. The Ford Foundation's Fund for the Republic was a particular target of Senator Joseph McCarthy's House Un-American Activities Committee. The foundations may not have been able to escape such scrutiny, but they did survive it. By 1954 they were able to resume an agenda of generous support for higher education.

The major foundations differed from the assorted federal agencies in having flexibility and a charter that allowed them to focus on two kinds of projects that were not well suited to the customary constraints of government programs. The foundations could devote themselves, if they wished, to strengthening a particular campus—or an institutional genre, such as liberal arts colleges or private research universities. A variation on this theme was that they could set out to develop a new academic field or to reshape the character of an existing one, such as administrative science, religious studies, or experimental psychology. They would do so by providing incentive grants for curricular innovation or for hiring new faculty, by funding laboratories, or by subsidizing an institute or center. The result was that more institutions and more fields were able to partake in academic entrepreneurial pursuits than was likely to occur with the selective emphases of federal research programs, where the bulk of resources were connected to military-related projects. The Ford Foundation, in conjunction with other foundations, redressed some of the imbalances of federal patronage by choosing two foci in the 1950s and early 1960s: major private universities, and social and behavioral sciences. As Robert Bremner has noted, the Ford Foundation's largest gift was widely praised. It was a "special appropriation of $560 million [$3.6 trillion in 2000 dollars] announced in December 1955 to assist privately supported colleges and universities to raise teachers' salaries, to help privately supported medical schools strengthen instruction, and improve services. Toward the end of the 1950s in addition to conducting foreign aid and fellowship programs, supporting experiments in educational television, and supplying venture capital to both the more and less venturesome areas of scholarship, the foundation began to make grants to novelists, poets, artists, musicians, composers, and dramatists."[21]

The Ford Foundation strategy was particularly effective in the field of business administration. Long popular as a major among undergraduates, it was held in low esteem as a locus of scholarship and advanced study. To change this image (and reality), the Ford Foundation provided generous subsidies to institutions — the University of Chicago, Stanford, Harvard, Cornell, and Columbia — to invigorate the field by drawing from such disciplines as economics, political science, statistics, and sociology. The rationale was that these exemplary universities would then inspire other institutions to emulate their innovations.

The Ford Foundation also devoted serious attention to issues that scholars had raised as early as the late 1930s. Before the war, the Swedish sociologist Gunnar Myrdal had written a provocative study for the Carnegie Foundation that dealt with racial inequality as a pervasive problem facing American culture.[22] Likewise, the 1947 Truman Commission Report had devoted substantial attention to the inequities of educational opportunities for African Americans. It remained for the Ford Foundation in the 1950s and 1960s to invest large amounts in historically black colleges and universities, institutions that had long suffered from inadequate funding.

The Ford Foundation also contributed to the transformation of American higher education in another way: by using incentive programs and matching grants to prompt colleges and universities to develop a permanent, sophisticated fund-raising machinery.[23] The Ford Foundation initiatives exposed just how weak most colleges and universities were in systematic development activities beyond perfunctory alumni giving. Even such prestigious, wealthy universities as Harvard fell short in their capital campaigns in the late 1930s and into the early 1950s. By 1960, Harvard and virtually all other institutions (especially in the private sector) had come to recognize that they no longer had the luxury of treating the science and art of fund-raising as a peripheral activity. The administrative solution was to create a vice president for development, complete with a large staff, as a permanent officer who reported directly to the president.

From Capital to Campus: Coordination and Diffusion

The cumulative result of the postwar innovations undertaken by the federal government and the private foundations was that by the early 1950s, colleges and universities' problems pertained less to money than to limits of time and space. Numerous state legislatures had made generous provisions for expanding higher education. The question was whether colleges and their allies could respond quickly enough to accommodate the increases in enrollment due first to the returning veterans, then to the initiatives to increase civilian access to higher education, and finally to the projected "baby boom" of students who would soon be progressing through the educational system.

One solution widely brokered between university presidents and legislators, especially in the West and Midwest, was the mechanism of "formula funding." The practice had been around for decades as a way for taxpayers and state government to provide stable, predictable support for the public campus. What reenergized the concept now was its ideal suitability to an era of enrollment growth. According to economists of education, the major burdens of higher-education expense came with the initial expenditures on a campus, both for its physical plant and for instruction. Building a lecture hall and staffing it with an instructor to accommodate a single student was expensive. Each subsequent student, however, added only a marginal cost. And since the funding formula paid the same amount per student, a campus could enjoy a greater surplus of discretionary money with each additional student it admitted. The important detail was that many state governments, led by California, were predisposed to set the per capita student subsidy at a realistic and even generous amount. This was the stroke of genius that provided the fuel to run the engines of mass higher education, especially in the state universities, in the 1950s and throughout the 1960s.

In such states as California, New York, and New Jersey, legislatures also looked for mutually beneficial alliances with private colleges and universities. If the public colleges and universities were not able to accommodate the growing student population, legislatures believed, independent colleges and universities should be viewed as a source of relief. The logic was that an institution located within a state was a valuable resource, worthy of appreciation and state support. If, for example, Stanford University or Pomona College was able to educate a California high school graduate via a state tuition grant, why was this any less a contribution to the state's future than a state subsidy to cover the expense of educating a student at UCLA or the University of California at Berkeley? This feat was accomplished by means of state tuition grant programs that were scaled to an institution's tuition charge, awarded to a qualified student, and then carried to an institution of choice within the state. The benefits were multiple: it saved the state government the expenses of building more public campuses; it increased institutional choice for the scholarship student; and it allowed private colleges to charge tuition fees competitive with those at the state-subsidized public universities.

The Case of California, 1947 to 1970

During the 1950s, citizens of California were deluged with the messages of a state government campaign to avoid forest fires and litter, marked by the slogan "Keep California Green and Golden." Most Californians — and the rest of the nation — understandably mistook the campaign as an appeal to boost the state's affluence, whether in currency (green) or coin (gold). This unintended plan worked marvelously well, and a formidable combination of aerospace, agriculture, shipbuilding, automobile manufacturing, and electronics, along with numerous military bases and naval stations, began to power the engine of the state economy. And since California had been a major point of embarkation and return for military personnel, it was an obvious, pleasant place for veterans to settle — especially with the availability of low-interest Veterans Administration housing loans. The result was a demographic and economic boom that stimulated a comparably energetic investment in education at all levels.

The period between 1945 and 1970 represented the peak of investment in mass higher education in California.[24] The state benefited from a fortuitous combination of timing, demographic change, prosperity, and educational innovation. The crown of this unprecedented venture was the University of California, especially its historic flagship campus at Berkeley. The nationwide fascination with the California experiment in higher education was reflected in photojournalism. The 6 October 1947 issue of *Time* magazine devoted a lengthy cover story to new trends in public higher education, focusing on the University of California president, Robert Gordon Sproul. In the same spirit of public enthusiasm, the cover story for *Life* magazine's 25 October 1948 issue was Ralph Crane's fifteen-page photographic essay, "The University of California: The Biggest University in the World Is a Show Place for Mass Education." The vital statistics were staggering: 43,600 full-time students, eight campuses, no tuition charges for state residents, an annual operating budget of $44 million ($314.7 million in 2000 dollars), and an endowment of $40 million ($286.1 million). Proving once and for all that "Big was Better," the University of California was a place "where professors are famous, equipment fabulous, and educational opportunity almost unbounded." Its Nobel laureate science professors shared the limelight with a Rose Bowl football team and a national championship baseball squad at Berkeley.[25]

These two articles magnified a point that the 1947 Truman Commission Report had cited: of all the states, California boasted the highest per capita expenditure on students. That it was such a populous state made the statistic all the more impressive. Photographs of the magnificent campus facilities at both Berkeley and the newer UCLA drove home the point that publicly funded higher education need not be austere or inferior to the historic private colleges and universities.

The *Time* and *Life* articles both noted that this great university and university system were predicated on certain deliberate pedagogical decisions. Undergraduates could not count on having small classes or close working relationships with professors. President Sproul justified this arrangement as more than a matter of mere efficiency. The rationale was that students gained more from large courses taught by the best scholars in the country than from lesser lights in a smaller setting. At the Berkeley campus, with an enrollment surpassing twenty-three thousand students, students were viewed as either "swimming" or "sinking." The university tried to provide resources and assistance to those who were sinking, but its foremost obligation was to those who showed that they were able to swim in the demanding academic waters. So although the university's official motto was "Fiat lux!" (Let there be light!), entering undergraduates were warned, "Sink or swim!" Better advice for freshmen would have been, "Think and swim!"

Even though the University of California's historic campus at Berkeley received most of the attention, the photojournalism of the late 1940s and early 1950s gave increasing coverage to UCLA and to such sites as the agricultural research centers and special research institutes that gave the University of California such statewide presence. But another important development was going on outside the magazine editors' field of view: the expansion of and growing popular support for junior colleges and state colleges. The result was that the intrastate rivalries among the university campuses, state colleges, and junior colleges that had prompted the Carnegie Foundation to intervene in California policy discussions during the 1930s resurfaced after World War II, with greater intensity and higher stakes. Much of the decade of the 1950s was consumed with negotiating a workable governance structure that provided accommodations for each educational sector, along with some statewide coordination. The end product was the Master Plan of 1960, hailed nationally as a model of statewide governance.[26] It catapulted the University of California's new president, economist Clark Kerr, to national prominence, including a cover story in *Time* magazine.[27] The essential resolution of the Master Plan was its division of labor and mission. The University of California retained its exclusive right among public institutions to confer the doctoral degree. Its undergraduate admissions would be drawn from the top 10 percent of high school graduates. Meanwhile, the system of state colleges earned the right to confer master's degrees and to draw undergraduates from the top third of high school classes. The community college system was to have statewide presence and to provide a port of first entry for all students. The plan included language about articulation (in particular, transfer of students) from one institutional segment to another.

As evidence of the sustained educational growth within the state, by 1965 the University of California had nine degree-granting campuses — Berkeley, Los Angeles, Davis, Santa Barbara, Riverside, San Diego, Irvine, Santa Cruz, and San Francisco — along with dozens of special institutes, observatories, and field stations. Its total annual enrollment was over one hundred thousand. Tuition remained free for state residents. The state also supported a large number of state colleges, ultimately merged to form the California State University and College System of nineteen campuses with an annual enrollment of over 150,000. Extending this commitment to mass higher education, California had over one hundred junior colleges, primarily subsidized through local property taxes. And there was one other crucial element in the California higher-education success story, one frequently overshadowed by the state-supported initiatives: the thriving private colleges and universities. At the level of Ph.D.-granting institutions with a research emphasis, these included Stanford, the University of Southern California, California Institute of Technology, and Claremont Graduate School. Also within their rank of over sixty accredited institutions were such prestigious campuses as Pomona College, the Claremont Colleges, and Occidental College.

The end products of compacts and Master Plans masked crises in governance and funding that percolated throughout the "golden age."[28] For example, the crisis of overcrowding led some faculty representatives at the University of California to consider the proposition that a great university ought to abandon undergraduate education in order to concentrate on research and graduate students. Why not purge the major state university of responsibility for the "thankless task" of freshman- and sophomore-level instruction? Since one good (or bad) turn deserved another, perhaps *all* undergraduate instruction should be removed from the university and dispersed to the public junior colleges and the regional state colleges. Representatives of the California state colleges and junior colleges applauded this proposed division of labor.

Fortunately for the University of California, President Clark Kerr got wind of this faculty initiative and squelched it before its formal presentation for statewide consideration. Had this measure gone forward, it might well have freed busy research faculty for their projects and doctoral students. From the point of view of the university president, however, it would have been a disaster. It provided a timely reminder that although an institution's most advanced degree level might be its crowning achievement, it was not its sole mission. Designation as a doctoral-degree-granting campus hardly precluded commitment to the bachelor's degree programs. Even an institution that prided itself on research and graduate programs could not survive without the tuition and subsidies provided by undergraduate enrollments. And beyond the finances of enrollment-driven subsidies, few American universities were willing to forfeit the round of undergraduate life marked by intercollegiate sports, fraternities and sororities, and myriad other student activities.

California was only one of many states to invest substantially in expanding public higher education, both in size and in new structural arrangements. In New York the new creation was the State University of New York, known as the SUNY system—a massive statewide network of sixty-four diverse campuses whose total enrollment was over three hundred thousand in 2000. It included a flagship research campus in Buffalo as well as medium-sized and small sites created by upgrading existing state institutions and annexing existing private colleges, in addition to building new ones. New York was also home to a large urban system in New York City: the City University of New York, or CUNY, which included nineteen campuses and a total enrollment of more than one hundred thousand in 2000. The multicampus statewide system model gained popularity elsewhere as well, in such states as Texas, North Carolina, and Georgia.

The Massachusetts Model

Like California, Massachusetts embodied an extreme commitment to higher education. It did so, however, in a way that stood in marked contrast — geographically, spiritually, and financially — to the "California idea." Whereas California represented a geographically huge expanse that relied on generous public funding of a relatively young system, Massachusetts was a fairly compact state whose population and campuses were concentrated in the Boston area. Most important, Massachusetts never approached the California commitment to public, tuition-free higher education. It relied on its historic colleges and many private colleges and universities, especially in the urban area on the Atlantic coast. By 1960 there were no fewer than sixty degree-granting institutions in the greater Boston area, with numerous other campuses in the western part of the state.

Richard Freeland, in his historical study of universities in Massachusetts from 1945 to 1970, has documented a pattern markedly different from (and equally important as) the California experience.[29] At each university — Harvard, Tufts, Boston College, Boston University, Northeastern University, and the Massachusetts Institute of Technology — the president recognized that competition for students and donors within the greater metropolitan area would be intense. The result was that each institution, without the aid of any state mechanism, carved out a distinctive mission aimed at a specific constituency. Northeastern University, for example, avoided head-to-head competition for prep school graduates, opting instead to showcase its distinctive work-study curriculum. This kind of deliberate decision allowed Northeastern to assert a philosophy of education and simultaneously to keep its tuition charges low — a combination that was attractive to a substantial number of Boston-area high school graduates.

Competing institutions in the Boston area worked out compacts and voluntary cooperative arrangements. Boston College, for example, worked out mutually beneficial agreements with Harvard that included a plan for young Boston College faculty members to enroll in doctoral programs at Harvard. Although most of the established universities were concentrated in the easternmost part of the state—that is, in Boston—the major public university, the University of Massachusetts, was a hundred miles to the west, at Amherst. The University of Massachusetts followed the national pattern of growth, jumping from an enrollment of about six thousand in 1955 to over twenty thousand in 1965. Its expansion also included the creation of a medical center in Worcester, midway between Amherst and Boston. In this new environment, lobbying for scarce state resources pitted the rural, western part of the state against the urban, eastern section. Enrollments did increase in the private colleges and universities, as did research activities and degrees conferred. Despite this success, accounts written by the presidents and deans of the era indicate that the "golden age" was marked by continual tension and institutional uncertainty.

The period from 1945 to 1970 was especially demanding for tuition-dependent private colleges and universities. The need to attract qualified students left little room for complacency. And although the Boston area developed a substantial electronics industry fueled by the abundance of talent from nearby MIT and other engineering programs, Massachusetts as a state never attracted the statewide concentration of defense plants and aerospace production that brought large federal contracts to California.

The "Plight" of Private Colleges and Universities

The case of the universities in the greater Boston area suggests that after World War II the nation's private sector of higher education faced a distinctive situation that some at the time thought bordered on crisis. Some of the concerns expressed by these institutions' presidents and trustees turned out to be exaggerated if not unfounded. Nonetheless, they were justifiably concerned about how the flood of new public policies at the federal and state levels between 1945 and 1955 would influence their institutional options.

Prior to World War II the private colleges and universities enjoyed two advantages over public higher education: a longer history that tended to promote strong alumni loyalty, especially as expressed in donations; and a freedom from meddling by governors and state legislatures. The autonomy to set tuition, whether up or down, was illustrative of a flexibility in responding to admissions markets. However, by the late 1940s some presidents felt that these advantages were overshadowed by the benefits that were accruing to public higher education. Foremost was the increasingly generous state subsidy provided to public colleges and universities, which allowed them to keep the price of tuition artificially low. In 1950, private colleges and universities represented slightly more than half of overall student enrollments. Most projections indicated that this parity would fade in the forthcoming years as institutions stretched to accommodate mass access to higher education.

Why this was a concern to the private colleges is not altogether clear. Even though many new institutions such as junior colleges and state regional colleges had been built to accommodate large new enrollments, there is not much evidence to suggest that private colleges had lost students. To the contrary, even small colleges had to expand the size of their freshmen classes.

Williams College in the western part of Massachusetts was a typical case. Featured in an article in the 24 January 1949 issue of *Life* magazine, Williams College was the "poster child" of the liberal arts college set. Its president and faculty agreed that optimal enrollment ought to be 850 students—all undergraduates, pursuing the bachelor of arts degree full time. To accommodate the influx of veterans, Williams temporarily expanded enrollment to 1,123. The problem was this: "In a time when U.S. Colleges are moving more and more toward mass education, this sort of custom-made learning is an expensive luxury. Today hundreds of small liberal-arts colleges like Williams, unable to depend on state funds and unwilling to expand or raise tuition, must now get out and beg for money, or shut up shop."[30]

Williams' annual operating budget before and after World War II was as follows:

Category	1939–40	In 2000 Dollars	1948–49	In 2000 Dollars
Instruction	$465,467	$5,771,343	$665,021	$4,757,528
Administration	$99,966	$1,239,482	$197,050	$1,409,686
Maintenance	$167,961	$2,082,554	$295,000	$2,110,416
Health	$36,085	$447,419	$60,312	$431,469
Athletics	$47,459	$588,446	$101,193	$723,929
Scholarships	$66,027	$818,671	$70,700	$505,784
Other	$28,035	$347,607	$42,331	$302,833
Total	$911,000	$11,295,524	$1,431,607	$10,241,648

These figures represent an increase of about 57 percent in less than a decade—at first glance, a seemingly huge increase. However, it was due primarily to a surge in inflation nationwide after World War II, caused by pent-up savings and prosperity combined with a shortage of purchasable goods and products. Williams had actually kept educational costs down. The national inflation rate in that decade was 73 percent (1939 CPI = 41.6; 1948 CPI = 72.1; 72.1 ÷ 41.6 = 1.733, a 73.3 percent inflation rate)—far higher than the college's 57 percent increase. In other words, even though Williams had not indulged in lavish new spending on undergraduates, the institution was losing ground in the effort to balance its budget. To educate a student at Williams cost $1,300 ($9,300 in 2000 dollars) per academic year in 1948–49. With tuition at $600 ($4,292) and room and board at $180 ($1,287), the college was required to provide about $500 ($3,576) per student per year from its endowment fund. Part of the problem, according to the president of Williams College, was the allegedly unfair advantage that a state university enjoyed because of per-student subsidies. Educational philosophies were demonstrated in economies of scale. Educating a student for one year at the University of California cost $600, less than half what it cost at Williams. The small college also believed itself to be at a disadvantage in the market to hire new professors.

Henceforth presidents of private colleges and universities involved in public-policy discussions would refer to a "tuition gap" that they felt imposed upon them an artificial and unfair disadvantage in setting the price of undergraduate education. The response of state and federal legislators to this argument was mixed and mild. And, not surprisingly, most presidents of state colleges and universities turned a deaf ear to requests for fair play. Despite such problems, private colleges and universities were remarkably resourceful and effective in adjusting to the market of student choice in the 1950s and 1960s.

Their first initiative was to build strong, systematic fund-raising programs. Their second was to take the lead in designing and implementing a novel approach to financial aid. The most prestigious and prosperous colleges, especially those in the Northeast and Pacific Coast region, announced policies of need-based financial aid combined with "need-blind" admissions. This combination of initiatives transformed their ability to recruit talent across the nation—and across the socioeconomic spectrum. The essential feature of need-blind admissions as practiced at the Ivy League institutions, as well as at such colleges as Amherst, Williams, Wesleyan, Stanford, Pomona, Reed, Carleton, Swarthmore, Duke, and the University of Chicago, was that applicants were assured that a decision about admission would be made without regard to their family income. The crucial corollary was that an applicant who received an offer of admission based on talent was guaranteed to receive from the institution a financial package of grants, loans, and work-study jobs based on financial need. The program was intended to make college realistically affordable. The need-based aid policies were significant because they were developed by the institutions themselves and relied largely on institutional resources. These private colleges and universities were ahead of federal programs and policies in making admission more a matter of talent than of family income.

The external functions of fund-raising, admissions, and student financial aid were then harnessed to curricular refinements. Honors programs, special-topic seminars, accelerated programs, independent study, study abroad, and small class size were qualitative measures that provided an attractive alternative to the large, impersonal lecture courses usually associated with the state universities. And during a decade of population growth and expanded encouragement to go on to colleges, numerous private colleges and universities were now in a position to adopt policies of "selective admissions."

By about 1958 the overall rush to go to college, any college, had evolved into a rush to go to a prestigious college. These dynamics put academically strong colleges in the right place at the right time. Institutional reputation came to be set in large part by the number and percentage of applicants a college admissions office rejected. Scarcity and selectivity set off a flurry of magazine articles about getting into college. One example was Katherine Kinkead's lengthy piece in the New Yorker about "how an Ivy League college decides on admissions"—so popular that it was soon thereafter published as a book.[31] In revealing the mystique of admissions considerations, such articles kindled even more public interest in these colleges. They also spawned a flourishing cottage industry of manuals and books offering advice on "how to get into the college of your choice." The result was that private colleges were faring well by 1960, an achievement marked by irate letters from disappointed parents whose children had been denied admission.

Contrary to the pessimism voiced by presidents and trustees in 1950, private colleges joined the research universities in enjoying a "golden age." Indeed, many faculty and presidents at the large research universities looked with envy at the teaching and learning environment offered by a Dartmouth, a Brown, a Pomona, a Swarthmore, a Carleton, a Davidson, or a Reed.[32] In this era of mass higher education, there was ample room for donors and well-prepared students to support the "great books" and classical languages at a revived St. John's College in Annapolis, Maryland. The interest was sufficiently great that St. John's was able to extend its academic missionary work to the Southwest with a second campus in Santa Fe, New Mexico.[33]

One sign of this respect for the liberal arts college ideal was the zeal with which the research universities recruited recent graduates of the liberal arts colleges for their doctoral programs. Systematic studies of the origins of American scientists have pointed out that although the large universities were the capstone of advanced studies, the small, selective colleges made an inordinate contribution to the education and development of scientific talent at the undergraduate level.[34] The clamor to go to college by high school graduates was sufficiently high that newspapers ran articles alerting parents and guidance counselors to colleges that still had vacancies in their next entering freshman class.

The significant product of this interdependence between the research university and liberal arts education was what Christopher Jencks and David Riesman have called the "university college"—a selective undergraduate college that might be either a freestanding institution or part of a university.[35] In both models, it had success. Again contrary to the pessimism of 1950, private universities pioneered this model and garnered both accolades and applications. Columbia College within Columbia University demonstrated that it was possible to have a coherent curriculum and liberal arts setting within one of the world's most eminent research universities. The model was mirrored in undergraduate colleges established at medium-sized Ph.D.-granting universities, such as the Johns Hopkins University and Brown University. Princeton University followed the reverse route to a comparable end, adding a small number of superb doctoral programs in such fields as history, civil engineering, biology, physics, and psychology to its incomparable heritage of serious commitment to liberal arts undergraduate education. The undergraduate college that Robert Maynard Hutchins championed as president of the University of Chicago proved that liberal education need not be eclipsed by a galaxy of nationally respected graduate and professional schools. Rice Institute, once known as the "Cal Tech of the Southwest," added nationally praised Ph.D. programs in mathematics and engineering to a cohesive undergraduate residential college system as it became Rice University—and charged no tuition to any student it admitted. As frosting on the cake, Rice demonstrated that a commitment to rigorous, coherent undergraduate education for a student body of about twelve hundred need not be inconsistent with having a nationally recognized football team that routinely filled a sixty-thousand-seat stadium.

Liberal arts colleges exerted another influence on all of American higher education in the 1960s: they offered an antidote to the "impersonality" and alleged abuses of the large multipurpose university. The "cluster college" movement was one embodiment of this effect. In 1956 at the University of California, the Riverside site, which had historically been devoted to citrus research, was transformed into a state college, an "Amherst of the West" that would offer California students the experience of a small, liberal arts college close to home. Eventually the University of California at Riverside abandoned its special identity to pursue numerous doctoral programs and become one of many medium-sized research universities. With that transition, President Clark Kerr transferred the inspiration for a small, collegial college within the state university system to its new campus at Santa Cruz. This was the pet project of Kerr's one-time graduate school roommate and later UCLA professor Dean McHenry. It drew inspiration from Oxford, Cambridge, Swarthmore, and the Claremont Colleges to create a honeycomb of residential colleges intended to "make the university seem smaller as it grew larger."[36]

The "cluster college" model caught the attention of other presidents elsewhere. The University of the Pacific opened its Raymond College, and the University of Michigan provided its students with the option of a Justin Morrill College. The dominant model of the research university had kindled widespread interest in a countervailing reform impulse whose underlying principle was to advance the residential college virtues associated with commitment to meaningful undergraduate education. The good times for private colleges were not confined to the academically selective institutions. Some, such as Parsons College in Iowa, offered both a small-campus atmosphere and close attention for students who were having academic problems—a message of hope for the upwardly mobile parents of underachieving high school students.[37]

Undergraduates and Campus Life in the 1950s

Despite the differences in campus ambience that distinguished a state university from a small college, popular images of undergraduate life in the 1950s converged upon a common theme: "Joe College" and "Betty Co-ed."[38] According to this image, the typical "college man" was a full-time student who entered college immediately after high school, planned to graduate in four years, chose a major field in his junior year, looked forward to marrying his college sweetheart ("Betty Co-ed"), and sought a career position in a large corporation. This model of collegiate life was interdependent with a flush American economy—what one historian has called the era of "when the going was good." Sociologists such as David Riesman characterized the college students of the 1950s as a "quiet generation," interested in stability and ostensibly well suited for what William F. Whyte called the life of the "organization man."[39]

As with all such characterizations, this image of collegiate life was reasonably accurate yet glossed over numerous variations and departures. One different and increasingly important pattern was that of the public junior colleges and commuter institutions. Perhaps the most glaring omission was that the "Joe College"/"Betty Co-ed" model represented the percentage of undergraduates who succeeded in their college studies. It overlooked the high attrition rate, especially in the freshman and sophomore years. Exactly how American society and its economy received such former students was the subject of little public discussion at the time.

The dominant image of a "quiet generation" of collegians also tended to gloss over pockets of ingenuity and innovation. A good illustration of this, and of American attitudes toward college, may be found in novelist Philip Roth's 1988 essay "Joe College," a memoir of his undergraduate days at Bucknell College in the early 1950s. Roth's high school education and family background precluded academic distinction. A graduate of an urban New Jersey public high school, young Roth's initial notion of "going to college" was to take classes at the Rutgers branch campus in downtown Newark. Quite outside the formal channels of high school advisors, however, Roth acquired a vague knowledge of prestigious colleges from an unlikely source: the betting line on college sports run by local bookies. Roth recalled that beyond the obvious elite colleges such as Yale, Princeton, and Harvard, he learned about other institutions, "hundreds of them: Wake Forest, Bowling Green, Clemson, Allegheny,

Baylor, Vanderbilt, Colby, Tulane—I knew their names." A high school friend who attended Bucknell in Lewisburg, Pennsylvania, struck the impressionable Roth as the very model of the "college man"—at ease, quietly confident, and at home in the enticing world of classrooms, fraternities, lecture halls, and laboratories bordered by the green lawns of a prototypical American campus. For Roth, the son of Jewish parents who prized education but had not gone to college themselves (his father was an insurance company branch manager), Bucknell provided the delightful experiences and associations that led to what he called collegiate "poise and savoir-faire." When visiting the campus, Roth discovered to his surprise that his parents shared his enchantment with the place. Even though he did not qualify for a scholarship, he had good grades, and his parents and uncles were adamant that they could come up with the money necessary for Philip to go to a "real college."[40]

Over the next four years Roth the enthusiastic collegian would undergo a succession of experiences inside and outside the classroom that constituted an education in the fullest sense of the word. This socialization into the company of college-educated men and women was different from, and more substantive than, the "poise and savoir-faire" Roth had anticipated as a college applicant. It ranged from navigating the subtleties of anti-Semitism to finding an intellectual home in the extracurricular worlds of campus journalism and the literary magazine. Above all, it was a biography of college life that had hundreds of thousands of variations and replications in the expanded orbit of American higher education in the 1950s.

Philip Roth's individual case was indicative of a larger phenomenon. Economic prosperity, educational aspiration, and a demographic boom gave most colleges and universities many reasons for celebration—and little reason to be preoccupied with potential problems. There were, however, some storm warnings of substantial problems looming in undergraduate education, as revealed in the systematic research studies of psychologist Nevitt Sanford, formerly a tenured professor at Berkeley who resigned his faculty position to protest the imposition of the loyalty oath. What Sanford and his colleagues discerned in the late 1950s and early 1960s was a normlessness and floundering among college students. His pioneering anthology, *The American College: A Psychological and Social Interpretation of the Higher Learning,* sounded an alert in 1962 for deans and professors to heed the growing concerns voiced by students.[41]

Most campus administrators, however, opted for "business as usual" in the early 1960s.

One area of undergraduate extracurricular life that reached its nadir in the 1950s was intercollegiate athletics. Between 1948 and 1952, college presidents struggled in vain with attempts to draft a satisfactory code of conduct for varsity athletes and athletics administrators. A point-shaving scandal in basketball brought infamy to such prominent programs as the University of Kentucky and several New York City–area college teams. The West Point football program was decimated by revelations of systematic cheating on academic examinations. Although representatives from the Pacific Coast Conference led a successful campaign to approve a "sanity code" of student-athlete conduct in 1948, its attempt to construct a national policy to ensure that student athletes were genuine students soon collapsed, for two opposing reasons. Academically strong institutions with relatively clean varsity sports programs, led by the University of Virginia, resented an external group's intrusion into university policies. At the other extreme, presidents at numerous colleges and universities relished big-time sports and its system of special privileges for athletes, and hence balked at any measures that would threaten their sports powerhouses. No national group of academic leaders, including the American Council on Education, was able to put together a coalition and policy that brought reasonable oversight to college sports. The last-ditch attempt to solve the problem was to give, by default, new regulatory powers to the National Collegiate Athletic Association — a body whose primary purpose had been to help promote national championship games. It was a compromise that tended to propel the momentum of big-time college athletics and promote an economic cartel in the coming decades.

From Junior College to Community College

As suggested above, one inherent limit of the "Joe College" and "Betty Co-ed" images of college life was that they were grossly mismatched with the college experience of a growing number of students. This disparity between image and reality was most acute with the expanding constituency of the public two-year institutions. In 1950, enrollment in public two-year colleges was 168,043. The figure more than doubled over the next ten years to 393,553. Then, between 1960 and 1970, enrollments increased more than fivefold, reaching about 2.1 million. One estimate was that on the average, a new public community campus opened each week during the decade starting in 1960. This incredible growth masks some interesting developments. Foremost was the relative decline of private two-year colleges. Second was the changing missions of the public institutions.

Developments in California were significant because of the sheer numbers involved and also as a forerunner of policies and practices more or less emulated in many other states—captured in the name change from "junior college" to "community college." To recap a trend mentioned in the preceding chapter, by 1940 advocates of vocational education and terminal programs had gained a strong position in California's policy debates. After World War II, however, determining the purposes of the two-year institutions became increasingly complicated. The immediate crisis that elicited change was the urgent need to accommodate both veterans and then an enduring flow of high school graduates seeking postsecondary education. Not even the most growth-oriented university could accommodate all its applicants. Hence the junior college regained what had been a diminishing role as a transfer institution that provided the first two years of a bachelor's degree curriculum. Most reports from state university officials indicate that junior college transfer students did well in their upper-division work, including their ability to graduate on time.

At the very least, then, a typical junior college served two distinct constituencies: terminal students and transfer students. Addition of new missions and new constituencies ultimately meant that the "junior college" was transformed into the "community college." In a state such as California, the idea that the two-year public institution should be exclusively or even primarily a transfer institution and a handmaiden to the state university was anathema. This was so because in California, junior colleges were funded largely through local property taxes—an arrangement comparable to extending K-12 public school funding an additional two years beyond high school. The analogy was reinforced by prevalent terminology: the head administrator of a public junior college was often called a "superintendent," bringing to mind a school district. Faculty were referred to as "instructors" rather than "professors," and most hiring relied on a local pool of applicants. The result was that in the 1960s most two-year public colleges combined the academic transfer role with a range of courses, programs, and curricula. This proliferation of missions directed toward nearby constituencies led to the name "community college."

Here was an institutional structure that claimed to fulfill in the 1960s Ezra Cornell's motto from a century before: "I would found an institution where any one could study any thing." Welding classes coexisted with courses in philosophy, real estate licensing courses with calculus. At many community colleges the aim was to provide a port of entry for the underserved. This meant that often a high school diploma was not required to take certain courses. It also meant that students at community colleges were quietly and steadily transforming the profile of the college freshman and sophomore—even though this transformation was slow to be acknowledged either by higher education researchers or by the general public.

Data from the University of California indicate that from about 1955 to 1965 those students who opted to transfer from community colleges to upper-division bachelor degree work at the state university did well in terms of grade-point average and degree completion—or at least as well as their counterparts who entered the university as freshmen. This profile seemed to confirm the community college's promise as a transfer institution. However, the picture is incomplete because only a small percentage of community college students sought such articulation or transfer. Furthermore, community college transfer students as a percentage of total state university enrollments declined steadily after 1960. It was difficult for planners to construct an accurate profile of the major student types or principal academic goals within the community college sprawl. The biggest uncertainty was the wisdom of investing large sums of public monies in two-year institutions that seldom offered dormitories or a residential campus experience to the large percentage of students who had no prior family experience of higher education—and who would be pursuing their postsecondary education living at home or in an off-campus setting devoid of the extracurricular learning and living experiences that were so crucial in enhancing cognitive skills and changes in attitudes and values. The flourishing of the commuter two-year public college after World War II demonstrated the generosity and innovation of American state legislatures in supporting new higher-education structures that were affordable and accessible—and whose educational effectiveness was unknown.

Testing and Tracking: The Sophistication
of Selective Admissions

A common thread that connected the academically selective institutions with the regional state colleges and the open-admissions community colleges was the universal reliance on standardized testing as one component of an application to help admissions officers make categorical decisions about who should go to college where. The result was the emergence of a potent testing industry guided primarily by the College Entrance Examination Board and its widely used tool, the Scholastic Aptitude Test. The CEEB had been around since early in the century, primarily working with a small group of prestigious colleges in the Northeast. Shortly after World War II, advances in mass standardized testing allowed the CEEB to develop a version of the SAT that replaced its traditional essay exams and individually graded components with electronically scored multiple-choice tests.[42]

The SAT had multiple influences on American life. For institutions, it facilitated the bulk processing of large numbers of applications. For American high school students and their parents, it came to symbolize the high stakes of college admissions and the ritual pleasure-pain of receiving "thick" or "thin" envelopes from deans of admission. Advocates of the SAT praised its utility for helping colleges identify talent, as measured by verbal and quantitative aptitudes scored on a scale of 200 to 800. In the early 1950s Charles McArthur's research on Harvard undergraduates suggested that the SAT was effective in helping to identify intellectual talent in public high school graduates — a group that historically had been at a disadvantage in admissions to the elite private colleges when competing against alumni from exclusive prep schools.[43] In a more general sense, the rise of the SAT introduced into the national vocabulary such phrases as "bands of confidence" to depict the range of implications for a student's score. As Joel Spring has put it, such testing and tracking helped higher-education officials construct an educational "sorting machine."[44]

The CEEB and its SAT faced disagreements even within the circle of national researchers and campus administrators. The disputes often played out along geographical lines. In the Midwest, for example, psychologists at the University of Iowa developed the "ACT," the American College Testing service, as a test whose intent was to combine admissions decisions with informed decisions about field of study and choice of major. Whereas the SAT was viewed primarily as a means to facilitate admissions decisions and selection, the ACT was as much an internal placement resource as a gatekeeper to keep unwanted and unworthy applicants at bay. Testing patterns reflected both regional and philosophical differences. The Ivy League campuses of the East Coast were seen by academics in other regions as exclusive — and hence their reliance on the SAT.

The test-makers' confidence in the SAT's validity was matched by campus administrators' appreciation for its convenience. Admissions officers valued it as a useful source of timely, concise data that could be correlated with other measures, including grade-point average, as a predictor of college-level performance. Confidence in the SAT, however, was never universal among scholars, who critically examined the validity and significance of standardized tests. One criticism was that few if any institutions ever relied wholly or consistently on SAT scores as a tool to guide admissions. Favoritism, whether bestowed on a star athlete or the child of a wealthy alumnus, always played a part along with high school transcripts and SAT scores in deliberations about selective college admissions. The corollary to that criticism was the concern that the SAT may have tended to reward the benefits of high socioeconomic status and its educational advantages.

One controversial contribution to this discussion was the observation in 1968 by sociologists Christopher Jencks and David Riesman that "tests are not unfair to the poor. Life is unfair to the poor — tests merely measure the results."[45] That observation might have explained the actual workings of testing and sorting in higher education, but it did not vindicate the process. A persistent, and warranted, doubt was whether the SAT was truly an "aptitude" test. Despite the CEEB's assurances that it was, the gradual but persistent drift in the scholarly analysis of the test suggested that it was more accurately described as an achievement test. Furthermore, there was growing evidence that coaching and gaining familiarity with the SAT enhanced performance. It was all yet another example of the partial triumph of meritocracy in American education.

Confronting Racial Segregation in Higher Education

One important initiative undertaken by the Rockefeller Foundation's General Education Board was to address funding disparities in higher education in the South. This effort included particular attention to private and public colleges whose historical constituency was black students,[46] and it was supplemented by institutional incentive funding from the Ford Foundation. After World War II, seventeen states in the South had legally segregated public educational systems. Racial integration in these states was marginal at best, and typically slow. In some cases voluntary integration of the all-white state university took place before the 1954 *Brown v. the Board of Education of Topeka, Kansas* court case. One example was the University of Kentucky, whose board opted to admit Lyman T. Johnson to the graduate program in history in 1949, a decision followed shortly thereafter by the admission of several other black students to a range of degree programs. Elsewhere the racial integration of state universities was contentious, even hostile, with violent student protests and gubernatorial opposition accompanying efforts at the University of Alabama, the University of Georgia, and the University of Mississippi.

The desegregation efforts of state legislatures and state universities during the 1960s were largely a matter of halfhearted, token compliance. According to Peter Wallenstein, by 1968 racial integration had been nominally achieved at all state flagship universities in the South, often as the result of litigation. But changes in admission policies at these institutions did not necessarily mean that black students were accepted in campus life, for segregation and exclusion often continued in dormitories, dining halls, and classroom seating arrangements.[47] Wallenstein's thoughtful research also systematically documents the uncertainty and slow pace of the progress toward some semblance of racial equality and social justice in American colleges and universities. Black students who opted to be pioneers in racial desegregation in the two decades between 1948 and 1968 often endured isolation, shunning, and sabotage, along with exclusion from "real college life" and the opportunity to participate in sports teams, dramatic productions, residence hall life, and dining commons. In some instances fellow undergraduates deliberately supported strategies that turned the newcomers into second-class citizens of the campus. Elsewhere, students tried with varying degrees of effort and success to evade or overturn the race-based restrictions imposed on black students by deans and presidents. According to Wallenstein's survey, the prevalent aim at most campuses was to comply quietly in an attempt to minimize conflict with either external audiences or internal campus constituencies.

In many cases graduate and professional schools became the vanguard of black admission to historically off-limits colleges and universities. There were two overlapping but distinct reasons for this phenomenon. By picking a graduate program and a field of study not offered at a state's historically black college or university, a black student and his or her supporting group could highlight flaws in the "separate but equal" doctrine. If the state's black institution did not offer a particular field of study or degree program, then how could it be equal? At times this strategy led universities to scramble to provide ridiculous solutions. The University of Kentucky, for example, went so far as to have some of its law professors drive by personal automobile several times a week to another site to provide a surrogate "law school" for a black applicant. Mercifully, this transparent "solution" soon collapsed. At some state universities the guardians of racial purity took consolation in admitting black students to, say, the law school or the doctoral program in education because it kept the historic undergraduate college — the "real heart of the institution" — unsullied in composition.

Studies by Melissa F. Kean, Clarence Mohr, and Nancy Diamond show that ending their policies of racial exclusion was a matter of little concern to the well-endowed private universities of the South that had aspirations to national prominence.[48] In the decade after World War II, Tulane, Vanderbilt, and Emory were going full speed ahead in the activities that marked prestige: selective undergraduate admissions, enhanced doctoral programs and professional schools, and above all emphasis on research in medical centers. But racial integration, let alone any meaningful partnership in helping to improve race relations in the host city and region, was an effort almost always dismissed by governing boards as a nuisance to institutional advancement. At best an ambitious president might from time to time express concern that a policy of strict racial segregation might count against a Southern campus that was being considered for awards and honors among a nationwide circle of established universities. But ironically, between 1950 and 1965 concerns about race were incidental at almost all prestigious colleges and universities in the United States — not just in the South.

The result was that black students remained marginal and proportionately underrepresented at almost all racially desegregated campuses in the United States. Furthermore, the so-called HBCUs, the historically black colleges and universities, continued to enroll and confer degrees to a large proportion of black high school graduates who pursued a bachelor's degree between 1945 and 1970. In addition to fulfilling this academic function, the historically black institutions played another important role in the 1960s: their students were the risk takers and leaders in numerous civil rights demonstrations, especially in efforts to integrate restaurants, stores, and bus stations throughout the South. Ironically, the shops and lunch counters that were adjacent to black colleges often refused to serve black students. These early efforts by black student groups had inordinate influence on all college and university civil rights movements throughout the 1960s.

The efforts of the black students and alumni who were leaders in national civil rights efforts were laudable—but, unfortunately, also insufficient to solve the chronic problems faced by the historically black colleges and universities. A small group known during the 1960s as the "Negro Ivy League"—Howard, Spelman, Morehouse, and Hampton Institute—had the cachet of historic presence and relatively large endowments. But for most of the 110 black colleges, whether public or private, endowments were low, faculty workloads heavy, laboratories antiquated, libraries understocked, and the future uncertain. Perhaps these institutions did educate a cohort of young adults and socialize them into the middle class, including professional ranks. But they did so in a largely undistinguished fashion. Undergraduate life on the black campuses was usually dominated by a preoccupation with fraternities and sororities akin to the hackneyed features of student culture at most white colleges. And when the most prestigious and affluent white colleges, such as the Ivy League, started to make a concerted effort to recruit and provide financial aid for academically strong black high school seniors, the traditionally black institutions were placed at an additional disadvantage in the competition for talent. Finally, their relatively few advanced degree programs, especially in the sciences and engineering, tended to preclude black institutions and their faculty from being strong contenders for federally sponsored research and development grants between 1945 and 1970.

Mass Higher Education and Student Discontents

The increasing variety of models for undergraduate education that thrived in the early 1960s—liberal arts colleges, "cluster colleges," honors colleges, and junior colleges—was symptomatic of both the health and the weakness of American higher education. The fact that the innovations emphasizing small size and personal contact between instructors and students were so popular threw into dramatic relief the undeniable fact that a large, growing number of undergraduates were pursuing their studies amid what was called the "impersonality of the multiversity." The model that had proved to be an effective structural accommodation for increased college enrollment and a way to garner resources for high-priced graduate programs was an increasingly unsatisfactory experience for many students.

A long season of discontent started to percolate into active student unrest at a few major state universities — most conspicuously, the University of California at Berkeley. In addition to voicing concern over large lecture classes, an articulate minority started to question the regulations imposed by deans of students. The flash point centered on students' rights of self-determination in hosting campus speakers and in simply speaking out on political issues. As campus administrators imposed restrictions, students showed organized resistance.

This was not an altogether new phenomenon, either at the University of California or at the University of Chicago, the University of Wisconsin, the City University of New York, and Columbia. The American campus of the twentieth century had long provided a thin but tenacious lifeline for radical scholarship and dissenting politics. Student activism had been effective in extending student rights to selected issues. From time to time over several decades at Berkeley, undergraduates and the university administration had clashed over the question of who ultimately had control over student activities, including the daily student newspaper. University administrators were caught in their own historic web in that they had long given lip service to the claim that the large-university experience brought out the best in students in terms of resilience and the ingenuity needed to survive and flourish. At those state universities where administrators lacked either the resources or the inclination to provide ample on-campus dormitories, students formed enduring autonomous housing cooperatives, complete with charters and governing boards.

Perhaps the best formal manifestation of this administrative invitation to undergraduate organization was the ability of students to incorporate and then operate elaborate student associations. At Berkeley, for example, the Associated Students of the University of California, known by the acronym ASUC, ran the student union, sponsored the newspaper, had an elaborate budgeting process, collected mandatory student fees, and even had its own lobbyist at the state capital. In the 1930s the ASUC committed time and resources to such campus-community issues as labor, housing, health, and racial discrimination. Through such collective strategies, including successful cooperation with the city council, students were integral to implementing "Fair Bear" rental codes for students and landlords as well as the "Clean Bear" campaign to bring restaurants adjacent to the campus up to ASUC standards of public health and cleanliness — initiatives in which students combined political savvy with economic sanctions to shape campus life largely apart from the university administration. The ASUC's counterpart at UCLA was involved in the same kind of activities and was even responsible for contracts and payrolls for varsity coaches. And periodically, when university administrators attempted to intervene in the activities of a student association — either by censoring a student newspaper or steamrolling a coach's salary contract through the student board — the student associations proved to be quite effective at fending off what they considered to be illegal administrative intrusions.[49]

Given the high degree of organized student power that was already in place in the 1950s, it is not completely surprising that students at the large research universities eventually sought to protect their rights and space. The activity of the 1950s was a distant early warning signal that students — or at least some students — sought relief from the predictable, festering problems of undergraduate education as something of a neglected stepchild within the university scheme. By 1963, local campus events at Berkeley, Michigan State University, and a handful of other universities started to attract nationwide attention through coverage in newspapers and evening news broadcasts.

University managers took pride in their increasing use of technology to handle the problems of course enrollments. Yet to some vocal students, these administrative solutions were part of the problem. Computer punch cards, for example, were one of the technological tools that came to be elevated into a symbol of bureaucratic indifference. Undergraduates pinned the cards to their lapels along with the motto "Do not fold, spindle, or mutilate" — referring to themselves as students, not the computer cards. The enduring slogan of undergraduates at large institutions was that they "did not want to be known only as a number" — an implicit demand for such reforms as small class size and humane living environments. In a subsequent series of firm but well-behaved protests, students — the men carefully dressed in sports coats and ties, their beards neatly trimmed — started to make demands on trustees, presidents, chancellors, and deans for changes in the conduct of campus affairs.

What started out as essentially a demand for curricular reform eventually was linked to growing concerns about university policies on classified research for government agencies. In the dramatic depiction by student dissidents, the university was a "knowledge factory" committed to providing trained personnel and research expertise for the "military-industrial complex."

A strange feature of the melodramatic student slogans is that they were remarkably consistent, in vocabulary if not tone, with descriptions that adult leaders of the "establishment"—namely, university administrators and even the president of the United States—had used. The phrase "military-industrial complex" had been coined not by a radical thinker like Thorstein Veblen or Karl Marx but by President Dwight D. Eisenhower, in one of his farewell addresses from the White House. Moreover, Clark Kerr, the economist who had served as professor, then chancellor, and finally president of the University of California, had talked matter-of-factly about the university as part of a "knowledge industry." And in other settings such as addresses to business leaders and the citizens of California, he had spoken unabashedly and positively about the ability of the university to meet the needs for developing talent and placing it in the economy of a technological society.

The disagreements between undergraduates and university administrators that escalated between 1961 and 1965, then, were not about the facts of the university's role in society but rather the appropriateness of that role. Questions about the university as a home for research sponsored by the Department of Defense reached a new level of volatility in 1964 and 1965, when they became linked to growing political dissent about the United States' military presence in Southeast Asia. For years students in junior high or secondary school might have had sporadic exposure to readings and discussions about "Indochina" when a current-events class happened to devote some attention to international affairs. But for most Americans, including college students, the subject remained peripheral. This would change dramatically when what had until now been known only as a distant French colony came to be familiar in newspaper articles and political discussions as Vietnam.

Between 1963 and 1968, student protests were highly publicized news events that gained nationwide attention. That intense participation, however, tended to be confined to a handful of campuses. And even at a campus like Berkeley, life for most students and faculty remained markedly conservative and predictable. On the afternoon of a peace march or even a violent demonstration, engineering students still worked on their projects, music recitals took place, and varsity athletics attracted large crowds. Student strikes at Columbia and Cornell in 1968 and then at Harvard in 1969 contributed to the visibility and momentum of a national antiwar movement that owed much of its initial impetus to campuses. In May 1970, however, the confrontations at Kent State University in Ohio and Jackson State University in Mississippi between student protesters and National Guard troops — confrontations in which undergraduates were shot at and even killed — propelled the campus movement into the mainstream of American news and life with a force that was wrenching and riveting.

A peculiar feature of the campus turmoil of the late 1960s is that the opposing factions both tended, each in its own way, to threaten academic freedom and intellectual integrity. The violence and coercive tone of the intense student radicals tended to quash reflection, analysis, and open discussion — especially if a student or professor disagreed with the orthodoxy of reform. Slogans like "If you are not part of the solution, you are part of the problem" epitomized the false dichotomy and the pressure to conform that stifled academic freedom and repelled thoughtful students and faculty who might have shown some sympathetic interest. Less visible yet equally restrictive were the special accommodations that university presidents and boards had given to numerous federal and industrial research projects whose intellectual suitability within a genuine university was dubious. The net result was that the coincidence of these two extreme adversarial groups shrank the middle ground for the genuine, appropriate teaching and learning that were part of the university ideal, if not always of the reality.

Professors and Prosperity

At most colleges and universities, the biggest gains in income, power, prestige, and protections between 1945 and 1970 were those accumulated by the faculty. The prospect of a shortage of qualified college teachers, combined with the deference to expertise in some fields, gave a generation of professors unprecedented opportunities. The robust academic marketplace also had some spin-off in that faculty were sometimes able to negotiate gains in shared governance with presidents and boards, although this development remained highly uneven across the institutional landscape.

What did gain widespread acceptance was the codification of the calendar and criteria for promotion and tenure. Arbitrary dismissals by a president or board of trustees became less likely in part because the procedural requirements impeded a quick, unquestioned punitive action. At some kinds of institutions, especially state regional colleges and community colleges, prospects for creation of faculty unions surfaced — an option that presidents would find far less palatable than the conventions of collegial governance and professional custom.

However, these gains were untested outside a sustained period of growth in higher-education enrollments, general economic prosperity, and an expanding academic market for virtually all professors. An academic vice president in 1966, for example, whose biggest problem was to hire a dozen new tenured professors during the summer months before classes started in September was more likely to be amenable to individual faculty contract demands for reduced teaching loads, added laboratory space, and an increased book budget than would a dean or vice president in any preceding era in the history of American higher education. And for a generation of new faculty members who enjoyed being hired under such circumstances, it was not difficult to imagine that such conditions were the norm — and might even improve over time, given the American public's support for higher education. Economic abundance, however, provided little insight as to the political and legal protections professors would face in the future.

Crises and Contradictions: Which Academic Revolution?

One intriguing characteristic of American higher education between about 1960 and 1970 was that its general circumstances, including strengths and weaknesses, were remarkably similar in both years, but with markedly different consequences and public responses. Abundance combined with overcrowding, prestige combined with a proliferation of activities, spanned the decade. But whereas university advocates in 1960 were confident that the institution was able to balance the numerous, often conflicting, roles of the prototypical American university, by 1970 most universities had become clumsy and were beginning to falter in this precarious juggling act. The heavy price was a rise in distrust among some constituencies and a loss of confidence within the institution itself.

Contrary to the accounts of some student leaders, students were neither the first nor the foremost group to abandon the university. Indeed, the insistence of antiwar groups on using the campus as a forum for dissent testified to their underlying faith in the goodness and importance of higher education. Their numerous attempts at university reform indicated that they may have been disappointed and disillusioned, but they were not disbelievers in higher education. The group that first bailed out on universities were the federal funding agencies, especially those aligned with classified research and projects for the Department of Defense. Sabotage, disruptions, fire-bombings, and other violent student acts did not force government officials to abandon their research agenda; they simply shifted their site from a campus office or laboratory to an independent institute. This was essentially a business decision. Externally sponsored research had no symbolic or spiritual allegiance to the campus as a sacred place.

University officials viewed the departure of federal projects differently. At the most basic level, it meant the potential loss of what had been generous annual funding, including both direct support for specific projects and the discretionary monies associated with the federal government's allowances for institutional overhead expenses. The loss of such lucrative "soft money" institutes created an immediate financial problem—and a long-term concern about dependable funding sources. And at a higher level of institutional self-analysis, the loss of the federal research grants signaled that the university had forfeited the trust of the peacetime government, including the armed services, that had been so carefully cultivated after World War II. The problem of how to provide fuel for the self-proclaimed "knowledge factory" raised philosophical questions and prompted the kind of administrative soul-searching that had been conspicuously absent a decade earlier when funds readily flowed from Washington and from business corporations to the campus research institutes.

The events at universities after 1965 also wore out the patience of state legislators, who became disgusted with campus administrators' failure to show that they could maintain control of student life and campus activities. Certainly much of this legislative disgust was directed at the excesses of students themselves. The familiar caricature of long hair, sloppy dress, free love, and disrespect for the "establishment" persuaded many general assemblies to rethink their uncritical support of state appropriations for higher education. To exacerbate the problem, the so-called student movement had become an omnibus for all manner of unrelated social and political grievances. Curricular reform, civil rights, financial accountability, scrutiny of research contracts, policies on university investments, displeasure with ROTC as well as foreign policy — all had come to be viewed by legislators and the general public as being somehow associated with student unrest.

Some politicians, including Governors Ronald Reagan in California and James Rhodes in Ohio, used campus unrest as a convenient issue from which to launch "get-tough" reform campaigns that appealed to voters statewide. Many state officials did not go to such extreme lengths but simply became fed up and worn out with the weekly news reports about student demonstrations. At some point, their ire extended beyond the disruptive students to include campus administrators. The political orthodoxy was that, regardless of the issues, presidents and deans had not demonstrated an ability to maintain campus civility and order. From time to time in the late 1960s there were a few flashes of self-proclaimed academic leadership in which a president or a chancellor depicted himself as a heroic figure who balanced reason (listening to student rebels with calm, pipe-smoking deliberation) with responsibility (drawing the line at inexcusable behavior, such as class disruption or physical violence). One example of this leadership style is described in William J. McGill's *The Year of the Monkey* — a firsthand account by the chancellor of the University of California at San Diego, who tried to steer such a course.[50]

In fact, Chancellor McGill and his counterparts at most other institutions — and their administrative staffs and deans of students — were ill prepared to provide effective leadership during these tumultuous years. There was little in their academic or professional experience that prepared them to cope with student dissent, external accountability, or funding shortfalls. Perhaps the most resilient and innovative campus presidents of the late 1960s and early 1970s were Kingman Brewster of Yale and John William Ward of Amherst College. Brewster, for example, brought all the pragmatism and disciplined organization of a lawyer and energetic fund-raiser to the presidency of his alma mater. The difference was that even in prosperous times, he pushed trustees, faculty, students, and alumni to consider serious questions about what a university education *ought* to be. And when student demonstrations, the antiwar movement, and civil rights activism altered the traditional rhythm of campus life, he acknowledged the forces of change and prompted old grads and current students to consider the new issues together. Brewster's approach was exceptional. The norm for presidents of this period was early retirement, heart attacks, and disbelief that these contentious groups, numerically so small, had come to exert such a disproportionate influence on the image and reputation of the campus.

By 1970, changes in sponsored research and development funding patterns and priorities had altered "business as usual" at universities, and even at colleges. The alienation of a variety of external groups — federal agencies, state legislatures, and older alumni — left presidents and deans in the uncharacteristic position of having to scramble for funds, and to explain and even justify their institution. What such introspection ought to have revealed was a fundamental weakness in the institutional philosophy. Universities in the United States after World War II were hard pressed to identify a central, cohesive mission. In 1963 Clark Kerr dryly noted that central heating was about the only unifying element in a contemporary multipurpose campus.[51] Such an observation could be taken with good humor so long as all groups were reasonably satisfied and the institution had an abundant flow of funds to support its myriad endeavors. But between 1965 and 1970 the university structure — and its complex bureaucratic arrangements for funding and systems maintenance — creaked and groaned, unable to maintain the historic balance that for two decades had been a source of pride as a "managerial revolution."

One reason for this susceptibility is that few universities had devoted much attention to the question of clarity of mission — or even missions. Abraham Flexner had raised the issue as early as 1930. But to a generation of university presidents between 1945 and 1970, there seemed to be little time or need for clarifying the matter of mission. About the only approximation of a mission that the research universities could state in the 1960s was a commitment "to advance knowledge." Unfortunately that was a vague, relativistic statement that raised hard questions: Knowledge for what purpose, and for whom? By 1969, American colleges and universities had not precisely crashed, but their philosophical and financial weaknesses had been exposed, leaving them off balance and uncertain. And in less than a decade, what university officials had envisioned as their coming "best of times" turned out to be their "worst of times."

The confusion and unexpected turns of events in American higher education during the 1960s were best captured in Christopher Jencks and David Riesman's provocative *The Academic Revolution*. The book's release in 1968 coincided with some of the high points in student rebellion.

Hence it sold well as readers eagerly sought "inside answers" to explain what they thought was an "academic revolution" fomented by student rebels. This reasonable expectation, however, was not at all what the authors had in mind. Their research since the early 1960s had probed a very different "academic revolution"—namely, the rise to power of the academic profession. The power and prestige of academic expertise, not the campus as a battleground, lay at the heart of Jencks and Riesman's "academic revolution." Perhaps it should have been described as an "academic transformation"—a nuance, however, that displayed little of the drama that might attract readers and reviewers.

Intended or not, this collision of meanings regarding "academic revolution" actually enhanced the book's contribution to discussions about higher education. In some ways it deflated the hubris of a generation of confident professors and presidents enjoying an era in which they were hailed as experts and specialists. Jencks and Riesman soberly pointed out that such inventions as standard-gauge railroad tracks probably had more impact on jump-starting the national economy than did the extension of higher education. They also deflated the facile notion that education had transformed American society into a haven for upward mobility. Prosperity over several decades may have raised the spending power of most Americans, but it did not necessarily alter the relative prestige of a family or individual in the social hierarchy. Conversely, a college degree could bestow some measure of prestige and social reward to an individual without assuring affluence.[52]

These candid analyses threw into suspense many of the attractive slogans that higher education had generated since World War II. To Jencks and Riesman, going to college had relatively little to do with teaching and learning. Its essential social role was to provide certification and socialization into an upper-middle-class orbit. And this it had done reasonably well. One of the major, unprecedented problems colleges had inherited was how to help prosperous, successful American parents deal with the alarming prospect that their children, despite high grades and SAT scores, might face downward mobility.

The sociological and historical perspective that Jencks and Riesman provided on this "academic revolution" enhanced public discussion about higher education and society, but ultimately—and understandably—their reasoned arguments would be blocked out by the graphic depictions of campus unrest projected by the daily news media. The indelible character of American higher education, both on and off the campus, became that of the "other" academic revolution, the one domi-nated by the violence and strife spawned by recent student activism. A prodigious flurry of news articles, books, and television documentaries addressed such themes as "The Embattled Campus," "Berkeley at War," and "Academics at the Barricades." Painful as these dramatic news re-ports were, academic leaders had to confront a less sensational but equally chilling prospect. For those American colleges and universities that were financially overextended and whiplashed by both internal and external groups, the painful discovery was that an annual budget marked by a deficit was the most philosophical of documents.

By 1970, one piece of conventional wisdom was that the prototypical American university was under duress because "its center had failed to hold." A more discerning variation on this observation was the reminder by academic critics that the essential source of malaise had been mis-understood, and hence misstated. The problem was not that the center had failed, but rather that the modern American university had no center at all.

8 Coming of Age in America
Higher Education as a
Troubled Giant, 1970 to 2000

A Proliferation of Problems, 1970 to 1980

What was the best explanation for the widespread good fortune experienced by American higher education in the quarter-century after World War II? To McGeorge Bundy, the former dean of arts and sciences at Harvard who served in U.S. president John F. Kennedy's cabinet and then joined the Ford Foundation, the answer was clear: "A rising tide lifts all boats."[1] If that was a reasonably good description of the buoyant era American higher education had enjoyed, the converse was true for the next decade. All institutions experienced turbulent waters between 1970 and 1980. One omen of this abrupt shift was that in 1970 the Institutional Investor Conference brought together two thousand of the nation's top money managers. They picked the National Student Marketing Corporation as their prediction for stock of the year. However, over the next five months the NSMC share price fell from $140 to $7. This, along with other events, signaled the end of higher education's "golden age."[2] A fitting new slogan for higher education would have been Bette Davis's line in the 1950 Hollywood film *All About Eve,* "Fasten your seat belts! We're in for a bumpy ride."

That warning would have been disconcerting to academic leaders because it would have been unexpected. Wasn't higher education, after all, a large, successful enterprise when judged by its 1970 profile? Enrollments were healthy, having reached an all-time high of 8.65 million students taught by 383,000 full-time instructors at 2,573 institutions. These same institutions conferred 1,072,581 bachelor's degrees during the 1969 – 70 academic year. Whereas two decades earlier, economists had warned of a looming shortage of Ph.D.'s, by 1970 universities had resolved that problem, as demonstrated by the awarding of 29,872 doctorates in the academic year 1969 – 70, in contrast to the 6,420 awarded in 1949 – 50. Total current fund income for American higher education in 1969 – 70 was $21.5 trillion ($98.1 trillion in 2000 dollars), an increase of a bit more than $9 trillion since 1965 – 66. At the same time, changes in access included major enrollment gains for racial minorities and women. These cumulative gains led Clark Kerr to call the period from 1960 to 1980 "the great transformation in higher education."[3]

The robust statistical profile, however, was misleading because it did not depict details that indicated fundamental crises percolating within higher education. If American higher education in 1970 was a huge enterprise, it was also a troubled giant. Foremost among the problems was a decline in confidence, both within its own ranks and among external groups. One obvious weak point was that the higher-education community had very little systematic information about itself, let alone thoughtful analyses to assist planning. A partial remedy came about in 1967, when the Carnegie Corporation established the Carnegie Commission on Higher Education. Led by Clark Kerr, the former president of the University of California, the group published an extensive series of commissioned research reports on the condition and character of higher education in the United States. The Carnegie Commission expired in 1973, and the Carnegie Council on Policy Studies in Higher Education succeeded it from 1974 to 1979.[4]

The studies were good, but the news in their findings was not. Economist Earl Cheit, who served as dean of the business school at Berkeley, presented the sobering, unexpected conclusion that higher education was on the brink of a "new depression."[5] This finding was in stark contrast to the public image of higher education as a "growth industry," its stability reflected in solid buildings and sound values. According to one account, "Cheit's probing of financial trends was as unwelcome and unexpected as a termite inspection report warning of a deteriorating foundation under a magnificent edifice."[6] In fact, colleges and universities in all sectors were overextended in their annual operating budgets and long-term endowments. They were ill equipped to handle sustained declines in funding. And although higher education claimed to have undergone a "managerial revolution" since World War II, there were indications that institutions were not always informed or fluid in their responses to changing situations. The so-called knowledge industry was characterized as cumbersome, not altogether unlike the troubled automobile and steel manufacturers elsewhere in American industry. This institutional lethargy was conveyed graphically by Lewis Mayhew when he wrote in 1980, about one large university, "As late as 1967 its financial records seemed to be maintained in pen and ink in schoolboy notebooks. The cautious thrift of the place was well revealed by its maintaining balances of several million dollars in non-interest gathering checking accounts, with the business manager pleased that the bank did not charge for checks written."[7]

One syndrome related to this lack of fiscal fitness was that the pervasive appeal of expansion across all institutions had led to a proliferation of new degree programs and fields of study. It was predicated on a belief in continued enrollment growth and generous funding over the coming decade — presumptions that turned out to be incorrect. A secondary consequence of this overexpansion in higher education in the United States that caused some alarm was homogenization and loss of institutional distinction. Harold L. Hodgkinson's comprehensive 1971 study *Institutions in Transition* received front-page coverage in virtually every major newspaper in the country. Its findings were that American colleges and universities were drifting toward an "omnibus model" in an attempt to be all things to all constituencies. The underlying theme was that many institutions were scrambling to add new programs and enroll new kinds of students in a haphazard effort to be attractive and to imitate rival colleges.[8]

How, then, was one to make sense out of the more than twenty-five hundred institutions that were loosely lumped together as "postsecondary education"? One step was the annual collection of standardized data from each college and university. The federal government helped by developing the Higher Education General Information Survey, or HEGIS, an instrument that included enrollments, basic budgets, and degrees conferred. It was a start, and later it was expanded and then renamed Integrated Postsecondary Education Data Systems, or IPEDS. Yet even the comprehensive statistics were perplexing in that they lumped together disparate institutions. The familiar categories of "college" and "university" were vague. The response of the Carnegie Corporation was to sponsor a task force whose product was the so-called Carnegie Classifications: operational definitions that distinguished a "research university" from a "doctoral-granting university," a "comprehensive university," a "liberal arts college," or a "two year college." The system's authors had intended to create a neutral categorization of institutions, but their format was quickly misinterpreted. Institutional spokesmen and the external public saw it as a hierarchical ranking scheme. Over the next two decades this attempt at creating order actually increased the chaos among institutions. What was intended to bring descriptive order to higher education had the unintended consequence of setting off a competitive rush by institutions to meet the operational criteria that would qualify them to be placed in another allegedly more prestigious category.

Between 1970 and 1980, however, the habitual push for prestige was muted by national studies whose findings emphasized the shortfalls of American higher education. The Newman Report (1971), sponsored by the Department of Health, Education, and Welfare, concluded, "It is not enough to improve and expand the present system. The needs of society and the diversity of students now entering college require a fresh look at what 'going to college' means." The panel of authors elaborated: "As we have examined the growth of higher education in the postwar period, we have seen disturbing trends toward uniformity in our institutions, growing bureaucracy, overemphasis on academic credentials, isolation of students and faculty from the world—a growing rigidity and uniformity of structure that makes higher education reflect less and less the interests of society."[9] The solution was not merely to refine existing structures. Indeed, the relatively new multicampus systems were depicted as inflexible and dysfunctional. Frank Newman and his fellow commissioners argued that higher education needed to change course, and to that end they encouraged new educational enterprises whose features included achieving equality for women, expanding minority access, and promoting diverse structures and funding mechanisms. Their recommendations represented a shift toward what was termed "social justice" and away from academic "business as usual."

Along with being stuck in this structural quagmire, colleges and universities inherited a succession of problems caused by external crises over which they had little control. "Stagflation," the unusual phenomenon of double-digit annual inflation coexisting with declining productivity in the national economy, translated into a situation in which college revenues were flat at the same time that prices of goods and services were increasing. One source of the problem was the OPEC oil embargo, which caused fuel prices to soar—a fourfold increase in three years. This was an especially difficult proposition for colleges whose abundant new construction projects during the 1960s had included temperature systems and other maintenance features that relied on cheap energy. Electricity that had been highly affordable in 1967 was prohibitively expensive in 1974.

The initial response of college and university presidents was to look for immediate ways to cut expenses, including deferring maintenance on buildings and grounds and then reducing departmental budgets for photocopying and postage. After a few years it became clear that such tactics were inadequate, even counterproductive. An unkempt campus, for example, was a false economy if it repelled prospective students and their parents. And postponing repairs and replacements meant facing extraordinarily higher costs down the road, thanks in part to the double-digit inflation.

Demographics also played havoc with the assumptions of sustained growth. A declining birth rate coupled with the end of the mandatory U.S. military draft meant that going to college decreased as an attractive option to many Americans between the ages of eighteen and twenty-two. Another factor was that migration of families out of the Rust Belt of the upper Northeast and Midwest and into the Sun Belt states of the South and Pacific Coast meant that colleges and universities were maldistributed. Vacancies in the dormitories and classrooms of Our Lady of the Elms College in upstate New York were of little use in accommodating high school seniors proceeding through the educational system in Arizona or Texas. The scope of the external problems was brought home in 1975 –76, when higher-education enrollment declined by 175,000 — the first drop since the tapering off attributed to the waning of GI Bill participation in 1951.

Demographics as Destiny

One of the more perceptive accounts of the growing pains that plagued higher education around 1970 was written by sociologist Martin Trow, who concluded that the uncertainty and structural overload of higher education were largely rooted in demographics. Higher education in the United States had worked reasonably well when asked to make the transition from elite to mass higher education (i.e., to try to accommodate 40 – 50 percent of high school graduates). However, the structures started to buckle when expected to fulfill a commitment to universal higher education, a challenge that had been exacerbated in the 1960s by an overall population increase, especially in the eighteen- to twenty-two-year-old age cohort.[10]

In short, quantitative changes had elicited qualitative changes in the character of the American campus. What this revealed was that Americans, as taxpayers, legislators, governors, and donors, had been successful in building structures that extended postsecondary education in such a way that programs were reasonably accessible and affordable to virtually any American who sought formal instruction beyond high school. However, this was a hollow victory in that it left the inner workings of colleges and universities in disarray, with diminishing coherence of curriculum and declining confidence in what the college experience meant.

The extension of higher education from mass toward universal access was indicative of a trend toward consumerism. In response to the allegation that colleges had long been relatively impervious to student needs and the changing academic demands of new constituencies, the competition for students, donors, and grants prompted many institutions to offer programs that were attractive. Within the aggregate data, other important developments warranted attention. Whereas in 1950, higher-education enrollment was about equally divided between state-supported institutions and independent colleges, by 1970 the balance had shifted substantially, with public higher education accounting for about three-fourths of the enrollments. The trend continued over the next decade so that by 1980 a bit over 78 percent of all students attended public institutions. And if one looked at the enrollment of first-time freshmen, the national profile showed that more than half were enrolled at public community colleges in 1980.

This is not to say that four-year colleges, especially four-year private colleges, declined in enrollments between 1950 and 1980. Indeed, their freshmen enrollments more than doubled, having increased from about 206,252 to 435,604 in that thirty-year span. The proportional change was due to the unprecedented expansion (and appeal) of low tuition at nearby public institutions. Freshman enrollments at the two-year community colleges and technical institutes grew from 82,000 in 1950 to 494,000 in 1965 and 1.3 million in 1980—more than a fifteen-fold increase over three decades. The significant (and often overlooked) corollary was that most "freshmen" did not attend a four-year residential campus. The two year, part-time public commuter campus had quietly but persistently come to have a strong presence in shaping what was entailed in "going to college"—even though the dominant image of the "real college experience" remained indelibly linked to the four-year, full-time residential tradition.

Federal Funding and the Transformation of Student Financial Aid

Student consumerism induced another substantial transformation in the conduct of American higher education in the early 1970s by bringing the federal government into higher education as a major source of need-based student financial aid. Heretofore the bulk of federal funding for higher education had been directed at sponsored research and development along with periodic special projects for capital construction. Even though the 1947 Truman Commission Report had emphasized the importance of affordable tuition, fulfilling that mandate had received little attention from the federal government. The immensely popular GI Bill of 1944 did not become the model for a program extended beyond the immediate postwar period and expanded to serve students other than military veterans. The primary apparatus for affordable college-going had been state government, via per capita subsidies and low in-state tuition charges for state residents. Between 1964 and 1971 the few signs of federal provision for student financial aid were confined to competitive fellowship programs and some entitlements for children of military veterans. Work-study programs, in contrast, had been attractive to Congress and taxpayers because their spirit of self-help and productive labor seemed more palatable than an investment in grants. But this resistance to direct student grants changed as the price of going to college increased in the late 1960s.

The pendulum swing from federal emphasis on competitive research grants toward undergraduate need-based financial aid came about gradually and unexpectedly. In the mid-1960s the high-powered research universities were confident that generous funding from U.S. agencies for research would eventually be supplemented by direct institutional aid.[11] Their optimism was based on the high regard in which universities were held. Public confidence in their conduct and public satisfaction with their ability to deliver research products suggested that the United States Congress would soon follow suit with thanks for a job well done. However, the campus unrest, the tensions over the federal presence on campus, and the ensuing loss of trust by Congress in the ability of university administrators to run their own institutions cooled the mutual admiration between Capitol and campus. The established research universities faced another source of tension: grumbling among members of Congress as well as numerous campus presidents. The concentration of re-

search grant dollars among a relatively small number of prestigious institutions rankled legislators from such regions as the Southwest and the
Southeast — and from all regions when their constituents included university presidents whose institutions were not in the charmed circle of
"federal grant universities." The net effect of this imbalanced research
patronage was to weaken the consensus of support for emphasizing
peer-review research and development programs — and to kindle some
interest in funding alternatives.

Even though major universities and such groups as the Association of
American Universities and the American Council on Education had a
strong lobbying presence in Washington, D.C., relatively young student
lobbying initiatives quietly upstaged them between 1970 and 1972. The
subsequent campaigns have been considered the most contentious battle
within the ranks of higher education. Most interesting about the student
groups is that they went about their work outside the formal umbrella
of university presidents and boards — an action that generated increasing uncertainty about precisely who "spoke for" higher education. The
Carnegie Commission and the Rivlin Commission were the only established national higher-education groups that endorsed emphasis on
portable student financial aid rather than direct federal subsidies to institutions — a position that many higher-education officials considered
to be tantamount to "treason."[12] The student coalitions had little recognition within the established higher-education associations housed in
Washington, D.C. What they did have was great appeal to members of
Congress, especially those facing reelection. The conventional support
of federal research programs now had the potential to disappoint several
constituencies. The unexpected and pleasant alternative was need-based
student financial aid that was portable and readily available to a large
number of constituents.

The resultant Basic Educational Opportunities Grants (BEOG) program, soon renamed the Pell Grants in honor of Senator Claiborne Pell
of Rhode Island, represented a belated fulfillment of the 1947 Truman
Commission Report's recommendations. Enacted as a 1972 amendment
to the 1964 Higher Education Act, the BEOG was entitlement. This meant
that any applicant who complied with its terms was guaranteed financial
aid. Typically compliance required that one would have to have been
accepted by and enrolled in an accredited institution of postsecondary
education. One would have to be a full-time student, as demonstrated
by enrolling for twelve credit hours per semester. One would have to

maintain good academic standing. If these criteria were met, then a student could qualify for up to $1,250 per year in federal student financial aid (this 1972 amount is equivalent to about $5,100 in 2000 dollars). It is important to note that the program dealt with grants, as distinguished from student loans. Also, eligibility was confined to full-time undergraduates.

The program's most novel feature was that the financial aid was portable. It was awarded to the individual student, not to an institution. True, the money would be deposited into the student's college account once he or she enrolled. But the portability feature meant that hundreds of thousands of recipients now had both the means to go to college and a choice as to which college to attend. The reciprocal effect on colleges and universities was that they now had to compete to attract applicants who could bring their Pell Grant dollars to the bursar's office. At a time when many colleges feared rising operational costs and declining numbers of students, the enactment of the BEOG / Pell Grant Program was a lifesaver—provided that college administrators took the initiative to reach out to potential students. Not only did the federal program cast a wide net across the socioeconomic landscape, it simultaneously encouraged all accredited institutions to participate. Citrus Community College in California, for example, could work to enroll Pell Grant students at the same time that Stanford University could. Neither institution was rewarded or punished for its particular academic admissions requirements. And since the Pell Grant program was an entitlement that accommodated all qualified students, there was no "zero sum" that made a gain for the community college a loss for the elite university.

Much to the delight of incumbent United States senators and representatives, the Pell Grant program and other subsidiary federal student aid programs made many parents and voters happy, and allowed all accredited institutions to compete for students awarded federal aid. Access to and support of undergraduate education had been quickly transformed to show substantial commitment to incentives and choice. Between 1972 and 1978 the Pell Grant program was popular with students and institutions, and it helped promote the appeal of "going to college" to a new generation of students at a time when colleges needed this boost. By 1990 the program typically served 3 million students, with awards totaling $4 billion, per year ($5.2 billion in 2000 dollars). In 1997–98 the figure had increased to 3.8 million students, with total funding of $3.8 billion ($4 billion in 2000 dollars).

The large scope and success of the federal student financial aid program did not mean an end to, or even a reduction in, the various federal research grant programs offered by U.S. departments and agencies. It did establish student financial aid as one of the two enduring planks of federal support for higher education, the other being sponsored research and development. The program's other legacy was that since most postsecondary institutions in the country were receiving monies via the Pell Grant program, they were now subject to the conditions of federal regulation that went along with accepting such monies. Perhaps the most significant legacy was that the Pell Grants positioned the federal government's higher-education policies and programs to give serious attention and resources to civil rights and social justice.

Starting in 1978, however, the focus of federal programs for student financial aid changed, from an emphasis on grants for students with financial need toward an emphasis on readily available student loans. The Guaranteed Student Loan Act was especially attractive both to banks and to students from relatively prosperous families. As such, it extended the net of participants. The price of this short-run popularity, however, was that in the coming decades the emphasis on federal loans meant that an increasing number of recent college graduates would be saddled with large amounts of debt.

The Changing Profile of Students after 1970

Student unrest persisted into the early 1970s but had waned by about 1973. One enduring legacy of the organized student movement was recognition by students of their rights as consumers and as members of the campus community. The result was that many institutions created a slot for students on their governing boards. In some cases administrators overestimated the enduring political commitment of undergraduates. The "Princeton Plan," for example, proposed to allow students a break from class attendance to be used for volunteer work in the presidential electoral campaigns. It expired quietly for lack of interest.

The enrollment decline of 1975–76—and the fear of a continued downward slide—had two consequences for campus administrators. First, they paid increasing attention to students and their parents in their provision of services and curricula. Second, colleges started to acknowledge part-time students and returning, older students as constituencies that warranted courtesies and accommodations. Terminology like "nontraditional student" worked its way into admissions offices and student affairs centers. Psychologist Patricia Cross published a profile of the "new learners" that served as a guidebook.[13] Deans and faculty increasingly acknowledged that their student constituencies would not always be dominated by full-time, residential students between the ages of eighteen and twenty-two. Nor could college officials assume that their constituency planned to finish a bachelor's degree in four years and then go on for an advanced degree.

Even though many public universities had entered into articulation agreements with public community colleges, a student who wished to transfer and complete a bachelor's degree at a four-year institution faced snags of incongruence and uncertainty in the review of course credits and fulfillment of bachelor degree requirements. At the same time, numerous independent four-year colleges took the initiative to recruit and enroll two-year college transfer students. The quest for upper-division students who sought to complete a bachelor's degree also prompted four-year colleges to offer courses and degree programs at off-campus locations convenient to a critical mass of transfer students. In this scheme of academic consumerism, classrooms at a military base or evening courses in a downtown location expanded access for nontraditional students and enabled many colleges to maintain undergraduate enrollments at a time when the customary pipeline of high school graduates was shrinking.

If the generation of undergraduates in college in the mid- and late 1970s had turned away from the political activism of their predecessors, they had not forgotten the 1960s' lessons about the power of collective strength to influence the character of the campus. Faculty noticed a "new vocationalism"—in particular, an obsession with preprofessional studies. Enrollments soared in such fields as business administration, management, accounting, and anything else thought to confer an edge in admission to graduate programs in law, medicine, or business. Within the extracurriculum, students and their parents simply were no longer satisfied with the lean services the campus of the 1960s had offered. Career-planning offices and a host of other student services proliferated. Dank, sweaty gymnasia were replaced by state-of-the-art health and fitness centers that rivaled Club Med. The Spartan dormitory, characterized by cinder-block walls, a pay phone in the corridor, and public bathrooms, was replaced by apartment suites complete with kitchens, lounges, and ample wiring for stereo systems and, later, computers.

New services were not the only changes in campus life. Deans of students increased the options undergraduates had for living arrangements. "Theme houses" that brought together students who shared an interest in such fields as Russian studies or theater arts supplemented dormitories and the fraternity-sorority offerings. Most dramatic was the introduction of coeducational dormitories. Squeamish parents and outraged clergy complained that college officials had abdicated moral responsibility by endorsing such residential patterns. Critics' fears about wild sexual abandon were unfounded—at least, wild sexual abandon as a consequence of the coeducational dormitories. At Rutgers University, for example, anthropologist Michael Moffat's 1989 study *Coming of Age in New Jersey* detected a surprising countereffect. Men and women in coeducational dorms tended to form caring relationships more akin to the brother-sister bond. Amorous relations between suite mates were considered taboo, and students from outside the dorm who came in as dates would be subjected to concerned scrutiny. Gender proximity in campus housing, contrary to parental predictions, had not eliminated modesty and self-consciousness.[14]

More intriguing than the dynamics of coeducational residence halls were the other changes that Moffat found in the undergraduate culture of the large university of the 1980s. Students in the dorms often had only incidental connection to or allegiance with the organized, university-wide student activities and services. Varsity teams, for example, were viewed by most undergraduates as a world apart. The Rutgers football team was described by a range of undergraduates as a distant professional activity that commanded no more (and no less) loyal rooting than the nearby New York Giants professional football team. Moffat's study also affirmed for the 1980s what Laurence Veysey had found for undergraduates a century earlier: there persisted a wide gulf between students and faculty as to what the college experience was all about. Even achievement-oriented undergraduates had scant notion of what professors did or what an academic career entailed.[15]

Professors and students on a large campus did share one characteristic: few in either group knew the name of the dean of student affairs. The "hidden curriculum" of the contemporary university was that students learned how to navigate large organizations—an acquired skill that would be indispensable in adult life. Each student carved out subculture alliances, geographical turf, and a strategy for academic survival. Study was but one of many activities that competed for students' time and attention, with a choice of major and degree objectives being part of an elaborate student pecking order and code. In an interesting aside, Moffat explored the charge that students of 1987 studied less than their counterparts of an earlier generation had done. His surprising finding was that although students often saw courses as obstacles to be hurdled or dodged, most undergraduates seemed to be as diligent and concerned about "getting ahead" as students had been a century earlier.[16]

During the 1980s there were indications of a substantial change in what had been known for almost a century as the "collegiate culture." Whereas the campus had once been a crucible of undergraduate fashions and values, it was now overwhelmed by a larger "youth culture" of music, tastes, and vocabulary that enveloped students while they were in high school and continued to pervade student life even in college. This meant that the ground rules of initiation into college life had changed. Once colleges and universities had accommodated the creature comforts of students, they had to face the more difficult task of dealing with a new set of instructional problems fostered by this cultural change. Perhaps the biggest change in institutional attitudes toward undergraduates between 1950 and 1970 was concern about retention and degree completion. Administrative indifference to attrition rates of 25 percent or more of an entering freshman class had ceased to be acceptable. Professional advising, new teaching and learning centers, expanded student services, and a variety of other institutional tools were implemented to increase the odds that a student persisted and graduated. One state government strategy was to divide its per capita subsidies. Part would be paid on entering enrollments, with the remaining payment to the institution being calculated on such measures as course completion or degree conferral.

Each campus faced another incentive to analyze and then respond to student attrition—namely, the exorbitant cost of undergraduate instruction. Careful audits at some state universities in the late 1970s revealed that weak performance by freshmen and sophomore students was disrupting the fundamental resource allocation strategy. The original plan was that a large undergraduate base reduced per capita expenditures, thus freeing up more tuition dollars for advanced courses and seminars for upper-division students and graduate students. The dynamics of the lower-division undergraduate culture dismantled this logic and turned the actual costs upside down. This internal revelation included the discovery that even prestigious research universities were interdependent with the character of American high schools. The rising failure rates in freshman-level English composition, mathematics, and science courses were attributed in part to secondary schools. Although a student may have received an A in high school calculus, the frequent dilution of the high school curriculum provided no assurance that a student had the requisite knowledge a university mathematics instructor presumed. Revelations of such gaps in academic preparation were not confined to open-admissions institutions. The dean of admissions at Stanford, for example, alerted professors in 1978 that although they had the luxury of selective admissions, even their academically talented entering students showed alarming signs of uneven analytical and writing skills.[17]

When underprepared freshmen dropped courses—or failed them—they came back to haunt the funding procedures by reenrolling a semester later and, often, dropping the course yet again. The university had already spent the state student subsidy but now was "churning" by devoting increased time, course slots, and classroom space to underachieving students. The syndrome was extended by such undergraduate practices as "going shopping" early in the semester: enrolling in, say, six courses on the first day of class, then reducing that number to four a few weeks later. The pragmatic message was that a flagship state research university was unintentionally investing a large proportion of its limited resources in freshmen students who often did not persist.[18]

To save money, colleges and universities had to spend money. Resources first had to go into a variety of support services that would help undergraduates stay afloat academically. What had been left to chance in 1950 was a matter of deliberate concern—and investment—in 1980. The effort also extended into increasingly sophisticated student-centered programs and activities beyond the teaching and learning of the classroom. Deans—and, later, faculty—acknowledged the growing diversity of the undergraduate body in numerous dimensions, including age, gender, income level, and academic preparation. In place of assumptions about a typical undergraduate experience involving four years of full-time study, academic advising increasingly came to accommodate diverse patterns. "Stopping out" joined "dropping out" in the lexicon. Internships, field experiences, study abroad, and numerous other innovations gradually came to be accepted components of the bachelor's degree experience. One of the more decisive acknowledgments of these changing conceptions of the college experience was that federal data collection extended its compilations on "bachelor's degree completions" from four years to five years and then to six years as the norm. A windfall of this institutional scrutiny was that universities were eventually forced to rediscover the importance of undergraduate education. Creating honors colleges, freshman seminars, and interdisciplinary fields and rewarding faculty who showed commitment to teaching and advising undergraduates were signs of at least partial reform within the research university.

Profile of the Faculty

To gain a sense of the changed climate of American higher education after 1970, it is useful to consider how the American professorate saw itself as well as how it was depicted in the national press. For example, Christopher Jencks and David Riesman had gained both fame and infamy for their 1968 book *The Academic Revolution,* which charted the rise to power of faculty and the academic profession, both within institutions and as influential, well-paid experts in American society. David G. Brown had painted a similar picture in *The Mobile Professors* (1967), which projected a long-term shortage of college teachers. But the celebration was short lived. A provocative, timely study published just a few years later was entitled *Academics in Retreat.*[19] By 1972 the end of a fifteen-year hiring boom had left the academic profession with reduced mobility and little leverage in their power to influence institutional decisions.

The academic job market had dried up in all but a few fields. Whereas in 1965 a new Ph.D. from a major university usually received three or four tenure-track job offers, by 1972 there often were no job vacancies posted.[20] It was not unusual for a tenure-track faculty vacancy to attract hundreds of qualified applicants. Neil Smelser and Robin Content, for example, documented how an announcement of two positions in the sociology department at Berkeley in the late 1970s attracted over three hundred applicants.[21] The hiring boom of the 1960s had saturated most institutions, with little prospect for vacancies for years to come. This professional clogging was due to the peculiar dynamics of faculty careers. A tenure-track job offer followed five or six years later by promotion to associate professor with tenure typically represented a twenty- to thirty-year investment between institution and individual. At the same time that the national job market for academics was reaching saturation, the expanded number of Ph.D.-granting programs were tooled up to assure a constant flow of new Ph.D.'s into the academic market for years to come. What would have been a marvelous solution to higher education's needs in 1960 had become the millstone of a glutted market in 1980.

In the array of problems facing presidents and boards, faculty were not a primary object of concern. One reason was that presidents and provosts enjoyed a buyer's market. Established as well as ascending institutions had the luxury of choice in hiring new professors. Now they could compete for faculty credentials of a kind that in the 1960s they might have been unlikely to land. And since few tenured professors had the option to consider good jobs elsewhere, the balance of governance power shifted away from the faculty back to the administration.

As Roger G. Baldwin and Jay L. Chronister documented, one disturbing institutional response to the glutted market for faculty was to rely increasingly on adjunct faculty—"teaching without tenure," a practice that heralded an administrative erosion of academic freedom.[22] This undermining of customary academic rank and tenure was particularly problematic for faculty at community colleges. Norton Grubb and his research associates concluded that professors at the public two-year institutions were becoming "honored but invisible."[23] And the short-term solution of consolidating departments with low enrollments tended to evade essential questions about what a college or university ought to offer in order to be legitimate. The net result was that the morale of professors was not high. The situation led Howard Bowen and Jack Schuster to conclude a national study with the observation that faculty were "a national resource imperiled."[24]

The Community College

The community college was the institution that stood poised to gain from the flux in American higher education in the 1970s. In many states, funding for construction and operation was available, even ample. Since many community colleges were "open admission," they could accommodate a range and variety of students. The academic transfer function coexisted with vocational programs. Furthermore, the public two-year colleges started to add new missions and new constituencies. Providing recreational or community-interest courses—with or without degree credit—ascended as an option. Continuing education and certification for a variety of business and professional fields constituted another attractive domain. To another extreme, the community colleges frequently took on remedial education. And the community college's most incongruous and interesting innovation was to offer advanced courses that provided retooling for applicants who already had bachelor's or master's degrees.

This proliferation of missions and constituencies was fueled by a state funding formula that provided a per capita subsidy for each student enrolled in a course. The formula's weakness was its lack of guidance on what was—and what was not—appropriate for the community college to offer.[25] Eventually signs of concern surfaced. The first alarm came from state universities that historically had relied on the public two-year colleges to provide the lower-division academic work that then led to transfer to the four-year campus. In some states, especially California, the concern was twofold. First, the number of community college students who applied for transfer to the four-year colleges declined drastically. Second, the academic record of those who did transfer lagged in comparison to earlier generations of transfer students—and in comparison to those students who entered the university as freshmen. The result was that four-year institutions lost a great deal of confidence in the community college as a reliable transfer institution.

The reservations the four-year institutions had about the community colleges' effectiveness extended to the more general question of retention and attrition. The convenient catchall explanation among community college officials was that since their students were diverse in background and preparation, it was difficult and perhaps inappropriate to subject the institution to conventional models of monitoring student retention patterns. One counter to that statement was the allegation that the two-year public colleges often institutionalized a predictable abuse of ill-prepared students, becoming "revolving-door" colleges or promoting a "cooling-out" function whereby students who stood little chance of academic survival blamed themselves for their eventual academic failure.

A second source of concern emerged when a number of research studies examined the community colleges' claims to being a source of good training for entry-level vocational jobs. One example of the philosophical disarray was the paradox that when a student dropped out of a technical course, it might actually be proof that the community college was doing a good job. The example most frequently invoked was that of air-conditioning repair classes. If a student quickly acquired the requisite skills for a well-paying job in this field, why bother to complete the course, let alone the two-year degree? Such models created a nightmare for assumptions about enrollment and curriculum planning. Equally perplexing was the lack of certainty that the vocational courses had much direct connection with the local economy. Many college officials predictably and understandably dismissed the analyses as flawed, and hence unfair. What did endure was uncertainty about the clarity of the community college's missions and their ability to demonstrate educational effectiveness, however defined.

Debates over effectiveness were incidental during times of economic prosperity. However, in the late 1970s, when most states were facing revenue shortfalls, academic accountability became an enormous factor in deliberations over funding. Nowhere was this problem more acute than in California, where in 1978 Proposition 13 placed a cap on local property taxes and reduced the flow of funding for the state's 120 community colleges. For the first time a California governor asked taxpayers whether it was reasonable to charge even modest tuition for a community college course. Or, put another way, if community colleges charged no tuition, ought there to be a limit on the number of times a citizen could enroll in and then drop a particular course?

Budget constraints also forced community colleges to rethink their omnibus mission. What was more important: to serve as a port of first entry for underserved and undereducated individuals, or to provide postgraduate refresher courses or retooling for citizens who already had bachelor's and master's degrees? The opportunity to be the "people's college" in every sense of the phrase was a source of institutional ascent in prosperous times but a millstone during a state recession. Community college advocates argued forcefully that posing the policy question in that manner was foul play because it was a false dichotomy. Why not do both?

Doubt about the educational efficacy of community colleges was most extreme in the research of Alexander Astin. He expressed his first reservations in his 1977 book *Four Critical Years*, in which he concluded that widespread reliance on the public two-year college as the port of entry for a first generation of college-going students was a recipe for low gains in cognitive skills and changes in beliefs and values.[26] Then, in his 1993 sequel study, *What Matters in College?*, Astin made the matter-of-fact comment that he had excluded community college students from his survey data on the impact of the college experience.[27] His rationale was that community colleges were not real colleges. This was only one researcher's opinion. Yet Astin was influential, and it is disconcerting that he had written off the institutions at which almost half of all college freshmen enrolled.

Budget Problems and Trade-offs: Brown University in 1980

Hard questions about educational equity and effectiveness were not confined to the public two-year colleges. Even the members of the Ivy League were confronting budget problems that raised essential philosophical questions. The ways in which the macro issues filtered down to campus governance were graphically captured in the situation Brown University faced in 1979 – 80. According to Debra Shore, "Soaring energy costs and a larger-than-expected enrollment of freshmen needing financial aid have thrown Brown's balanced budget into a precarious position and the University now faces some difficult questions. Can Brown afford financial aid to students? If this were so, then at what cost? And if not, what does that mean for diversity—racial, geographic, economic—in the student body at Brown?"[28]

Most presidents would have loved to have had Brown's problem: more qualified applicants than slots; a relatively high per capita endowment; a supportive, established alumni; and an attractive niche within higher education as a small university whose faculty combined scholarship with teaching. But institutional health is relative. Within the Brown administration, the concern was that resources were stretched, especially in contrast to the strength of its fellow members of the Ivy League. The price of tuition and expenses for one year had risen to $10,000 in 1981 (about $18,900 in 2000 dollars)—making Brown one of the most expensive colleges in the country. It was also one of the most generous, fulfilling its commitment to need-blind admissions and need-based financial aid. The budget crunch brought about by rising energy consumption and operating costs seared through the soul of the campus, forcing a reconsideration of whether Brown could continue its admissions and financial aid policies. Increases in tuition and other charges simultaneously helped and hurt the university's revenues. Since more than 30 percent of Brown's undergraduates received substantial financial aid, any increase in tuition increased the university's expenses if it was to meet the recalculated financial aid needs of its students.

The obvious question with no obvious answer was, What were sources within university expenses from which money could be saved and then be shifted to student financial aid? Options included decreasing faculty and staff salaries, reducing operating hours and budgets for libraries, and other internal curtailments—each of which would have made Brown less effective as a teaching and research institution. One of the more controversial proposals to save money was that Brown step back from its universal commitment to need-blind admissions. In other words, the university administration could claim the prerogative of not offering financial aid to all its applicants who were offered admission.

There was, of course, no response that would satisfy all constituents. Brown's tradition of need-based financial aid was important in both real and symbolic terms for its commitment to meritocracy. To turn away from that policy at this time was particularly risky because an increasing number of education-minded and prosperous families were giving increasing attention to the ascending state universities with low tuition charges as an option for their college-bound children.[29] Some independent colleges opted for "merit scholarships" that had no financial need requirement as a strategy to compete for the brightest students, regardless of family income—a policy that was most attractive to affluent parents who would not qualify for need-based aid. The net result was the emergence of new ground rules and new student constituencies in the rough-and-tumble market of college recruitment in which deans of admissions came to rely on proactive techniques and strategies to attract potential students.

Learning from Adversity

Starting in the early 1970s, articles about higher education, whether in the popular press or in professional journals, broadcast a message of woe. Colleges, along with hospitals, social service agencies, museums, performing arts centers, and charitable organizations, were depicted as an "endangered sector," stuck in what Waldemar Nielsen called the "crisis of the nonprofits."[30] Higher education's new depression, whose clouds had been sighted on the horizon as early as 1973, threatened to be an extended monsoon season. The sobering postscript was that captains of the campus were told not to expect much in the way of financial flood relief from the federal government. By 1975 most presidents and boards had to face the undeniable fact that their institutions faced problems that were chronic, not transient. Articles published in 1978 in such national magazines as *Time* and *U.S. News and World Report* warned that colleges faced a "life and death struggle" and that it was a "buyer's market as colleges scramble to fill space." Systematic studies also concluded with projections about a potentially high rate of institutional mortality. Symptomatic of this extended concern was the popularity of Lewis Mayhew's thoughtful advice manual, *Surviving the Eighties,* and the Carnegie Commission's concluding report, *Three Thousand Futures.*[31]

So although higher education had been hailed for its "managerial revolution" of the 1960s, it was an incomplete transformation because it had never been tested in a time of adversity. The prospect of declining high school graduation populations in some regions of the country, combined with double-digit inflation, rising energy costs, and an expensive, intractable campus infrastructure, signaled the need for change. What one had, then, was a consolidation of a managerial and planning approach combined with the university and college becoming a genuinely enterprising institution. One of the most influential analysts of higher education's predicaments (and solutions) was economist Howard J. Bowen. Bowen had served as dean of the business school at Illinois, president of the University of Iowa, and president of Grinnell College before devoting full attention to the economics of higher education as a professor at the Claremont Graduate School in California. At a time when legislatures and a skeptical public questioned the efficacy of higher education, Bowen presented detailed analyses of the costs of higher education and a comprehensive rationale for what he termed an "investment in learning" not only as a benefit for individuals but, more important, as a societal gain.

Despite the predictions around 1980 that large numbers of colleges and universities were doomed to close, the actual institutional survival record was impressive. Recovery was due in large part to a shift from a "managerial revolution" to an "enterprising evolution" in campus governance. Works such as George Keller's *Academic Strategy* made the case that a thoughtful connection of data to decisions was preferable to incremental scrambling.[32] It was a timely prescription because federal and state governments were moving toward emphasis on "privatization" and incentives in the allocation of funding. In addition to the impact of this approach to student financial aid starting in 1972, which altered admissions and student recruitment, there was a comparable emphasis on incentives in institutional fund-raising. The basic vehicle to promote campus initiative was the "matching grant"—a strategy pioneered by John D. Rockefeller almost a century earlier but rediscovered by both government agencies and private foundations as they challenged colleges to "meet the match" in a mix of resources. In the effort to stimulate support, governments also suspended distinctions between "state" and "private" institutions. In Indiana, for example, the state legislature gave an incentive to individual and corporate philanthropy toward higher education with its generous dollar-for-dollar state income tax deduction to donors who made contributions to accredited colleges and universities in the state.

Changing policies meant that an increasing number of institutions started taking grantsmanship seriously in their quest to make a case for receiving awards from state governments and foundations for new projects beyond "business as usual." Donor prospect research, analysis of demographic trends, and careful monitoring of agency requests for proposals prompted campus fund-raising offices to cultivate a new breed of development professional. And many universities added a vice president for government relations to the presidential cabinet.

The changes in getting and spending in higher education that surfaced in the early 1980s altered not only the campus but also the granting agencies themselves. First, a new generation of individual donors and foundations emerged—exemplified by California's Irvine Foundation—that gave priority to a new agenda of educational issues rather than focusing on individual campuses. Second, the established foundations, such as the Ford Foundation, defined themselves less as a replica of major federal agencies and opted instead to stake their awards on projects that were both innovative and exploratory, with an eye toward the future—including projects devoted to issues such as minority and women students or international studies and global interdependence.[33] Perhaps the most important change was that colleges and universities could no longer assume that they were either the exclusive or the primary beneficiaries of individual or corporate giving.

The States and Higher Education: Coordination and Centralization

One plank in the 1972 amendments to the Higher Education Act of 1964 sought to alter the governance of higher education. Its strategy was for the federal government to provide incentive funds to each of the fifty states that created state higher-education coordinating agencies to act as a liaison between institutions and the federal government. The emphasis was on long-range planning, with an eye toward avoiding duplication of academic programs. The program to fund these agencies—often called "1202 commissions"—had mixed results. In some states, coordinating agencies already existed. Elsewhere, the incentive funding stimulated new agencies. There was also variation from state to state in the character of the agencies, which ranged from highly centralized arrangements (e.g., the Regents of the State University of New York or the North Carolina University System) to systems of voluntary coordination. The distinguishing feature of the state councils was to rely on some combination of suasion and coercion to prompt institutions to address statewide questions that an individual campus was unlikely to consider on its own. One novel feature of the 1202 commission funding was its explicit provision that independent colleges and universities were to be included along with state institutions in discussions of statewide public policy. The national organization for leaders was SHEEO, the State Higher Education Executive Officers. SHEEO worked in conjunction with governors in such associations as the Education Commission for the States.

For university presidents, especially at the established flagship state universities, a state council often was a nuisance or a nemesis. The idea that the state university had to file reports and make requests via a state agency represented a departure from customary lobbying in the state capital. At best, state coordinating commissions prompted individual colleges and universities to consider collective questions about mission that campus presidents on their own seldom considered. State councils, however, often found themselves in a bind because their mandate was to make recommendations on budgets, capital construction, closing down archaic programs, and endorsing new programs either to the governor or to the state legislature. But in most cases there was no guarantee that their recommendations would be followed. Even though rational planning might indicate that creating a new law school would be expensive and unnecessary, logic could be derailed by a coalition of state legislators who were adamant that the state university in their home district needed a law school. The upshot was that the state councils changed the dynamics and vocabulary of statewide policy deliberations. Some contributions that emerged during the financially strapped years of the 1970s included incentives for "intersegmental cooperation"—that is, providing some funding for ventures that encouraged, for example, the flagship state university to cooperate with the community colleges and the state colleges. Another innovation was the notion of "steady-state growth," whereby a campus would be informed that it could add a new academic program only if it eliminated an established one. The state councils also inserted a new layer of bureaucracy between campus and the capital.

Although most of the publicity went to the increasing federal role in higher education during this period, the states, not Washington, D.C., remained the pillar of government support for the instruction and annual operating budgets of public higher education.

The Development of a Formidable For-Profit Sector

The generous provisions of the Pell Grant program and other student financial aid initiatives had another important consequence for extending the scope of postsecondary education. Because the program had not explicitly defined the kinds of institutions that were eligible, many proprietary schools now petitioned for eligibility to participate in student financial aid programs. Despite objections from "established" colleges and universities, ultimately the newcomers gained a seat at the table and became eligible for student financial aid programs ranging from grants to loans. These gains, however, were continually subjected to scrutiny and attempts at curtailment. Accreditation groups and traditional colleges cited the high default rates among students at some proprietary schools as evidence of lax educational standards and even outright exploitation of at-risk students. The requirement that an institution be accredited provided by itself little assurance that the institution was educationally sound and responsibly operated. By the late 1970s this waning confidence in accreditation as an effective checkpoint had two consequences. First, many state governments undertook their own initiatives to identify and then curb "diploma mills." Second, growing dissatisfaction about the efficacy of voluntary accreditation bodies in policing suspect institutions led to the dissolution of the umbrella agency, the Council on Postsecondary Accreditation, or COPA.

Representatives of the proprietary schools countered allegations about diluted standards and dubious financial practices by pointing out the uncertain quality of many "regular" colleges and universities. They also relied on lobbying and political donations to gain increasing support in Congress. Inclusion spread, and by 1996 one could speak of a formidable new sector known as "Higher Ed, Inc."—a phenomenon that

Richard Ruch has called the "rise of the for-profit university."[34] Foremost among such institutions was the University of Phoenix, with a multistate network of sites along with reliance on "distance learning" technology to offer both coursework and degree programs. Like it or not, the presidents of established colleges and universities were forced to acknowledge that proprietary colleges and institutes were unwelcome guests who were going to stay for dinner, especially when the main course was federal student aid.

From Retrenchment to Recovery, 1980 to 1989

Higher-education associations continued in their public relations campaigns to remind citizens and politicians that investment in higher education not only was beneficial to the economy but also promised numerous other social advantages.[35] The efforts bore fruit. As inflation dropped and the nationwide economy started to rebound by around 1983, appropriations for higher education picked up. One sign of recovery was that by the mid-1980s most gubernatorial candidates campaigned as "higher-education governors"—calling for partnerships among state government, private industry, and higher education as a way to foster a strong "high-tech" state economy. The governors and university presidents appeared to be looking to the future, but in fact they relied on the historical examples of "Silicon Valley" near Stanford and Berkeley, the "Route 128 Electronics Belt" in the Boston-Cambridge area, and the "Research Triangle" of the University of North Carolina, Duke University, and North Carolina State University. Between 1985 and 1990, numerous universities joined with their state governments to sponsor (and subsidize) research parks and new entities with such intriguing names (and vaguely implied missions) as the "Center for Innovative Technology."

Universities too started to believe their own public relations about their destiny as economic incubators. Economist Charles Clotfelter examined four institutions—Harvard, Duke, Carleton, and the University of Chicago—as part of a 1996 study of cost escalation in elite higher education. He found that institutional ambition and the drive for both quality and prestige prompted institutions to spend generously in the mid-1980s. "Buying the best" became the credo of the elite institutions. The message spread throughout higher education and extended to the quest for top students and faculty along with a commitment to meritocracy and social justice. Moreover, since many institutions had deferred purchases and maintenance in the late 1970s, by 1985 there was a pent-up purchasing drive, which escalated until the October 1987 stock market crash and then the 1989 drop in state revenues.[36]

Government Relations and Regulation

The "partnership" between higher education and the federal government worked reasonably well so long as it meant that the campus received what it considered to be adequate funding. In such circumstances, government regulation was viewed as a nuisance, but still a necessary price to pay. By the late 1970s this acquiescence had started to dissolve. In 1982 a study group commissioned by the Carnegie Foundation for the Advancement of Higher Education prefaced its report on campus governance with the observation, "There remains in the control of higher education an inherent tension. Colleges and universities are expected to respond to the needs of society of which they are a part—while also being free to carry on, without undue interference, their essential work."[37] To university presidents who at that time faced double pressures of increased government regulation and decreased federal funding for research and student financial aid, this characterization was painfully accurate—and familiar.[38] Influential spokesmen, including officials with higher-education associations as well as university presidents, brought the issue center stage, arguing that governmental regulation had become unreasonable and excessive. Implicit in this argument was that colleges and universities could be counted on to "do the right thing," with minimal oversight. Federal regulation was wrong, and wrongheaded.

Sociologist Nathan Glazer compared federal regulation in higher education and in business in a study that took up the same theme but brought a historical perspective to the litany of academic complaints. To Glazer, the important historical dimension was that business and higher education had essentially traded places with respect to the federal government between 1910 and 1980. Whereas President Theodore Roosevelt had focused on "trust busting" and bringing large business corporations to heel, colleges and universities of that era were almost always exempted from federal regulatory measures. This tradition of federal restraint continued through the New Deal. Colleges and universities, for example, originally were not required to pay social security taxes or workmen's compensation, or even to provide employees with clean drinking water.

In addition to these basic matters of institutional operation, Congress and the courts had extended great latitude to the American campus in the name of academic freedom. Prior to 1970, for example, it was highly unusual for courts to hear cases involving individual faculty grievances connected with tenure and professional termination. Likewise, hiring decisions and the conduct of academic search committees were considered outside the purview of the courts. Disputes over admissions and graduation were considered intramural matters as well. Nor did institutions have to disclose student records to students themselves.[39]

According to Glazer, by 1980 the role of the federal government with respect to business and colleges had in many cases reversed. Businesses were increasingly given exemptions and incentives. Colleges and universities, in contrast, were subjected to a growing list of regulations and procedures. An interesting wrinkle in the growing amount of litigation that involved colleges and universities as defendants was that the plaintiffs varied, ranging from disgruntled outsiders to insiders who as members of the campus community felt that the administration and board had treated them improperly. The university had always had critics from outside. More novel was the idea of insiders—faculty, students, staff, alumni—becoming sufficiently organized to mount a formal challenge to the alma mater. These gradual inroads into higher education's autonomy raised two fundamental questions: Who "speaks for" the campus, and whom, ultimately, does the campus represent? And, second, if governmental regulation and intervention were not invoked, how would colleges and universities respond to problems of social justice when left to their initiative? On balance, higher-education institutions continued to retain a great deal of autonomy. Yet there was growing belief that college and universities ought to be publicly accountable for their decisions.

Derek Bok, president of Harvard, expressed concern on behalf of his fellow college and university presidents about the intrusion of the federal government into the basic activities of higher education, reaffirming Supreme Court Justice Felix Frankfurter's commentary in a 1957 case that asserted the "four essential freedoms" of a university: the freedom to determine for itself who may teach, what may be taught, how it should be taught, and who may be admitted to study. Bok's preference was for federal regulations that relied on incentives and subsidies as a means of inducing colleges and universities to comply. The least desirable approaches were rigid rules, procedural requirements, and coercion. To Bok, the federal agencies' insatiable demands for data had reduced the university to a Gulliver bedeviled by Lilliputians who were binding it with the red tape of contradictory, even inappropriate government mandates. He conceded that some federal regulations had helped curb the most odious kinds of discrimination but felt that on balance, universities were reasonable and responsive.[40]

Despite the fuming by presidents about federal intrusion and micromanagement, many constituencies close to higher education had come to rely on federal regulation as their best hope for a fair hearing and perhaps redress in disputes about institutional conduct. Federal regulation had joined with student financial aid programs as a partner in the promotion of social justice on the American campus. The difficult question was how colleges and universities would have behaved if they had been left alone, without litigation or regulation. Would, for example, the composition of higher-education faculty in 1980 or 1990 have differed much in gender and race from its profile in 1960? Even Clark Kerr and other academic leaders conceded that the American university was liberal in its advocacy for others yet conservative in its own conduct. And as Chester Finn pointed out in his 1978 discussion of the "regulatory swamp" in *Scholars, Dollars, and Bureaucrats,* a federal regulation pertaining to higher education arose only in response to some decisive complaint by a constituent.[41]

Regulatory Issues and Equity: Women in Higher Education

The status of women in higher education during the 1970s was summed up well by Bernice Sandler and Roberta Hall, who observed that there was a pervasive "chilly" climate for women.[42] To return to the rudimentary statistical profile of higher education in 1970, at first glance women seem to have achieved reasonable accommodation as undergraduates. Their share of overall enrollments was 41 percent, up from 32 percent in 1950. There was a bit more disparity in figures for graduate enrollments, though again the women's share had increased over time. Women represented 39 percent of graduate students in 1970, compared with 27 percent in 1950. Their representation in faculty appointments beyond lecturer, however, was minuscule.

In 1975 P. J. Bickel, E. A. Hammel, and J. W. O'Connell conducted a careful study of patterns of application and enrollment in Ph.D. programs to plumb the riddle of gender discrimination. Their surprising finding was that when one analyzed each department, men and women applicants were accepted at about the same rate. Yet in the aggregate, women constituted a fraction of Ph.D. enrollments. How to explain — and correct — this overall disparity? The first step was to explain the gap between departmental and university-wide trends. The answer was that a large number of women tended to apply to oversubscribed departments that accepted only a small percentage of applicants and had a tradition of lengthy years to completion of the doctoral degree. Men, on the other hand, tended to apply to fields that had vacancies and fellowship funding and relatively fast tracks to degree completion. It was the difference between, say, an English department and an engineering department. When women did apply to engineering or chemistry or physics, they were accepted for doctoral study at about the same rate as men. The crucial implication was that undergraduate women were not applying to certain graduate fields.[43]

Explanations for this phenomenon went deep into the educational system. One finding was that if an undergraduate had not studied calculus as a high school student or as a college freshman, about 50 percent of the undergraduate majors would be off limits. Research by Sheila Tobias found that in the American public school system, girls who excelled in mathematics through middle school and into high school algebra and geometry were suddenly suspending their mathematics studies. Their being steered out of mathematics, not their lack of achievement or aptitude, was creating the critical gap. The transformation of doctoral study enrollments — including bringing more women into the sciences, engineering, and mathematics — depended on changes in advising and mentoring well before undergraduate enrollment.[44]

Incorporating such reforms into the educational system would require years of incubation. In the meanwhile, women in graduate school in the early 1970s were disproportionately represented in selected fields. Their presence was most conspicuous in the humanities, education, library science, home economics, and to some extent the biological sciences, with relatively low figures for graduate programs in law, medicine, business, engineering, and the physical sciences. Surveying all academic fields, women constituted a negligible proportion of the faculty — about 21 percent of the teaching positions in four-year institutions in 1972–73. Furthermore, this presence was skewed toward untenured instructorships, where women represented 44 percent of the faculty. At the same time, women constituted 10 percent of the full professors, 16 percent of the associate professors, and 24 percent of the assistant professors.

By any measure, the difference between women as a proportion of undergraduates and their representation among doctoral degree recipients and campus faculty represented a shortfall. By 1974 –75, however, there were signs of significant change. The first professional school to show this was law, followed by medicine. In 1997– 98, women accounted for 43 percent of all professional degrees conferred. Within that broad category, women received 45 percent of the law degrees, 42 percent of the medical degrees, 38 percent of the dental degrees, and 66 percent of the veterinary medicine degrees. Whereas women received 10 percent of the Ph.D.'s conferred in 1949 – 50, by 1984 – 85 the figure had increased to 37 percent.

Connected to the various discussions about graduate school recruitment was the fundamental issue of educational effectiveness and equity, as played out in the contrast between single-gender colleges versus coeducation. To continue the theme Harold Hodgkinson emphasized in his 1971 commissioned study *Institutions in Transition,* most women's colleges opted to become coeducational. The same was true for historic men's colleges. In one *New Yorker* drawing of the 1970s a stereotypic weary business executive arrives home, slumps in a chair, and notes with incredulity, "My daughter goes to West Point and my son goes to Vassar." The list of historically single-gender institutions that opted for coeducation was long: Radcliffe College merged its undergraduate program with that of Harvard College; Pembroke College was dissolved, and women became a plurality of undergraduates at Brown University. Women had two options for undergraduate education at Columbia University. Columbia College, traditionally all-male, had become coeducational and now admitted women, while Barnard College retained its historical commitment to admitting only women. Amherst, Dartmouth, Princeton, Yale, Wesleyan, Williams, and the University of Virginia were prestigious all-male institutions that opted to shift to coeducation.

Coeducation was not always an even exchange. The formerly all-male institutions tended to gain while the former women's colleges lost. The women who applied to Dartmouth, for example, tended to have SAT scores and high school grade-point averages higher than those of their male counterparts. In contrast, when Vassar College opted to admit men, the admissions staff suffered a double whammy. Male applicants tended to lag behind women applicants in their academic credentials. Even more demoralizing, the college had evidently forfeited its special appeal to highly qualified women who sought the distinctive attributes of an all women's campus. Meanwhile, the women's colleges that made a deliberate decision to continue their specific mission did well.

One of the more significant episodes of gender equity dealt less with exclusion at the admissions office than with educational programs and opportunities within a campus. Center stage was the 1972 legislation known as Title IX. Its original language set forth terms to prohibit discrimination in educational programs. It also included some exemption for selected institutional categories, including military academies. In practice, though, its terms were unclear. One surprising turn of events was its application to gender equity and intercollegiate athletics. The National Collegiate Athletics Association, which initially had strongly opposed Title IX's being tied to college sports, abruptly changed its strategy in 1981 when it added women's championships and teams to its jurisdiction. Over the next decade several court cases jumped erratically on the question of whether intercollegiate athletics were covered by Title IX if athletics departments were not direct recipients of federal funds. When colleges did make token gestures to include women as student athletes, they were subject to litigation by dissatisfied women's groups. The culmination came in 1997 when the Supreme Court refused to overturn a lower-court ruling in *Brown v. Cohen,* a decision that established elaborate statistical criteria by which a college or university could demonstrate compliance with Title IX.

The ascendancy of women, in terms of both numbers and skill, as intercollegiate athletes was one of the remarkable transformations in American higher education. It was also an unresolved issue that continued to be contentious. Many athletics directors contended that overzealous enforcement of Title IX was causing the financial ruin of intercollegiate athletics. What was often left out of the discussion was the fact that most intercollegiate athletics programs, including the "big-time" programs, had been sources of enduring financial problems and budget shortfalls since the early 1970s—before women's sports programs became a factor.[45]

Regulatory Issues and Equity: Minorities in Higher Education

Affirmative action in hiring initially applied to business and industry. Eventually it was incorporated into higher education personnel decisions, with particular attention to faculty appointments. In a distinct but related development, it was extended to include decisions about students, namely admissions policies and practices. After the civil unrest associated with the assassination of Martin Luther King, Jr., and other incidents that brought racial tensions to the fore, numerous colleges and universities initiated measures to promote racial access and diversity. And enrollment patterns for African Americans and other minority groups indicated substantial change. Ultimately, programs geared to increase minority enrollments were challenged in the courts—including the cases of *DeFunis v. Odegaard* and *Bakke v. the Regents of the University of California.* The resolution emerging from the *Bakke* case was that race alone was not allowable as grounds for admissions decisions. However, race taken into consideration with other factors was permissible.

Integration and desegregation had troubling implications for the future of the historically black colleges and universities, the so-called HBCUs. As Henry N. Drewry and Humphrey Doermann reported in *Stand and Prosper,* these institutions had long provided access and instruction for an inordinate percentage of black students—and had done so without benefit of abundant facilities and resources.[46] Even after nominal integration of higher education in the South and elsewhere, the HBCUs continued to be available, effective, and attractive sources of undergraduate education. However, in the post-*Bakke* era, as well-endowed historically white colleges demonstrated sustained interest in recruiting black students, the HBCUs stood to lose in bidding wars. Could a Howard or a Hampton compete against a Princeton or a Harvard? The answer was yes—sometimes. But it was an expensive contest. The irony of Justice Powell's commentary in the *Bakke* case was his praise for Harvard's admissions program as a model for other colleges to emulate. Indeed, most admissions deans would have relished having Harvard's institutional resources and heritage.

A related irony came about in the late 1990s when former Harvard president Derek Bok joined with former Princeton president William Bowen—then president of the Mellon Foundation—to publish *The Shape of the River.* Here two of the onetime vocal critics of federal government policies and affirmative action sang the praises of the positive impact of affirmative action in promoting racial diversity within the student ranks of the academically elite American campuses.[47] Once again the solutions that might have been available and effective for a Harvard or a Princeton were not available to a state university in the West or an impoverished college in the South. Furthermore, even when historically white flagship universities did show commitment to recruiting and welcoming students from racial minorities, there was an avoidance and lack of trust by many black students. The result was that the HBCUs continued to make a disproportionate contribution in terms of both enrollments and bachelor's degree completions by black students.

Policy discussions about equity and minorities became increasingly complex in the 1980s as more constituencies asserted a distinctive heritage and political presence. To speak merely of "minorities" was no longer adequate, now that demographic and educational data on such groups as Asian Americans, Native Americans, Hispanics, and gays and lesbians had elevated awareness of the growing diversity of both the United States as a whole and its potentially college-bound students. Perhaps the best generalization about public policies was their attempt simultaneously to promote access and acknowledge diversity. The new higher-education policy environment included financial aid and scholarship programs that promoted access to mainstream campuses as well as fresh government funding initiatives dedicated to creating new categories of institutions, such as tribal colleges.

The legal environment of the late 1990s was significantly altered by concerted efforts on the part of groups of students and alumni of flagship state universities to dismantle affirmative action, with conspicuous cases unfolding at the University of Georgia, the University of Texas, the University of Michigan, and the University of California. The most dramatic twist in this course of events was the changing role of universities in the South. Whereas in 1950 or 1960 many flagship state universities resisted racial integration, by the year 2000 the opposite sentiment had come to dominate: academic leaders affirmed their commitment to racial equity. John T. Casteen III, president of the University of Virginia, took this courageous public stand in his 1999 "State of the University" address:

> The debate about affirmative action oversimplifies Virginia's legal history and the fact of what has been done here to build success in the last quarter century or so.
> ... [A] morally responsible view of Virginia's history, and specifically of actions taken by the state itself in defiance of law, must acknowledge a second reality of Virginia's actions in our time. Alone among the American states, the Commonwealth of Virginia seized, closed, and locked public schools in 1958 rather than desegregate those schools in accord with orders of the United States Supreme Court. . . . So a unique question needs to be addressed before anyone assumes that our Virginian concern about aca-

demic access for minority students is the same as all others: What effects linger across generations when children grow up in a culture where as a matter of defiant law, the General Assembly and the Governor chose to close schools and deny education over allowing those children's parents or grandparents to study in classrooms open to every child, regardless of race? . . . Regardless of lawyers' debates, however, the moral imperative is that Virginia and persons who care for her and her children, all her children, must assume an ongoing commitment to remedy the consequences of actions well within living memory.[48]

Casteen argued that in higher education, the past was indeed pertinent to the present and future of our public policies and institutional paths. Meanwhile, various court cases offered colleges and constituents little guidance for achieving equity in college admissions.

The College-Costs and College-Price Debates

Federal scrutiny of higher education intensified when U.S. Secretary of Education William Bennett (himself a former classics professor) raised questions about abuses in the financial aid system. Critical questions led to allegations about higher education's equivalent of the infamous "welfare Cadillac"—the anecdotal report of a financial aid recipient driving a red Corvette during spring break in Florida. On a more substantive note, the expansion of federal financial aid programs led to insinuations that some institutions were chasing federal dollars by artificially raising tuition charges so as to increase a Pell Grant recipient's "financial need."

The allegations prompted a spate of systematic research. As Chester Finn had noted in 1978, the issue was the difference between "price" and "cost."[49] One controversial finding was that the cost—that is, the actual expense—of educating an undergraduate for a year at a public institution was not much different from that at a private institution in the same geographical area. There was even some indication that state institutions often actually spent more per student than their private counterparts. The systematic research had cast doubt on the convenient stereotype that independent (or private) colleges were havens for students from affluent families. One study in California showed that the concentration of students from relatively high-income families was substantially greater in the flagship state university than in the private colleges. If this was so, then the logical extension was to ask what exactly a policy of "no tuition" at a state university accomplished. Independent colleges in turn argued that public colleges and universities benefited from a "tuition gap" created by taxpayer subsidies that kept public tuition prices artificially low for a large constituency that could indeed afford to pay a greater share of the actual costs.

Debate escalated when college tuition charges were correlated with inflation, usually as measured by the consumer price index (CPI). It was sometimes alleged that colleges were raising prices faster than the general rate of inflation. Few doubted that American colleges and universities were both expensive and excellent. Whether they were overpriced was less clear.[50] One thorny problem in answering that question was that the CPI and college tuition were a poor match because they measured markedly different kinds of purchases. Higher-education associations responded with the HEPI, the higher-education price index. And for some comparative policy discussion, higher-education advocates pointed out that the cost of taking care of a prisoner for a year was greater than the expenses of educating a college student at a high-tuition campus. Overlooked in the debates of the mid-1980s were the historical data showing that from around 1975 to 1980, increases in college tuition and charges tended to be less than the annual increases in the CPI. One result of over a decade of double-digit inflation and deferred maintenance was that by the early 1980s, colleges had a backlog of projects; expenses were only now catching up. Another complication that emerged from marketing research was the so-called Mount Holyoke phenomenon: the surprise finding that higher tuition tended to increase the number and academic quality of applicants. Evidently price and prestige were connected in the college applicant's mind.

The college-costs debates hinted at a central fundamental weakness of higher education as a part of public policy: internal conflicts within the higher-education ranks tended to pit the independent institutions against the state colleges and universities. The various sectors within higher education devoted most of their time to waging war against one another. As a result, higher education was seldom able to present a coherent, unified front to Congress. Although senators and representatives were in favor of colleges and universities, they often felt torn on higher-education issues. In contrast, lobbying groups such as the National Rifle Association or the National Association of Manufacturers were able to mobilize requests — and thanks — to legislators on short notice.

The Curricular Wars

Higher-education associations located at One DuPont Circle in Washington, D.C.—such as the American Council on Education, the National Association of Independent Colleges and Universities, and the associations representing public higher education in lobbying and public policy efforts—bickered among themselves about political matters. In some ways the bickering mirrored the curricular debates that had been going on at campuses since 1970. It was characterized by ideological clashes over what was to be taught and according to which perspectives.[51] The conflict was healthy in that it elicited a "marketplace of ideas" within departments and across academic units.

Regardless of how academic administrators or faculty argued about the appropriate content of the curriculum, many of these disputes were settled by another constituency—namely, students who exercised their rights as consumers. Soaring enrollments in such "employable" fields as business, computer science, engineering, and various entry-level professional degree programs prompted colleges and universities to devote increasing resources to funding faculty lines and facilities in these popular fields.

Meanwhile, some of the most bitter ideological debates about the curriculum during the 1980s and 1990s took place outside the popular "employable" fields. Disagreements among faculty about the direction of what was entailed in being an English major, how one defined a canon in literature, or the ideological clashes in history and sociology kindled an interesting energy within traditional fields that were by and large outside the mainstream of massive federal grant funding. To faculty and students in the schools of medicine, engineering, agriculture, and pharmacy, the internal battles of the liberal arts departments were distant and curious, tempests in a teapot. Yet to the faculty in those departments, the battles over "political correctness" and the definition of a field were crucially important, especially if one assumed that ideas and instruction mattered.

The ideological debates within the liberal arts signaled the flourishing of new perspectives and multidisciplinary approaches in such thematic areas as women's studies, African-American studies, and Hispanic studies. This took two forms: the creation of permanent departments dedicated to such fields, and the integration of these new perspectives into existing departments. Ultimately the intradepartmental debates had an impact on public policy discussions held in such federal agencies as the National Endowment for the Humanities as their advisory boards and directors reviewed their statements on funding criteria for grant proposals. These curricular debates also led to the creation of numerous splinter groups. What became muddled was whether the typical department of English or history in an American college or university was a champion of allegedly leftist political advocacy or, to another extreme, a bastion of conservatism.

One ironic consequence of the curricular wars was the emergence of a conservative voice among young alumni, especially at the elite historic institutions. Prolific commentators like Dinesh D'Souza and new alumni groups at Princeton and Dartmouth expanded their curricular concerns into charges that colleges had abdicated their traditional sense of reason. For perhaps the first time in memory, recent graduates charged the editors of alumni magazines with having moved too far to the left.

Ambitious undergraduates and their parents largely avoided these curricular debates. However, the debates did prompt the Carnegie Foundation for the Advancement of Teaching, led by Ernest Boyer, to undertake a series of reports that tried to persuade faculty and campus administrators to rethink the undergraduate curriculum and the nature of the college experience. Provocative as these discussions were, they tended to be overrun by certain dominant trends in funding for higher-education research and development.

Research Universities and the Federal-Overhead Controversy

Advocates for the major research universities made the case that these institutions were a bargain for taxpayers and the federal government. Failure to invest in funding for programs, instrumentation, and so on represented a false economy.[52] Although federal programs were devoting new, expanding resources to student financial aid, it is not clear that advanced research programs had been abandoned. Clark Kerr has pointed out that when indexed for inflation, federal research and development grants to universities went from $1.3 trillion in 1960 to $4.3 trillion in 1980 ($7.5 trillion to $8.9 trillion in 2000 dollars).[53] The rate of annual increases had tapered, even though the actual dollar amounts had not.

Emphasis on social justice had made some inroads even into federal research programs. In response to complaints by university officials and members of Congress who believed that their favored institutions and regions were being left out, Congress established such programs as Ep-Scor, whose intent was to ensure that research funding was distributed to institutions without a strong federal research record in underserved states. Agencies like the National Science Foundation also dedicated research funds to historically black colleges or to programs encouraging women scientists.

Along with such innovative programs that were concessions to social justice, highly competitive peer-reviewed grants in the sciences remained at the heart of federal research and development. In March 1991, however, this line hit an unexpected snag in a public forum when Congressman John Dingell of Michigan probed Navy Department research grants, especially at Stanford University.[54] Among the findings was that grant overhead and recovery costs were equivalent to 70 percent of federal research grant dollars awarded. In other words, if a principal investigator applied for—and received—a federal research grant of $100,000, the host university would receive an additional $70,000 as indirect recovery and overhead costs for that grant. These grants seemed to be in the tradition of the "Golden Fleece" awards popularized by William Proxmire in response to periodic revelations of seemingly inane research studies funded by federal agencies. But the congressional critics did not consider comparative data. For example, cost overruns on federal contracts with commercial companies that manufactured aircraft or other products for the Department of Defense far exceeded the overhead charges of research universities. Even though Stanford's procedures were eventually vindicated, research universities lost ground in the forum of public opinion.[55] Elsewhere, anecdotes about the alleged excesses of grants made good copy for investigative reports. For example, the University of Michigan was scolded for having used federal research grant money to help pay football bowl game expenses, including travel and lodging for alumni boosters and the marching band.[56]

While the foremost research universities were mobilizing to defend their honor and refute their critics, a familiar question about prestige resurfaced. Were the universities historically at the top of the list holding their own, or was there room at the top for newcomers? The conventional wisdom was that the original members of the Association of American Universities, founded in 1900, had maintained their position and prestige. Yet there was also some commentary suggesting that they had used such customs as "peer review" as a means to limit the likelihood that new grant applicants or researchers outside the elite, established universities would be competitive for prestigious federal grants. Hugh Davis Graham and Nancy Diamond brought the issue to the fore in a study that tackled the question of what had been happening in ratings and rankings among research universities since World War II.[57] They found that there was indeed some room at the top. Certainly there was a great deal of continuity: Johns Hopkins, Harvard, Columbia, Berkeley, Stanford, Wisconsin, Cornell, and Penn were strong both in 1910 and in 1997. If one extended the roster to fifty institutions, however, the profile was markedly different. Some historic institutions had dropped out of the stakes — for example, Catholic University and Clark University, both charter members of the AAU.

Graham and Diamond noted that the ratings and rankings game tended to emphasize opinions about reputation as well as total federal research dollars a campus received. To counter these tendencies, they devised a fresh ranking system based on scholarly achievements (awards, publications, and honors as well as grant dollars). They also reduced some of the inadvertent tendency for listings of university grant dollars to treat size as a proxy for quality. To overcome this syndrome, they analyzed institutions on a per capita basis. In other words, universities were ranked on the basis of productivity in publications and research grant dollars per faculty member, rather than aggregate number of publications and grants. They found thirty-two universities among the top fifty that could be seen as relative newcomers or "challengers" to the elites. Foremost among these were some of the young University of California campuses: Santa Barbara, San Diego, and Irvine. Other "rising stars" included Brandeis, UCLA, and SUNY Stonybrook.

The comprehensive analysis of changing institutional performance since World War II identified some regional readjustments. Whereas the South had long been dismissed as an academically underdeveloped higher-education environment, the data from Graham and Diamond's study prompted reconsideration. Emory University, the University of Florida, and Texas A&M joined Duke, Vanderbilt, the University of North Carolina, the University of Texas, Rice University, Tulane University, and the University of Virginia as Southern institutions that were among the sixty-two members of the prestigious Association of American Universities. A corollary of the new ratings data was that when evaluated on a per capita basis, some "obvious" institutions slipped in the rankings (e.g., Ohio State University and Pennsylvania State University).

This slippage sent the message that bigger was not always better in research effort. The intriguing conclusion was that the diffusion of research talent had reached far throughout American higher education.

The preoccupation with research rankings elicited some less favorable responses. The Carnegie Foundation for the Advancement of Teaching, for example, grew weary of ambitious universities using its "Research I" category as a model for aspiration. To defuse this tendency, the Carnegie Foundation reworked its categories, substituting such measures as "doctorates conferred" for "federal research dollars spent" as an organizing principle. Despite this reform, few university presidents or professors heeded the change. Research grants continued to prevail as the currency of the realm.

The impact of these episodes extended beyond the immediate circle of established research universities. More than ever they set the tone and pace for institutional aspiration. At universities where faculty believed that their projects had not received fair consideration in applications to the National Science Foundation or the National Institutes of Health, ambitious presidents devised a strategy to circumvent the tradition of scholarly peer-review boards. The alternative route to federal grant funding was to persuade a supportive member of Congress to attach a "rider bill" to establish a research project as an obscure part of some larger federal works legislation. Who would notice or object to a $3 million provision to fund an Institute for Asphalt Research to be housed at a state university in one senator's home state if its enabling language were buried in the draft of a billion-dollar highway construction bill? This form of direct appropriations helped some universities close the research dollar gap—and drew the ire of the scholarly research establishment.

The thirst for research resources and accomplishments influenced campus behavior in another way. The expectation that professors should publish and should obtain external research funding worked its way increasingly into both the customary and formal codes for tenure and promotion at the state regional comprehensive universities and at many liberal arts colleges—institutions that had little if any involvement in doctoral programs. This expectation had some plausibility because these institutions increasingly hired new professors who had studied for the Ph.D. at major research universities and understood what research was about. Often they brought with them to their new professional home a demand for the kinds of resources and equipment requisite for serious research projects. A less compelling rationale was that some presidents viewed research grant dollars as a convenient way to get an infusion of funds for ordinary operations, not new projects.

Whether the pressure for systematic research was originating from the administration or the faculty, the comprehensive state universities and liberal arts colleges were in a bind. They were unclear on a crucial question about institutional mission: Were large-scale research and grantsmanship an obligation, rather than an option, for professors at institutions outside the circle of research universities and Ph.D.-granting universities? According to Martin J. Finkelstein's study of the American academic profession, faculty at the state colleges and other institutions that were belatedly attempting to gain recognition for research encountered the highest degree of ambiguity, if not contradiction, in their roles.[58] Faculty with heavy teaching loads at institutions whose primary constituents were open-admissions undergraduates were also required to publish books and articles and write successful grant applications — all without much in the way of institutional support. This was the widespread scenario that resulted when the excesses of the research university were mistaken as a model for all of American higher education.

Preoccupation with the elite research universities also distracted attention from some important trends that shaped the character of American higher education at the end of the twentieth century. First, although doctoral degrees were the most coveted academic programs, the under-acknowledged "silent success" was the master's degree programs, as documented by Clifton Conrad, Jennifer Grant Hayworth, and Susan Bolyard Miller's 1993 study.[59] The master's degree was important because it was a staple offering not only at the research universities but also at the comprehensive universities and state colleges. With the addition of a range of master's programs, the state colleges had extended their strong presence within postsecondary education. Whereas in the late 1960s they might have been taken lightly as the "invisible colleges" or the "colleges of forgotten Americans," by the 1990s they had substantial power in their enrollments, in their alumni, and in the politics of higher education. In many states they were responsible for expanding if not creating an educated middle class.

Themes for the Twenty-first Century

The prototypical American campus of the twenty-first century, whether a college or university, was a formidable organization in its local and state community. Often a college was the largest employer in what was, of course, a "college town." This presence even extended to major cities: Johns Hopkins in Baltimore, Brown University in Providence, Harvard in Cambridge-Boston, the University of Kentucky in Lexington, Indiana University in Bloomington, Northwestern University in Evanston, and so on. Part of this heritage was that the American campus continued to enjoy a variety of tax benefits, including exemption from local property taxes and federal and state income taxes. But the size and success of the American campus also meant that between 1970 and 2000, these traditional privileges were subject to continual review and renegotiation. Necessity often was the impetus to reconsider property tax policies. In Boston, for example, a college, a church, a museum, a charity, or some other not-for-profit organization owned over 60 percent of the land. Ironically, the consequence was that municipal largesse to one group tended to reduce resources for another educational group—namely, public school systems. The intriguing historical change was that some municipal and county governments gave serious consideration to levying property taxes on local colleges and universities.[60]

Some university presidents responded by making voluntary annual payments to the host local government, all the while being careful to avoid using a term, *taxes,* that might set a precedent. Although this measure provided a temporary truce of sorts, it left open another avenue of scrutiny by municipalities, by business owners, and even by the Internal Revenue Service: monitoring campus activities to make certain that they were appropriate to the institutions' educational nonprofit status. The crucial legal criterion was UBIT, an acronym for "unrelated business income taxes." From the point of view of a shop owner, the question was, Why should a college that has a travel agency or a computer sales center in its student union be treated any differently from a private business? Similarly, the property-taxing authorities asked, Why should a university arena that is often used for rock concerts be exempted as an "educational facility"? These were fair, overdue questions. In many cities the university had become not only the largest employer but also the largest landowner and landlord for a wide range of property holdings. As county and city budgets became strapped in the early 1990s, local governments often considered repealing some of the historical wholesale tax exemptions once given to universities. One New York initiative was to levy local taxes on Syracuse University's Carrier Dome. At Indiana University the university golf courses were subject to property taxes.

Predictably, college and university officials tried to turn public opinion against this new wave of fiscal obligation. To do so, however, required the campus to take on the character of Janus, the Roman god with two faces looking in opposite directions. A university could not resist the temptation to share the good news of its successes in fund-raising and grant acquisition and the robust health of its endowment and budget. It was equally quick to remind all constituencies that its fiscal fitness was precarious. Fund-raising and philanthropy had often rescued the American campus in this tension between private demands to provide more, better services while relying less on tax subsidies and public funds. The result was that at a time when its capital campaign was in high gear, a university would still claim that it was hard to make ends meet. In 1994 when the University of Pennsylvania completed its $1 billion fund-raising campaign ($1.1 billion in 2000 dollars), the Development Office was obliged to explain to both deans and donors that the university faced a tight budget because most of the money was marked for either endowments or deferred gifts.[61]

Even the established, well-endowed colleges and universities relied on accounting tricks to project an image of woe. In 1992, for example, Harvard's annual report taken at face value would have led one to conclude that the cupboard was bare. This was not necessarily the case, however, according to one financial analyst who pointed out the peculiar message Harvard's reports were broadcasting to the public. Despite an endowment of almost $5 billion ($6.1 billion 2000 dollars), its annual operating budget was $42 million ($51.5 million) in the red. One reason for this profile was the university's use of "fund-accounting" reports, leading to the interpretation that Harvard was "managing its bottom line in such a way as to appear poorer than it really is. The university is in the midst of a plan to reportedly raise $2.5 billion on top of what is already the world's largest private endowment. Harvard is a bit like the rich man who wears scuffed shoes and a frayed collar when he visits his doctor."[62]

The private universities such as Penn and Harvard had no monopoly on this sort of public relations effort to persuade various constituencies that higher education was, for all its accomplishments, bordering on starvation. The flagship state university presidents of the 1990s were all singing the same chorus: "We used to be state supported; then we were state assisted; and now we are state located." The claim was not necessarily incorrect. Public higher education in Virginia, for example, could document how a succession of governors and legislatures had reneged on their pledges to restore severe budget cuts made during the crises of the early 1990s and then allowed to persist during the state's return to prosperity at the end of the decade.[63] Presidents of the regional state colleges in Illinois and elsewhere were hamstrung by legislatures that demanded that tuition charges be kept low when per capita state subsidies leveled off.[64] The Permanent University Fund for the University of Texas and Texas A&M systems was worth more than $7 billion in 2002. Facilities at the flagship universities are massive, often lavish. As the president of Texas A&M told reporters, "It looks like we must be filthy rich. You need to see all of that and look through it."[65]

These arguments, however, started to wear thin when flagship state university presidents hinted that their state governments had treated them better early in the twentieth century than at the start of the twenty-first century. One president of a Big Ten university, for example, noted in the *Chronicle of Higher Education* that the percentage of the university's operating budget borne by the state government was greater in 1914 than in 2001, having gone from 75 percent just before World War I to about 19 percent at the start of the twenty-first century. But such unadorned percentages, invoked without accompanying institutional data from both eras, are unconvincing, and possibly misleading. Perhaps historical research can leaven the polemics of higher-education discussions. The pleas of poverty begin to stretch credibility when one considers, for example, that in 2002 the University of Michigan had an annual operating budget of $3.8 billion and a diversified operation of federal research grants, an endowment of more than $2.5 billion, generous alumni support, out-of-state tuition income, commercial ventures, and patent rights to supplement its state per capita subsidies. One wonders if a professor or administrator at the University of Iowa or the University of Michigan would truly wish to exchange their contemporary workload and compensation with those of their university counterparts of about a century ago.

This chronic whining seems to have sprung from a historical lag between the institutions' self-image and reality. In the minds of college and university presidents, their institutions still languished in a state of being underfunded, underappreciated, and vulnerable — despite having large endowments, high admission standards, and high enrollments. Vice presidents for development celebrated the completion of successful fund-raising campaigns but quickly cautioned legislators and faculty that this was still not enough to provide all the programs a campus ought to seek. In contrast to this perception of struggling fragility, many constituencies in American society had come to view colleges and universities as what Arthur Levine in 1997 called a "mature industry."[66] A 1988 article in the *Washington Post* about university competition for multi-million-dollar federal research grants referred to the company of such universities as MIT, Stanford, Berkeley, Wisconsin, Cornell, and Chicago as the "big leagues of science."[67]

The self-serving vacillations of the established colleges and universities, pleading for enhanced funding at one moment and boasting of their abundant good fortune the next, lost them the respect of groups both on and off the campus. One dysfunctional consequence of the continual complaining by presidents at the major research universities was that it drew attention away from institutions that had genuine concerns about adequate support—that is, community colleges and private colleges with small endowments. One explanation that perhaps partially reconciles the paradox of such hunger amid such abundance is that American colleges and universities have wandered into a state of continual expansion characterized by overextension of functions without clarity of purposes, a pattern that has fostered administrative bloat and other spending excesses. It has also created an aura of confusion as to what our colleges and universities ought to assert as their real purposes and appropriate missions. As Bruce C. Vladeck, professor of public health and political science at Columbia University, has observed, "The competition for students and faculty is closely interwoven with the general drive for institutional prestige. Like most people, administrators and trustees are generally eager to do a good job and to appear to be doing a good job. But in higher education, as in most nonprofit services, it is extremely difficult to tell what a good job is, since it is so extraordinarily difficult to evaluate the quality of the 'product.'"[68]

This dilemma warrants little sympathy when colleges and universities are unclear and inarticulate about their primary purposes. If the higher-education community cannot make sense of itself and explain itself to external audiences, who can? The resilience of American colleges and universities over the centuries, especially their capacity to add and absorb new constituencies, new institutions, and changing fields of teaching and research, endures as a remarkable heritage. Yet the ambiguity and uncertainty displayed in recent years with respect to societal roles indicates a drift in mission and character. This was a line of critical analysis raised by Abraham Flexner in 1929 in his series of lectures at Oxford

University, published in 1930 as *Universities: American, English, German*.[69] And it was a timely concern raised again at the end of the twentieth century by such historians of higher education as George M. Marsden and Julie A. Reuben.[70] The challenge for higher education in the United States during the twenty-first century is to acknowledge its historical good fortune and to accept its role as a mature institution, along with the responsibilities that accompany that maturity. This task is not a matter of money but of rediscovering essential principles and values that have perhaps been obscured in the recent blurring of educational activities and commercial ventures. By going back to the basics of these fundamental matters of institutional purpose, the diverse constituencies in American higher education can once again connect past and present as a prelude to creating an appropriate future.

9 A New Life Begins?

Reconfiguring American Higher Education in the Twenty-first Century

The first decade of the twenty-first century was a good time to take stock of, even celebrate, the historic achievements of American higher education over the preceding century. At the start of the new millennium, colleges and universities shared in the larger national optimism of economic and educational ascent. And 2010 was an especially fortuitous year for higher-education anniversaries. It was, for example, the centennial of two landmark works that heralded the rise of American higher education: first, the Flexner Report for the Carnegie Foundation on the reform of medical education and, second, the publication of Edwin Slosson's book, *Great American Universities*. It also marked the fiftieth anniversary of the famous California Master Plan for Higher Education, which had provided an internationally acclaimed blueprint for the transition to mass higher education.[1]

These heroic anniversaries, however, were small consolation to college and university presidents in 2010. Despite the achievements in American higher education since about 1900, the contemporary developments that surfaced by 2010 were crises that dampened enthusiasm for celebrating the heritage of higher education. The first decade of the millennium did not end well for American colleges and universities because they encountered a combination of financial problems as endowments, state appropriations, and donor contributions declined. At the federal level, student financial programs were mired in contentious congressional debates about renewal of loan and grant programs. Federal support for campus-based research and development had tapered at a time when a growing number of scholars and institutions competed for a fixed allocation for grants from such agencies as the National Institutes of Health (NIH) and the National Science Foundation (NSF). The outlook was sufficiently dire that the president of the Association of American Universities worked to have federal agencies assure support for the established research universities, arguing that they were both more expensive and more deserving than other kinds of institutions. And, although he did not state explicitly that perhaps there now were too many institutions aspiring to the stature of research universities, he did urge Congress and colleagues at least to start discussing the matter.[2]

There was even more sobering news. In October 2009 the Knight Foundation Commission announced, in a news release, their finding that most university presidents conceded that they had lost control of spending for big-time intercollegiate athletics programs.[3] At about the same time several studies simultaneously documented that, for more than thirty years, American colleges and universities had been showing a decline in their retention rates for undergraduates and their bachelor-degree graduation rates.[4] Even the heralded Flexner Report on Medical Education was now regarded as old news because the battle for academic standards had long been won. In contrast, the Carnegie Foundation for the Advancement of Teaching's 2010 report, *Educating Physicians*, sounded a "call for reform of medical school and residency" that urged medical college deans and professors to make certain a new generation of medical students were being taught to emphasize cooperation and patient empathy—evidently, characteristics that were sorely lacking among many American medical doctors.[5]

American higher education in the twenty-first century had taken on a defensive posture, as illustrated by the book jacket of Jonathan Coles's 616-page book about "The Great American University." Its sequence of subtitles documented a downward spiral, starting with "its rise to preeminence," followed by a reminder of "its indispensible national role," and concluding with the warning, "Why it must be protected."[6] How to reconcile these glaring differences between past achievements and present problems? Were the severe economic downturns and crises of confidence of 2010 a temporary problem or symptomatic of a new set of systemic dislocations for higher education in the United States that threatened its future excellence? According to Andrew Delbanco of *The New York Review of Books*, his epitaph for the era was no less than "The Universities in Trouble."[7] Mark Bauerlein writing in the *Wall Street Journal* concluded that these unresolved problems meant that "higher education may be heading for a reckoning."[8]

The Past as Prologue: From 1900 to 2010

When the characteristics of American higher education at the start of the twentieth century were juxtaposed with the conditions of colleges and universities early in the twenty-first century, it placed into bold relief how remarkable were the changes and innovations in colleges and universities as part of the life of the nation. At the end of the nineteenth century, presidents of American universities were painfully self-conscious, even apologetic, about their institutions' dubious academic standards for graduate study and research when compared to European and British universities. This preoccupation with shoring up scholarly reputation was the impetus for the founding of the Association of American Universities in 1900. A century later international academic ratings and rankings had flip-flopped. American research universities were ranked high, perhaps the highest, of universities worldwide. Scholarly journals published in the United States—in English—had replaced the primacy of German scholarship as the international gold standard of advanced research.

The net assessment was that, when it came to quality and academic reputation in higher education worldwide, the period from 1900 to 2010 represents no less than a world turned upside down for American higher education. The quality and quantity of Ph.D. programs offered by universities in the United States were firmly established as a model and a marvel for higher-education systems elsewhere—stretching across its undergraduate degree programs to Ph.D.'s and to a vast array of professional schools. By 2000 university-affiliated medical schools in the United States had addressed those weak points and, indeed, were cited internationally not only for their academic rigor but also for their integration of high-stakes research and development with all facets of medical education and nationwide health care. Whereas in 1900 most medical schools were free-standing and often did not even require a high school diploma for entrance, in the twenty-first century they had become the home and host for a variety of new, rigorous academic disciplines, such as biochemistry, physiology, bioengineering, and biogenetics.

As suggested in chapter 8, American higher education at the start of the new millennium was successful, prestigious, prosperous, and pervasive. Given this condition in 2000, what was the subsequent trajectory of the dominant trends of our colleges and universities in the first decade of the twenty-first century? To explore and perhaps even answer this question, the approach will have two distinct parts. First, to monitor how some of the salient trends of the late twentieth century—the recent past, as noted in the preceding chapter—have fared between 2000 and 2010. Second, the approach will be to conclude with some overarching comparisons and contrasts of higher education in the United States between the twentieth and twenty-first centuries.

Higher Education's Unfinished Business from 1990 to 2010

The problems that surfaced in the 1990s for American higher education remained unsolved. Indeed, between 2000 and 2010, they became more rather than less troublesome to the health and vitality of established colleges. As noted in the preceding chapter, the sore spots included competition from the for-profit sector; the dilemma of whether to acknowledge—and incorporate—new media, such as internet distance learning, into the traditional curriculum and degree programs; the achievement of diversity throughout all institutions; the reliance on underfunded community colleges as a convenient catch-all; and belated recognition of changes in the gender representation among students, faculty, alumni, and administration.

One of the foremost concerns facing established colleges and universities that carried over from the 1990s was the persistent growth and self-confidence of the for-profit colleges.[9] By 2010 this sector had "changed the landscape of American higher education," as it enrolled more than 10 percent of college students in the United States, marked by an increase by about 2 percent each year. These institutions elicited sufficient fear and criticism that they were the object of three months of congressional hearings starting in July 2010. The bill of particulars was three-fold. First, their record of recruiting and enrolling students with a disproportionate number of federal loans cut into the availability of program funding for students at "real" colleges; second were allegations that their students tended to leave programs with heavy indebtedness plus a high default rate on federal loans. And, third was the concern by established four-year colleges and universities that the "for profit" institutions made exaggerated claims about the employment opportunities awaiting students who completed their certification or degrees in a variety of technical and vocational fields. According to Peter Goodman's feature article in the *New York Times*, these institutional abuses were accentuated during a period of national economic recession, as he noted that in "hard times" marginal students were lured into trade school and debt.[10] Hence, the litmus of "gainful employment" became the watch-word of congressional inquiries into for-profit college operations.[11]

The rising popularity of the "for profit" colleges demonstrated the pervasiveness of the work ethic in American life. Even high school grad-uates with undistinguished academic records understood well that in the United States eventually one had to find a path or a place related to jobs. The promotional posters attested to this—with slogans such as "This College *Works . . .*" as prelude to program descriptions for busi-ness administration, equine studies, health care administration, medi-cal assisting, medical coding, mining management and safety, nursing, public safety administration, sports management, and teacher educa-tion. In a similar vein, Sullivan University projected itself as "We Mean Business" to an audience of late adolescents who most likely had been ignored by selective, established academic institutions. And, for adult students, the promise of an "MBA ASAP" was alluring.

No doubt there were documented reasons for concern about poor records of student job placement coupled with loan indebtedness. However, much to the chagrin of established colleges, the for-profit sec-tor fought back with strong, effective lobbying and public relations ini-tiatives.[12] For example, an effective counter was that one could raise the same questions about the performance of "real colleges." First, by 2006 a senior in college had acquired on the average a debt of over $17,000. Sec-ond, most of the degree programs at American colleges and universities were tied to some form of professional preparation or formal licensure and certification. And during the summer of 2010 national newspapers featured stories about graduates of prestigious law schools who re-mained unemployed. This was especially disturbing because heretofore the legal profession had exhibited an unusual capacity to absorb new recipients of law degrees.

In another prestigious, learned profession—medicine—medical school deans showed increasing concern over the problem of young doctors, especially those specializing in pediatrics, incurring hundreds of thousands of dollars in medical school debts and then facing a pro-fessional future of relatively low income compared to their classmates in such specialties in orthopedics or dermatology. The crisis was suf-ficiently grave that medical schools worried about the future of attract-ing medical students to the practices of primary care and pediatrics. Indictments against the "for profit" colleges had to be balanced with recognition that the nonprofit colleges gave inordinate attention to the study of business administration at both the undergraduate and graduate levels. At the College of William and Mary in Virginia, for example, business persisted as the most popular major (20%) at an institution considered among the most committed to the liberal arts among public institutions. Nationwide the master's degree in business administration had been the success story of academic programs for over thirty years—even though it carried with it neither professional licensure nor any certainty as to just how the degree improved decisions or productivity at companies. In sum, most American colleges and universities had succumbed to what sociologist Ivar Berg called *The Great Training Robbery*—the misplaced belief that there was an indelible connection between academics and employment.[13]

The congressional hearings' preoccupation with the success or failure of professional preparation and job placement tended to draw attention away from one of the most distinguishing characteristics of some "for profit" institutions, especially the University of Phoenix. What the established colleges and universities failed to appreciate was that the University of Phoenix had attracted an underserved, growing constituency—namely, working adults who yearned to earn a bachelor's degree. The University of Phoenix was serving a category of students that traditional colleges had often ignored or neglected. For many of these students, the bachelor's degree was incidental to employment, since they already were in midcareer. Their persistence in pursuing collegiate studies through the University of Phoenix actually was a testimony to the real and symbolic importance in American life of a college degree as a rite of initiation and achievement and personal stature—sometimes, but not always, connected to vocational prospects.

A distinct yet overlapping issue often associated with for-profit colleges was the expansion of distance education formats for college courses and degrees. Distance education—in this case, courses and programs offered via internet instruction—represented one of the transformational innovations in American higher education. Important to note is that the locus of innovation often was in the for-profit sector—with the University of Phoenix standing out as the most highly developed, sophisticated provider. At first, many established universities dismissed such instruction as anathema to the residential or in-person course. By 2010, however, the vast majority of traditional colleges and universities offered internet courses for degree credit, as they followed rather than led the for-profit sector. Indeed, one could earn an M.B.A. from

Duke University via an internet program—which, although not relying on campus services and facilities that would drive costs up, actually
charged students a higher price than for a traditional M.B.A. program
in residence at Duke. Prestigious universities had found a good deal
with internet programs for professional degrees. They were relatively
inexpensive to provide, yet their "branding" power meant that they
could command a high tuition—thus, becoming a "cash cow" for the
university. For better or worse, all colleges and universities had become
involved in the technological transformation of academic programs.

Demographics and Diversity: The Changing Profile of Students

Higher education continued to be a "growth industry" in the early
twenty-first century, as total enrollment in more than three thousand
institutions rose to 16 million, with enrollments projected to surpass
20 million in 2010. In 2007–8 colleges and universities in the United
States conferred 1.6 million bachelor's degrees.[14] Within this aggregate
enrollment there were reconfigurations in the demographic profiles of
students—and, ultimately, in the composition of the faculty and administration of colleges and universities. By 2000, for example, at two
large, prestigious state flagship universities—the University of Texas at
Austin and the University of California, Berkeley—minorities were a
majority. In other words, white students constituted less than half of the
undergraduate student body and increasingly shared campus lecture
halls and dormitories with a persistently increasing number of students
who were Asian, Hispanic, or African American.

Within the undergraduate world, Hispanic and Latino students became an increasingly visible and vocal constituency. Obviously Latino
students represented a substantial critical mass at colleges and universities in such states as California, Arizona, Texas, and New Mexico. Yet
geographical mobility and family migration across states meant that
by 2010 Latinos as a distinct college group had ceased to be regional
in character and now were a significant proportion of enrollments in
higher education nationwide, representing more than 12 percent of total enrollments in 2007–8. Changes in college attendance by Latinos
represented a formidable change in reducing some of the exclusion
factors that had been predominant two or three decades earlier. The
irony of this shift from exclusion to increased access was not without

its historical ironies. As historian Christopher Tudico has documented, in decades prior to the formal and informal exclusion of Latinos from, for example, California and Texas public higher education, an earlier generation of Latinos had in the early twentieth century enjoyed full campus citizenship. Puerto Rican students had a long record of attending colleges across the continent. In southern California, the Mexican American Movement (MAM) from 1934 to 1950 promoted the value of higher education "among the larger Mexican American community."[15] The importance of this historical context is the reminder that, in the concerted efforts of Latino advocacy groups to increase college access and choice for their sons and daughters, they are in large part working to reclaim opportunities they once had—and which have since been taken away.[16]

Student diversity and college access, cutting across all underserved groups, were inseparable from controversies involving federal student financial aid programs between 2000 and 2010. The most disturbing development was a shift in national priorities: many banks and lenders were given terms that tended to place more attention on assuring that federally subsidized student loans were a lucrative and safe enterprise rather than a primary vehicle for increasing college affordability for a new generation of students from backgrounds of modest income. The customary debates over federal student financial aid policy typically had pitted advocates for designating the federal government as the lender to students versus those who championed a program in which the lenders were banks whose student loans were subsidized and guaranteed by the federal government. Between 2000 and 2005, the competition showed a new wrinkle within the ranks of private lenders, as new, upstart loan companies such as "My Rich Uncle" vied to get a share of the loan market in competition with established banks. This intense rivalry among private lenders tended to marginalize the welfare and access of students as a priority. This situation changed dramatically in the congressional elections of November 2006, when a large number of Democratic candidates unexpectedly won over incumbent Republicans. The result was fresh attention to restoring the federal government as a lending agency that assured students low-interest loans along with increases in the Pell Grant program.[17]

The most significant quantitative and qualitative changes in American higher education were the increases in and ascent of women in all roles—as undergraduates, graduate and professional school students, administrators, and professors. The 1972 federal Title IX legislation had had little immediate effect on opportunities for women on campus. By the early twenty-first century, however, Title IX enforcement and litigation in conjunction with requirements by the NCAA and various intercollegiate athletics conferences had drastically altered the roles of women as student-athletes and as coaches.[18] At the same time, the changing patterns of enrollment and choices of academic fields meant that women gained influence, power, and leadership in all dimensions of campus programs and life. Women represented about half of medical students and law students.[19] Women were a majority of bachelor's degree recipients in several fields, including biology, anthropology, and health sciences. And, when one looks at Ph.D. degrees awarded in 2007, one finds that women earned 44 percent of the doctoral degrees in biological sciences, 29 percent in geology and mathematics, and 33 percent in chemistry.[20] One of the most astonishing records of academic achievement was that by 2010 women were more than 90 percent of the students in veterinary schools.

At four-year coeducational colleges nationwide, women were in the majority of undergraduate enrollments. In some instances, this was a substantial differential, such as 55 percent women and 45 percent men. As faculty retirements finally led to a revitalization of the academic job market, women increasingly gained appointments in tenure track positions. What one found was a progression of representation as one ascended the academic ladder. In 2007, for example, women were 47 percent of the assistant professors, 40 percent of the associate professors, and 27 percent of the full professors.[21] At the same time one finds women as academic deans and provosts at a growing number of institutions. In 2010, women were presidents of four of the eight Ivy League institutions—Harvard, Brown, Penn, and Princeton—as well as at the University of Michigan, the University of Iowa, Syracuse University, and the University of Virginia.

There were some unexpected consequences—or, at least adjustments—associated with these gains. If a coeducational college sought some particular balance of men and women in its entering class, it meant that high-achieving women often were put at a disadvantage in admissions even though their academic and extracurricular records surpassed those of male applicants.[22] Gender imbalances within a student body also altered the dynamics and proportionalities of traditional student life by creating what was called "the new math on campus," es-

372 A History of American Higher Education

pecially in dating and women's relationships with men.[23] Nor did extracurricular programs always reflect the changed student body. At a regional state campus where women were 60 percent of the enrollment, one might find that the intercollegiate athletics program continued to place disproportionate resources into a football team, with full athletic grants-in-aid for eighty-five male student-athletes.

The Emergence of Global Universities: The Internationalization of Higher Education

Nowhere were the ambivalences facing American higher education in the twenty-first century more evident than in the issue of globalization. It was simultaneously a source of prestige and doubt for colleges and universities in the United States. A feature article in the *New York Times* noted, "Once a Leader, U.S. Lags in College Degrees."[24] In a similar vein a *Christian Science Monitor* headline asked, "US college degrees: Still the Best among the World's Top Universities?" The uncertainty among American higher-education leaders was fueled by what one scholar called the "Post American Era" in education—along with economics and politics. Cara Lovett, writing about American business schools in the post-American world, characterized this new era of economics and education with the observation, "In his 2008 best seller, *The Post-American World,* Fareed Zakaria argued that the salient feature of the twenty-first century is not the decline of America's power and influence in the world but rather 'the rise of the rest.'"[25]

True, the United States had been the leader since World War II in expanding higher education in a concerted effort to promote mass and then universal access to postsecondary studies. Given this exemplary blueprint, many countries watched and then emulated the American model. In 2000, for example, Turkey's massive investment in campus construction and its related strategic planning to link higher education with economic development bears a striking resemblance to the Master Plan that Clark Kerr drafted for California a half century earlier. International imitation of American higher education was a sign of flattery. In a comparable initiative, faculty from the University of Georgia's Institute for Higher Education were invited by university leaders in Croatia to share ideas on academic planning. In Belgium, the new University of Louvaine La Neuve drew much of its inspiration and plans for design from the prototypical American campus town plus student affairs staff—a marked departure from the European tradition of urban universities melded into an old city.[26] Oxford and Cambridge universities, battered by years of lean appropriations from government, looked to development offices in the United States for advice on how to initiate systematic private fund-raising. Above all, higher education—including the construction of new universities—was a growth industry worldwide. Little wonder, then, that several nations made real and relative gains in terms of university access and degree completion.

What was surprising was that many American academic leaders found this development to be either unexpected or unsettling. Since the end of World War II, American universities and foundations had been involved in scholarly exchanges worldwide with such programs as Fulbright Fellowships, Marshall Scholarships, Danforth Fellowships, and Rhodes Scholarships. Land-grant colleges in the 1950s and 1960s sent agronomists to Africa and Asia to spread "the American way" in crop production and the "Green Revolution." Furthermore, the ministries of education in several nations in Asia and Latin America enthusiastically provided full fellowships for their promising students to pursue doctoral degrees at leading American universities. By the 1980s most American colleges and universities recruited and welcomed international students not only for advanced degree studies but for undergraduate programs, especially in the applied sciences, technology, and mathematics. Over time program participants and alumni followed career paths involving numerous institutions and national settings. Hence, a predictable development in the early twenty-first century has been the expansion of academic cooperation and cross-fertilization in multiple directions and numerous geographic sites.

American universities, especially their graduate and professional programs, faced a paradox of popularity as universities in other nations often used American academic models to create their own home-based programs. Hence, over time, universities in the United States had to share the wealth of innovations and ideas in the new competition for talent. A good snapshot of these energetic developments is Ben Wildavsky's *The Great Brain Race,* in which he documents and interprets how "global universities" were "reshaping the world."[27] At one level this meant that American universities were establishing branch campuses and extended programs in such distant sites as Malaysia or Singapore. At the same time, it also meant that universities in Europe and elsewhere had learned their lessons well from observing U.S. higher education and now were establishing their own new programs in such fields as business administration. The new euro currency reforms included emphasis on higher education, including the so-called Bologna Plan. Also, within Europe, university students in affiliated nations were able to participate in the new Erasmus Plan, which allowed migration and enrollment at universities across national borders. The net result was that the balance of academic trade no longer tilted in one direction—that is, toward the United States. Accepting and adjusting to these new dynamics required reorientation for American colleges and universities that failed to realize that the academic imperialism of the immediate post–World War II era, which had placed the United States center stage, had moved into a new international commonwealth format.

The most problematic elements of this global innovation in higher education were not the activities and growth in other nations but rather the pilot projects in which American universities established new campuses abroad. Why, for example, was Dubai such an instantaneous, attractive magnet for American universities starting around 2000? Was this interest fostered by a genuine interest in international understanding? Or were the new ventures seen as an opportunity for fresh revenue streams? Did sound academic priorities suggest that a state university in the United States that failed to send admissions officers to all the counties in its home state should suddenly acquire urgency about establishing business and engineering degree programs in Dubai? The meteoric attraction of Dubai—and the subsequent rapid collapse of its inflated economy—suggested that many American higher-education entrepreneurs in their haste had failed to study closely the politics and economy (and even location) of Dubai. This belated discovery was evident in 2009, when news reports of its financial crash indicated that not only was Dubai *not* a source of oil, its ostentatious city building and educational expansion rested on an embellished foundation of banks and illusory financial leveraging. The economic crash plus its declining student demand for degree programs meant that by 2009 several American universities had quickly pulled back on what were supposed to have been their long-term academic enterprises there.[28]

Big-Time Intercollegiate Sports: Education's Entertainment

American universities' increased support for big-time intercollegiate athletics between 2000 and 2010 illustrated the perils of publicity and prestige. The conventional wisdom, as told to boards of trustees and presidents, was that a powerful football and basketball team brought many good things to a university—visibility on television, affiliation for alumni and donors, half-time promotionals to attract students, and revenues that would support numerous Olympic sports. Furthermore, athletics directors claimed that a winning sports program stimulated donations to the whole university, including academic programs.

At best, the strategy worked in a few exceptional places. The University of Florida drew from its revenues from championship football and men's basketball teams to funnel massive funding into such sports as volleyball, swimming and diving, soccer, and track—for both men's and women's squads.[29] Ohio State University offered thirty-six varsity sports and had an operating budget of more than $100 million per year.[30] And the athletics director noted that "all athletics dollars were university dollars"—a genuine commitment that included marking $9 million for university library improvements over a three-year period, along with other annual transfers for educational programs. The problem was that, by 2010, the examples of the University of Florida and Ohio State University were the exception, not the rule. Only 17 athletics programs among the more than 300 NCAA Division I institutions were truly self-supporting. Even this estimate was dubious, as a reporter in 2010 for Portland's newspaper, *The Oregonian,* described the University of Oregon's athletics department financial profile as follows:

> The Oregon football program's rise in national prominence has brought an increase in donations and ticket sales. For the better part of a decade, University of Oregon officials have touted the athletic department's economic self-sufficiency, a rarity in the world of big-time college sports. But for at least nine years, athletics has used hundreds of thousands of dollars annually from the university's general fund to cover the cost of academic support for athletes, according to files obtained by the Oregonian. The general fund has paid nearly $8.5 million over the past nine years for academic support for athletes, which includes exclusive tutoring and counseling, increasing six fold from less than $300,000 in 2002–03 to a budgeted $1.8 million this academic year. Meanwhile tuition has nearly doubled and state support has plummeted to 7 percent of the university's overall budget.[31]

Most athletics departments, including those with high-profile programs associated with the Bowl Championship Series (BCS), lost money each year. Particularly surprising was that varsity football, intended to be the golden goose of intercollegiate sports revenue, often cost more to operate than it brought in from ticket sales, television contracts, product endorsements, and alumni donations. Most big-time football programs relied on subsidies from the educational side of the university budget. One would be hard-pressed to find a more dysfunctional, disappointing outcome for such an expensive, long-term university investment. In contrast to the enhanced funding for Olympic Sports at the University of Florida, most universities looked to reduce their nonrevenue sports, while making certain that they had protected—and enhanced—funding for football and men's basketball. For example, in September 2010 the University of California, Berkeley, announced that it was cutting five of its twenty-four varsity teams.[32] This in part was a concession to faculty discontent upon discovering that the chancellor had been authorizing annual subsidies of about $13 million per year, flowing from the campus general fund to the athletics department.

Such was the context of a series of critical reports issued by the Knight Foundation's Commission on the Future of Intercollegiate Athletics. Whatever the athletics balance sheet showed, athletics directors and boards of trustees were prepared to offer yet another justification for funding the arms race in big-time sports. If a program fell short of its mandate to be self-supporting, the deficit was justified because, after all, a Homecoming game boosted campus morale and brought alumni and donors back to Alma Mater—and it was unfair for critics to try to put a price tag on such important intangibles. Meanwhile, universities also were in a legal bind that impeded cost reductions. Compliance with both Title IX guidelines and the even more stringent NCAA requirements meant that an athletics department was required to maintain a large number of sports and to approach some measure of equity between men and women student-athletes in the areas of scholarship grants-in-aid, training facilities, and coaching salaries. Selective pruning of teams or soliciting for subsidies from the university was the temporary solution. Such measures, however, begged the fundamental question of university priorities and payments. A few fortunate conferences such as the SEC, the Big Ten, the Atlantic Coast Conference, and the PAC 10 received a reprieve of sorts by negotiating new, lucrative television contracts. Yet even with revenue sharing within these conferences, some member institutions strained to keep pace financially. Outside these conferences, the vast majority of intercollegiate athletics programs were struggling—and evading genuine resolutions.

The trends within the big-time varsity sports associated with the

NCAA's Division I gave rise to what came to be known as "College Sports, Inc."—an institutional commitment to winning teams—which tended to position the athletic department as an increasingly special entity within the university structure.[33] It had consequences for the intercollegiate athletics programs of all colleges and universities. There was a trickle-down effect in which athletics directors and coaches nationwide tended to mimic the entitlement associated with the most powerful programs.[34] It included such practices as preferential admissions for student applicants who were recruited as athletes, allocation of financial aid for athletics scholarships, construction of elaborate new training facilities, and high pay for high-profile coaches. At both the University of Texas and Amherst College, for example, the "branding" of winning teams to market the institution as well as to attract students and please alumni had become a common denominator across higher education. By 2005 presidents and board members at several financially stressed small, unselective private liberal arts colleges—such as Adrian College in Michigan—relied on investment in new athletics facilities, coaches salaries, the addition of new varsity teams, and aggressive recruitment of athletes both to bolster athletics reputation in NCAA Division III and as a strategy to rescue the entire college from its pattern of declining student enrollments and sinking tuition revenues.[35]

Research Universities in an "Era of Big Bets" Federal Grants

Clark Kerr's 1963 book *The Uses of the University* simultaneously described the history of and outlook for a small number of high-powered "federal grant" universities in the United States. Over the next half century it was often invoked by ambitious university presidents as a manifesto of change at their own institutions. It provided a model (and a dream) for aspiring universities that were newcomers to competition for sponsored research grants from federal agencies. Typically, these institutions were *not* members of the prestigious Association of American Universities (AAU) but sought to be invited while also pursuing such goals as being a "Top Twenty Public Research University." In 2009 sociologist Gaye Tuchman described this institutional type as "Wannabe U"—illustrative of a new model of an aggressive corporate university.[36] One attractive feature of joining in this grants competition was the prospect of creating a new revenue stream for university operations. When one looks at the 2009 rankings of universities' research and development federal grant expenditures, the sums were impressive, if not enticing:

The Johns Hopkins University	$1,587,547,000
University of Michigan	$636,216,000
University of Washington	$619,353,000
Massachusetts Institute of Technology	$532,618,000
University of California, San Diego	$511,428,000
University of Wisconsin, Madison	$507,898,000
University of Colorado	$500,123,000
University of Pennsylvania	$499,498,000
University of California, San Francisco	$483,667,000
Columbia University	$483,111,000
Stanford University	$477,507,000

Following these top eleven universities, those ranked between 50th and 100th showed dollar amounts ranging from $207,216,000 to $102,903,000. Within the top one hundred universities, there was re-markable diversity in geography and institutional age—suggesting that several newcomers to the federal research enterprise had been reason-ably successful. On closer inspection, the rankings revealed some trou-bling features. First, there were great disparities within the ranks of the research universities. The top-rated institution, the Johns Hopkins University, had federal grant expenditures that were more than twice the amount noted for the second-place University of Michigan. Only thirty-one universities had $300 million or more in annual federal grant expenditures as part of a total university operating budget ranging from $2 billion to $3 billion per year. The concentration of federal research grants in a relatively small cluster of universities meant that entering into this competition was both risky and expensive. Above all, the an-nual reports of federal research grant dollars were silent on the matter of how much each university spent from other sources in order to have competed for and then administered the federally sponsored research and development. The ability of a particular department or professor to land a large federal research grant may have been impressive but it was incomplete. One must also consider how much that project spent—be-cause the latter often surpassed the former.

The alarming finding between 2000 and 2010 among vice presidents for research was that the research enterprise was costly—and at many universities it ended up losing money year after year. Consider, for example, the situation of a mediocre physics department at a research university. Many of its necessary initial basic expenses for faculty salaries, laboratory technicians, and start-up funds for newly hired professors, laboratory space, equipment, conference travel, and utilities were fixed even before receipt of a single federal research grant dollar. Furthermore, federal agencies such as the National Science Foundation seldom covered such predictable costs as capital construction or even academic term release time for faculty who were principal investigators. Drafting research grant proposals took a lot of faculty and staff time—expenses that had to be absorbed by the university from sources other than the grant itself. If a physics department had happened to land a federal grant, it was immediately obligated to pay a substantial amount to reimburse the university's research foundation for infrastructure support, indirect costs, grant proposal writing, as well as for the formidable expenses of grant administration, including accounting, record keeping, and compliance with institutional and federal regulations. If this same team of physics professors were not successful in pursuit of the federal grant, university administrators had to draw from other budgetary lines to pay the bills associated with the rejected grant application. Since most federal research grant competitions relied on academic peer review and showed a higher rate of successful grant awards from universities and programs that had a track record of success, universities that were relative newcomers to the grants game were less likely to land the coveted grants that would enable them to recoup the venture costs of their application.

Universities that had invested heavily in providing the infrastructure and staff to compete for sponsored research grants faced another pitfall: changing priorities of federal agencies. It was not unusual for a specific research team at a campus to have a long, successful run of several years in getting an initial grant award followed by generous renewals. However, if the research topic faded in luster at, for example, the National Science Foundation, a university's vice president for research had the dilemma of determining the fate of highly specialized "research professors" whose contracts were tied to "soft money." Did one "float" the now unfunded research team in hopes of their future success in landing a grant? If so, for how many years? What incumbent projects or personnel would be reduced to subsidize the empty-handed research team? This scenario was complicated by the fact of academic life that research specialties were so arcane that they often had little transferability to other fields or new projects. There were no academic labor hiring halls at which each morning a personnel supervisor would call out to unemployed scientists, "Hey! I need two physicists for a three-day project at the Genex Institute . . . Must specialize in cold temperature studies and be available to perform odd jobs such as cleaning up dirty data as well."

The risks and expenses that increased between 2000 and 2010 were due in part to an innovative feature in the competitive ground rules. In the twenty-first century large-scale science projects sponsored by federal agencies explicitly emphasized multidisciplinary cooperation, as faculty from disparate departments converged in such new combinations as bioengineering, biochemistry, biogenetics, nanotechnology, or neurosciences. Traditional departments, such as chemistry, biology, botany, and geology, were "old hat" and uncompetitive. The price to pay for interdisciplinary projects was that these collaborations had grown to rely on new administrative and physical structures within the campus. Each time a provost or a vice president for research approved the creation of a new research institute, it committed to recurrent administrative expenses for such nonresearch personnel as a center director and accompanying staff. A 2009 report from the University Leadership Council, *Competing in the Era of Big Bets,* reported serious concerns that many research universities would not be able to sustain the level of institutional funding necessary to support the proliferation of campus research centers and institutes.[37] Furthermore, most university-sponsored research parks intended to fuse academics and industry in applied research seldom showed a surplus—and often required recurrent annual subsidies from the university to continue operating. Although a few of the original university research park ventures—such as the North Carolina Research Triangle, Stanford's Silicon Valley, Texas's "Austin Miracle," and the University of Utah's Research Park—had thrived, among 116 cases, more than half lost money. Worst of all, most failed to stimulate the promised regional economic development.[38]

The expensive uncertainty of federally sponsored research, both at an individual campus and nationwide, was illustrated by the case of genome research. Hailed in the 1990s as the promising frontier of multidisciplinary research involving biologists, chemists, physicists, and statisticians, it received priority funding from the National Institutes of Health and several other federal agencies and private foundations. Review of the results from this massive research effort in 2010 suggested disappointment with its applications to products and problem solving and other indices of its cost-benefits.[39] The policy implication for the twenty-first century was that a university that undertook wholesale entry into the federal research arena faced high costs and high risks. These pursuits and projects often drained the overall resources of a campus and of national research agencies—with little guarantee of having contributed significant new knowledge, as one would reasonably expect from a university that called itself a "knowledge factory." Historian Roger L. Geiger's study, *Knowledge and Money*, pointed out that even the most prominent of the research universities faced what he called the "paradox of the marketplace":

> Market forces have profoundly affected the contemporary research university's fundamental task of creating, processing, and disseminating knowledge. They arguably have provided American universities access to greater wealth, better students, and stronger links with the economy. Yet they also have exaggerated inequalities, diminished the university's control over its own activities, and weakened the university's mission of serving the public.[40]

State Universities and the New "A&M": Athletics and Medicine

Despite the high-stakes risk of focusing on big-time athletics and federally sponsored research in the health sciences, these two enterprises came to define a new type of public research university. It was a hybrid that sprouted in part as an attempt to revitalize the traditional state land-grant campus. In 1981, for example, the University of Maryland commissioned a planning report titled, *The Post–Land Grant University*. The argument was that the historic features associated for more than a century with the Morrill Acts of 1862 and 1890 were no longer adequate to define the modern multipurpose flagship state university.[41] By 2010 American public higher education had drifted into a new "A&M." Instead of the historic "Agriculture and Mining" or "Agriculture and Mechanics," the 2010 model stood for "Athletics and Medicine."

These new emphases provided a ray of hope to restore prestige and morale to beleaguered flagship state universities. By having "A&M" stand for "Athletics and Medicine," university presidents and provosts thought they had rescued the modern public university from the archaic nineteenth-century meaning, "Agricultural and Mechanical." This revised branding provided state universities with both a jump start and truth in advertising about their priorities. After more than a quarter century of grumbling by presidents that they were losing resources and falling behind their elite private research university counterparts, public higher education has an opportunity to put new wine into the old A&M bottle. After all, "Athletics and Medicine" were hailed by the campus public relations office as the front doors and neon signs that showcased an enterprising, dynamic state university.

The institutional strategy was based on the premise that few would miss the old "A&M." Historic programs that once defined the land-grant model showed signs of decline. For example, in 2010 a number of articles reported that colleges of agriculture at state universities were selling off their livestock and reducing their farms for agricultural re-search and extension.[42] The change was timely because at many land-grant universities the traditional "A" already had tended to disappear. Consider the case of the University of California, Berkeley, for example, where the historic, famous College of Agriculture has changed its name to the "College of Natural Resources." What about the "M"? Originally it meant "mechanics"—a nineteenth-century usage that approximates our notion of "engineering." But "mechanics" had little name recogni-tion today and was confusing because it brought to mind the vocational training programs in auto repair or air conditioning service provided by community colleges. In other words, the old "A&M" shell is vacant and ready to accommodate the new contenders, "Athletics and Medicine."

What were the strengths of this coupling? First, both areas represented high-profile units of the university. Second, both were not only highly visible but also seen as indispensable. Third, both were expensive—they brought in a lot of resources and also spent a lot. Fourth, both activi-ties were integral to the local economy through services, construction, and employment. The new "A&M" also retained fidelity to the historic land-grant service mission. Hospitals and clinics certainly represented health service to the public. And big-time athletics even made a case for itself as a public utility. In 2008 the commissioner of a major athletics conference said in earnest that, at the state universities in his confer-ence, football ought to be regarded as a form of public service. True, this was not exactly the same as providing extension assistance on crop rota-tion—but who in the modern era could not agree that a state university team in the BCS championship or in the NCAA basketball Final Four had not reached out to the entire state's population?

Academic medical centers (AMCs) were a success story of growth after 2000. A college of medicine and its affiliates no longer were to be described as merely one among many academic units because it had now achieved a size, prestige, and power that transformed its presence. In 2010 it was not unusual for a medical center and related health sciences units to constitute somewhere between one-third and one-half of a flagship university's faculty positions. Furthermore, for a university with an annual operating budget of about $2 billion, the academic medical center often accounted for 40 percent or more of the total university expenditures.

Athletics and medicine provide an interesting symmetry in hiring, as both share the ability to compete for talent in a high-priced market. Hiring a new coach was, for example, sometimes balanced by hiring a researcher with an M.D. and Ph.D. whose work dealt with finding a cure for a serious disease. And both new hires commanded a retinue of assistants, staff, and incentive bonuses that supplemented base salaries. They were together the superstars of academia. A flagship state university anchored on one end of the campus with the big "A" and anchored on the other end by the big "M" was formidable. Both units commanded new, expensive facilities—which often became obsolete relatively quickly. And the expanding, large facilities meant that the two units occupied a substantial percentage of campus real estate—usually without either leasing or purchasing the land. In fact, there were cases where big-time athletics provided the model and vocabulary for creating strong academic programs. Consider the following account of academic recruitment at one state flagship university:

> To land its latest prized recruit, the University of Kentucky launched an intense six-month courtship that included a weekend stay at Gainesway Farm and the promise to invest more than $80 million. All this wasn't for a McDonald's All-American basketball player for UK's much-ballyhooed, newly hired coach . . . University officials pulled out all the stops to reel in an even rarer commodity: a big-name surgeon-researcher to head its Markey Cancer Center . . . The process of wooing a nationally known expert to a university's faculty is a high-stakes, pressure-packed effort that rivals, and in some cases, surpasses, college basketball coaching searches.[43]

There were liabilities in showcasing athletics and medicine as the new A&M. Although both brought in a lot of money, whether in television revenues, ticket sales, major donations, Medicaid payments, federal grants, or fees from clinics, these fertile sources could be precarious. In 2003, for example, an article in the *Los Angeles Times* reported that UCLA's medical center "struggled for months with wobbly finances and internal dissension," characterized by a consulting firm's report as "problems ranging from inconsistent billing and plummeting revenues to a disorganized administration in which job duties overlapped."[44] Perhaps the best example of the financial fragility of the expensive university medical centers came about at Georgetown University in Washington, D.C., where a shortfall in the medical center income led the university president to try to impose an internal tax on the law school and business school as a convenient source of medical center fiscal fitness.[45]

A university medical center in the twenty-first century typically faces three sources of financial risk: first, a downturn in number of patients and empty hospital beds run up expenses quickly. Second, any reduction in the federal Medicaid or Medicare reimbursement rate requires university medical centers to reduce drastically their income projections. Third, although many academic medical centers enjoyed financial autonomy due to their own large endowments, these quickly became undependable in the volatile national economy around 2008 to 2010. It was not unprecedented, for example, that a university medical center endowment of $250 million in 2007 (most of which was earmarked to pay for an aggressive capital expansion and building program) by 2009 had shrunk about 40 percent down to $150 million—a one-year loss of $100 million due to unproductive investment choices. The gamble from the point of view of a vice president for an academic medical center was that if and when these shortfalls did occur, it was likely that the state government or the university, or both, would bail out the medical center. The presumption was that an AMC was too big, too visible, and already represented too much of an investment to be abandoned by its host university or state.

The same dynamics held for flagship state universities with NCAA Division I intercollegiate athletics programs. A losing season in a revenue sport such as football or men's basketball quickly brought about a decline in ticket revenues and fewer invitations to be selected for nationally televised games. However, even if this happened, it's hard to imagine a state university abandoning football or basketball. The programs had become so important that their expenses had to be covered, even if that were to mean transferring resources from other parts of the university.

The consequences for other academic units located on campus between the anchors of Athletics and Medicine were formidable and undeniable. One possible concern was the endurance of the traditional "A&S" acronym for "Arts and Sciences." Since this unit probably had difficulty in claiming primacy in the state university of the twenty-first century, a possible reform was to amend their branding to reflect a new, diminished status. "A&S" could be rebranded as "a & s"—lower case to connote shrinking budgets, deteriorating centrality, and reduced visibility. This real and symbolic marginality within the budget and curriculum of the total university operation meant that the historic academic core of the multipurpose state university became literally a step-child. Nowhere was this more evident than in the problems of deferred maintenance of older buildings and facilities in contrast to the capital expenditures for new facilities in the health sciences.[46]

The Gridlock of Funding for State Universities

Even though the "new A&M" model provided hope for some state universities to revitalize, by 2010 the indication was that most state flagship universities were unable to solve their financial problems.[47] Public-university presidents continued their familiar complaint about how little money they've received from their state legislatures. Some even suggested the need to seek direct federal aid. Whether or not state universities qualified for federal relief followed a script of pleas—followed by some questions and considerations. Unfortunately for the future of legislative support for public higher education, the case presented by state university presidents was a tiresome and unpersuasive litany.

Typically, the first claim made by a state university president was, "Our state government has been giving us less and less—and we are falling behind our counterparts in other states." The weakness in this plea was that by 2010 *all* state universities had faced hard times in appropriations because, of course, all state economies were hurting. When the revenues of major states like California, Florida, and Michigan were down, public-university presidents there can hardly claim that they were being singled out unfairly for cuts among all state agencies and services. A study published in 2009 by the Delta Project on Postsecondary Education Costs, Productivity, and Accountability helped provide informed discussion on policy deliberations because it gave profiles of how public higher education had fared in each state.[48] The Commonwealth of

Kentucky, to cite one case, was small in population and poor in income and earnings. Yet the Delta Project data indicated that the state government had been relatively generous to public colleges and universities. The state subsidy per student was $8,960—the twelfth highest dollar figure among the fifty states and two territories. It would be fair to say that the state had done right by higher education—support that public institution presidents had not always adequately acknowledged.

State universities relied on a sleight of hand to justify their complaint that state appropriations have become a shrinking part of their annual operating budgets. They glossed over the fact that the size and complexity of a university had become markedly different from years ago. New, federally sponsored research programs, medical centers, auxiliary services, research parks, and foundations are self-initiated ventures that expand the overall base budget. That then, by logic and definition, made the state contribution decline as a percentage of the budget—even if appropriations increased in actual dollars.

To see how little the flagship state universities had changed in their polemics and pleas over the course of the first decade of the twenty-first century, one has only to revisit the 2002 profile that Ben Gose wrote about the University of Texas and the "Fall of the Flagships" in the *Chronicle of Higher Education:* "The President of Texas A&M University commented, 'It looks like we must be filthy rich . . . You need to see all of that and look through it.'"[49] In August 2010 Paul Fain, also writing in the *Chronicle of Higher Education,* visited Seattle and observed almost the identical scenario, as he noted,

> Washington's flagship university doesn't look like it has money problems. The picturesque campus, a blend of Gothic architecture and the lush greenery of the Pacific Northwest, draws more federal research dollars than any other public university in the country. And the University of Washington raised $2.7-billion in a recent campaign from its perch in this entrepreneurial city. But cracks are appearing under the surface. The state is not paying for the many construction projects here, and severe budget cuts are now threatening quality at the university, particularly for undergraduates who are going with larger classes and fewer research opportunities, one of the institution's core strengths.[50]

The result is that the state flagship university pitted itself against the state's community colleges, with the complaint that state legislators were favoring the increased funding of two-year degree programs at the expense of four-year bachelor degree programs plus other offerings at the University of Washington. No longer could a flagship state university president assume that state legislators gave first funding priority to the historic, prestigious research university.

Given this setback in state lobbying, the next proposition by a state university president was, "We need more money to educate our students." That may have been true, but the Delta Project study showed that, in many states, an increasing percentage of state subsidies and tuition dollars had been directed into noninstructional costs. One read about administrative plans to eliminate academic programs and cut faculty positions or to convert them from tenure-track to adjunct status. Yet there was no indication that state universities had reduced the number of vice presidents. Indeed, several national reports released in 2009 and 2010 identified "administrative bloat" as a troubling source of rising institutional costs. It included the estimate that, over the past two decades, the number of administrative positions at universities had risen 39 percent, whereas the increase in number of faculty positions was 18 percent—indicating that new administrative offices had a growth rate more than double that of the faculty.[51]

This widespread trend was illustrated by the case of one flagship state university that was medium in size, with an enrollment of about twenty-five thousand, and, although its public relations emphasized its ambitions as a "research university," it was *not* one of the sixty-two universities who were members of the prestigious Association of American Universities. In 2010 its top administration included, in addition to a president, fifteen vice presidents. Even though located in a relatively poor state and in a city with a reasonable cost of living when compared to Boston or New York or Chicago, its administrative salaries were generous, as listed below:

Executive Vice President for Health Affairs & Hospital	$706,291
Executive Vice President for Finance and Administration	$458,999
Vice President and Dean of the Medical College	$585,663
Vice President for Clinical Operations/Hospital	$543,479
Senior Vice President for Health Affairs	$467,230
Provost and Vice President for Academic Affairs	$275,000
Vice President for Commercial and Economic Development	$255,999
Vice President for Institutional Diversity	$210,000

Vice President for Research	$210,000
Vice President for Financial Operations & Treasurer	$210,000
Vice President for Institutional Advancement	$191,759
Vice President for Student Affairs	$170,214
Vice President for Facilities Management	$153,453
Vice President for Human Resources	$151,422
Vice President for Institutional Research & Planning	$143,967

Furthermore, the university paid in 15 percent of a vice president's salary as a contribution to the individual's TIAA CREF account. The steel czar and philanthropist Andrew Carnegie would have found this latter practice surprising. He had created and funded TIAA CREF exclusively for professors—whom he believed were underpaid—not for campus administrators. Each top administrator also had substantial support in such roles as assistant vice president or associate vice president. The president had the services of a full-time chief of staff who, although not in a "line" or decision-making office, received a salary of $145,923 plus the 15 percent TIAA CREF contribution. In comparison to these compensation packages, the average salary for full professors with tenure was slightly over $100,000. The trends of rising administrative salaries and expansion of the number of top administrative positions was endemic in American universities nationwide.

Charges of administrative bloat and overstaffing usually led a state university president to counter, "Our university has a freeze on salaries." For many campus employees, that may have been the case, but not for all. In 2009 the football coach at the University of Florida signed a six-year contract that raised his annual salary from $3.25 million to $4 million, making him the conference's highest-paid coach. The coach at Louisiana State University invoked a clause in his contract that guaranteed him $1,000 more than any other coach in the league if he led the team to a national championship. And higher compensation during lean times was hardly confined to the football stadium or basketball arena. At many state flagships it was common practice for some top-ranking administrators like the vice president of the medical center to receive substantial annual bonuses. Indicative of the curious priorities of American universities was that at many state universities some assistant football coaches made a higher salary than the provost and academic vice president.

A state university president often tried to persuade taxpayers and legislators that the campus was working to reduce expenses by imposing a freeze on hiring. That drastic measure was, indeed, a cause for concern. But what was unclear was whether it applied to selected high-profile academic or administrative superstars who, because of "market forces," had to be wooed with large salaries, laboratory facilities, and expensive state-of-the-art equipment, along with a retinue of their own support staff. And it was probably a safe bet that such special hires weren't for professors in the French department or the school of social work.

Perhaps the most dubious claim by the president of a flagship state university was, "Our university has limited funds." On closer inspection, a more accurate characterization was that, even though total funds were ample, there were pockets within the university structure and budget that were lacking adequate resources. The problem of state support for higher education in the twenty-first century was comparable to a mechanical system with valves that are stuck so that fuel flows only one way. The problem for a public university in 2010 was not only lack of external appropriations but also imbalances of financial resources within the campus. For example, consider the situation of those state universities who were members of the Southeastern Conference. In August 2009 the conference commissioner's office announced that the twelve member universities would receive revenues for television contracts of $2.25 billion over fifteen years, a figure that supplemented the existing $825 million contract with CBS. As Ben Volin, a sportswriter for Cox Newspapers, observed, "Thanks to ESPN, SEC teams now have significantly more money to spend on recruiting, upgrading facilities, and luring top-notch coaches."

There was no sound reason why that largess could not be shared with educational programs central to the mission of those universities. Reallocation was neither impossible nor unreasonable for a president to implement administratively because athletics programs were beholden to their host institutions. Such a recommendation predictably led to the presidential chorus proclaiming, "But that's different! That's private money!"

State university presidents lamented, "Large portions of our budget are restricted." That was true. It also was neither indelible nor insoluble. Presidents, business officers, and trustees had many administrative tools readily available to redistribute at their discretion the allegedly confined funds. For instance, given the abundance in athletics revenues, the president and trustees could have required the athletics association, a privately incorporated body, to pay fair-market-value rent on all of its facilities located on university property. Institutions could have also billed the association for use of the university name, the university logo, and university affiliation. After all, it was neither the athletics association nor the athletics department that belonged to the National Collegiate Athletic Association—it was the *university*. Because the athletics association often charged groups and organizations, including the university, for use of its logo and mascot, turnabout was fair play.

Most disappointing in these executive excuses was that university presidents were supposed to educate donors about the mission of the university. But if donors still preferred to give generously to athletics and not to academic causes, presidents did have in hand a partial solution: they could have imposed a processing fee or overhead charge of, say, 15 percent on all major gifts to the university and its affiliated foundations. The president and provost could have then redistributed those indirect-cost funds as they deemed appropriate. The money might have gone back to the original unit or to another department. Whatever the reallocation, it would have allowed the president, not donors, to set the university's course. That strategy was not far-fetched. It would have been comparable to the policy that professors encountered when applying for federal research grants. A principal investigator was required to add on average 47 percent in overhead expenses to the grant budget. The administration, not the professor, then determined how that money would be redistributed. That practice of institutional overhead and indirect costs had not deterred professors from applying for grants—so it could have been feasible in application to other units.

Such internal realignments would not have been a total solution for public higher education's financial plight. But at least public universities could have sent a signal to their state legislature or to the U.S. Congress that, before they apply for the federal relief program or lobby for increased state appropriations, finally they were trying to put their own houses in order to better match their resources with their educational missions.

The Millennium in Perspective: American Higher Education from the Twentieth to Twenty-first Centuries

One theme that resonated throughout the entire twentieth century was the perennial rhetorical question that really was a challenge: "Why

can't a college be run like a business?" That slogan provided a good litmus of changes in the institutional gyroscope between 1900 and 2000.
Foremost was the prevalence of business leaders and corporate executives as trustees on the boards of almost all colleges and universities,
large and small. This was a dramatic, documented transformation away
from the preponderance of clergy as both board members and institutional presidents.[52] More often than not, unfortunately, colleges and
universities in the United States in the late twentieth and early twenty-
first century had not fared well when they attempted to imitate business corporations in selecting projects and setting priorities. University
presidents all too often adopted—and internalized—slogans that depicted the university as an "economic engine" or a "knowledge factory"
that held out the promise of state prosperity and job creation. Two conspicuous examples of the enterprising strand in academia—university
research parks and big-time athletics programs—seldom fulfilled their
promises. In the same vein, was it really appropriate or effective for a
college or university to establish a "for profit" corporation as part of
its organizational structure and educational mission? This was no idle
musing because city and county governments increasingly pressed to
impose property taxes on universities, especially if the campus had extended to include commercial activities that veered sharply from the
traditional justifications for academic land's tax exemption.[53] The net
result of such concerns was that, in 2010, reports from the Delta Group
and other policy analysis groups indicated that the business as usual
that has characterized most universities would not be sustainable in-
definitely.

Ironically, the disproportionate news coverage and publicity given
to the research university as an economic engine tended to obscure
some "best practices" models of academic institutions. Small liberal
arts colleges, for example, had been remarkably resilient in their ability to maintain clarity of educational mission and remain financially
solvent.[54] Even though the large research universities had received publicity and funding for "Big Science," the private liberal arts colleges persisted in their tradition as the undergraduate alma mater of a disproportionate percentage of Ph.D. recipients in the sciences. This was not
altogether surprising because this category of colleges had been effective
in winning and then implementing National Science Foundation grants
that focused on science education for undergraduates—projects that
meshed well with their faculty tradition of including undergraduates

as research assistants and coauthors in laboratory work and scholarly publications.[55]

College Students in an Era of Commercialization and Consumerism

The emphasis on academic commercialism had substantial albeit mixed consequences for undergraduate education. To the delight of entering students, colleges and universities had invested mightily in services and facilities that made college life increasingly attractive to the daughters and sons of affluent America. Fitness centers, apartments rather than ascetic dormitory rooms, study abroad programs, tutoring services, career placement offices, computer sites, restaurants and coffee shops, recreational offerings, and tickets for big-time intercollegiate sports events meant that the American campus of the twenty-first century competed effectively in an environment of up-scale shopping and leisure. Colleges also increased their budgets for recruiting students and courting applicants. The trade-off was that disproportionate spending on noninstructional items rose higher and faster than commensurate investment in core academic programs. A number of undergraduate admissions offices shifted student financial aid offerings from need-based aid to merit scholarships, justified on the grounds that a college ought to be able to participate in the talent hunt for new students—meaning that it was all right to award a full scholarship to a bright student from a prosperous if not wealthy family.

The result was that there were signs of increasing schisms within and between colleges in the socioeconomic composition of their student bodies. At the University of Virginia, for example, the percentage of students who received Pell Grants fell below 3 percent. This was significant because a Pell Grant was the best litmus for estimating that a student was from a modest-income family. A relatively small number of academically prestigious and selective institutions came to be skewed toward the able and affluent, if not the rich and famous. The inequalities of admissions and student life were captured in the fiction of the era—notably Tom Wolfe's 2004 novel set at "DuPont University," *I Am Charlotte Simmons*. Further evidence of this pronounced trend was Andrew Hacker's finding that, although tuition and expenses for an academic year at Williams College had risen to more than $50,000, 60 percent of the students required no financial aid because their families were able to pay the full bill.[56] A further testimony to the institutional ambition for prestige was that administrators placed resources into activities and achievements in the academic arms race that would help Alma Mater rise in the annual rankings published by *U.S. News and Report*. Stanford law professor Deborah L. Rhode's 2007 book, *In Pursuit of Knowledge: Scholars, Status, and Academic Culture* analyzed the changing proportions of college expenditures and concluded that she had grave doubts as to whether students at expensive colleges were receiving a substantive education for their investment of time and money.[57]

Rethinking the Historic Role of Governing Boards and Trustees

In reviewing the continuity in American higher education over six centuries since the founding of Harvard College in 1636 and the College of William and Mary in 1692, one distinctive feature has been the inordinate power and faith that our institutions and public policies vest in college and university boards of trustees. The colonial colleges, along with universities in Scotland, were unique and innovative in devising a legal structure of governance that gave ultimate authority to an external lay board—which in turn worked closely and almost exclusively with the president, who was the head of a strong administrative structure. The driving force for this innovation was distrust of and disgust with faculty governance at Oxford and Cambridge universities. Reliance on the external board plus a powerful president was designed to promote a "tight ship" character to the colleges in the New World. Indeed, the model was immediately effective and enduring. James Blair, the founding president of the College of William and Mary, worked well with "his" board of visitors—so much so that they named him "President for Life." And, although the original statutes for the college had provision for faculty governance via an "Academic Senate," in fact, the president conveniently usurped this by designating the board of visitors as the incumbents for the so-called "Academic Senate." Such constitutional and legal deliberations ensured that well into the twenty-first century the formal and informal arrangements for a strong presidency joined at the hip with an ultimately powerful board of trustees would dominate governance in American higher education.

A peculiar consequence of this model was the inverse relation between the ultimate authority given to boards in marked contrast to their low profile and negligible accountability. Boards of trustees were silent partners who had been seldom analyzed—and only infrequently covered in the press. There were a few colorful exceptions. The regents of the University of California—each of whom was appointed for a sixteen-year term—were described by one historian as "the world's largest unhappy family." This characterization was stimulated by their proclivity for suing one another after yet another contentious meeting of name calling, after which some regents presided over their own individual press conferences to berate fellow regents with whom they disagreed on policy matters.[58] In the main, however, academic boards of trustees were quiet, relatively unengaged, and, most unfortunately, uninformed about the character and context of the colleges and universities that they governed. In recent decades there have been readily available resources such as the Association of Governing Boards (AGB), plus such hard print and electronic daily and weekly publications as the *Chronicle of Higher Education* and *Academe Today*—all intended to provide convenient, timely information and education for board members. There certainly has been no requirement for board members to read these sources to be informed about higher education—nor is there any assurance that most board members have voluntarily accepted invitations or opportunities to learn substantively about academic life and work. In contrast, it was doubtful that board members of a business corporation were uninformed about the industries or companies they served and led. In sum, boards of trustees of many universities were good candidates to be the "straight men" in the old vaudeville routine where a news reporter asked, "What do you think about ignorance and apathy in governance of higher education." According to the script, their stock answer would be, "I don't know—and I don't care." Whatever humor this may have elicited among theater audiences, by 2010 it had ceased to be a laughing matter for the proper governance of American colleges and universities.

This problem was especially acute at large flagship state universities, where appointments to the board were often a source of political patronage for governors. Indeed, politics literally spilled into the university board in some states such as Kentucky, where there was a requirement that board composition be monitored so that there was a balance of Democratic and Republican appointees. To be a state university board member often emphasized the perks of prime, free tickets for intercollegiate football and basketball games. State university board members were less likely than their independent or private college and university counterparts to be generous donors and fund-raisers for the institution. Curiosity about the genuine teaching and learning of the institution was an expendable topic. Indeed, the conventional wisdom of university presidents was to keep the board occupied with diversions—and certainly at arms length from academic affairs.

The resulting syndrome was that uninformed and marginally involved board members were the Achilles heel of higher education for two reasons: first, there were few (if any) checks and balances on board actions and decisions; second, state university presidents gained by default inordinate control over policy deliberations. Board interactions with—and knowledge about—various constituencies and activities within the university tended to be constricted to the information filtered by the president and administrative staff.

What was wrong with trustees transferring so much power to the university president? Whatever the situation facing the heroic university presidents of 1910 as visionary pioneers, a century later one had a generation of presidents who by their own admission had little control over such areas as intercollegiate athletics, the medical center, or the research enterprise. In 1996 the retired president of Cornell noted good-naturedly to a gathering of his fellow elite university presidents, during his after-dinner remarks at Princeton's 250th anniversary forum, that the increased responsibility for fund-raising meant that contemporary university presidents were "beggars who lived in big houses."[59] College and university residents did have prestige and publicity, as board members usually were drawn from the ranks of corporate executives, and approved salaries and bonuses for presidents and vice presidents that emulated those of corporations and industry. If a state university president were to be fired, usually it was due to some gaffe about the hiring of a coach rather than a substantive academic or curricular matter. At a handful of universities—such as the University of Chicago in 1999 and Harvard University in 2006—the academic culture was sufficiently strong and self-confident that presidential disagreements with faculty over academic practices led boards to oust a president.[60] More typical, however, were the experiences of John DiBaggio at Michigan State University and David Rozelle at the University of Kentucky, where presidential attempts to reform varsity sports and to rein in an arrogant coach led presidents to fall from favor with the board of trustees—and, eventually, to resign for presidential appointments elsewhere.[61]

The preponderance of a business corporation outlook among university boards succeeded in redefining the presidency and its relation to the academic profession. When there was a presidential vacancy, the applications increasingly came from administrators who had never held faculty appointments and whose experience was in the nonacademic areas of university life, such as fund-raising and development or business affairs. Conspicuously absent—or, at least, declining—in the presidential applicant pool were provosts, academic deans, and professors.[62] The void in many American universities in the early twentieth century was presidential vision and propriety in educational mission. So long as the historic governance structure of a strong external board and president remained intact, many state universities were mortgaged into an arrangement that made conventional academic operations unsustainable. Boards of trustees at both public and private universities also lost some measure of public trust when investigative reporters documented that at numerous institutions trustees often entered into business contracts with their university that represented a conflict of interest.[63] Structures for decision making and responsibility in American higher education warranted no less than a thorough "new deal." The defining question, perhaps bordering on academic heresy was, "Perhaps a university could be great in spite of, rather than because of, its academic corporation?"

If the historic system of external boards was not serving higher education well in the twenty-first century, where was genuine reform incubating? Perhaps the foremost example of conventional support for targeted universities was the William and Flora Hewlett Foundation's 2007 award of a $113 million grant to the University of California, Berkeley, in a matching gift program for endowed faculty chairs.[64] Although this generosity was admirable, it favored an institution that already had enjoyed public and private support for almost a century. Furthermore, this infusion of funds begged the essential question of how prominent state flagship universities were going to survive in the future. Other established foundations opted more for scrutiny than charity. For example, the Mellon Foundation, the Spencer Foundation, the College Board, and the Carnegie Foundation for the Advancement of Teaching not only continued but also stepped up their critical analysis of higher education. Elsewhere in the orbit of established foundations, however, there were signs of decreasing interest in and funding for higher-education projects.[65] Some of the slack was taken up by the initiatives of newcomers, such as the Bill and Melinda Gates Foundation and the Lumina Foundation. An interesting change, however, was that these new initiatives focused more on the broad issue of student access and retention and less on providing direct support to particular colleges and universities. The established higher-education associations of One DuPont Circle, such as the American Council on Education, persisted in effective advocacy for higher education, especially in federal legislation to enhance student financial aid programs. However, some organizations, such as the American Association of Higher Education, closed up shop. The Association of American Universities, representing the sixty-two most prestigious research universities, was disappointing in its inability or unwillingness to depart from a predictable orthodoxy that advocated special support for its member institutions.

For long-term higher-education reform, less visible yet exciting was the flourishing of a cluster of new, flexible, and imaginative institutes and organizations in Boston and Washington, D.C., that relied on relatively small core teams of leaders who often were analysts, editors, writers, and strategists who had left campus settings to focus on harnessing new technology and sophisticated databases to address issues of serving students, lobbying for equity and social justice at the levels of state and federal government, and providing an independent, informed voice in higher-education policy deliberations. The names, albeit unfamiliar to either the American public or even to college and university leaders, included such entities as the Institute for College Access and Success, the Delta Cost Project, the Education Trust, the American Enterprise Institute's Higher Education Reform Group, the Center for American Progress, Connect Edu, Excelencia in Education, and the Kaufman Foundation. Another fertile source of critical analysis and fresh information was the excellent daily and weekly journalistic coverage along with detailed, in-depth analyses of all facets of college and university trends provided by the *Chronicle of Higher Education* and *Inside Higher Ed*. The collective impact of these innovative organizations and publications was to reinforce the messages that it was time for "A Reset for Higher Education" and that "As Students Change, Colleges Must Follow."[66] Another timely source of informed criticism and warning came from some retired university presidents—including William F. Bowen of Princeton University, James Duderstadt of the University of Michigan, and Derek Bok of Harvard University. Bok's 2003 book, *Universities in the Marketplace*, dissected the foibles of the commercialization of higher education. Bowen and Duderstadt, respectively, focused on the need to address the abuses of college sports at all levels. These retired university presidents provided good companion pieces for the reform initiatives of the Knight Foundation's Commission on the Future of Intercollegiate Athletics.

Conclusion

A dominant theme that emerged from the recent past in the United States was that many of the conventional practices and policies that characterized American higher education's approaches to funding and resources, along with fundamentals of leadership and vision at the start of the twenty-first century, were strained and ineffective. They had become inappropriate because they caused our educational institutions to drift from essential educational purposes. How might this be set aright? One partial answer is that this book, an extended historical analysis of higher education since 1636, will have been most pertinent if its narrative of context and cases informs a new generation of higher-education readers and leaders of the insights that make all stakeholders thoughtfully concerned about connecting past and present to assure a sound future. One legacy of the history of American higher education is that colleges and universities in 2010 would do well to draw inspiration from the motto of Scripps College: *Incipit Vita Nova,* which translates as "A New Life Begins."

Notes

Preface

1. Edwin Slosson, *Great American Universities* (New York: MacMillan, 1910), p. 75.

2. Philip G. Altbach, "Training University Administrators: Should Management Schools?" *Inside Higher Ed,* 5 November 2010.

3. Edwin Slosson, *Great American Universities* (New York: MacMillan, 1910), p. 347.

4. See, for example, "Brown University's Debt to Slavery" (editorial), *New York Times,* 23 October 2006. Primary sources from Brown University include *Slavery and Justice: Report of the Brown University Steering Committee on Slavery and Justice* (2006) and *Report of Commission on Memorials* (March 2009).

5. James Axtell, *The Making of Princeton University: From Woodrow Wilson to the Present* (Princeton: Princeton University Press, 2006).

6. John R. Thelin, "Archives and the Cure for Institutional Amnesia: College and University Saga as Part of the Campus Memory," *Journal of Archival Organization* 7, no. 1 (2009):4–15.

7. S. Williams, "The Architecture of the Academy," *Change: The Magazine of Higher Education* 17 (March–April 1985):14–30, 50–55.

8. See, for example, Stephanie Russell, "When Campus and Community Collide," *Historic Preservation,* September/October 1983, pp. 36–41.

9. Gay Brechlin, "Classical Dreams, Concrete Realities," *California Monthly,* March 1978, pp. 12–15.

10. Eric Hoover, "Application Inflation: Bigger Numbers Mean Better Students, Colleges Say—But When Is Enough Enough?" *Chronicle of Higher Education* 57, no. 12 (12 November 2010):A1, A20–A22.

11. John Thelin, "Why Can't Businesses Be Run More Like a College?" *Planning for Higher Education* 24, no. 3 (Spring 1996):58–60.

12. David F. Swensen, *Pioneering Portfolio Management: An Unconventional Approach to Institutional Investment* (New York: Free Press, 2000).

13. Andrew Delbanco, "The Universities in Trouble," *New York Review of Books* 56, no. 8 (14 May 2009).

14. Geraldine Fabrikant, "As Donors Retrench, Challenges for Universities," *New York Times*, 11 November 2010, p. F17.

15. Nicholas Wade, "Rare Hits and Heaps of Misses to Pay For," *New York Times*, 9 November 2010, pp. D1, D8. See also Sheldon Krimsky and Cat Warren, eds., "The Conflicted University," special issue of the AAUP's *Academe* (November 2010).

Introduction

1. *Information about Harvard College for Prospective Students* 60 (5 September 1963):1–2.

2. No one disputes Brown University's 1764 charter as the College of Rhode Island and Providence Plantations. Although Hampden-Sydney now lists its founding date as 1776, in the 1980s it claimed an earlier date based on the chartering of an academy that may well have been a forerunner to the later college.

3. "Two Colleges Assert Right to Use 'College of New Jersey' as Name," *Chronicle of Higher Education*, 12 July 1996, p. A6.

4. Robert K. Durkee, letter to the editor, "The Name of a College in New Jersey," *Chronicle of Higher Education*, 16 August 1996, p. B5.

5. "History," College of New Jersey website, 1999.

6. Walter L. Creese, "Remembering Mayor Charles P. Farnsley," in *The University of Louisville*, ed. Dwayne D. Cox and William J. Morison (Lexington: University Press of Kentucky, 2000), pp. 8–9.

7. George Santayana, *The Last Puritan: A Memoir in the Form of a Novel* (New York: Charles Scribner's Sons, 1936).

8. Earl F. Cheit, *The Useful Arts and the Liberal Tradition* (New York: McGraw-Hill, 1975).

9. Ben Gose, "The Fall of the Flagships: Do the Best State Universities Need to Privatize to Thrive?" *Chronicle of Higher Education*, 5 July 2002, pp. A19–A23.

10. Edwin E. Slosson, *Great American Universities* (New York: Macmillan, 1910).

11. Christopher Jencks and David Riesman, introduction to *The Academic Revolution* (Garden City, N.Y.: Doubleday Anchor, 1968), pp. xii–xiii.

12. John R. Thelin, "Rudolph Rediscovered: An Introductory Essay," in *The American College and University: A History*, by Frederick Rudolph (1962; reprinted Athens: University of Georgia Press, 1990), pp. ix–xxiv.

13. Richard Hofstadter and Wilson Smith, eds., *American Higher Education: A Documentary History* (Chicago: University of Chicago Press, 1961).

14. Merle Curti and Roderick Nash, *Philanthropy in the Shaping of American Higher Education* (New Brunswick, N.J.: Rutgers University Press, 1965); Jesse

Brundage Sears, *Philanthropy in the History of American Education* (Washington, D.C.: Government Printing Office, 1922); Robert H. Bremner, *American Philanthropy*, 2d ed. (Chicago: University of Chicago Press, 1988).

15. Burton R. Clark, "Belief and Loyalty in College Organization," *Journal of Higher Education* 42 (June 1971):499–515. See also Burton R. Clark, *The Distinctive College: Antioch, Reed, and Swarthmore* (Chicago: Aldine, 1970).

16. Allan Nevins, *The State Universities and Democracy* (Champaign-Urbana: University of Illinois Press, 1962), p. 82.

17. For a collection of such materials, see A. C. Spectorsky, ed., *The College Years* (New York: Hawthorn, 1958).

18. John R. Thelin, "Cliometrics and the Colleges: The Campus Condition, 1880 to 1910," *Research in Higher Education* 21, no. 4 (1984): 425–37.

19. Seymour E. Harris, *A Statistical Portrait of Higher Education* (New York: McGraw-Hill, 1972); Seymour E. Harris, *The Economics of Harvard* (New York: McGraw-Hill, 1970).

20. Colin Burke, *American Collegiate Populations: A Test of the Traditional View* (New York: New York University Press, 1982).

21. Margery Somers Foster, *"Out of Smalle Beginings . . .": An Economic History of Harvard College in the Puritan Period* (Cambridge, Mass.: Belknap Press of Harvard University Press, 1962).

22. The key reference source for dollar indexing upon which I relied was the U.S. Bureau of the Census, *Historical Statistics of the United States, Colonial Times to 1970*, bicentennial ed. (Washington, D.C.: U.S. Government Printing Office, 1970). I owe special thanks to Dexter Alexander for historical analysis of the higher education financial data.

23. Ed Crews, "How Much Is That in Today's Money? One of Colonial Williamsburg's Most-Asked Questions Is among the Toughest," *Colonial Williamsburg*, Summer 2002, pp. 20–25.

1. Colleges in the Colonial Era

1. Quoted in Ralph Nading Hill, *Dartmouth, the College on a Hill: A Dartmouth Chronicle* (Hanover, N.H.: Dartmouth College, 1964), p. 280.

2. W. F. Craven, *The Legend of the Founding Fathers* (Princeton, N.J.: Princeton University Press, 1956).

3. Parke Rouse, Jr., *When Williamsburg Woke Up* (Williamsburg, Va.: Colonial Williamsburg Foundation, 1981).

4. John Stewart Bryan, "A Dedication," in *The Colonial Echo* (Williamsburg, Va.: College of William and Mary, 1936), pp. 6–7.

5. Russell T. Smith, "Distinctive Traditions at the College of William and Mary and Their Influence on the Modernization of the College, 1865–1919," Ed.D. diss., College of William and Mary, Williamsburg, Va., 1980.

402   Notes to Pages 6–15

6. "What Is Brown?" *Bulletin of Brown University,* 1956, pp. 9–10.

7. Budd Schulberg, *The Disenchanted* (New York: Random House, 1950), p. 77.

8. *Building Harvard: Architecture of Three Centuries* (Cambridge, Mass.: Information Center of Harvard University, 1971), pp. 6–7.

9. Frederick Rudolph, "The Collegiate Way," chap. 5 of *The American College and University: A History* (New York: Knopf, 1962).

10. *Information about Harvard College for Prospective Students* 60 (5 September 1963):11–12.

11. George W. Pierson, *Yale: A Short History* (New Haven: Yale University, 1976), p. 41.

12. B. A. O. Williams, "College Life," in *The Handbook to the University of Oxford* (Oxford: Clarendon Press, 1968), pp. 275–88; Jasper Rose and John Ziman, *Camford Observed* (London: Gollancz, 1964).

13. Kenneth Cooper, "The Colleges," in *Cambridge* (Norwich, Great Britain: Jarrod Publishing, 1985), p. 10.

14. "Statutes of the College of William and Mary, 1727," in *American Higher Education: A Documentary History,* ed. Richard Hofstadter and Wilson Smith (Chicago: University of Chicago Press, 1961), 1:39–49.

15. Lawrence Stone, "The Size and Composition of the Oxford Student Body, 1580–1909," in *The University in Society: Oxford and Cambridge from the Fourteenth Century to the Early Nineteenth Century,* ed. Lawrence Stone (Princeton, N.J.: Princeton University Press, 1974), 2:3–110.

16. James Axtell, *The School upon a Hill: Education and Society in Colonial New England* (New Haven: Yale University Press, 1974).

17. Hugh Kearney, *Scholars and Gentlemen: Universities and Society in Preindustrial Britain* (Ithaca: Cornell University Press, 1970); see esp. chap. 8 for a discussion of the Scottish universities and their influence.

18. Quoted in Pierson, *Yale,* p. 9.

19. See Margery Somers Foster, *"Out of Smalle Beginings . . .": An Economic History of Harvard College in the Puritan Period* (Cambridge, Mass.: Belknap Press of Harvard University Press, 1962).

20. Seymour E. Harris, *The Economics of Harvard* (New York: McGraw-Hill, 1970), p. 509. I am indebted to Dexter Alexander for bringing this episode to my attention.

21. "Charter of Rhode Island College (Brown University), 1764," in *American Higher Education,* ed. Hofstadter and Smith, 1:134.

22. Jurgen Herbst, "From Religion to Politics: Debates and Confrontations over American College Governance in the Mid-Eighteenth Century," *Harvard Educational Review* 46, no. 3 (1976): 397–424. See also Jurgen Herbst, *From Crisis to Crisis: American College Government, 1636–1819* (Cambridge, Mass.: Harvard University Press, 1982).

23. Merle Curti and Roderick Nash, *Philanthropy in the Shaping of American Higher Education* (New Brunswick, N.J.: Rutgers University Press, 1965), pp. 31–35. Cf. Robert H. Bremner, *American Philanthropy*, 2d ed. (Chicago: University of Chicago Press, 1988), pp. 24–28; Jesse Brundage Sears, "The Colonial Period," in *Philanthropy in the History of American Higher Education* (Washington, D.C.: Government Printing Office, 1922), pp. 10–32.

24. Wilford Kale, *Hark upon the Gale: An Illustrated History of the College of William and Mary* (Norfolk, Va.: Donning, 1985).

25. Pierson, *Yale*, pp. 6–7.

26. Curti and Nash, *Philanthropy in the Shaping of American Higher Education*, pp. 13–18. Cf. Bremner, "Doing Good in the New World," in *American Philanthropy*, pp. 5–18; Sears, "The Colonial Period," pp. 10–32.

27. Foster, *"Out of Smalle Beginings."*

28. "Samuel Johnson Advertises the Opening of King's College (Columbia), 1754," in *American Higher Education*, ed. Hofstadter and Smith, 1:109–10.

29. Axtell, "The Collegiate Way," chap. 6 of *The School upon a Hill*.

30. "Commencement Exercises at King's College, 1758," in *American Higher Education*, ed. Hofstadter and Smith, 1:130.

31. See Nicholas Phillipson, "Culture and Society in the Eighteenth Century Province: The Case of Edinburgh and the Scottish Enlightenment," in *The University in Society*, ed. Stone, pp. 407–48.

32. "Charter of Rhode Island College (Brown University), 1764," in *American Higher Education*, ed. Hofstadter and Smith, 1:136. For a more complete version of that document, see appendix A in Walter C. Bronson, *A History of Brown University* (Providence, R.I.: Brown University, 1914), p. 493.

33. Phyllis Vine, "The Social Function of Eighteenth Century Higher Education," *History of Education Quarterly* 16 (Winter 1976):409–24.

34. See Kathryn M. Moore, "Freedom and Constraint in Eighteenth Century Harvard," *Journal of Higher Education* 17 (November–December 1976):649–59; Sheldon S. Cohen, "The Turkish Tyranny," *New England Quarterly* 47 (December 1974):564–83.

35. Howard H. Peckham, "Collegia Ante Bellum: Attitudes of College Professors and Students toward the American Revolution," *William and Mary Quarterly*, January 1971, pp. 50–72.

36. Jay Barry and Martha Mitchell, *A Tale of Two Centuries: A Warm and Richly Pictorial History of Brown University, 1764–1985* (Providence, R.I.: Brown Alumni Monthly, 1985), pp. 10–33.

37. Oscar Handlin and Mary F. Handlin, "Colonial Seminaries, 1636–1770," in *The American College and American Culture: Socialization as a Function of Higher Education* (New York: McGraw-Hill, 1970), pp. 5–18. See also Vine, "Social Function of Eighteenth Century Higher Education."

38. Barry and Mitchell, *A Tale of Two Centuries*, pp. 10–33.

39. Jackson Turner Main, *The Social Structure of Revolutionary America* (Princeton, N.J.: Princeton University Press, 1965).

40. Vine, "Social Function of Eighteenth Century Higher Education."

41. Bernard Bailyn, *Education in the Forming of American Society* (Chapel Hill: University of North Carolina Press, 1960).

42. John Randolph, quoted in David Hackett Fischer, *Albion's Seed* (New York: Oxford University Press, 1989), p. 412.

43. Quoted in "History and Background," in *About Columbia* (New York: Columbia University, 1999), n.p.

44. John Witherspoon, "Address to the Inhabitants of Jamaica and Other West-India Islands on Behalf of the College of New Jersey" (1772), in *American Higher Education,* ed. Hofstadter and Smith, 1:137.

45. Winthrop S. Hudson, "The Morison Myth Concerning the Founding of Harvard College," *Church History* 8 (1939):148–59.

46. See George M. Marsden, *The Soul of the American University: From Protestant Establishment to Established Non-belief* (New York: Oxford University Press, 1994).

47. James Axtell, "Dr. Wheelock's Little Red School," chap. 4 of *The European and the Indian: Essays in the Ethnohistory of Colonial North America* (New York: Oxford University Press, 1981), pp. 87–109. See also Curti and Nash, *Philanthropy,* pp. 34–35.

48. Benjamin Franklin, *Remarks Concerning the Savages of North America* (ca. 1784), reprinted in *Guide to the College of William and Mary* (n.p., 1983).

49. Pierson, *Yale,* p. 56.

50. Herbst, *From Crisis to Crisis,* p. 128.

51. Curti and Nash, *Philanthropy,* pp. 34–35; John Whitehead, *The Separation of College and State* (New Haven: Yale University Press, 1973).

52. John R. Thelin and Marsha Krotseng, "The Paper Chase: Charters and the Colleges," *Review of Education* 9 (Spring 1983):171–75.

53. Carl Bridenbaugh, *Vexed and Troubled Englishmen, 1590–1642* (Oxford: Oxford University Press, 1968).

54. Handlin and Handlin, *American College and American Culture,* pp. 9–10.

55. Gordon S. Wood, "The Greatest Generation," *New York Review of Books,* 29 March 2001, pp. 17–22. Cf. Joseph J. Ellis, *Founding Brothers: The Revolutionary Generation* (New York: Knopf, 2000).

56. Charter of Rhode Island College (Brown University), 1764, reproduced as appendix A in Bronson, *History of Brown University,* p. 493.

57. Curti and Nash, *Philanthropy,* p. 31.

58. Thomas G. Dyer, "Antecedents and Beginnings," in *The University of Georgia: A Bicentennial History* (Athens: University of Georgia Press, 1985); see esp. pp. 3–6.

59. George Isidore Sanchez, *The Development of Higher Education in Mexico* (Westport, Conn.: Greenwood Press, 1970).

60. See Leslie S. Domonkos, "History of Higher Education," in *International Encyclopedia of Higher Education* (San Francisco: Jossey-Bass, 1977), pp. 2017–40.

61. Walton Bean, "The Spanish Colonial Frontier" and "Spanish Settlement of Alta California," chaps. 4 and 5 of *California: An Interpretive History* (New York: McGraw-Hill, 1968).

62. "The Public Image(s) of Harvard," in *Admissions to Harvard College: A Special Report by the Committee on College Admissions Policy* (Cambridge, Mass.: Harvard University, February 1960), p. 14.

63. "Signs of Modernity: The New Look in Harvard's Official Publications," *Harvard Bulletin*, 16 November 1970, p. 57.

2. Creating the "American Way" in Higher Education

1. Jurgen Herbst, *From Crisis to Crisis: American College Government, 1636–1819* (Cambridge, Mass.: Harvard University Press, 1982), pp. 244–53.

2. Colin Burke, *American Collegiate Populations: A Test of the Traditional View* (New York: New York University Press, 1982), pp. 15–17.

3. Robert H. Bremner, *Philanthropy in America*, 2d ed. (Chicago: University of Chicago Press, 1988), pp. 50–51.

4. See James McLachlan, "The American College in the Nineteenth Century: Toward a Reappraisal," *Teachers College Record* 80 (December 1978): 287–306; Burke, *American Collegiate Populations*; and Roger L. Geiger, ed., *The American College in the Nineteenth Century* (Nashville: Vanderbilt University Press, 2000), pp. 91–114.

5. Robert T. Blackburn and Clifton F. Conrad, "The New Revisionists and the History of U.S. Higher Education," *Higher Education* 15, nos. 3–4 (1986):211–30.

6. Jean Evangelauf, "Where Did U.S. Public Higher Education Begin? Georgia and North Carolina Claim the Honor," *Chronicle of Higher Education*, 23 October 1985, p. 1; Linda Williams, "We Just Can't Picture Pep Rallies for This Intercollegiate Match," *Wall Street Journal*, 3 October 1985, p. 1; Bill McAllister, "UNC Carries a New Card," *Washington Post*, 3 September 1993, weekend section, p. 62.

7. Merle Borrowman, "The False Dawn of the State University," *History of Education Quarterly* 1, no. 2 (1961):6–22.

8. See, for example, John D. Wright, Jr., *Transylvania: Tutor to the West* (Lexington, Ky.: Transylvania University Press, 1975), and Walter Wilson Jennings, *Transylvania: Pioneer University of the West* (New York: Pageant Press, 1955).

9. William A. Bowden, "The Jefferson Connection," *Transy Today* 15 (Fall 1997):18–19.

10. Jon Wakelyn, "Antebellum College Life and the Relations between Fathers and Sons," in *The Web of Southern Social Relations: Women, Family, and Education,* ed. Walter J. Fraser, Jr., R. Frank Saunders, Jr., and Jon L. Wakelyn (Athens: University of Georgia Press, 1985), pp. 107–26.

11. Michael Sugrue, "'We Desired Our Future Rulers to be Educated Men': South Carolina College, the Defense of Slavery, and the Development of Secessionist Politics," in *American College,* ed. Geiger, pp. 91–114; McLachlan, "American College in the Nineteenth Century."

12. Philip Lindsley, "The Problems of the College in a Sectarian Age" (1829 baccalaureate address), in *American Higher Education: A Documentary History,* ed. Richard Hofstadter and Wilson Smith (Chicago: University of Chicago Press, 1961), pp. 232–37; quotation at pp. 233–34.

13. See Jennings L. Wagoner, Jr., "Honor and Dishonor at Mr. Jefferson's University: The Antebellum Years," *History of Education Quarterly* 26 (Summer 1986):155–79.

14. David F. Allmendinger, *Paupers and Scholars* (New York: St. Martin's Press, 1974).

15. Dwayne D. Cox and William J. Morison, "First among Medical Schools of the West," in *The University of Louisville,* ed. Dwayne D. Cox and William J. Morison (Lexington: University Press of Kentucky, 2000), pp. 11–19.

16. Linda Eisenmann, "Rediscovering a Classic: Assessing the History of Women's Higher Education a Dozen Years after Barbara Solomon," *Harvard Educational Review* 67 (Winter 1997):689–717; Burke, *American Collegiate Populations,* p. 341; Roger L. Geiger, "'The Superior Instruction of Women,' 1836–1890," in *American College,* ed. Geiger, pp. 183–95.

17. Helen Lefkowitz Horowitz, "Plain though Very Neat: Mt. Holyoke," in *Alma Mater: Design and Experience in the Women's Colleges from Their Nineteenth-Century Beginnings to the 1930s* (New York: Knopf, 1984), pp. 9–27.

18. Christie Anne Farnham, *The Education of the Southern Belle: Higher Education and Student Socialization in the Antebellum South* (New York: New York University Press, 1994).

19. See Andrew F. Smith, "'The Diploma Pedler': Dr. John Cook Bennett and the Christian College, New Albany, Indiana," *Indiana Magazine of History* 90 (March 1994):26–47.

20. Merle Curti and Roderick Nash, *Philanthropy in the Shaping of American Higher Education* (New Brunswick, N.J.: Rutgers University Press, 1965), p. 29.

21. Announcement of 12 December 1792 published in the *North Carolina Journal,* reproduced in William S. Powell, *The First State University: A Pictorial History of the University of North Carolina,* 3d ed. (Chapel Hill: University of North Carolina Press, 1992), p. 12.

22. Cadet journal entries cited in Sidney Forman, "Cadets," in *The College Years,* ed. A. C. Spectorsky (New York: Hawthorn, 1958), pp. 58–68, passim.

23. Howard Miller, *The Revolutionary College: American Presbyterian Higher Education, 1707–1837* (New York: New York University Press, 1976).

24. McLachlan, "American College in the Nineteenth Century"; David B. Potts, "Curriculum and Enrollment: Assessing the Popularity of Antebellum Colleges," in *American College,* ed. Geiger, pp. 37–45.

25. Allmendinger, *Paupers and Scholars.*

26. Henry Adams, "The Harvard Stamp," from *The Education of Henry Adams,* as presented in *The College Years,* ed. A. C. Spectorsky (New York: Hawthorn, 1958), pp. 348–59.

27. Frederick Rudolph, "The Extracurriculum," chap. 7 of *The American College and University: A History* (New York: Knopf, 1962).

28. Leon Jackson, "The Rights of Man and the Rites of Youth: Fraternity and Riot at Eighteenth Century Harvard," in *American College,* ed. Geiger, pp. 46–79.

29. Rudolph, "The Extracurriculum."

30. James McLachlan, "The Choice of Hercules: American Student Societies in the Early Nineteenth Century," in *The University in Society: Oxford and Cambridge from the Fourteenth Century to the Early Nineteenth Century,* ed. Lawrence Stone (Princeton, N.J.: Princeton University Press, 1974), pp. 449–94.

31. Burton R. Clark and Martin Trow, *Determinants of Collegiate Subcultures* (Berkeley: Center for Research and Development in Higher Education, 1967). See also Helen Lefkowitz Horowitz, *Campus Life: Undergraduate Cultures from the End of the Eighteenth Century to the Present* (New York: Knopf, 1987), esp. pp. 1–60.

32. Burke, *American Collegiate Populations.*

33. Robert T. Blackburn and Clifton F. Conrad, "The New Revisionists and the History of U.S. Higher Education," *Higher Education* 15 (1986):211–30.

34. Edwin D. Duryea with Don Williams, *The Academic Corporation: A History of College and University Governing Boards* (New York: Falmer Press, 2000), p. 105.

35. President Joseph McKeen at Bowdoin College in Maine (1802), quoted in Rudolph, *American College and University,* pp. 58–59.

36. John Whitehead, *The Separation of College and State* (New Haven: Yale University Press, 1973). See also John Whitehead, "How to Think about the Dartmouth College Case," *History of Education Quarterly* 26 (Fall 1986):333–49.

37. Courtney Leatherman, "New York Regents Vote to Remove 18 of 19 Adelphi U. Trustees," *Chronicle of Higher Education,* 21 February 1997.

3. Diversity and Adversity

1. Donald G. Tewkesbury, *The Founding of American Colleges and Universities* (New York: Columbia University Teachers College Press, 1932), pp. 185–90.

2. Earle D. Ross, *Democracy's College: The Land Grant Movement in the For-mative Stages* (Ames: Iowa State University, 1942).

3. Eldon L. Johnson, "Misconceptions about the Early Land Grant Colleges," *Journal of Higher Education* 52 (July–August 1981):331–51.

4. Scott Key, "Economics or Education?" *Journal of Higher Education* 67 (March–April 1996):196–220.

5. Nancy Beadie, "From Academy to University in New York State: The Genesee Institutions and the Importance of Capital to the Success of an Idea, 1848–1871," *History of Higher Education Annual* 14 (1994):13–38.

6. Daniel W. Lang, "The People's College, the Mechanics Mutual Protec-tion, and the Agricultural College Act," *History of Education Quarterly* 18 (Fall 1978):295–321.

7. Thomas Kevin B. Cherry, "Bringing Science to the South: The School for the Application of Science to the Arts at the University of North Carolina," *His-tory of Higher Education Annual* 14 (1994):73–100.

8. Margaret Nash, "'A Salutory Rivalry': The Growth of Higher Education for Women in Oxford, Ohio, 1855–1867," in *The American College in the Nine-teenth Century*, ed. Roger L. Geiger (Nashville: Vanderbilt University Press, 2000), pp. 169–82.

9. Christie Anne Farnham, *The Education of the Southern Belle: Higher Edu-cation and Student Socialization in the Antebellum South* (New York: New York University Press, 1994).

10. James C. Albisetti, "American Women's Colleges through European Eyes, 1865–1914," *History of Education Quarterly* 32 (Winter 1992):439–58.

11. Jurgen Herbst, *And Sadly Teach: Teacher Education and Professionaliza-tion in American Culture* (Madison: University of Wisconsin Press, 1989).

12. Earl F. Cheit, "Business Administration: Trade Comes to the University," chap 5. of *The Useful Arts and the Liberal Tradition* (New York: McGraw-Hill, 1975).

13. Francis Wayland, "Report to the Brown Corporation" (1850), in *American Higher Education: A Documentary History*, ed. Richard Hofstadter and Wilson Smith (Chicago: University of Chicago Press, 1961), pp. 478–87.

14. John Henry Newman, *The Idea of a University*, ed. Frank M. Turner (New Haven: Yale University Press, 1996). See also Jaroslav Pelikan, *The Idea of the University: A Reexamination* (New Haven: Yale University Press, 1992), and John R. Thelin with Todd Cockrell, "Reasonable Doubts about Newman's University," *The Review of Higher Education* 17 (Spring 1994):323–30.

15. Lytton Strachey, *Eminent Victorians* (1918; reprinted London: Folio Soci-ety, 1967), pp. 84–85.

16. Hugh Hawkins, "The University-Builders Observe the Colleges," *History of Education Quarterly* 11 (Winter 1971):353–62.

17. Roger L. Geiger, "The Crisis of the Old Order: The Colleges in the 1890s," in *American College,* ed. Geiger, pp. 264–76, esp. p. 270.

18. James Axtell, "The Death of the Liberal Arts College," *History of Education Quarterly* 11 (Winter 1971):339–52.

19. Marilyn Tobias, *Old Dartmouth on Trial: The Transformation of the Academic Community in Nineteenth-Century America* (New York: New York University Press, 1982).

20. George Peterson, *The New England College in the Age of the University* (Amherst, Mass.: Amherst College Press, 1963).

21. W. Bruce Leslie, *Gentlemen and Scholars: College and Community in the "Age of the University," 1865–1917* (University Park: Pennsylvania State University Press, 1992).

22. Christopher Beckham, "Toward an Appreciation of the 'Denominational College': Three Innovative Approaches to Baptist Higher Education in the Post–Civil War South," unpublished manuscript, August 2001.

23. Lyman C. Bagg, *Four Years at Yale: By a Graduate of '69* (New Haven: Charles C. Chatfield and Company, 1871), p. iii.

24. Leslie, *Gentlemen and Scholars.*

25. See James McLachlan, *American Boarding Schools: A Historical Study* (New York: Charles Scribner's Sons, 1970).

26. Charlotte Williams Conable, *Women at Cornell: The Myth of Equal Education* (Ithaca: Cornell University Press, 1977).

27. Patricia Palmieri, *In Adamless Eden: The Community of Women Faculty at Wellesley* (New Haven: Yale University Press, 1995).

28. Helen Lefkowitz Horowitz, *Alma Mater: Design and Experience in the Women's Colleges from Their Nineteenth-Century Beginnings to the 1930s* (New York: Knopf, 1984).

29. See Wayland, "Report to the Brown Corporation."

30. George Keller, *Academic Strategy: The Management Revolution in American Higher Education* (Baltimore: Johns Hopkins University Press, 1983), pp. 5–8.

31. Merle Curti and Roderick Nash, *Philanthropy in the Shaping of American Higher Education* (New Brunswick, N.J.: Rutgers University Press, 1965), p. 91.

32. Ibid., p. 105.

33. Ibid., pp. 46–49.

34. Ibid., pp. 47–49.

35. Jesse Brundage Sears, *Philanthropy in the History of American Higher Education* (Washington, D.C.: U.S. Government Printing Office, 1922), pp. 82–83.

36. Curti and Nash, *Philanthropy,* pp. 168–70.

37. See Michael Dennis, "Architects of Control: Progressives and the Education of Blacks in the New South," chap. 3 of *Lessons in Progress: State Universities*

and Progressivism in the New South, 1880–1920 (Urbana: University of Illinois Press, 2001).

38. Eric Anderson and Alfred A. Moss, Jr., *Dangerous Donations: Northern Philanthropy and Southern Black Education, 1902–1930* (Columbia: University of Missouri Press, 1999).

39. See James D. Anderson, "The Hampton Model of Normal School Industrial Education, 1868–1915," in *The Education of Blacks in the South, 1860–1935* (Chapel Hill: University of North Carolina Press, 1988), pp. 33–78.

40. Daniel J. Kevles, "A Time for Audacity: What the Past Has to Teach the Present about Science and the Federal Government," in *Universities and Their Leadership,* ed. William G. Bowen and Harold T. Shapiro (Princeton, N.J.: Princeton University Press, 1998), pp. 199–240.

41. Daniel J. Boorstin, "The Booster College," in *The Americans: The National Experience* (New York: Harper and Row, 1965), pp. 152–61.

42. See David Potts, "American Colleges in the Nineteenth Century: From Localism to Denominationalism," *History of Education Quarterly* 11 (Winter 1971):363–80.

4. Captains of Industry and Erudition

1. William K. Selden, "The AAU—Higher Education's Enigma," *Saturday Review,* 19 March 1966, pp. 76–78. See also Hugh Hawkins, *Banding Together: The Rise of National Associations in American Higher Education, 1887–1950* (Baltimore: Johns Hopkins University Press, 1992).

2. Thorstein Veblen, *The Higher Learning in America: A Memorandum on the Conduct of Universities by Businessmen* (New York, 1918), pp. 63–71.

3. See Merle Curti and Roderick Nash, "Great Gifts for New Universities," in *Philanthropy in the Shaping of American Higher Education* (New Brunswick, N.J.: Rutgers University Press, 1965), pp. 107–35.

4. David B. Tyack, *The One Best System: A History of American Urban Education* (Cambridge, Mass.: Harvard University Press, 1974).

5. Curti and Nash, "Great Gifts for New Universities." See also Robert H. Bremner, "Benevolent Trusts and Distrusts," in *American Philanthropy,* 2d ed. (Chicago: University of Chicago Press, 1988), pp. 100–15.

6. Jesse Brundage Sears, "The Late National Period, 1865 to 1918," in *Philanthropy in the History of American Higher Education* (Washington, D.C.: U.S. Government Printing Office, 1922), esp. p. 60.

7. Daniel J. Boorstin, *The Image: A Guide to Pseudo-events in America* (New York: Harper Colophon, 1964).

8. James C. Stone and Donald P. DeNevi, eds., *Portraits of the American University, 1890 to 1910* (San Francisco: Jossey-Bass, 1971).

9. John R. Thelin, "Picture Perfect: Postcards and the Image of the American

Campus," in *"Having a Great Time . . .": The John B. Hawley Higher Education Postcard Collection*, ed. John B. Hawley and Craig Kridel (Columbia: University of South Carolina Museum of Education, 2001), pp. 13–38.

10. "The Old Century Plan," *California Monthly*, June 2000, p. 24.

11. Paul Venable Turner, "The University as City Beautiful," in *Campus: An American Planning Tradition* (Cambridge, Mass.: M.I.T. Press, 1984), pp. 163–214.

12. D. Balmori, "Campus Works and Public Landscapes," in *Beatrix Farrand's American Landscapes: Her Gardens and Campuses*, ed. D. Balmori, D. K. MacGuire, and E. M. Peck (Sagaponack, N.Y.: Sagapress, 1985), pp. 127–96.

13. A. D. F. Hamlin, "Recent American College Architecture," *The Outlook*, August 1903, reprinted in *Portraits of the American University*, ed. Stone and DeNevi, pp. 357–66.

14. Laurence Veysey, *The Emergence of the American University* (Chicago: University of Chicago Press, 1965).

15. Ibid., part 2.

16. Quoted in James Howell Smith, "Honorable Beggars: The Middlemen of American Philanthropy," Ph.D. diss., University of Wisconsin, Madison, 1968, p. 176.

17. "Gilman Recalls the Early Days of the Johns Hopkins, 1876," in *American Higher Education: A Documentary History*, ed. Richard Hofstadter and Wilson Smith (Chicago: University of Chicago Press, 1961), 2:643.

18. Andrew D. White, *Autobiography*, quoted in *American Higher Education*, ed. Hofstadter and Smith, 2:549–50.

19. Smith, "Honorable Beggars," pp. 113–56.

20. Jean F. Block, *The Uses of Gothic: Planning and Building the Campus of the University of Chicago, 1892–1932* (Chicago: University of Chicago Library, 1983), p. 2.

21. See Milton Mayer, *Young Man in a Hurry: The Story of William Rainey Harper, First President of the University of Chicago* (Chicago: University of Chicago Alumni Association, 1941); Edwin E. Slosson, "The University of Chicago," in *Great American Universities* (New York: Macmillan, 1910), pp. 405–41; Veysey, *Emergence of the American University*; and Richard J. Storr, *Harper's University: The Beginnings* (Chicago: University of Chicago Press, 1966).

22. Incident described in Veysey, *Emergence of the American University*, pp. 379–80.

23. Curti and Nash, "Toward a Practical Higher Education," chap. 4 of *Philanthropy*.

24. Smith, "Honorable Beggars," pp. 156–82.

25. Frederick T. Gates, "Rules of Procedure" (memorandum of 26 May 1890), in ibid., appendix I, pp. 256–65.

26. Ibid.

27. A Wall Street financier describing Dwight L. Moody, quoted in ibid., p. 108.

28. Ibid., pp. 156–82.

29. Curti and Nash, *Philanthropy,* pp. 136–67.

30. Robert McCormack, quoted in Jefferey P. Bieber, Janet H. Lawrence, and Robert T. Blackburn, "Through the Years: Faculty and Their Changing Institution," *Change* 24 (July–August 1992):32.

31. John Higham, *History: The Development of Historical Studies in the United States* (Englewood Cliffs, N.J.: Prentice-Hall, 1965), pp. 21–28.

32. Lincoln Steffens, "Sending a State to College," *American Magazine,* February 1909, reprinted in *Portraits of the American University,* ed. Stone and De-Nevi, pp. 118–33.

33. Merle Curti and Vernon L. Carstensen, *The University of Wisconsin, 1848–1925* (Madison: University of Wisconsin, 1949).

34. Harold Wechsler, *The Qualified Student: A History of Selective College Admissions in America* (New York: Wiley, 1977).

35. John Aubrey Douglass, *The California Idea and American Higher Education: 1850 to the 1960 Master Plan* (Stanford: Stanford University Press, 2000). See also John R. Thelin, "California and the Colleges," *California Historical Quarterly* 56 (Summer 1977):140–63 (part 1); 56 (Fall 1977):230–49 (part 2).

36. See Carolyn B. Matalene and Katherine C. Reynolds, "Struggling to Survive: The Old College from 1880 to 1906," in *Carolina Voices: Two Hundred Years of Student Experiences,* ed. Carolyn B. Matalene and Katherine C. Reynolds (Columbia: University of South Carolina Press, 2001), pp. 66–103.

37. Edward L. Ayers, *The Promise of the New South: Life after Reconstruction* (New York: Oxford University Press, 1992).

38. Michael Dennis, *Lessons in Progress: State Universities and Progressivism in the New South, 1880–1920* (Urbana: University of Illinois Press, 2001).

39. Eric Anderson and Alfred A. Moss, Jr., *Dangerous Donations: Northern Philanthropy and Southern Black Education, 1902–1930* (Columbia: University of Missouri Press, 1999).

40. Ronald Isetti, *Called to the Pacific: A History of the Christian Brothers of the San Francisco District, 1868–1944* (Moraga, Calif.: St. Mary's College Press, 1979).

41. Lynn D. Gordon, *Gender and Higher Education in the Progressive Era* (New Haven: Yale University Press, 1990), p. 87.

42. Geraldine Joncich Clifford, *Lone Voyagers: Academic Women in Coeducational Institutions, 1870–1937* (New York: Feminist Press at the City University of New York, 1989).

43. Maresi Nerad, *The Academic Kitchen: A Social History of Gender Stratification at the University of California, Berkeley* (Albany: State University of New York Press, 1999). See esp. chap. 3, "Institution Builder: Agnes Fay Morgan."

44. Ibid., pp. 139–42.

45. Jana Nidiffer, *Pioneering Deans of Women: More Than Wise and Pious Matrons* (New York: Teachers College Press, 2000).

46. Margaret W. Rossiter, *Women Scientists in America: Struggles and Strategies to 1940* (Baltimore: Johns Hopkins University Press, 1982).

47. Linda Eisenmann, "Creating a Framework for Interpreting US Women's Educational History: Lessons From Historical Lexicography," *History of Education* 30 (2001):460.

48. Biographical profile presented in Clifford, *Lone Voyagers*, p. 17.

49. Joyce Antler, *Lucy Sprague Mitchell: The Making of a Modern Woman* (New Haven: Yale University Press, 1987).

50. Eisenmann, "Creating a Framework," pp. 453–70.

51. Ellen Condliffe Lagemann, *Private Power for the Public Good: A History of the Carnegie Foundation for the Advancement of Teaching* (Middletown, Conn.: Wesleyan University Press, 1983).

52. Barry D. Karl, "Andrew Carnegie and His Gospel of Philanthropy: A Study in the Ethics of Responsibility," in *The Responsibilities of Wealth*, ed. Dwight F. Burlingame (Bloomington: Indiana University Press, 1992), pp. 32–50.

53. See Peter Krass, *Carnegie* (New York: John Wiley, 2002).

54. Michael Schudson, "Organizing the 'Meritocracy': A History of the College Entrance Examination Board," *Harvard Educational Review* 43 (1972): 34–69.

55. Lagemann, *Private Power for the Public Good*.

56. Robert Wiebe, *The Search for Order, 1877–1920* (New York: Hill and Wang, 1967).

57. David S. Webster, *Academic Quality Rankings of American Colleges and Universities* (Springfield, Ill.: Charles C. Thomas, 1986), pp. 3–10.

58. Abraham Flexner, *Medical Education in the United States and Canada*, Bulletin no. 4 (New York: Carnegie Foundation for the Advancement of Science, 1910). See also Thomas Bonner, *Iconoclast: Abraham Flexner and a Life in Learning* (Baltimore: Johns Hopkins University Press, 2002).

59. Paul Starr, *The Social Transformation of American Medicine: The Rise of a Sovereign Profession and the Making of a Vast Industry* (New York: Basic Books, 1982), pp. 117–27. See also Lagemann, *Private Power for the Public Good*, pp. 61–71.

60. John R. Thelin, "Left Outs and Left Overs: The Limits of Education and Social Reform since 1890," *Reviews in American History* 20 (1992):222–28.

61. Clark Kerr, *The Uses of the University* (Cambridge, Mass.: Harvard University Press, 1963).

62. Richard Angelo, "The Social Transformation of American Higher Education," in *The Transformation of Higher Learning, 1860–1930*, ed. Konrad H. Jarausch (Chicago: University of Chicago Press, 1983), pp. 261–92; Paul H. Mattingly, "Structures over Time: Institutional History," in *Historical Inquiry in Ed-*

ucation: A Research Agenda, ed. John Hardin Best (Washington, D.C.: American Educational Research Association, 1983), pp. 34–55.

63. Dorothy E. Finnegan and Brian Cullaty, "Origins of the YMCA Universities: Organizational Adaptations in Urban Education," *History of Higher Education Annual* 21 (2001):47–78.

64. Mattingly, "Structures over Time."

65. Adam R. Nelson, "Setting Students Free," *Brown Alumni Monthly,* September–October 2001, pp. 50–55; quotation at pp. 51–52.

66. Earl F. Cheit, *The Useful Arts and the Liberal Tradition* (New York: McGraw-Hill, 1975).

67. Nathan Glazer, "Regulating Business and Higher Education: One Problem or Two?" *Public Interest* 54, no. 56 (1979):43–65. See also Eugene D. Gulland and Sheldon E. Steinbach, "Antitrust Law and Financial Aid: The MIT Decision," *Chronicle of Higher Education,* 6 October 1993.

68. Christopher Jencks and David Riesman, *The Academic Revolution* (Garden City, N.Y.: Doubleday Anchor, 1968).

69. See Hugh Hawkins, "The University-Builders Observe the Colleges," *History of Education Quarterly* 11 (Winter 1971):353–62.

5. Alma Mater

1. Edwin E. Slosson, *Great American Universities* (New York: Macmillan, 1910), p. 374.

2. Henry Adams, *The Education of Henry Adams* (Boston: Houghton Mifflin, 1918), pp. 305–6.

3. George Santayana, "The Spirit and Ideals of Harvard University," *Educational Review,* April 1894, reprinted in *George Santayana's America: Essays on Literature and Culture,* ed. James Ballowe (Urbana: University of Illinois Press, 1967).

4. Henry Seidel Canby, *Alma Mater: The Gothic Age of the American College* (New York: Farrar and Rinehart, 1936), p. 24.

5. "University Competition," *Brown Alumni Monthly,* June 1900, p. 5.

6. John R. Thelin, "Ivy's Roots, 1890 to 1910," in *The Cultivation of Ivy* (Cambridge, Mass.: Schenkman, 1976), pp. 5–19.

7. James C. Stone and Donald P. DeNevi, eds., *Portraits of the American University, 1890 to 1910* (San Francisco: Jossey-Bass, 1971).

8. James W. Alexander, "Undergraduate Life at Princeton—Old and New," *Scribner's Magazine,* June 1897, p. 64.

9. Hamilton Holt, "A College Professor's Wife," *The Independent* 59 (30 November 1905):1279–83. See also David M. Katzman and William M. Tuttle, Jr., eds., *Plain Folk: The Life Stories of Undistinguished Americans* (Urbana: University of Illinois Press, 1982), pp. 82–96.

10. Canby, *Alma Mater,* p. 24.

11. *As a College Man Thinks: Being a Letter from a Pomona College Student to a High School Senior* (Claremont, Calif.: Pomona College, ca. 1924). See also John R. Thelin, "California and the Colleges," *California Historical Quarterly* 56 (Summer 1977):140–63 (part 1).

12. David B. Chamberlain and Karl P. Harrington, eds., *Songs of All the Colleges: Including Many New Songs,* 4th ed. (New York: Hinds and Noble, 1903), flyer and p. 26.

13. F. Scott Fitzgerald, *This Side of Paradise* (New York: Charles Scribner's Sons, 1920), chap. 1.

14. Santayana, "Spirit and Ideals of Harvard University," p. 58.

15. William Sloane, "Princeton," in *Four American Universities* (New York: Harper and Brothers, 1895), p. 95.

16. Quoted in Forrest J. Hall, "Nightshirt 'Peerade,'" *Dartmouth Alumni Magazine,* April 1954, p. 83.

17. *Harvard Advocate* (n.d., ca. 1910), quoted in William Bentinck-Smith, *The Harvard Book* (Cambridge, Mass., 1953), p. 13.

18. Canby, *Alma Mater,* pp. 23–26.

19. Ibid., p. 50.

20. Adam R. Nelson, "Setting Students Free: Who Was Alexander Meiklejohn and Why Does He Still Matter?" *Brown Alumni Monthly,* September–October 2001, pp. 50–55. See also Adam R. Nelson, *Education and Democracy: The Meaning of Alexander Meiklejohn, 1872–1964* (Madison: University of Wisconsin Press, 2001). Cf. "University Fees" and "Financial Aid to Students," *Catalogue of Brown University for 1907–1908,* pp. 160–65.

21. Laurence R. Veysey, *The Emergence of the American University* (Chicago: University of Chicago Press, 1965).

22. Slosson, *Great American Universities,* p. 363.

23. Jennings L. Wagoner, Jr., "The American Compromise: Charles W. Eliot, Black Education, and the New South," in *Education and the Rise of the New South,* ed. Ronald K. Goodenow and Arthur O. White (Boston: G. K. Hall, 1981), pp. 26–46.

24. John R. Thelin, "Cliometrics and the Colleges: The Campus Condition, 1880 to 1910," *Research in Higher Education* 21, no. 4 (1984):425–37.

25. Ronald Smith, *Sports and Freedom: The Rise of Big-Time College Athletics* (New York: Oxford University Press, 1988).

26. Frederick Rudolph, "The Rise of Football," in *The American College and University: A History* (New York: Knopf, 1962), pp. 373–93.

27. Michael Oriad, *Reading Football: How the Popular Press Created an American Spectacle* (Chapel Hill: University of North Carolina Press, 1993).

28. John R. Thelin, *Games Colleges Play: Scandal and Reform in Intercollegiate Athletics* (Baltimore: Johns Hopkins University Press, 1994).

29. See Robin Lester, *Stagg's University: The Rise, Decline, and Fall of Big-Time Football at Chicago* (Urbana: University of Illinois Press, 1995).

30. See Smith, *Sports and Freedom,* esp. pp. 38–42 and 110–14.

31. Horowitz, "Acting a Manly Part: The Beginnings of College Life" and "The Life," in *Alma Mater,* pp. 56–68 and 147–78.

32. Lynn D. Gordon, "Sophie Newcombe and Agnes Scott Colleges, 1887–1920: From Dutiful Daughters to New Women," in *Gender and Higher Education in the Progressive Era* (New Haven: Yale University Press, 1990), pp. 165–88.

33. Gordon, "Women at the University of California, 1870–1920: From Pelicans to Chickens," in *Gender and Higher Education,* pp. 52–84.

34. Dorothy Hayden et al., "A Model College Girl," in *Songs of All the Colleges,* ed. Chamberlain and Harrington, pp. 230–31.

35. Karen J. Blair, "The Women's Club Movement Creates and Defines the Women's College," in *The Search for Equity: Women at Brown University, 1891–1991,* ed. Polly Welts Kaufman (Hanover, N.H.: Brown University Press with the University Press of New England, 1991), pp. 27–54.

36. See Linda Eisenmann, "'Freedom to Be Womanly': The Separate Culture of the Women's College," in *Search for Equity,* ed. Kaufman, pp. 55–86.

37. James D. Anderson, *The Education of Blacks in the South* (Chapel Hill: University of North Carolina Press, 1988), p. 112.

38. Ibid., pp. 238–78; quotation at p. 276.

39. Canby, *Alma Mater,* p. 50.

40. Aleck Quest, "The Fast Set at Harvard University," *North American Review,* November 1888, p. 542; Woodrow Wilson, quoted in Slosson, *Great American Universities,* p. 506.

41. Theodore Roosevelt, paraphrased in Rudolph, *American College and University,* pp. 376–77.

42. *Yale College Book of 1904* (New Haven: Yale University, 1904), p. 180.

43. Literary editor Brockhurst, quoted in Owen Johnson, *Stover at Yale* (New York: Frederick Stokes, 1912), pp. 238–39.

44. Charles W. Eliot to Henry James, quoted in Veysey, *Emergence of the American University,* p. 438.

45. George Anthony Weller, *Not to Eat, Not for Love* (New York: Robert Haas, 1933), p. 114.

46. Fitzgerald paraphrased in John Davies, *The Legend of Hobey Baker* (Boston: Little, Brown and Company, 1964), pp. viii–ix.

47. Cornelius Howard Patton and Walter Taylor Field, *Eight o'Clock Chapel: A Study of New England College Life in the Eighties* (Boston: Houghton Mifflin, 1927), p. 332.

48. Marcia G. Synnott, *The Half-Opened Door: Discrimination and Admissions at Harvard, Yale, and Princeton, 1900–1970* (Westport, Conn.: Greenwood Press, 1979).

49. Gordon, *Gender and Higher Education*, pp. 81–82.

50. Norris E. James, "Passing Show: Each Carefree Generation Develops Customs and Traditions of Its Own," in *Fifty Years on the Quad: A Pictorial Record of Stanford University and the 35,000 Men and Women Who Have Spent a Part of Their Lives on the Campus, 1887–1937*, ed. Norris E. James (Palo Alto, Calif.: Stanford Alumni Association, 1938), pp. 90–93.

51. David O. Levine, "The College Goes to War," in *The American College and the Culture of Aspiration, 1915–1940* (Ithaca: Cornell University Press, 1986), pp. 23–44. See also Carol S. Gruber, *Mars and Minerva: World War I and the Uses of the Higher Learning in America* (Baton Rouge: Louisiana State University Press, 1976).

52. Jonathan Frankel, "The Ivory Boot Camp," *Harvard Magazine* 94 (September–October 1991):71–74; quotation at p. 74.

53. Levine, "The College Goes to War."

54. Frankel, "Ivory Boot Camp."

55. See Davies, *Legend of Hobey Baker*.

6. Success and Excess

1. "The Colleges Turn out Their 1937 Models: American Boy and Girl," *Life*, 7 June 1937, p. 23.

2. See Robert E. Durden, *The Launching of Duke University, 1924–1949* (Durham, N.C.: Duke University Press, 1993).

3. David O. Levine, *The American College and the Culture of Aspiration, 1915–1940* (Ithaca: Cornell University Press, 1986).

4. See Steven Brint and Jerome Karabel, *The Diverted Dream: Community Colleges and the Promise of Educational Opportunity in America, 1900–1985* (New York: Oxford University Press, 1989), and Thomas Diener, *Growth of an American Invention: A Documentary History of the Junior and Community College Movement* (Westport, Conn.: Greenwood Press, 1986).

5. "Into College Plants Has Poured $2,250,000,000," *Life*, 7 June 1937, pp. 52–57.

6. See Earl F. Cheit, "Agriculture: The Search for a Dual Purpose Cow," in *The Useful Arts and the Liberal Tradition* (New York: McGraw-Hill, 1975), pp. 31–56.

7. F. N. Boney, *A Pictorial History of the University of Georgia* (Athens: University of Georgia Press, 1984); Thomas G. Dyer, *The University of Georgia: A Bicentennial History* (Athens: University of Georgia Press, 1985).

8. "Sports Records Move West," *Life*, 7 June 1937, p. 72.

9. Howard J. Savage, *American College Athletics*, Bulletin no. 23 (New York: Carnegie Foundation for the Advancement of Teaching, 1929).

10. John R. Thelin, "The Reform Canon," in *Games Colleges Play: Scandal*

and Reform in Intercollegiate Athletics (Baltimore: Johns Hopkins University Press, 1994), pp. 13–37.

11. John R. Thelin, "Looking for the Lone Star Legacy," *History of Education Quarterly,* Summer 1977, pp. 221–28; Mary Martha Hosford Thomas, *Southern Methodist University: Founding and Early Years* (Dallas: Southern Methodist University Press, 1974).

12. Murray Sperber, *Onward to Victory: The Crises That Shaped College Sports* (New York: Henry Holt and Company, 1998), pp. 91–284. See also John R. Thelin, "Academics on Athletics," *Journal of Higher Education* 73 (May–June 2002):409–19.

13. "Champions of the Ivy League," advertisement for Macy's Men's Store, *New York Times,* 26 November 1938, p. 5.

14. Article in the *Boston Sunday Advertiser,* ca. January 1921, reprinted in *Gentlemen under the Elms,* ed. Jay Barry (Providence: Brown Alumni Monthly, 1982), pp. 11–13.

15. "Junior College: At Stephens in Missouri Girls Are Taught to Solve Women's 7,400 Problems with Classes in Beauty, Riding, Voice," *Life,* 7 June 1937, pp. 66–67.

16. Levine, *American College.*

17. August Brunsman (editor, *Daily Ohio State Lantern*), letter to the editor, *Life,* 7 June 1937, p. 6.

18. Morris Bishop, "—And Perhaps Cornell," in *Our Cornell,* ed. Raymond Floyd Hughes (Ithaca, N.Y.: Cayuga Press, 1939), pp. 76–77.

19. Charles Homer Haskins, *The Rise of the Universities* (New York: Henry Holt, 1923), pp. 90–91.

20. *The Report on Undergraduate Education of the Dartmouth College Senior Committee* (Hanover, N.H.: Dartmouth College, 1924), part 1, p. 16.

21. Lucius Beebe, "The Boston *Telegram,*" in *The Lucius Beebe Reader,* ed. Charles Clegg and Duncan Emrich (New York: Doubleday and Company, 1967), p. 66.

22. William Bentinck-Smith, ed., *The Harvard Book: Selections from Three Centuries* (Cambridge, Mass.: Harvard University Press, 1953), pp. 13–14.

23. Tracy Campbell, "Banishment to Paradise," in *Short of the Glory: The Fall and Redemption of Edward F. Prichard, Jr.* (Lexington: University Press of Kentucky, 1998), pp. 24–43.

24. James Thurber, "University Days" (1934), in *The College Years,* ed. A. C. Spectorsky (New York: Hawthorn, 1958), pp. 436–41.

25. Robert Benchley, "What College Did to Me" (1927), in *The College Years,* ed. Spectorsky, pp. 183–93.

26. Ibid., pp. 189–90.

27. Thurber, "University Days," p. 476.

28. George Anthony Weller, *Not to Eat, Not for Love* (New York: Robert Haas, 1933), pp. 93–94.

29. Statistics compiled from *Harvard College, Class of 1929: First Report* (Cambridge, Mass.: Crimson Printing Company, 1930).

30. Edward Shils, "The University: A Backward Glance," *The American Scholar*, May 1982, pp. 163–79; quotations at p. 164.

31. Brendan Gill, *Here at the New Yorker* (New York: Random House, 1975), pp. 63–71.

32. Weller, *Not to Eat*.

33. Campbell, "Harvard Law School," in *Short of the Glory*, pp. 44–58.

34. John Kenneth Galbraith, memoir in *There Was Light: Autobiography of a University: Berkeley, 1868–1968*, ed. Irving Stone (Garden City, N.Y.: Doubleday and Company, 1968), pp. 19–31; see esp. p. 28.

35. Weller, *Not to Eat*, pp. 47 and 280.

36. Galbraith, in *There Was Light*, p. 22.

37. Levine, "Women on Campus," in *American College*, pp. 123–26.

38. Louise Blecher Rose, "The Secret Life of Sarah Lawrence," *Commentary*, May 1983, pp. 52–56.

39. Linda M. Perkins, "The African American Female Elite: The Early History of African American Women in the Seven Sisters Colleges, 1880–1960," *Harvard Educational Review* 67 (Winter 1997):718–56.

40. *The Illio* (Champaign-Urbana: University of Illinois, 1946), p. 156.

41. Burton R. Clark and Martin Trow, *Determinants of Collegiate Subcultures* (Berkeley: Center for Research and Development in Higher Education, 1967); Helen Lefkowitz Horowitz, *Campus Life: Undergraduate Cultures from the End of the Eighteenth Century to the Present* (New York: Knopf, 1987), esp. pp. 3–23.

42. *University Bulletin: Louisiana State University and Agricultural and Mechanical College*, n.s., 28 (June 1936):91–92.

43. See Vernell Denae Larkin, "Dreams Denied: The Anderson Mayer State Aid Act, 1936–1950," Ed.D. diss., University of Kentucky, Lexington, 2001.

44. Levine, "Black Students," in *American College*, pp. 158–61.

45. Robert Maynard Hutchins, *The New College Plan* (Chicago: University of Chicago Press, 1931), p. 16. See also Robert Maynard Hutchins, *The Higher Learning in America* (New Haven: Yale University Press, 1936).

46. Burton R. Clark, *The Distinctive College: Antioch, Reed, and Swarthmore* (Chicago: Aldine, 1970).

47. Gerald Grant and David Riesman, *The Perpetual Dream: Reform and Experiment in the American College* (Chicago: University of Chicago Press, 1978).

48. See William Clary, *The Claremont Colleges: A History of the Development of the Claremont Group Plan* (Claremont, Calif.: Claremont University Center, 1970).

49. Clyde W. Barrow, *Universities and the Capitalist State: Corporate Liberalism and the Reconstruction of American Higher Education, 1894–1928* (Madison: University of Wisconsin Press, 1990).

50. Barrow, "Who Owns the Universities? Class Structure and the Material Means of Mental Production," in *Universities and the Capitalist State,* pp. 31–59.

51. See Barrow, "Corporate Power and Social Efficiency: The Industrialization of American Universities," in *Universities and the Capitalist State,* pp. 60–91, esp. pp. 86–87.

52. Barrow, *Universities and the Capitalist State,* pp. 50–53.

53. Abraham Flexner, *Universities: American, English, German* (New York: Oxford University Press, 1930).

54. See Rebecca S. Lowen, "Transforming the University: Administrators, Physicists, and Industrial and Federal Patronage at Stanford, 1935–1949," *History of Education Quarterly* 31 (Fall 1991):365–88. See also Rebecca S. Lowen, *Creating the Cold War University: The Transformation of Stanford* (Berkeley: University of California Press, 1997).

55. See, for example, the profile of David Packard in the Hewlett-Packard advertisement in *Chronicle of Higher Education,* 5 March 1999, pp. A8–A9.

56. Robert Sibley, "The University of Today: A Portfolio of Scenes from the Seven Campuses," in *The Golden Book of California, 1860–1936,* ed. Robert Sibley (Berkeley: University of California Alumni Association, 1937), p. 17.

57. *The World Almanac* (1940), as presented in *Report of Self-Study* (Williamsburg, Va.: College of William and Mary, 1974), p. 5.

58. Cheit, *Useful Arts.*

59. Brint and Karabel, "Organizing a National Educational Movement, 1900–1945," in *Diverted Dream,* pp. 23–66.

60. Levine, "The Junior College and the Differentiation of the Public Sector," in *American College,* pp. 162–84; John H. Frye, *The Vision of the Public Junior College, 1900–1940: Professional Goals and Popular Aspirations* (Westport, Conn.: Greenwood Press, 1992).

61. Claudia Goldin and Lawrence F. Katz, "The Shaping of Higher Education: The Formative Years in the United States, 1890 to 1940," *Journal of Economic Perspectives* 13 (Winter 1999):37–62; quotation at p. 50.

62. Seymour E. Harris, *A Statistical Portrait of Higher Education* (New York: McGraw-Hill, 1972), p. 687.

63. Stuart M. Stoke, "What Price Tuition?" *Journal of Higher Education* 8 (June 1937):297–303; quotation at p. 297.

64. Sperber, "World War II: The Deterioration of College Sports," in *Onward to Victory,* pp. 91–156.

65. Flexner, "American Universities," in *Universities,* pp. 64–66.

66. Oliver Jensen, *A College Album: Or, Rah, Rah, Yesterday* (New York: McGraw-Hill and American Heritage Press, 1974), p. 61.

7. Gilt by Association

1. American Council on Education, "Enrollments by Levels of Study, Selected Years 1899–1900 to 1990," in *1984–85 Fact Book on Higher Education* (New York: Macmillan 1984), p. 57.

2. Edwin Kiester, Jr., "The G.I. Bill May Be the Best Deal Ever Made by Uncle Sam," *Smithsonian* 25 (November 1994):128–39.

3. *What about Harvard?* (Cambridge, Mass.: Harvard University, 27 March 1945), p. 4.

4. Kiester, "G.I. Bill," pp. 130–33.

5. For example, see Sylvan Karchmer, "Hail Brother and Farewell" (1949), in *The College Years*, ed. A. C. Spectorsky (New York: Hawthorn, 1958), pp. 180–87; Sloane Wilson, "G.I.," ibid., pp. 160–62; and John R. Thelin, *Games Colleges Play: Scandal and Reform in Intercollegiate Athletics* (Baltimore: Johns Hopkins University Press, 1994), pp. 99–100.

6. Irwin Shaw, *Rich Man, Poor Man* (New York: Delacort, 1970), pp. 1–3.

7. President Harry S. Truman, "Letter of Appointment of Commission Members" (13 July 1946), in *Higher Education for American Democracy: A Report of the President's Commission on Higher Education,* ed. George F. Zook (New York: Harper and Brothers, 1947), n.p.

8. Paula S. Fass, *Outside In: Minorities and the Transformation of American Education* (New York: Oxford University Press, 1989).

9. United States Office of Scientific Research and Development, *Science, the Endless Frontier: A Report to the President by Vannevar Bush, Director of the Office of Scientific Research and Development, July 1945* (Washington, D.C.: U.S. Government Printing Office, 1945).

10. Rebecca S. Lowen, *Creating the Cold War University: The Transformation of Stanford* (Berkeley: University of California Press, 1997).

11. Edward Kifer, "Robert Maynard Hutchins," in *Encyclopedia of Education* (New York: Macmillan Reference for Thompson-Gale, 2002), pp. 1094–96.

12. William F. Buckley, *God and Man at Yale: The Superstitions of Academic Freedom* (Chicago: Regnery, 1951).

13. Ellen W. Schrecker, *No Ivory Tower: McCarthyism and the Universities* (New York: Oxford University Press, 1986).

14. See John Aubrey Douglass, "Rising Costs, the Red Scare, and the End of Postwar Consensus," in *The California Idea and American Higher Education: 1850 to the 1960 Master Plan* (Stanford: Stanford University Press, 2000), pp. 198–222. Cf. Verne A. Stadtman, "A Test of Loyalty," in *The University of California, 1868–1968* (New York: McGraw-Hill, 1970), pp. 319–38.

15. Mary McCarthy, *The Groves of Academe* (New York: Harcourt, Brace, 1952).

16. Roger L. Geiger, *Research and Relevant Knowledge: American Research Universities since World War II* (New York: Oxford University Press, 1993).

17. See Clark Kerr, "The Realities of the Federal Grant University," chap. 2 of *The Uses of the University* (Cambridge, Mass.: Harvard University Press, 1963); quotation at pp. 52–53.

18. Ibid., pp. 53–54.

19. Clark Kerr, "The Frantic Race to Remain Contemporary," *Daedalus* 93 (Fall 1964):1051–70.

20. Geiger, *Research and Relevant Knowledge.*

21. Robert H. Bremner, *American Philanthropy,* 2d ed. (Chicago: University of Chicago Press, 1988), pp. 168–69.

22. See Ellen Condliffe Lagemann, "Public Policy and Sociology: Gunnar Myrdal's *An American Dilemma,*" in *The Politics of Knowledge: The Carnegie Corporation, Philanthropy, and Public Policy* (Chicago: University of Chicago Press, 1989), pp. 123–40.

23. Dwight McDonald, *The Ford Foundation: The Men and the Millions* (New York: Reynal and Company, 1955).

24. See Stadtman, "Part IV: Dynamics of the Modern University," in *University of California,* pp. 363–510.

25. "The University of California: The Biggest University in the World Is a Show Place for Mass Education," *Life,* 25 October 1948, pp. 88–112. See also "Big Man on Eight Campuses—California's Sproul: Is Everyone Entitled to a College Education?" *Time,* 6 October 1947, pp. 69–76.

26. See Douglass, "Negotiating the Master Plan and the Fate of Higher Education in California," in *California Idea,* pp. 265–97.

27. "University of California's Clark Kerr" (cover story), *Time,* 17 October 1960. See also John R. Thelin, "California and the Colleges," *California Historical Quarterly* 56 (Summer 1977):140–63 (part 1) and 56 (Fall 1977):230–49 (part 2).

28. See Arthur G. Coons, *Crises in California Higher Education* (Los Angeles: Ward Ritchie Press, 1968).

29. Richard M. Freeland, *Academia's Golden Age: Universities in Massachusetts, 1945–1970* (Oxford: Oxford University Press, 1992).

30. "Williams College: In an Era of Mass Teaching It Considers Smallness a Virtue," *Life,* 24 January 1949, pp. 53–62; quotation at p. 53.

31. Katherine Kinkead, *How an Ivy League College Decides on Admissions* (New York: W. W. Norton, 1961).

32. Burton R. Clark, *The Distinctive College: Antioch, Reed, and Swarthmore* (Chicago: Aldine, 1970).

33. Gerald Grant and David Riesman, *The Perpetual Dream: Reform and Experiment in the American College* (Chicago: University of Chicago Press, 1978).

34. Robert H. Knapp and J. J. Greenbaum, *The Younger American Scholar: His Collegiate Origins* (Chicago: University of Chicago Press, 1953). See also Robert H. Knapp, *The Origins of American Humanistic Scholars* (Englewood Cliffs, N.J.: Prentice-Hall, 1964).

35. Christopher Jencks and David Riesman, "The University College," in *The Academic Revolution* (Garden City, N.Y.: Doubleday Anchor, 1968), pp. 2–27.

36. Clark Kerr, quoted in Thelin, "California and the Colleges," part 1, p. 158. See also *Solomon's House: A Self-Conscious History of Cowell College* (Felton, Calif.: Big Tree Press, 1970).

37. David Boroff, *Campus USA: Portraits of American Colleges in Action* (New York: Harper, 1961).

38. Russell Schoch, "As Cal Enters the '80s There'll Be Some Changes Made," *California Monthly*, January–February 1980, pp. 1, 20.

39. Jeffery Hart, *When the Going Was Good: American Life in the Fifties* (New York: Crown, 1982); David Riesman, Reuel Denny, and Nathan Glazer, *The Lonely Crowd: A Study of the Changing American Character* (New Haven: Yale University Press, 1950); William H. Whyte, Jr., *The Organization Man* (New York: Simon and Schuster, 1956).

40. Philip Roth, "Joe College: Memories of a Fifties Education," *Atlantic Monthly*, December 1987, pp. 41–61.

41. Nevitt Sanford, *The American College: A Psychological and Social Interpretation of the Higher Learning* (New York: John Wiley and Sons, 1962).

42. See Nicholas Lemann, *The Big Test: The Secret History of the American Meritocracy* (New York: Farrar, Strauss, and Giroux, 1999).

43. Charles McArthur, "Personalities of Public and Private School Boys," *Harvard Educational Review*, Fall 1954, pp. 256–62.

44. Joel Spring, *The Sorting Machine: National Educational Policy since 1945* (New York: David McKay, 1976).

45. Jencks and Riesman, *Academic Revolution*, p. 125.

46. See Sam P. Wiggins, *Higher Education in the South* (Berkeley, Calif.: McCutchan Publishers, 1966).

47. Peter Wallenstein, "Black Southerners and Non-black Universities: Desegregating Higher Education, 1935–1967," *History of Higher Education Annual* 19 (1999):121–48.

48. See Melissa F. Kean, "Guiding Desegregation: The Role of 'The Intelligent White Men of the South,' 1945–1954," *History of Higher Education Annual* 19 (1999):57–84; Clarence Mohr, "Opportunity Squandered: Tulane University and the Issue of Racial Desegregation in the 1950s," ibid., pp. 85–120; and Nancy Diamond, "Catching Up: The Advance of Emory University since World War II," ibid., pp. 149–84.

49. Verne A. Stadtman, "The Students between Two Wars," in *The University of California, 1868–1968* (New York: McGraw-Hill, 1970), pp. 281–300.

50. William J. McGill, *The Year of the Monkey: Revolt on Campus, 1968–69* (New York: McGraw-Hill, 1982).

51. Kerr, *Uses of the University*, pp. 20–21.

52. Jencks and Riesman, *Academic Revolution*, pp. 61–154.

8. Coming of Age in America

1. The quotation sometimes attributed to McGeorge Bundy also appears in the speech delivered by President John F. Kennedy in 1962 in Pueblo, Colorado.

2. Louis Menand, "College: The End of the Golden Age," *New York Review of Books,* 8 October 2001.

3. Clark Kerr, *The Great Transformation in Higher Education, 1960–1980* (Albany: State University of New York Press, 1991).

4. See *The Carnegie Council on Policy Studies in Higher Education: A Summary of Reports and Recommendations* (San Francisco: Jossey-Bass, 1980).

5. Earl F. Cheit, *The New Depression in Higher Education: A Study of Financial Conditions at Forty-one Colleges and Universities* (New York: McGraw-Hill, 1971).

6. John R. Thelin and Amy E. Wells, "Important Books about Higher Education," in *Higher Education in the United States: An Encyclopedia,* ed. James J. Forest and Kevin Kinser (Santa Barbara, Calif.: ABC-CLIO, 2002), pp. 719–36; quotation at p. 729.

7. Lewis B. Mayhew, *Surviving the Eighties: Strategies and Procedures for Solving Fiscal and Enrollment Problems* (San Francisco: Jossey-Bass, 1980), pp. 76–77.

8. Harold L. Hodgkinson, *Institutions in Transition: A Profile of Change in Higher Education* (New York: McGraw-Hill, 1971).

9. Frank Newman et al., *Report on Higher Education* (Washington, D.C.: U.S. Department of Health, Education, and Welfare, March 1971), p. vii.

10. Martin Trow, "Reflections on the Transition from Elite to Mass to Universal Higher Education," *Daedalus* 99 (Winter 1970):1–42.

11. Homer D. Babbidge and Robert M. Rosenzweig, *The Federal Interest in Higher Education* (New York: Macmillan, 1962). See also Lawrence E. Gladieux and Thomas R. Wolanin, *Congress and the Colleges: The National Politics of Higher Education* (Lexington, Mass.: D.C. Heath, 1976).

12. Kerr, *Great Transformation,* pp. xvii–xix.

13. Patricia Cross, *Accent on Learning* (San Francisco: Jossey-Bass, 1976).

14. Michael Moffat, *Coming of Age in New Jersey: College and American Culture* (New Brunswick, N.J.: Rutgers University Press, 1989).

15. Ibid., pp. 25–61.

16. Ibid., pp. 29–34.

17. Fred A. Hargadon, "A Memo to Secondary Schools, Students, and Parents" (Stanford, Calif.: Stanford University Office of Admissions, 1978).

18. Russell Schoch, "As Cal Enters the '80s There'll Be Some Changes Made," *California Monthly,* January–February 1980, pp. 1, 2.

19. Christopher Jencks and David Riesman, *The Academic Revolution* (Gar-

den City, N.Y.: Doubleday Anchor, 1968); David G. Brown, "College Teacher Shortage," in *The Mobile Professors* (Washington, D.C.: American Council on Education, 1967); Joseph Fashing and Steven E. Deutsch, *Academics in Retreat: The Politics of Educational Innovation* (Albuquerque: University of New Mexico Press, 1971).

20. See Dorothy E. Finnegan, "Segmented Labor Markets," *Journal of Higher Education*, November–December 1993, pp. 621–56.

21. Neil Smelser and Robin Content, *The Changing Academic Market Place: General Trends and a Berkeley Case Study* (Berkeley: University of California Press, 1980).

22. Roger G. Baldwin and Jay L. Chronister, *Teaching without Tenure: Policies and Practices for a New Era* (Baltimore: Johns Hopkins University Press, 2001).

23. W. Norton Grubb, ed., *Honored but Invisible: An Inside Look at Teaching in Community Colleges* (New York: Routledge, 1999).

24. Howard R. Bowen and Jack Schuster, *American Professors: A National Resource Imperiled* (New York: Oxford University Press, 1986).

25. California Postsecondary Education Commission, *Missions and Functions of the California Community Colleges* (Sacramento: CPEC, May 1981).

26. Alexander W. Astin, "Implications for Policy and Practice," in *Four Critical Years: Effects of College on Beliefs, Values, and Knowledge* (San Francisco: Jossey-Bass, 1977), pp. 242–62.

27. See foreword to Alexander W. Astin, *What Matters in College? Four Critical Years Revisited* (San Francisco: Jossey-Bass, 1993).

28. Debra Shore, "What Price Egalitarianism?" *Brown Alumni Monthly*, February 1981, pp. 12–19; quotation at p. 12.

29. David Riesman, *On Higher Education: The Academic Enterprise in an Era of Rising Student Consumerism* (San Francisco: Jossey-Bass, 1981).

30. Waldemar Nielsen, "The Crisis of the Nonprofits," *Change* 12, no. 1 (1980):23–29.

31. Lewis B. Mayhew, *Surviving the Eighties* (San Francisco: Jossey-Bass, 1979); Carnegie Council on Policy Studies in Higher Education, *Three Thousand Futures: The Next Twenty Years for Higher Education* (San Francisco: Jossey-Bass, 1980).

32. George Keller, *Academic Strategy: The Management Revolution in American Higher Education* (Baltimore: Johns Hopkins University Press, 1983).

33. Goldie Blumenstyk, "New Head of the Ford Fund's Educational Program Is Champion of Women and Minority Students," *Chronicle of Higher Education*, 9 December 1991, pp. A27–A28.

34. Richard S. Ruch, *Higher Ed, Inc.: The Rise of the For-Profit University* (Baltimore: Johns Hopkins University Press, 2001).

35. See Howard J. Bowen, *Investment in Learning: The Individual and Social Value of American Higher Education* (San Francisco: Jossey-Bass, 1977).

36. Charles T. Clotfelter, *Buying the Best: Cost Escalation in Elite Higher Education* (Princeton, N.J.: Princeton University Press, 1996).

37. Carnegie Foundation for the Advancement of Teaching, *Control of the Campus: A Report on the Governance of Higher Education* (Princeton, N.J.: Carnegie Foundation for the Advancement of Teaching, 1982), pp. 3–4.

38. John R. Thelin, "Campus and Commonwealth: A Historical Interpretation," in *Higher Education in American Society,* ed. Philip G. Altbach, Robert O. Berdahl, and Patricia J. Gumport (Amherst, N.Y.: Prometheus Press, 1994), pp. 21–36.

39. Nathan Glazer, "Regulating Business and the Universities: One Problem or Two?" *Public Interest,* Summer 1979, pp. 42–65.

40. Derek C. Bok, "The Federal Government and the University," *Public Interest,* Winter 1980, pp. 80–101.

41. Clark Kerr, *The Uses of the University* (Cambridge, Mass.: Harvard University Press, 1963); Chester E. Finn, *Scholars, Dollars, and Bureaucrats* (Washington, D.C.: Brookings Institution, 1978).

42. Bernice R. Sandler and Roberta M. Hall, *The Classroom Climate: A Chilly One for Women* (Washington, D.C.: American Association of Higher Education, 1982).

43. P. J. Bickel, E. A. Hammel, and J. W. O'Connell, "Sex Bias in Graduate Admissions: Data from Berkeley," *Science* 187 (7 February 1975):393–404.

44. Sheila M. Tobias, *Overcoming Math Anxiety* (New York: W. W. Norton, 1978).

45. See John R. Thelin, "Good Sports? Historical Perspective on the Political Economy of Intercollegiate Athletics in the Era of Title IX, 1972–1997," *Journal of Higher Education* 71 (July–August 2000):391–410.

46. Henry N. Drewry and Humphrey Doermann, *Stand and Prosper: Private Black Colleges and Their Students* (Princeton, N.J.: Princeton University Press, 2001).

47. William J. Bowen and Derek Bok, *The Shape of the River: Long-Term Consequences of Considering Race in College and University Admissions* (Princeton, N.J.: Princeton University Press, 2000).

48. John T. Casteen III, "The State of the University" (Charlottesville: University of Virginia, 14 April 1999).

49. Finn, *Scholars, Dollars, and Bureaucrats.*

50. John R. Thelin, "Why College Costs So Much," *Wall Street Journal,* 11 December 1985, p. 32. See also Ronald G. Ehrenberg, *Tuition Rising: Why College Costs So Much* (Cambridge, Mass.: Harvard University Press, 2000).

51. John R. Thelin, "The Curriculum Crusades and the Conservative Backlash," *Change* 24 (January–February 1992):17–23.

52. Robert M. Rosenzweig with Barbara Turlington, *The Research Universities and Their Patrons* (Berkeley: University of California Press, 1982).

53. Kerr, *Great Transformation,* p. xv.

54. Robert M. Rosenzweig, *The Political University: Policy, Politics, and Presidential Leadership in the American Research University* (Baltimore: Johns Hopkins University Press, 1998).

55. William Celis III, "Navy Settles a Fraud Case on Stanford Research Costs: Part of Claim Is Paid: No Wrong Is Found," *New York Times*, 19 October 1994, p. A11.

56. Kenneth J. Cooper, "Rose Bowl Expenses Billed as Research Costs: University of Michigan Charges Questioned," *Washington Post*, 11 September 1991, p. A21.

57. Hugh Davis Graham and Nancy Diamond, *The Rise of American Research Universities: Elites and Challengers in the Postwar Era* (Baltimore: Johns Hopkins University Press, 1997).

58. Martin J. Finklestein, *The American Academic Profession: A Synthesis of Social Scientific Inquiry since World War II* (Columbus: Ohio State University Press, 1990).

59. Clifton F. Conrad, Jennifer Grant Hayworth, and Susan Bolyard Miller, *A Silent Success: Master's Education in the United States* (Baltimore: Johns Hopkins University Press, 1993).

60. Lois Therien, "Getting Joe College to Pay for City Services," *Business Week*, 16 July 1990, p. 37; Goldie Blumenstyk, "Town-Gown Battles Escalate as Beleaguered Cities Assail College Tax Exemptions," *Chronicle of Higher Education*, 29 June 1988, n.p.

61. Robert S. Shepard, "How Can a University That Raises a Billion Have a Tight Budget?" *Chronicle of Higher Education*, 12 January 1994, p. A48.

62. Rhoula Khalaf, "Customized Accounting," *Forbes*, 25 May 1992, p. 50. See also John R. Thelin, "Institutional History in Our Own Time: Higher Education's Shift from Managerial Revolution to Enterprising Evolution," *CASE International Journal of Educational Advancement* 1 (June 2000):9–23.

63. David Breneman, "The 'Privatization' of Public Universities: Mistake or Model?" *Chronicle of Higher Education*, 7 March 1997, p. B4.

64. Thomas Wallace, "The Age of the Dinosaur Persists," *Change* 25 (July–August 1993):56–63.

65. Roy Bowen, quoted in Ben Gose, "The Fall of the Flagships: Do the Best State Universities Need to Privatize to Thrive?" *Chronicle of Higher Education*, 5 July 2002, pp. A1, A19–A22.

66. Arthur Levine, "Higher Education's New Status as a Mature Industry," *Chronicle of Higher Education*, 31 January 1997, p. A48.

67. John R. Thelin, "Research Universities," in *Encyclopedia of American Social History*, ed. Mary Kupiec Cayton, Elliot J. Gorn, and Peter W. Williams (New York: Charles Scribner's Sons, 1992), pp. 2537–45; quotation at p. 2544.

68. Bruce C. Vladek, "Buildings and Budgets: The Overinvestment Crisis," *Change*, December 1978–January 1979, p. 39.

69. Abraham Flexner, *Universities: American, English, German* (New York: Oxford University Press, 1930).

70. George M. Marsden, *The Soul of the American University: From Protestant Establishment to Established Non-belief* (New York: Oxford University Press, 1994); Julie A. Reuben, *The Making of the Modern University: Intellectual Transformation and the Marginalization of Morality* (Chicago: University of Chicago Press, 1996).

9. A New Life Begins?

1. In 2010 the City University of New York chose "Investing in Futures: Public Higher Education in America" as the historic theme for its nationally distributed annual calendar.

2. Robert M. Berdahl, "Reassessing the Value of Research Universities," *Chronicle of Higher Education* 55, no. 14.

3. Knight Commission on Intercollegiate Athletics, "First of Its Kind Survey Reveals Dilemma of Reform," press release of October 26, 2009. See also the commission's subsequent report, *Restoring the Balance: Dollars, Values, and the Future of College Sports* (Miami: Knight Foundation, June 17, 2010).

4. William Bowen, Matthew Chingos, and Michael McPherson, *Crossing the Finish Line: Completing College at America's Universities* (Princeton: Princeton University Press, 2009). See also Frederick M. Hess, Mark Schneider, Kevin Carey, and Andrew P. Kelly, *Diplomas and Dropouts: Which Colleges Actually Graduate Their Students (and Which Don't)* (Washington, D.C.: American Enterprise Institute, 2009), and John R. Thelin, *The Attrition Tradition in American Higher Education: Connecting Past and Present* (Washington, D.C.: American Enterprise Institute, 2010).

5. Molly Cook, David M. Irby, and Bridget C. O'Brien, *Educating Physicians: A Call for Reform of Medical School and Residency* (Stanford, Calif.: Carnegie Foundation for the Advancement of Teaching, 2010). For headline news coverage, see Anemona Hartocollis, "In Medical School Shift, Meeting Patients on Day 1," *New York Times,* 2 September 2010, pp. A1, A12.

6. Jonathan R. Cole, *The Great American University: Its Rise to Preeminence, Its Indispensable National Role, Why It Must Be Protected* (New York: Public Affairs, 2009).

7. Andrew Delbanco, "The Universities in Trouble," *New York Review of Books* 56, no. 18 (14 May 2009).

8. Mark Bauerlein, "Ignorance by Degrees: Colleges Serve the People Who Work There More Than the Students Who Desperately Need to Learn Something," *Wall Street Journal,* 2 August 2010.

9. Thomas Bartlett, "Phoenix Risen: How a History Professor Became the Pioneer of the For-Profit Revolution," *Chronicle of Higher Education,* 10 July 2009, pp.

A1, A10–A13. See also Robin Wilson, "Profit Colleges Change Higher Education's Landscape," *Chronicle of Higher Education*, 12 February 2010, pp. A1, A16–A19.

10. Peter S. Goodman, "In Hard Times, Lured into Trade School and Debt," *New York Times*, 14 March 2010, pp. 1, 20.

11. Mary Beth Marklein, "For-Profit Colleges under Fire over Value, Accreditation," *USA Today*, 29 September 2010.

12. Jennifer Gonzalez, "Advocate of For-Profit Colleges Mounts a Strong Defense before Senate Hearing," *Chronicle of Higher Education*, 23 June 2010.

13. Ivar Berg, *The Great Training Robbery: Education and Jobs* (New York: Basic Books, 1972).

14. "Student Demographics," *Chronicle of Higher Education: Almanac Issue, 2010–11* 57, no. 1 (27 August 2010):25–26.

15. Christopher Tudico, "Beyond Black and White: Researching the History of Latinos in American Higher Education," in *The History of U.S. Higher Education: Methods for Understanding the Past*, ed. Marybeth Gasman (New York: Routledge, 2010), pp. 163–71.

16. Joseph Berger, "Why Latinos Are Left Behind," *New York Times Education-Life Magazine*, 25 July 2010, pp. 16–19.

17. John R. Thelin, "Higher Education's Student Financial Aid Enterprise in Historical Perspective," in *Footing the Tuition Bill: The New Student Loan Sector*, ed. Frederick M. Hess (Washington, D.C.: American Enterprise Institute, 2007), pp. 19–43.

18. Welch Suggs, *A Place on the Team: The Triumph and Tragedy of Title IX* (Princeton: Princeton University Press, 2005).

19. Jonathan D. Glater, "Women Are Close to Being Majority of Law Students," *New York Times*, 26 March 2001.

20. W. Michael Cox and Richard Alm, "Scientists Are Made, Not Born," *New York Times*, 28 February 2005.

21. "The Profession," *Chronicle of Higher Education: Almanac Issue, 2010–11* 57, no. 1 (27 August 2010):20.

22. Jennifer Delahunty Britz, "To All the Girls I've Rejected," *New York Times*, 23 March 2006.

23. Alex Williams, "The New Math on Campus: When Women Outnumber Men at a College, Dating Culture Is Skewed," *New York Times*, 7 February 2010, Style Section, pp. 1, 8.

24. Tamar Lewin, "Once a Leader, U.S. Lags in College Degrees," *New York Times*, 23 July 2010; Lee Lawrence, "US College Degrees: Still Among World's Top Universities?" *Christian Science Monitor*, 2 June 2010.

25. Clara M. Lovett, "American Business Schools in the Post-American World," *Chronicle of Higher Education*, 6 September 2010.

26. Gabriel Ringlet, ed., *Une aventure universitaire: Universite catholique de Louvain* (Bruxelles: Editions Racine, 2000).

27. Ben Wildavsky, *The Great Brain Race: How Global Universities Are Reshaping the World* (Princeton: Princeton University Press, 2010).

28. Tamar Lewin, "University Branches in Dubai Are Struggling," *New York Times,* 28 December 2009, p. A19.

29. Joe Draper and Katie Thomas, "As Colleges Compete, Major Money Flows to Minor Sports," *New York Times,* 2 September 2010, pp. A1, A20.

30. Welch Suggs, "How Gears Turn at a Sports Factory: Running Ohio State University's $79 Million Program Is a Major Endeavor, with Huge Payoffs and Costs," *Chronicle of Higher Education,* 29 November 2003, pp. A1, A32–A37.

31. Rachel Bachman, "Oregon Athletic Department Uses State Money for Academic Needs Despite Claims of Self-sufficiency," *Oregonian* (Portland), 7 October 2010.

32. Joe Drape, "Cal-Berkeley Cuts 5 Athletic Programs," *New York Times,* 28 September 2010.

33. Murray Sperber, *College Sports, Inc.: The Athletic Department vs. the University* (New York: Henry Holt and Company, 1990).

34. James L. Shulman and William G. Bowen, *The Game of Life: College Sports and Educational Values* (Princeton and Oxford: Princeton University Press, 2001; William G. Bowen and Sarah A. Levin, *Reclaiming the Game: College Sports and Educational Values* (Princeton and Oxford: Princeton University Press, 2003).

35. Libby Sander, "Athletics Raises a College from the Ground Up," *Chronicle of Higher Education,* 19 September 2008.

36. Gaye Tuchman, *Wannabe U: Inside the Corporate University* (Chicago: University of Chicago Press, 2009).

37. University Leadership Council, *Competing in the Era of Big Bets: Achieving Scale in Multidisciplinary Research* (Washington, D.C.: Education Advisory Board, 2009), 108 pp.

38. Michael I. Luger and Harvey Goldstein, *Technology in the Garden: Research Parks and Regional Economic Development* (Chapel Hill: University of North Carolina Press, 1991).

39. Andrew Pollack, "Awaiting the Genome Payoff," *New York Times,* 14 June 2010, p. A1

40. Roger L. Geiger, *Knowledge and Money: Research Universities and the Paradox of the Marketplace* (Stanford, Calif.: Stanford University Press, 2004).

41. Malcolm Moos, *The Post–Land Grant University: The University of Maryland Report* (College Park: University of Maryland, 1981).

42. Lisa Rathke, "Agriculture Colleges Sell Cow Herds to Cut Costs," *Associated Press,* 12 July 2010.

43. Ryan Alessi, "University of Kentucky Lands High-Profile Cancer Center Chief: Wooing Hit New Level for Doctor/Researcher," *Lexington Herald-Leader,* 14 April 2009, pp. A1, A5.

44. Steve Hymon, "Head of UCLA Medical Center Is Leaving Post," *Los Angeles Times*, 3 September 2003. See also "UCLA Hospital System Can't Heal Itself," *Los Angeles Times*, 2 March 2003.

45. Katherine S. Mangan, "An Unfair 'Tax'?: Law and Business Schools Object to Bailing Out Medical Centers," *Chronicle of Higher Education*, 15 May 1998.

46. Scott Carlson, "As Campuses Crumble, Budgets Are Crunched," *Chronicle of Higher Education*, 23 May 2008.

47. Ronald G. Ehrenberg, *Tuition Rising: Why College Costs So Much* (Cambridge, Mass.: Harvard University Press, 2000).

48. Donna M. Desrochers, Colleen M. Lenihan, and Jane V. Wellman, *Trends in College Spending, 1998–2008: Where Does the Money Come From? Where Does it Go? What Does It Buy?* (Washington, D.C.: Delta Cost Project, 2010); Jack Stripling, "Follow the Money," *Inside Higher Ed*, 9 July 2010.

49. Ben Gose, "The Fall of the Flagships?: Do the Best State Universities Need to Privatize to Thrive?" *Chronicle of Higher Education*, 5 July 2002, p. A19.

50. Paul Fain, "Cuts Intensify Identity Crisis for Washington's Flagship Campus," *Chronicle of Higher Education*, 29 August 2010, p. A1.

51. Scott Carlson, "As Campuses Crumble, Budgets Are Crunched," *Chronicle of Higher Education*, 23 May 2008.

52. Clyde W. Barrow, *Universities and the Capitalist State: Corporate Liberalism and the Reconstruction of American Higher Education, 1894–1928* (Madison: University of Wisconsin Press, 1990).

53. See, for example, "Boston May Ask Its Colleges to Pay More in Lieu of Taxes," *Boston Globe*, 6 April 2010. For analyses of precedents for taxing campus property, see Goldie Blumenstyke, "Town-Gown Battles Escalate as Beleaguered Cities Assail College Tax Exemptions," *Chronicle of Higher Education*, 29 June 1988; Lois Therrien, "Getting Joe College to Pay for City Services," *Business Week*, 16 July 1990, p. 37.

54. Alvin P. Sanoff, "Serving Students Well: Independent Colleges Today," in *Meeting the Challenge: America's Independent Colleges and Universities since 1956* (Washington, D.C.: Council of Independent Colleges, 2006), pp. 37–62; John R. Thelin, "Small by Design: Resilience in an Era of Mass Higher Education," in *Meeting the Challenge*, pp. 3–36.

55. Thomas R. Cech, "Sciences at Liberal Arts Colleges: A Better Education?" and Priscilla W. Laws, "New Approaches to Sciences and Mathematics Teaching at Liberal Arts Colleges," in Steven Koblik and Stephen R. Graubard, *Distinctively American: The Residential Liberal Arts Colleges* (New Brunswick, N.J.: Transaction Press, 1990), pp. 195–216, 217–40.

56. Andrew Hacker, "They'd Much Rather Be Rich," *New York Review of Books* 54, no. 15 (11 October 2007).

57. Deborah L. Rode, *In Pursuit of Knowledge: Scholars, Status, and Academic Culture* (Stanford: Stanford University Press, 2007).

58. Quoted in W. J. Rorabaugh, *Berkeley at War: The 1960s* (New York: Oxford University Press, 1989).

59. Frank T. Rhodes, Jr., Introductory remarks at Princeton University's 250th anniversary forum (April 1996). See also Rhodes's formal talk at the conference, "The University and Its Critics," in William G. Bowen and Harold T. Shapiro, eds., *Universities and Their Leadership* (Princeton: Princeton University Press, 1998), pp. 3–14.

60. For accounts of President Hugo Sonnenschein's curricular disputes with faculty and students—and ultimately his resignation from the University of Chicago, see Ben Gose, "University of Chicago President's Plan to Resign Doesn't Quiet Debate over His Agenda, *Chronicle of Higher Education*, 18 June 1999. For one of many articles about the Harvard board's firing of President Lawrence Summers in 2006, see Robin Wilson, "The Fall of Summers: Lawrence Summers Never Won over Harvard's Faculty, and That Cost Him His Job," *Chronicle of Higher Education*, 24 February 2006.

61. For accounts of board dismay over attempts at varsity sports reform with President John DiBaggio at Michigan State University and President David Rozelle at the University of Kentucky, see John R. Thelin, *Games Colleges Play: Scandal and Reform in Intercollegiate Athletics* (Baltimore: Johns Hopkins University Press, 1994), pp. 189–96.

62. Richard Ekman, "The Imminent Crisis in College Leadership," *Chronicle of Higher Education*, 24 September 2010, p. A88.

63. Paul Fain, Thomas Bartlett, and Marc Beja, "Divided Loyalties: One-Fourth of Private Colleges do Business with Trustees' Companies. Whose Interests Come First?" *Chronicle of Higher Education*, 14 March 2010. See also Julianne Basinger, "Boards Crack Down on Members' Insider Deals: Recent Scandals Trigger New Scrutiny of Trustees," *Chronicle of Higher Education*, 6 February 2004.

64. Elia Powers, "A Prominent Public Targets Faculty Retention," *Inside Higher Education*, 12 September 2007.

65. Mary B. Marcy, "Why Foundations Have Cut Back in Higher Education," *Chronicle of Higher Education*, 25 July 2003.

66. For an example of an effective combination of timely statistical information on higher education combined with informed critical analysis, see Joni E. Finney, "A Reset for Higher Education," Margaret Miller, "More Pressure on Faculty Members, from Every Direction," Sandy Baum, "As Students Change, Colleges Must Follow," and Michael S. McPherson, "Asking the Right Questions about College Access," all in *Chronicle of Higher Education: Almanac Issue* 57, no. 1 (27 August 2010):6, 17, 25, 34.

Essay on Sources

Sherlock Holmes, baffled by a difficult case, once complained to Watson that he needed clues if he was to continue his investigation. Scrounging for sources, he cried out in exasperation, "I cannot build bricks without straw!" Unlike Sherlock Holmes, I have enjoyed the benefit of exemplary scholarship from numerous sources while exploring the mysteries of American higher education over four centuries. The endnotes to each chapter provide citations directly connected to my historical narrative. The following commentary is intended to highlight key books and monographs that have been most pertinent to my interpretations. I have also given special attention to works that have been published recently and that are readily available.

During the past fifty years the history of higher education has been fertile ground for sound writing and research, much of it accomplished without the luxury of abundant external funding. Indeed, the decade from 2000 to 2010 has been especially impressive in both quantity and quality of works. One consistently good source of case studies and novel reinterpretations has been the articles published in the *History of Education Quarterly.* Illustrative of this contribution is the winter 1971 issue, devoted to the theme of the "liberal arts college in the age of the university." In the past decade editors Leonard Baird of the *Journal of Higher Education* and Philip Altbach of the *Review of Higher Education* have been receptive to historical analyses on significant issues for a general higher-education audience. One convenient volume for pulling together many of these influential journal articles is the 1997 (second) edition of the *ASHE Reader on the History of Higher Education,* edited by Lester Goodchild and Harold Wechsler. Also useful as a guide to the literature on higher education is *One Hundred Classic Books about Higher Education: A Compendium and Essays,* edited by Cameron Fincher, George Keller, E. Grady Bogue, and John Thelin (2001). The annual volume *Higher Education: Handbook of Theory and Research,* edited by John C. Smart, has included each year since its inception in 1985 a major historiographic essay on a significant higher-education topic. Researchers also have the benefit of two excellent comprehensive reference works published in 2002 whose contributing authors include leading higher-education scholars: *The Encyclopedia of Education,* edited by James W. Guthrie, and *Higher Education in the United States: An Encyclopedia,* edited by James J. Forest and Kevin Kinser.

Since the early 1980s another periodical, the *History of Higher Education Annual,* edited by Roger Geiger, has provided a forum for cutting-edge monographs. In some cases the impact of the articles in these volumes has been sufficiently great that they have then been refined and published as book-length anthologies, organized around such themes as a rethinking of the nineteenth-century American college (the focus for the 1994 volume) and southern higher education in the twentieth century (1999 volume).

Institutional histories, especially the officially sponsored anniversary volumes, have often been dismissed as shallow and constrained in candor. My experience of, and debt to, such works is different. The work in this genre that I found to be most valuable as a source of information and a model of scholarship is Thomas G. Dyer's *The University of Georgia: A Bicentennial History* (1985). Indeed, the history of selected universities in the South has followed Dyer's example, with works that show that institutional affiliation can effectively include critical analysis. Foremost in this group are Clarence L. Mohr and Joseph E. Gordon, *Tulane: The Emergence of a Modern University, 1945–1980* (2001) and Henry H. Lesesne, *A History of the University of South Carolina, 1940–2000* (2001). Paul Conkin's authorized history of Vanderbilt, *Gone with the Ivy* (1985), concludes a long, comprehensive chronicle with essential questions about a university's mission. It also includes an important analysis of social and literary history in its original interpretation of the "agrarians" and "fugitives" who found an unlikely home in the English department at a time when the Vanderbilt governing bodies and chancellor were steering the institution in a very different direction. Michael Dennis's *Lessons in Progress* (2001) connects historical studies of state universities in Virginia, Georgia, South Carolina, and Tennessee to show how Progressivism took root in higher education of the New South between 1880 and 1920. Rounding out this southern exposure, Dwayne D. Cox and William J. Morison's *The University of Louisville* (2000) is notable on several counts: its narrative is lively and good-humored, and it effectively connects the history of a municipal campus, with all its foibles and tensions, to that of its host city. Their account of the Louisville black community's effective voting strategies in the 1930s to expose the inequities of tax support for a racially exclusive municipal campus is refreshing in its candor. John Boles's *University Builder: Edgar Odell Lovett and the Founding of the Rice Institute* (2007) fuses the biography of a distinctive university with that of its founding president in a graceful work that allows Rice to take its rightful place in the higher-education pantheon. At the same time, Melissa Kean's *Desegregating Private Higher Education in the South: Duke, Emory, Rice, Tulane, and Vanderbilt* (2008) reconstructs the shameful heritage of how the boards of trustees at prestigious private universities in the South deliberately avoided taking responsibility or initiative to admit African-American students in the mid-twentieth century. Moving north, Morton Keller and Phyllis Keller's *Making Harvard Modern: The Rise of America's University* (2001) puts Harvard's legacy for the twentieth century into historical perspective. Harvard, of course, has not been the whole story. James Axtell's *The Making of Princeton University: From Woodrow Wilson to the Present* (2006) contributes both a sorely needed update on the remarkable transitions and traditions at Princeton and a model of institutional research that includes a focus on undergraduates and their changing studies and life within a historic campus. Jonathan Cole's massive analysis, *The Great American University: Its Rise to Preeminence, Its Indispensable National Role, Why It Must Be Protected* (2009), relies on 640 pages to provide a hundredth-anniversary update to Edwin Slosson's *Great American Universities*, with a tone of urgency and worry accompanying its catalogue of accomplishments. At Brown University, archivist Martha Mitchell and editor Jay Barry effectively used short sidebars to illuminate key episodes along with archival photographs in *A Tale of Two Centuries: A Warm and Richly Pictorial History of Brown University, 1764–1985* (1985).

I part company with many serious scholars in that I like and rely on the photographic essays that many colleges and universities have commissioned in the past decades. These works are rich sources for understanding and transmitting the visual legacy of campus architecture and landscaping. The single best such source I have found is Oliver Jensen's photographic compilations put together as part of a project sponsored by American Heritage in *A College Album: Or, Rah, Rah, Yesterday!* (1974). One theme I have emphasized throughout my text is that architecture persists as a distinctive part of American higher education's presence. Some essential works in this area include Jean F. Block, *The Uses of Gothic: Planning and Building the Campus of the University of Chicago, 1892–1932* (1983); Paul Venable Turner, *Campus: An American Planning Tradition* (1984); Thomas Gaines, *The Campus as a Work of Art* (1991); and Richard P. Dober's two works, *Campus Design* (1992) and *Campus Architecture: Building in the Groves of Academe* (1996).

Institutional case studies have flourished in number and in significance apart from commissioned histories. Rebecca S. Lowen's *Creating the Cold War University* (1997) focuses on Stanford to show how the strategies of fusing physics and engineering to the external environments of industrial projects and, later, federal research grants promoted the transformation of a comfortable California campus into a modern dynamo. If Stanford represents an important example from the Pacific Coast, it is complemented by Richard M. Freeland's multi-institutional study of Massachusetts universities circa 1945 to 1970, aptly titled *Academia's Golden Age* (1992). No discussion of the American "multiversity" can ignore Clark Kerr's influential slim volume *The Uses of the University* (1963), originally delivered as the Godkin Lectures at Harvard in 1962. An intriguing sequel to Kerr's classic work is the anthology edited by Stephen Brint, *The Future of the City of Intellect* (2002), which includes a twenty-first-century commentary by Clark Kerr himself. John Aubrey Douglass, *The California Idea in American Higher Education: 1850 to the 1960 Master Plan*, draws on state political history to elaborate on Clark Kerr and a host of other important institutions and individuals that made California a marvel and model for mass higher-education considerations.

Whereas Clark Kerr typifies the participant-observer who both makes and writes the history of the American research university, Roger Geiger's numerous works demonstrate how this focus on the research university can be nurtured to flourish as a mature, central theme of the comprehensive scholarship on American higher education. These works include *To Advance Knowledge: The Growth of American Research Universities, 1900–1940* (1986) and *Research and Relevant Knowledge: American Research Universities since World War II* (1993). Geiger has continued to be perceptive and prolific in the past decade, with publication of *Knowledge and Money: Research Universities and the Paradox of the Marketplace* (2004) and, coauthored with Creso M. Sa, *Tapping the Riches of Science: Universities and the Promise of Economic Growth* (2008). Geiger continues a tradition staked out in 1965 by Laurence Veysey in *The Emergence of the American University*. Julie A. Reuben revisits Veysey's thesis with a new interpretation in *The Making of the Modern University: Intellectual Transformation and the Marginalization of Morality* (1996).

For a critical analysis of the university research park enterprise in historical perspective, the indispensable study is Michael I. Luger and Harvey Goldstein, *Technology in the Garden: Research Parks and Regional Economic Development* (1991). In the twenty-first century, the 2008 report of the University Leadership Council, *Competing in the Era of Big Bets: Achieving Scale in Multidisciplinary Research*, documents an overextended and fragile structure for university-based research centers. Moving from the specifics of high-stakes, sponsored research, the topic of commercialization and the American campus has been a source of lively debate and critical analysis since 2000. Illustrative of this genre are the following works: Derek Bok, *Universities in the Marketplace: The Commercialization of Higher Education* (2003); Deborah L. Rode, *In Pursuit of Knowledge: Scholars, Status, and Academic Culture* (2007); and Gaye Tuchman, *Wannabe U: Inside the Corporate University* (2009).

Focus on the campus as the crucial unit has been tempered by the historical study of philanthropy and foundations whose resources and recommendations have cut across American higher education. A rediscovered pioneering work in this vein is Jesse Barnard Sears, *Philanthropy in the History of American Higher Education* (1922, reprinted 1990). Sears's book provided the groundwork of chronology and rudimentary statistical compilations about institutional endowments and major gifts. After 1960, established historians refined Sears's study to flesh out the narrative and interpretation. Merle Curti and Roderick Nash's *Philanthropy in the Shaping of American Higher Education* (1965) used support of higher education as an effective tool by which to integrate social and institutional history—in a book that warrants more praise and sustained use than it has received. Robert H. Bremner's *American Philanthropy* (1960, 2d ed. 1988) provides a readable survey and interpretation of philanthropy writ large. Although Bremner did not set out to focus on colleges and universities, one recurrent finding is that higher education has been both a pacesetter and a central institution in organized giving and receiving. Ellen Condliffe Lagemann refines the focus of large-scale philanthropy by focusing on important foundations in two enduring works: *Private Power for the Public Good: A History of the Carnegie Foundation for the Advancement of Teaching* (1983) and *The Politics of Knowledge: The Carnegie Corporation, Philanthropy, and Public Policy* (1989). A significant example of how the foundation representatives viewed the American campus—and wanted to reshape it—is found in Abraham Flexner's 1929 Oxford University lectures, published as *Universities: American, English, German* (1930). Two new books that graft the history of philanthropy and higher education to underrepresented (and underacknowledged) constituencies are Marybeth Gasman's *Envisioning Black Colleges: A History of the United Negro College Fund* (2007) and the anthology edited by Andrea Walton, *Women and Philanthropy in Education* (2005).

Since the commissioned studies sponsored by the major foundations often bore the imprimatur of an influential author, it is only fitting that biography has a crucial place within the systematic analysis of philanthropic organizations. Central to this domain is the Carnegie Foundation for the Advancement of Teaching—as shown by Thomas Bonner's *Iconoclast: Abraham Flexner and a Life in Learning* (2002). Other notable case studies of foundations and their key engineers include Eric Anderson and Alfred A. Moss, Jr., *Dangerous Donations: Northern Philanthropy and Southern Black Education, 1902–1930* (1999), and Donald Fisher, *Fundamental Development of the Social Sciences: Rockefeller Philanthropy and the United States Social Science Research Council* (1993). Fisher's most original contribution is to track down the cooperation between a private foundation and the federal government in developing official programs of data collection, especially those associated with economic indicators. A broader interpretation is Judith Sealander's *Private Wealth and Public Life* (1997), a history of foundation philanthropy and the reshaping of American social policy from the Progressive era to the New Deal.

The major foundations have been important for higher education not only as a means of financial support but also as a source of scholarly scrutiny. In the 1970s, for example, Clark Kerr led a well-funded Carnegie Foundation initiative to probe higher education. For those interested in studying American higher education's recent past, the culminating volume, *The Carnegie Council on Policy Studies in Higher Education: A Summary of Reports and Recommendations* (1980), provides a good roadmap to the contours and detours of higher education as a major presence in our national life.

The campus and the philanthropic foundation are not the only organizing structures in American higher education. In *Banding Together: The Rise of National Associations in American Higher Education, 1887–1950* (1992), historian Hugh Hawkins of Amherst College steers attention to the alphabet soup of voluntary groups formed by institutions, especially their presidents. The implication of Hawkins's account of associations is that usually their reason for being is to shape programs and policies. Hence, this collective effort connects to the theme of how American colleges and universities have been involved in—and influenced by—public policies put into motion by state and federal governments.

The role of public policy in higher education has received relatively little emphasis, perhaps in deference to the conventional wisdom that American higher education has a tradition of autonomy and decentralization. Perhaps so, but a number of historians have amended that simplistic characterization by taking a close look at government relations. John Whitehead's *Separation of College and State* (1973) relies on careful accounts of five colleges chartered in the colonial era and their institutional contours well into the nineteenth century to complicate our notions of "public" and "private" institutions. Jurgen Herbst's *From Crisis to Crisis: American College Government, 1636–1819* (1982) animates the external relations of colleges from the colonial era into the "new national" period, with the concluding account of the emergence of the "provincial college" as a distinctively American institution. Taken together, the works by Whitehead and Herbst leave thoughtful readers with the delightful dilemma of trying to resolve the enduring significance of the 1819 Dartmouth College case.

Although federal legislation dealing with higher education was relatively limited in the nineteenth century, its conspicuous landmarks include the Morrill Act of 1862. Roger Williams rescues this episode from superficiality with his study, *George W. Atherton and the Beginnings of Federal Support for Higher Education* (1989). His key finding is that the original legislation floundered until George Atherton, a political economist who became president of Pennsylvania State College, persuaded fellow land-grant institution presidents to join him to form a lobbying group in Washington, D.C. This was the origin of the succession of legislation between 1890 and 1920 that put federal funding into place and opened up the discussion between campus and capital. For those who wish to follow the emergence of proposed expanded federal policies regarding access and affordability in higher education, the pioneering work in compiling data and mounting a sustained, informed argument is *Higher Education in a Democracy*, edited by George F. Zook (1947)—popularly known as the Truman

Commission Report. Chester Finn's *Scholars, Dollars, and Bureaucrats* (1978) asked a basic (and embarrassing) policy question—namely, how to justify a $14 billion federal expenditure on higher education when higher education is reserved for the states. The good, long answer to a simple question is a political history of federal involvement, ranging from funding in sponsored research and student financial aid to regulation and paperwork compliance—all of which have become part of "business as usual" for colleges and universities.

Historians of higher education who have studied public policies have delighted in defying Bismarck's advice that one should avoid watching laws or sausages being made. The exercise gains in courage when one includes the dismal science of economics in the venture. Margery Somers Foster's *"Out of Smalle Beginings . . .": An Economic History of Harvard College in the Puritan Period* (1962) sets the standard for making sense out of cents—as well as farthings and shillings. Unfortunately, few historians have dared to write comparably complete accounts of accounts for other institutions in other eras. Economist Seymour Harris has paved the way for subsequent works, with two compendia: *A Statistical Profile of Higher Education* (1972) and *The Economics of Harvard* (1970). Howard J. Bowen's *Investment in Learning: The Individual and Social Value of American Higher Education* (1977) is a landmark work that brings together disparate sources in a comprehensive economic analysis of American higher education. In the past two decades a few scholars have provided some historical perspective on changing resources and allocations—for example, Ronald Ehrenberg's *Tuition Rising: Why College Costs So Much* (2000) and Charles T. Clotfelter's *Buying the Best: Cost Escalation in Elite Higher Education* (1996). The problem is that these works are uneven in their coverage of the various eras and epochs in American higher education. Their authors have more information on the present than they do on the past.

Despite this imbalance toward contemporary data, some of the recent statistical studies on revenues and expenditures across American higher education are illuminating for historical studies. An excellent example of such a work is the 2009 Delta Cost Project coauthored by Donna M. Desrochers, Colleen M. Lenihan, and Jane V. Wellman, *Trends in College Spending, 1998–2008: Where Does the Money Come From? Where Does it Go? What Does It Buy?*

One favorable consequence is that scholars of the twenty-first century have ready access to statistical databases from which they can then compile their own historical and contemporary analyses of the economic conditions of higher education, along with other demographic and institutional patterns. For several years such groups as the American Council on Education (and, later, the University of Chicago Press) have published these databases as the *Almanac of Higher Education*. Since 1995 the *Chronicle of Higher Education* has taken over this charge with its annual printed version and its on-line collection of higher-education data banks. The best fresh examination of higher education's statistical record concerns not finances or budgets but patterns of student enrollment and institutional survival. Colin B. Burke's *American Collegiate Populations: A Test of the Traditional View* (1982) represents over a decade of careful review and recompilation of basic data. The quantitative recasting led Burke to advance a revised qualitative depiction of the viability of the nineteenth-century colleges. He did not, however, subject his data to the sophisticated tests of a statistician. Hence, his provocative work remains more an invitation for additional analyses than a final word. Historians Hugh Graham and Nancy Diamond combined statistical databases with historical profiles in *The Rise of American Research Universities: Elites and Challengers in the Postwar Era* (1997) to analyze the perennial question as to who has risen—and fallen—in the ranks of the top research universities. Their focus on the recent past follows logically from David S. Webster's longitudinal study, *Academic Quality Rankings of American Colleges and Universities* (1986).

Statistics, of course, provide only one glimpse of higher education's track record. For readers who do wish to ground their thinking in sound essentials about higher education's European and colonial roots, some classic works provide a good foundation. Charles Homer Haskins's *The Rise of the Universities* (1923) was originally presented as a series of three lectures at Brown University. It endures as a succinct, lively account that connects the legacies of the medieval universities to twentieth-century higher education. In distilling the central features of the university, Haskins thoughtfully and good-naturedly dispels erroneous stereotypes by reminding us what the historic university did not include or promise. Several generations of American historians have been indebted to Bernard Bailyn's penetrating *Education in the Forming of American Society* (1960) as a model and a manifesto for looking at education beyond the strict construction and literalism of formal schools and official curricula. A delightful, expanded sequel to Bailyn's small, influential book is James Axtell's *The School upon a Hill: Education and Society in Colonial New England* (1974). In a later study Axtell extended the notion of acculturation as education in the colonial era to go beyond the interaction between England and the New World. In *The European and the Indian: Essays in the Ethnohistory of Colonial North America* (1981) Axtell reconstructs how Native Americans approached the education of the young—and also how they viewed the newcomers' comparable practices. Lawrence Stone of Princeton University brought together a team of scholars at the Shelby Cullom Davis Center to examine the intricacies of higher education and society on both sides of the Atlantic Ocean in a two-volume anthology, *The University in Society* (1974). An underappreciated lucid small book on a large topic is Oscar and Mary Handlin's *The American College and American Culture: Socialization as a Function of Higher Education* (1970).

A number of leading historians have incorporated the story of colleges and universities into the larger fabric of American social and political history.

These invaluable contributions include Daniel J. Boorstin's multivolume series *The Americans* (1965), Richard Hofstadter's *Anti-intellectualism in American Life* (1963), and Lawrence Cremin's three-volume *American Education* (1970). Clyde W. Barrow's *Universities and the Capitalist State: Corporate Liberalism and the Reconstruction of American Higher Education, 1894–1928* (1990) effectively resurrects and analyzes economic data as well as statistical trends on the composition of university boards to present a critical profile of American higher education at the start of the twentieth century. The most thorough account of colleges and universities during World War I is Carol S. Gruber's *Mars and Minerva: World War I and the Uses of the Higher Learning in America* (1976). David O. Levine's *The American College and the Culture of Aspiration, 1915–1940* (1986) remains the seminal work on the important albeit underappreciated era in American higher education between the world wars. In a compelling reconstruction of the interplay of government, campus administrators, and faculty in the Communist "witch-hunt" era immediately after World War II, Ellen W. Schrecker's *No Ivory Tower: McCarthyism and the Universities* (1986) connects campus and capitals.

Whereas Clyde Barrow's book demonstrates how historical statistics can raise essential questions about the politics of American higher education, a number of substantive works rely on insider experience in national agencies and campus boardrooms. Foremost in this genre is Homer D. Babbidge and Robert M. Rosenzweig, *The Federal Interest in Higher Education* (1962). Rosenzweig returned to this theme, with focus on an elite group of institutions, in *The Research Universities and Their Patrons* (1982).

Social and behavioral scientists often chide historians for their reliance on biographies, derided as "$n = 1$" research. In fact, such criticisms are off the mark because they gloss over the texture and insights about colleges and universities that biographies can provide. Irving Stone, famous for his historical biographies of artists and scientists, paid homage to the University of California at Berkeley in 1969 by editing a collection of alumni memoirs, *There Was Light* (the title refers to the university motto, "Fiat lux"). The disparate threads are tied together with the interesting subtitle, *Autobiography of a University*. Over time this approach has turned out to be one of the most productive veins of new scholarship on how colleges work—and their numerous, complex consequences.

Understandably, historic institutions with strong ties to the publishing industry are well represented in anthologies of alumni memoirs. These collections include Diana Dubois, editor, *My Harvard, My Yale: Memoirs of College Life by Some Notable Americans* (1982) and Jeffrey L. Lant, editor, *Our Harvard: Reflections on College Life by Twenty-two Distinguished Graduates* (1982). Unfortunately, the memoirs of unnotable and undistinguished alumni have been less likely to make their way into print, thus skewing the picture. One hopes that all institutions will follow Harvard and Yale's lead in collecting the memoirs and oral histories of their constituents. Editors Carolyn B. Matalene and Katherine C. Reynolds provide a model in their anthology about the University of South Carolina, *Carolina Voices: Two Hundred Years of Student Experiences* (2001). Studies of the campus as a source of "personal history" can profit from reliance on guides to local and state history, such as David E. Kyvig and Myron A. Marty, *Nearby History: Exploring the Past around You* (1982, 1996).

Historians looking beyond the confines of a single campus have compiled rich anthologies organized around a theme or shared experience. The unifying theme of Geraldine Joncich Clifford's *Lone Voyagers: Academic Women in Coeducational Institutions, 1870–1937* (1989) is the life and work of academic women both as a part of and apart from coeducational institutions. Maresi Nerad's *The Academic Kitchen: A Social History of Gender Stratification at the University of California, Berkeley* (1999) focuses on the case study of an important albeit understudied character, Alice Faye Morgan, to show how a woman navigated the uncharted waters of both the faculty ranks and administrative responsibility for building an academic department at Berkeley over four decades.

Nerad's fusion of institutional and individual biography illustrates the vitality of scholarship on women in higher education. Margaret Rossiter's *Women Scientists in America: Struggles and Strategies to 1940* (1982) documents the syndrome of double standards and underrecognition that faced women in the laboratory and the academy up to World War II. Jana Nidiffer's *Pioneering Deans of Women: More Than Wise and Pious Matrons* (2000) considers women as campus administrators. Central as an overarching resource is Linda Eisenmann's *Historical Dictionary of Women in Education in the United States* (1998). A generation of historians are indebted to Barbara Miller Solomon for having synthesized decades' worth of studies for her interpretive survey, *In the Company of Educated Women* (1985). *Gender and Higher Education in the Progressive Era* (1990), Lynn Gordon's collection of historical profiles of women at Berkeley, Chicago, Vassar, Agnes Scott, and Sophie Newcombe, complicates our understanding of women as undergraduates. Polly Welts Kaufman, editor of *The Search for Equity: Women at Brown University, 1891–1991* (1991), brings together original research on a range of case studies within a single university to illustrate how women participated centrally in the age of the university.

Whereas some historians have devoted primary attention to the tensions women faced in coeducation, Helen Lefkowitz Horowitz staked out a different focus in *Alma Mater: Design and Experience in the Women's Colleges from Their Nineteenth-Century Beginnings to the 1930s* (1984). Using the coincidence of curriculum and campus architecture as a lens, she reconstructed profiles of Mount Holyoke, Vassar, Wellesley, Smith, Bryn Mawr, and Radcliffe to elaborate on the complexity and change in institutions committed exclusively to the higher education of women. Linda Eisenmann's article, "Educating the Female Citizen in a Post-war World: Competing Ideologies for American Women, 1945–1965," published in *Educational Review* (2002), defines the recent themes in extending this line of inquiry. Eisenmann expanded her article to provide in 2007 the seminal work on a large, complex era and topic in her book, *Higher Education for Women in Post-war America, 1945–1965.*

A recurrent complaint about formal "house histories" is that their emphasis on official records and the actions of presidents and boards tends to eclipse the perspectives of other members of the campus community—namely, faculty and students. Over the past four decades a number of works have provided an antidote to this neglect. Helen Lefkowitz Horowitz's *Campus Life: Undergraduate Cultures from the End of the Eighteenth Century to the Present* (1988) introduces the model of "insiders," "outsiders," and "rebels" to reconstruct the worlds students made over three centuries. Useful case studies along this line include Marilyn Tobias's *Old Dartmouth on Trial: The Transformation of the Academic Community in Nineteenth-Century America* (1982), a reconstruction of an episode at Dartmouth in which students aligned with alumni and faculty to bring a stodgy administration to heel.

Historians have rediscovered the vitality of liberal arts colleges in an era in which the emergence of the university often received most attention. George M. Marsden's *The Soul of the American University: From Protestant Establishment to Established Non-belief* (1994) has prompted serious reconsideration of the drift away from deliberate education for values and character. Gerald Grant and David Riesman's *The Perpetual Dream: Reform and Experiment in the American College* (1978) organizes a gallery of institutional profiles to provide a historical overview of the preoccupation with reforming undergraduate education. Sociologist Burton Clark's *The Distinctive College* (1970) relied on historical case studies of three institutions—Swarthmore, Antioch, and Reed—to show how the acquisition and transmittal of a memorable "organizational saga" has helped to energize selective colleges over the long haul. Historian W. Bruce Leslie's *Gentlemen and Scholars: College and Community in the "Age of the University," 1865–1917* (1992) extends this line of analysis with gracefully written profiles of Princeton, Swarthmore, and Bucknell in the late nineteenth and early twentieth centuries. Fresh perspectives on historical and contemporary developments in independent liberal arts colleges are covered in two recent works: Steven Koblik and Stephen R. Graubard's anthology, *Distinctively American: The Residential Liberal Arts Colleges* (1990), and the Council on Independent College's fiftieth-anniversary collected essays, *Meeting the Challenge: America's Independent Colleges and Universities since 1956* (2006).

For those who wish to pursue research on students, the glimpses of campus life provided in fiction, movies, and memoirs are essential. A. C. Spectorsky's *The College Years* (1958) remains the exemplary anthology. It also awaits a sequel to make sense out of the autobiographical records of students since 1960 or thereabouts. A few years after publication of Frederick Rudolph's *The American*

College and University: A History in 1962, contemporary writing about higher education became understandably preoccupied with student unrest on campus. Amid the prodigious bulk of journalistic coverage, some works I find enduring include Stephen Kelman's *Push Comes to Shove* (1972) and W. J. Rorabaugh's *Berkeley at War* (1990). Commercially distributed documentaries, such as *Berkeley in the Sixties,* allow historians and their students to view vintage newsreels of campus unrest and political activism along with the highly self-indulgent recollections of former students who saw themselves as revolutionaries.

Anthropology also holds promise as a discipline that can assist historians in the study of student life. One highly original work, Michael Moffat's *Coming of Age in New Jersey: College and American Culture* (1989), shows how ethnographic study of a contemporary campus can supplement official documents to explain how a campus and its students come to terms with one another. Anthropologist Laura Wilkie relied on artifacts and ethnography to reconstruct the world of a Berkeley fraternity chapter from a century ago in *The Lost Boys of Zeta Psi: A Historical Archaeology of Masculinity at a University Fraternity* (2010). To gain a sense of the recent innovations in historical research methods and perspectives in studying various aspects of higher education, see the anthology edited by Marybeth Gasman, *The History of U.S. Higher Education: Methods for Understanding the Past* (2010). To another disciplinary extreme, historians today have the advantage of being able to draw upon the systematic data on college students' changing attitudes, values, and cognitive skills as analyzed by psychologists. A pioneering work in bringing the behavioral sciences to bear on the study of students is Nevitt Sanford, editor, *The American College: A Psychological and Social Interpretation of the Higher Learning* (1962). In a similar vein, Kenneth Feldman and Theodore Newcomb synthesized a large body of work from behavioral sciences in *The Impact of College on Students* (1969). Subsequent works that will be useful to historians who take the time to plumb the social and behavioral sciences literature include Alexander Astin's *Four Critical Years* (1977) and his sequel work, *What Matters in College?* (1993). Ernest T. Pascarella and Patrick Terenzini, *How College Affects Students: Findings and Insights from Twenty Years of Research* (1991), is the most current synthesis of behavioral science studies and will be welcomed by historians as a reference source for secondary data.

Intercollegiate athletics, long infamous as one of the sideshows that ran the American campus, has attracted serious attention. Ronald Smith's *Sports and Freedom: The Rise of Big-Time College Athletics* (1988) endures as the seminal work on college sports from their origins in the mid-nineteenth century up until about 1910. John Thelin's *Games Colleges Play: Scandal and Reform in Intercollegiate Athletics* (1994) picks up where Smith stops and extends the story into the 1990s. Michael Oriard's *Reading Football: How the Popular Press Created an American Spectacle* (1993) brings to life the evolution of a peculiarly American cultural phenomenon: reading about as well as watching college football. Robin Lester reconstructs the powerful innovations in the governance and performance of University of Chicago teams in *Stagg's University: The Rise, Decline, and Fall of Big-Time Football at Chicago* (1995). John Sayle Watterson's *College Football: History, Spectacle, Controversy* (2000) fleshes out this sports heritage in lucid prose. Murray Sperber's *Onward to Victory: The Crises That Shaped College Sports* (1998) plumbs the records of public relations firms and athletics departments to reconstruct the machinery of big-time sports in the twentieth century. For longitudinal data on the consequences of intercollegiate athletics for students at academically selective institutions, James L. Shulman and William G. Bowen have drawn on Mellon Foundation data to present a systematic analysis in *The Game of Life: College Sports and Educational Values* (2001). In 2003 Bowen, with coauthor Sarah A. Levin, continued this line of inquiry by drawing from comprehensive statistical records to probe the advantages often given to varsity teams and student-athletes at academically selective institutions that did *not* rely on athletic scholarships—including the Ivy League and New England's Little Three of Amherst, Williams, and Wesleyan. The residual reminder from their book, *Reclaiming the Game: College Sports and Educational Values,* was that the excesses of college sports were not confined to the highly visible big-time athletics programs. Reconstructing the history of women as intercollegiate athletes, coaches, and athletics directors holds great promise for a new generation of scholars. *Silver Era, Golden Moments: A Celebration of Ivy League Women's Athletics* (1999), edited by Paula D. Welch, provides one indication of the abundance of sources available on this understudied topic.

The discussion of the complexities of the 1972 Title IX legislation on equity in educational programs will shift from journalistic to historical analysis in coming years. One example of this accumulating historical perspective on gender and college sports is Welch Suggs, *A Place on the Team: The Triumph and Tragedy of Title IX* (2005). Social justice and civil rights as part of the serious study of intercollegiate athletics continued to accelerate in the early twenty-first century with publication of such works as Lane Demas, *Integrating the Gridiron: Black Civil Rights and American College Football* (2010), and Charles H. Martin, *Benching Jim Crow* (2010). Kurt Edward Kemper's *College Football and American Culture in the Cold War Era* (2009) delineates strong ties between the national political culture and the promotion of big-time college football following World War II. Michael Oriard continued his succession of original historical analysis with his 2009 book, *Bowled Over: Big-Time College Football from the Sixties to the BCS Era.* For historians of higher education who seek primary sources on the extended efforts at policy reform, a good source comes from the series of periodic reports published by the Knight Commission on Intercollegiate Athletics, such as the 2010 study, *Restoring the Balance: Dollars, Values, and the Future of College Sports.* Economist Andrew Zimbalist's *Unpaid Professionals* (1999) uses institutional and national data on college sports finances to refute and amend many of the convenient, albeit erroneous, justifications for uncontrolled spending on varsity sports.

I have deliberately included junior colleges and community colleges in my account of American higher education. Although these are uniquely American institutions, their story remains largely untold. The best critical perspective is Steven Brint and Jerome Karabel, *The Diverted Dream: Community Colleges and the Promise of Educational Opportunity in America, 1900–1985* (1989). Thomas Diener's anthology, *Growth of an American Invention* (1986), presents some essential documents. Anthropologist Howard London's *The Culture of the Community College* (1978) has left us a classic case study that too few scholars have chosen to heed as a model for replication elsewhere.

Access to—and social tracking within—American higher education is always close to the surface of the research questions historians ask about colleges and universities. Sociologists Christopher Jencks and David Riesman kindled controversy and reflection in 1968 with their historical analysis of what they called the "partial triumph of meritocracy" in *The Academic Revolution*. Harold Wechsler's *The Qualified Student* (1978) plumbs the historically and geographically changing variations on selective admissions to provide a coherent analysis of ways in which colleges and their constituencies have responded to the trend toward mass education. More recently, Nicholas Lemann's *The Big Test: The Secret History of the American Meritocracy* (1999) used the drama of the Scholastic Aptitude Test as the base from which to put into historical perspective the sorting and tracking machinery of postsecondary education.

Mitchell L. Stevens's *Creating a Class: College Admissions and the Education of Elites* (2007) combines sociological perspective and historical context to provide a fresh analysis of the American tradition of selective admissions and sorting in our national education sweepstakes. Perhaps the most significant addition to this scholarly literature in the early twenty-first century has been the attention to a downside of higher-education access—namely, the relatively dismal record of retention and bachelor's degree completion. Illustrative of this new line of research interest are such works as William Bowen, Matthew Chingos, and Michael McPherson, *Crossing the Finish Line: Completing College at America's Universities* (2009); Frederick M. Hess, Mark Schneider, Kevin Carey, and Andrew P. Kelly, *Diplomas and Dropouts: Which Colleges Actually Graduate Their Students (and Which Don't)* (2009); and John R. Thelin, *The Attrition Tradition in American Higher Education: Connecting Past and Present* (2010).

Admissions is only one step in the sequential pattern that has created genuine access to higher education. The indispensable partner has been student financial aid that promotes affordability. One of the major gains in research and policy analysis in the twenty-first century has been the perceptive historical research about how programs of student grants, loans, and work-study from federal, state, foundation, and institutional sources have attempted to redress the overt and latent obstacles to social justice in terms of student choice and access to undergraduate programs. A superb overview and interpretation of more than three centuries of continuity and changes in American provisions for student financial aid is provided by historian Rupert Wilkinson in his informed, provocative, interpretative book, *Aiding Students, Buying Students: Financial Aid in America* (2005). The American Enterprise Institute, under the editorial leadership of Frederick M. Hess, fused present and past in the anthology, *Footing the Tuition Bill: The New Student Loan Sector* (2007).

Tracking, of course, is inseparable from exclusion and discrimination associated with race and ethnicity in the United States. Studies of African Americans and access to higher education include James Anderson's *The Education of Blacks in the South, 1860–1935* (1988). Paula Fass's *Outside In: Minorities and the Transformation of American Education* (1989) extends the research net to connect patterns of discrimination (and change) in the U.S. armed services, public high schools, and colleges and universities. Henry N. Drewry and Humphrey Doermann combine historical and contemporary analysis of the historically black colleges and universities in *Stand and Prosper: Private Black Colleges and Their Students* (2001). Sam Wiggin's *Higher Education in the South* (1964) analyzes the underfunding and segregation of public and private colleges for African Americans as the foremost regional problem. A useful supplement to the historical books and articles is the PBS video documentary series on the civil rights movement, circa 1949 to 1969, *Eyes on the Prize*. Most pertinent to historians of higher education is the episode "Fighting Back," which includes original newsreel footage of episodes involving campus desegregation at the University of Alabama and the University of Mississippi, along with oral histories of key participants. Naturally, the documentary film footage gravitates toward the most volatile chapters in the saga. To flesh out the variations and nuances of the sustained efforts to achieve racial equality in access to all higher education, we also need the thoughtful work of historians. At the start of this essay I singled out editor Roger Geiger's *History of Higher Education Annual* as a useful source of fresh scholarship whose articles have the timeliness to alter our thinking about how higher education has behaved and developed. One such contribution to the study of institutions and race relations is Peter Wallenstein's concise yet thorough "Black Southerners and Non-black Universities: Desegregating Higher Education, 1935–1967," published in the 1999 issue (vol. 19) of Geiger's *Annual*. Wallenstein's survey provides a sequel and supplement to the intensive case study of desegregation that Thomas Dyer wrote as part of his candid, balanced book, *The University of Georgia: A Bicentennial History* (1985).

Although teaching and learning are allegedly at the heart of higher education, scholars have made relatively few attempts (and with limited results) to penetrate the changing classroom and curricula of the American campus. Bruce A. Kimball's *Orators and Philosophers: A History of the Ideal of Liberal Education*

(1986) is one important exception to the rule as he decodes the major debates about the purposes of undergraduate education in the late eighteenth and the nineteenth century. Frederick Rudolph's *Curriculum* (1986) leaves us a reasonably good survey over three centuries. The single best account of the rituals of classroom dynamics is Henry Seidel Canby's memoir about college of the 1890s, *Alma Mater: The Gothic Age of the American College* (1936). A good historical perspective on the comparable trends in the resolution of teaching and research in such disparate fields as history departments and medical schools is rendered by Larry Cuban, *How Scholars Trumped Teachers: Change without Reform in University Curriculum, Teaching, and Research, 1890–1990* (1999). The persistence of this tension in all professional graduate schools, especially medicine, is explicated in a report from the Carnegie Foundation for the Advancement of Teaching, by Molly Cook, David M. Irby, and Bridget C. O'Brien, *Educating Physicians: A Call for Reform of Medical School and Residency* (2010).

General treatments of institutions, ranging from "research universities" to "liberal arts colleges," tend to gloss over the nuances of graduate and professional schools. Fortunately, a number of studies have sharpened their focus to give graduate students and professional schools the attention they warrant. Earl Cheit's *The Useful Arts and the Liberal Tradition* (1975) concisely brings together salient events and reports that shaped such new university fields as agriculture, business, forestry, and engineering. Paul Starr's *The Social Transformation of American Medicine* (1982) connects professional organizations and educational initiatives with social history. W. Thorp, M. Myers, Jr., J. S. Finch, and James Axtell have written a model work on graduate and professional schools for a single university, *The Princeton Graduate School: A History* (2000).

To gauge the changing composition and view of college and university professors, researchers now have access to a number of excellent reference works, including Howard R. Bowen and Jack H. Schuster's *American Professors: A National Resource Imperiled* (1986). Martin J. Finklestein's *The American Academic Profession* (1990) synthesizes a voluminous body of scholarship in the social sciences published since 1945.

The most evasive group within American higher education has been one of its most powerful groups—namely, trustees. Two veteran historians of higher education, Edwin D. Duryea and Don Williams, have synthesized numerous studies of higher education's governance, resulting in the informative work, *The Academic Corporation: A History of College and University Governing Boards* (2000). Its limit, however, is that it drifts more toward the governance associated with campus presidents and court cases, with less revelation about boards and trustees. Beardsley Ruml, one of the most obscure yet interesting figures in twentieth-century American higher education, has left us *Memo to a College Trustee* (1959), which documents an orbit of institutional control far removed from deans and faculty. Hugh Hawkins's *Between Harvard and America* (1972) plumbs the complexities of both President Charles Eliot and imperial Harvard. W. H. Cowley's posthumous *Presidents, Professors, and Trustees: The Evolution of American Academic Government* (1980) represents the belated attempt of a former president and pioneering higher-education scholar to make sense out of the troubled heritage of shared governance. Robert Maynard Hutchins's *The Higher Learning in America* (1936) documents the independent, iconoclastic views Hutchins brought to his memorable tenure as president of the University of Chicago. William G. Bowen and Harold T. Shapiro, each of whom served as president of Princeton University, have edited essays in *Universities and Their Leadership* (1998) that allow readers to participate in the game of comparing campus presidents of the past and the present. In recent years there has been a ground-swell of memoirs by retired university presidents and other higher-education officials, such as Donald Kennedy's *Academic Duty* (1997) and Robert M. Rosenzweig's *The Political University: Policy, Politics, and Presidential Leadership in the American Research University* (1998). Their tone indicates that the heritage of mutual distrust between presidents and professors shows little sign of abatement. An unfortunate void in the history of how colleges work is the relative absence of memoirs and accounts by middle-level administrators. A partial antidote is Robert Birnbaum's *How Colleges Work: The Cybernetics of Academic Organization and Leadership* (1991). George Keller's *Academic Strategy: The Management Revolution in American Higher Education* (1983) was written foremost to inculcate thoughtfulness into the visions of a new generation of campus presidents and deans. One of its enduring contributions has been to provide unparalleled historical context on how some administrative practices and forms fell into place, and how others over time fell from favor.

Healthy historical writing about higher education must acknowledge new institutional forms in the national saga. I have already specifically mentioned community colleges as one example. Other contenders include correspondence schools, extension courses, "diploma mills," and now Internet "virtual universities," all of which have become part of the American way in extending educational access. The problem is that these ventures seldom receive much coverage in the historical accounts. One partial antidote is Richard S. Ruch's *Higher Ed, Inc.* (2001), a survey of the formidable "for-profit" institutions that are now part of higher education as a "knowledge industry."

Since the early 1990s, one of the watchwords of American politics and culture has been that "it takes a village." In fact, the sequel is that, for international economic and educational development, "It takes a campus," whether in College Park, Maryland, or Dubai. The undeniable fact of life of American higher education in the twenty-first century is that each and every college has shown increased awareness of the global educational environment. Fortunately for the history of higher education, several astute scholars have paid serious attention to this proposition, which will henceforth prompt academic leaders in the continental United States to acknowledge and respect the innovations and energy at academic institutions worldwide. Leading the way in this expanded perspective are such recent works as Ben Wildavsky, *The Great Brain Race: How Global Universities Are Reshaping the World* (2010), and D. Bruce Johnstone and Pamela N. Marcucci, *Financing Higher Education Worldwide: Who Pays? Who Should Pay?* (2010).

The works mentioned in this essay hint at rather than exhaust the good reading that awaits historians of higher education. Amid this abundance, however, there is one disappointing weak spot: a lack of freshly edited anthologies of historical documents. Richard Hofstadter and Wilson Smith provided superb service to several generations of scholars in 1961 with the publication of their two-volume work *American Higher Education: A Documentary History.* James Stone and Donald DeNevi's *Portraits of the American University, 1890 to 1910* (1971) allows readers to go back in time to the heroic era of national photojournalism about the emerging American university. Its limit, however, is that it does not reach into the individual experiences of the students, faculty, and alumni. We have no sequel to Hofstadter and Smith's compilation that extends their selections into the twenty-first century—or that reevaluates primary sources that might be added to their selections for the period 1636 to 1950.

One welcomed resolution is that two senior, highly respected historians —Wilson Smith and Thomas Bender—turned their attention to assembling and editing the outstanding documents about the missions of American higher education following World War II. The result was their masterful anthology, *American Higher Education Transformed, 1940–2005: Documenting the National Discourse* (2008). Unfortunately, this kind of documentary compilation is rare.

Whether these sorely needed additions to the arsenal are likely to be written and published is uncertain. On the one hand, the closing of such established archives as those of Columbia University's Teachers Colleges will tend to thwart new scholarship. On the other hand, innovations in electronic access to university and association archives via e-mail and the use of digital technology to transmit facsimiles of documents have greatly enhanced opportunities for primary-source research. Moreover, many college and university archivists have carefully assembled rich materials that remain largely untouched by historians of higher education. The American Council on Education records now housed at Stanford University are far more accessible to scholars than when maintained at the ACE offices in Washington, D.C. Similarly, the Association of American University records are both safe and accessible at the Johns Hopkins University's archives and special collections, providing a great opportunity to go beyond the perspective of a single institution. The University of California's Bancroft Library boasts a superb investment in making university photographs and other records available on the Internet. The University of South Carolina's Museum of Education sets a high standard in its holdings and its accessibility. Most interesting for higher-education scholars is the university's acquisition of the John B. Hawley Higher Education Postcard Collection.

Meanwhile, reading and writing about the history of American higher education continue to attract a dedicated, talented following whose members, despite the variety of their special interests, exhibit a common bond—namely, an enduring interest in significant issues and a combination of enthusiasm and expertise that assures a vital legacy.

Index